# Spanning the Bridge of Time

*Special Edition Iowa Cookbook
with Timeless Recipes, Stories,
History, Poetry and Music*

*1846-1996
By Diana L. Neff*

I

# Cover Picture

Shown on the cover is the Government Bridge which connects the city of Davenport, Iowa to the Rock Island Arsenal. Built in 1872, it was made of iron with a rail deck above the wagon deck. It measured slightly over 1500 feet and had five spans plus a draw span. The wagon deck was only 16 feet wide for 2-way wagon traffic. In 1896 a new bridge was constructed to handle larger and heavier locomotives and rail cars. It eventually handled street cars, railroad cars, vehicles, and foot traffic. Although most of the traffic is by automobile, the bridge is still used occasionally for railroad traffic.

The U.S. Ellen, built in 1907 in La Crosse, Wisconsin, began its days on the Mississippi River as a sternwheeler rafter. It was used in part for excursions and private parties and in 1911 was sold to the U.S. Corps of Engineers. The Ellen was a very sophisticated boat for its time. At one point it was air-conditioned with an elevator installed for an expected visit by U.S. President Franklin D. Roosevelt. Unfortunately it never occurred. The boat was sold to private owners in 1943 and converted to diesel the following year.

© copyright 1996

Diana L. Neff
806 2nd Street
Princeton, Iowa 52768-9752

Library of Congress Catalog Card Number 96-92521

# Introduction

In 1996 Iowans celebrate 150 years of Statehood with parades and pageantry. In the upcoming pages you'll find short histories of many of your favorite Iowa scenes, as well as timeless recipes passed down, in many cases, from generation to generation. My book is meant to not only "whet your appetite", but to teach about Iowa and hopefully serve as a valued keepsake. Stories, poetry, and music have added to the delight and variety of the book.

I've traveled to 41 of our 50 states. Nowhere would I rather live than right here. I love to travel, but also enjoy returning home. I feel very fortunate to live where I do. Each season, like each area of the state, from the Missouri to the Mississippi, is beautiful and unique in its own way.

It is my hope that "Spanning the Bridge of Time" will find a special place on your kitchen shelves for many years to come. Iowans are known for their strong sense of pride. Hopefully, this Special Edition will serve as a symbol of ongoing pride, respect, and appreciation for our different backgrounds and the contributions made by Iowans, both past and present, in creating our beautiful and bountiful state.

Please enjoy reading and preparing what I have enjoyed putting together for you!

Diana L. Neff

# Dedication

I wish to dedicate this book to my husband, David. Without his constant support, patience, and encouragement, completing a project of this size would have been nearly impossible. I found myself having back surgery along the way. David was always there to help out in any way that was needed. Thus, "Spanning the Bridge of Time" became a definite "team" effort.

So thank you, David, for everything.

# Acknowledgments

Gary Nauman, Madison, Wisconsin, for the cover and other specific illustrations; Carol Love, Madison, Wisconsin, for spot illustrations; Ben Neff, also Madison, Wisconsin, for typesetting cover and dividers; and Alan Shaw, Princeton, Iowa for cover photographs.

Scott County Sesquicentennial Commission for endorsement.

"An Illustrated History Of The Rock Island Arsenal And Arsenal Island", Parts One And Two by Mr. Thomas J. Slattery. Kris Gayman Leinicke, Curator of Collections, Rock Island Museum. Way's Packet Directory and Way's Steamboat Towboat Directory by Frederick Way Jr.

Buffalo Bill Museum, Le Claire, Otto Ewoldt, President and Curator; Buffalo Bill photo, Putnam Museum of History and Natural Science, Davenport, Iowa; the song, "A Great Scout Named Buffalo Bill", Cecil Fletcher.

Peggy Hansen, Danish Windmill, Elk Horn.

Mamie Doud Eisenhower Birthplace Foundation, Inc., Boone, Iowa; Mamie Doud Eisenhower Birthplace Museum and Library, Larry Adams, Curator; Mamie Eisenhower's birthplace drawing - William J. Wagner, Dallas Center; "Ike The Cook", Edward and Candace Russoli.

Herbert Hoover Museum & Library, West Branch, Iowa, "Dining With The Hoover Family: A Collection of Reminiscences and Recipes", by Dale C. Mayer.

The Little Brown Church in the Vale: Pastors Bob and Linda Myren, Nashua, Iowa; Bill Dunn Photos, Charles City.

The Lee P. Loomis Archive of Mason City Public Library, Mr. Arthur Fischbeck, Curator and Historian.

Kate Klimesh, Spillville, Spillville town council, Bily Clock Museum, Jim Ronan, Curator; "JOSEPH JAN KOVARIK", Dvorak's American Secretary by Dr. Jan Lowenbach.

Winterset Madisonian Newspaper: Tom Gorman, Publisher; Madison County Historical Society, Wendell Spencer, Manager; Bridge photographs by Gene Crawford.

*(Continued on Next Page)*

V

# (Acknowledgments - Continued)

The Fairfield Daily Ledger Inc., Fairfield, Iowa.

Don Peterson - Stanton Historical Society.

Billie Turley - Midwest Old Threshers, Mount Pleasant.

Terrace Hill Society, Des Moines, "Recipes and Recollections From Terrace Hill": Mrs. Chris Branstad, Editor-in-Chief.

Iowa State Fair Blue Ribbon Foundation; State Fair Drawings: William H. McNarney, Des Moines; State Fair Board.

National Czech & Slovak Museum & Library, Cedar Rapids; Logo Design by Marjorie K. Nejdl.

Vesterheim Norwegian - American Museum, Decorah.

Laura Ingalls Wilder Park & Museum, Inc., Ferneva Brimacomb, Director - Burr Oak, Iowa.

Iowa Pork Producers Association.

Maytag Dairy Farms, Newton - James W. Stevens, President and CEO.

JOLLY TIME Pop Corn, Sioux City.

Sioux Honey Association, Sioux City.

The Quaker Oats Company, Cedar Rapids.

Cookies Food Products, Inc., Wall Lake, Iowa.

"Dutch Touches: Recipes and Traditions", Penfield Press, Iowa City, Iowa. Pella Chamber of Commerce, Pella Iowa.
THE FARM IMPLEMENT NEWS, Chicago, Illinois
(January, 1889, Vol. X., No. 1)
"Princeton, Iowa, A Two-Rivers Township" by
Dorothy B. Lage and "From Out of the Past" by
Paul B. Dennis. Princeton drawing by Ruth Solter.

"Recipes From Iowa . . . with love", by Peg Hein and Kathryn Cramer Lewis.

Donna Glenn, Iowa's Championship Rodeo, Sidney, Iowa.

Margery Strom, Shenandoah, Iowa, "Mother's Hour Letter", Shenandoah, Iowa, July 1926, and "Kitchen Klatter News", Shenandoah, Iowa, January, 1928; "The Story Of An American Family" by Lucile Driftmier Verness.

# (Acknowledgments - Continued)

Betty Jane Shaw, President and Owner of Earl May Seed & Nursery, Shenandoah, Iowa.

Joanna Schanz, Amana Colonies.

Chamber of Commerce, Kalona, Iowa.

Lila Jean Jensen, Audubon, Iowa.

Thelma Nopoulos, Wilton Candy Kitchen, Wilton, Iowa.

Charlotte Fliehler, Strawberry Point Chamber of Commerce.

Dorothy Birdwell, Waterford, Ohio - "The Old Dinner Bell".

Betty Brotherton, Wall Lake, Iowa.

Mr. and Mrs. Jack Hawn, Perry, Iowa.

Mr. and Mrs. Vincent Pemble, Indianola, Iowa.

Wichita Eagle & Beacon.

Betty Stone, Ridgecrest Retirement Village, Davenport.

The County Extension Services that participated.

The Davenport Leader and North Scott Press for advertising.

Special thank you to Mom, Dad and Aunt Laurie.

Last, thank you to all those who contributed one or more recipes to help make this cookbook a success.

Enjoy, and Congratulations Iowa on your 150th!

# Table of Contents

BEVERAGES . . . . . . . . . . . . . . . . . . . . . . . . . . . . . . . . . . . . .1-14

APPETIZERS . . . . . . . . . . . . . . . . . . . . . . . . . . . . . . . . . .15-44

BRUNCH . . . . . . . . . . . . . . . . . . . . . . . . . . . . . . . . . . . . .45-72

BREADS . . . . . . . . . . . . . . . . . . . . . . . . . . . . . . . . . . .73-122
   Quick Breads, Yeast Breads, Biscuits, Dutch Letters, Rolls, Muffins

SOUPS AND SANDWICHES . . . . . . . . . . . . . . . . . . . .123-148

SALADS AND DRESSINGS. . . . . . . . . . . . . . . . . . . . .149-190

CASSEROLES . . . . . . . . . . . . . . . . . . . . . . . . . . . . . .191-224

MEAT DISHES . . . . . . . . . . . . . . . . . . . . . . . . . . . . .225-294
   Beef, Pork, Ham, Lamb, Seafood, Poultry, Wild Game

VEGETABLES, RICE AND POTATOES . . . . . . . . . . .295-330

PASTA . . . . . . . . . . . . . . . . . . . . . . . . . . . . . . . . . . . .331-340

DESSERTS . . . . . . . . . . . . . . . . . . . . . . . . . . . . . . . . .341-444
   Cakes, Pies, Puddings, Pastries, Toppings, Further Delights

COOKIES AND BARS. . . . . . . . . . . . . . . . . . . . . . . . .445-492

CANDY . . . . . . . . . . . . . . . . . . . . . . . . . . . . . . . . . . . .493-510

MISCELLANEOUS. . . . . . . . . . . . . . . . . . . . . . . . . . . .511-540

### First Edition
**First Printing - July, 1996**
**Second Printing - September, 1996**
**Third Printing - April, 1997**
**Fourth Printing - May, 1997**

## Brennan Printing
100 Main St. • Deep River, Iowa 52222

# Beverages

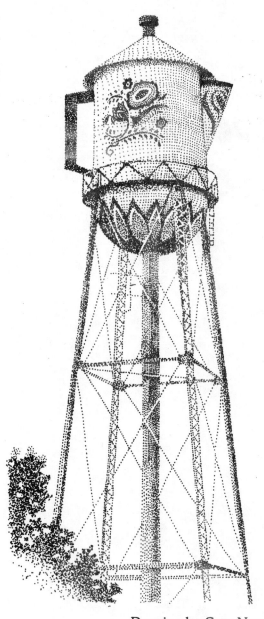

Drawing by Gary Nauman

# Largest Coffee Pot In The World
## Stanton, Iowa
*(With special thanks to Stanton Historical Society)*

Stanton is sometimes referred to as the Swedish capitol of Iowa. Its welcome to visitors is the Swedish "Coffee Pot", which rises almost 150 feet above the skyline of Stanton. At night it is lit. Actually a water tower, it could hold 640,000 cups of coffee or 40,000 gallons, which easily makes it the largest in the world. It seems to convey the message of hospitality to those entering the small town in southwest Iowa.

One of Stanton's famous personalities is Virginia Christine, or Mrs. Olson, the Hollywood and TV commercial star and the lovely Swedish lady, who served up a good cup of coffee to her viewing audience, along with a smile.

# BEVERAGES

**BEVERAGES**

Anise Milk . . . . . . . . . . . . . . 5
Spiced Milk . . . . . . . . . . . . . 5
Lo-Cal Hot Cocoa Mix . . . . 6
Powdered Hot Cocoa . . . . . 6
Hot Spiced
   Cranberry Juice . . . . . . . . 7
Just Like "Grandma's"
   Lemonade . . . . . . . . . . . . . 7
Hot Apple Cider Punch . . . 8
Lush Slush . . . . . . . . . . . . . . 8
Ginger Beer . . . . . . . . . . . . . 9
"As A Healthful
   Summer Drink" . . . . . . . . 9
Raspberry Roman
   Punch (1880's) . . . . . . . . . 10
Homemade Bailey's
   Irish Cream . . . . . . . . . . . 10
Blackberry Brandy Slush . . 11
Rumtopf (rum pot) . . . . . . 11
Dandelion Wine . . . . . . . . . 12
Early Household
   Hints . . . . . . . . . . . . . 13,14

# Anise Milk
*(Anijsmelk)*

*"In the Netherlands, hot anijsmelk is especially popular after ice-skating on a chilly winter night."*

| | |
|---|---|
| 1 quart milk | 1 teaspoon anise seed |
| 1 tablespoon sugar | (crushed) |

Heat milk just to boiling point. Stir in sugar and anise seed. Serve either hot or cold. Makes 4 servings.

Variation: To make Sage Milk (saliemelk), substitute 1 teaspoon powdered sage for anise.

Carol Van Klompenburg
(Pella, Iowa)

# Spiced Milk
*(Slemp)*

*"Slemp is the traditional drink for children at Sinterklaas parties."*

| | |
|---|---|
| 4 cups milk | Pinch of saffron |
| 6 cloves | Pinch of mace |
| 1 cinnamon stick or | ¼ to ½ cup sugar |
| ¼ teaspoon ground | 1 teabag or 1 teaspoon tea |
| cinnamon | (optional) |

Bring milk to a boil in heavy saucepan. Tie spices in cheesecloth. Drop into milk. Simmer for ½ hour. Add the sugar. Remove cheesecloth with spices, squeezing excess liquid into milk. Serve immediately.

Carol Van Klompenburg
(Pella, Iowa)

## Lo-Cal Hot Cocoa Mix

**BY THE BATCH:**

6½ cups non-fat milk
¾ cup cocoa

18 packets Equal or other sweetener equivalent to ¾ cup sugar

Use ⅓ cup mix to 8 ounces of hot water.

**BY THE CUP:**

⅓ cup non-fat dry milk
1 tablespoon cocoa

1 packet of Equal or other sweetener equivalent to 2 teaspoons sugar

Mix and add 8 ounces of hot water. You may add a drop of vanilla for flavor.

Dorothy Frazer
(Conrad, Iowa)

## Powdered Hot Cocoa

8 or 9 quarts powdered milk
16 ounces instant chocolate drink

8-10 ounces powdered cream
¾-1 cup powdered sugar

Use ⅓ cup in 1 cup of hot water. Use ⅔ cup in mug of hot water. Store in gallon jar or plastic bag. Keeps well.

Darlene Neff
(Pleasant Valley, Iowa)

## Hot Spiced Cranberry Juice

1 package cranberries
1 quart water
1 cup sugar
2 cups water

Juice of 1 lemon
3 cinnamon sticks
2 or 3 more cups water
   (to taste)

Cook cranberries and water until cranberries pop. Drain juice. Make syrup of sugar, water, lemon, cinnamon sticks and 2 or 3 more cups of water, to taste. Serve hot. (Best when made well ahead of serving time to allow cinnamon flavor to blend. Sometimes it's necessary to adjust amount of sugar, to taste. One quart bottle of cranberry juice cocktail can be substituted instead of cooking fresh cranberries.)

**Nadine Johnson**

## Just Like "Grandma's" Lemonade

1 tub Crystal Light Sugar
   Free Lemonade Mix

8 cups water
¼ lemon (unpeeled and
   unseeded)

In a large pitcher, combine dry lemonade mix and water. Pour 2 cups lemonade mixture into blender container. Chop lemon into small pieces. Add lemon pieces to lemonade mixture in blender. Cover and process on HIGH 45 to 60 seconds or until lemon is finely grated. Pour lemon mixture into remaining lemonade in pitcher. Mix well to combine. Serve over ice and savor every sip! Serves 8 (1 cup) - Each serving equals: HE: 1 optional calorie, 1 calorie, 0 gram fat, 0 gram protein, 0 gram carbohydrate, 1 milligram sodium, 0 gram fiber. DIABETIC: Free food. HINT: You can also use ¼ to ⅓ of an orange for lemon-orange ade, or 1/8 to ¼ of a lime for lemon-lime ade.

**JoAnna M. Lund**
*(JoAnna is the editor and publisher of the Healthy Exchanges Newsletter. Healthy Exchanges, JoAnna M. Lund, P.O. Box 124, DeWitt, IA 52742). Phone: 319-659-8234*

7

# Hot Apple Cider Punch

1 gallon apple cider
2 teaspoons whole cloves
2 teaspoons whole allspice
2 (3-inch) cinnamon sticks

⅔ cup sugar
2 oranges studded with
  cloves (optional)

Heat cider and sugar. Place cloves, allspice and cinnamon sticks in cloth or container that can be dipped into liquid and easily removed after the punch has simmered 20 minutes.

**Darlene Neff**
**(Pleasant Valley, Iowa)**

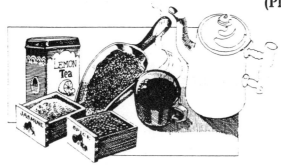

# Lush Slush

1 (12 ounce) can orange juice
  concentrate
4 cups ginger ale
1 cup sugar

1 small can crushed
  pineapple
1 or 2 (6 oz.) jars maraschino
  cherries

Drain cherries and cut in half. Thaw orange juice. Stir all ingredients together and freeze in plastic container. Thaw very slightly before serving in individual glasses. Very refreshing especially on hot days. Also good before a meal as an appetizer.

**Jean Rex**
**(Le Claire, Iowa)**

8

# Ginger Beer

¾ pound white sugar
1 ounce cream of tartar

1 ounce ginger
Juice and grated rind of 1
  lemon

Put these together in a jar, and pour over it, all 4 quarts of boiling water; let stand until lukewarm. Add 1 tablespoon of fresh yeast and nearly 1 tablespoon of wintergreen or sassafras; let this stand for 24 hours, then put in bottles. Cork tightly and seal. It will be ready for use in a few days.

## "As A Healthful Summer Drink"

Ginger beer is made of 2 pounds of white sugar, 2 ounces of tartic acid, 3 eggs (into the whites of the eggs beat ½ cup of flour), flavor with ½ ounce of the essence of wintergreen or of lemon. Put in bottles and keep in a cool place.

When you wish to have a refreshing drink, take 2 tablespoons of this syrup and a quarter of a teaspoon of soda, and add to one tumbler of cold water. Stir it vigorously and then drink.!

**Penelope Miller
(Princeton, Iowa)**

9

# Raspberry Roman Punch (1880's)

To 1 quart of water add, 1 pound and ¼ loaf of sugar. Take a gill measure and pour in some French brandy, peach brandy and Jamaica rum (about the same quantity of each until gill is full).

Add to the water, half a pint of raspberry juice and the grated rind and juice of 2 lemons. Stir together well and freeze like ice-cream. (Probably a winter treat)

**Penelope Miller**
**(Princeton, Iowa)**

# Homemade Bailey's Irish Cream

1 (14 ounce) can Eagle Brand
   Sweetened Condensed
   Milk
3 eggs
1 pint half & half

1 cup Irish Whiskey
⅓ cup dark rum
2 tablespoons chocolate syrup
2 teaspoons instant coffee
   crystals
1 teaspoon vanilla

Blend all ingredients until smooth. Store in tightly covered container in refrigerator for 2 weeks. Stir or shake gently before serving. Makes 5 cups of liqueur.

**Mrs. Chris Branstad**
**(Terrace Hill, Iowa Governor's Residence)**
**(Des Moines, Iowa)**

## Blackberry Brandy Slush

9 cups water
2 cups sugar
1 (12 ounce) can frozen
  lemonade

1 (12 ounce) can frozen grape
  juice
2 cups blackberry brandy

Bring water and sugar to a boil, then cool. Add concentrated cans of juices and brandy. Freeze (stirring occasionally.)

**LeAnne Schneckloth**

## Rumtopf (rum pot)

2 cups strawberries
2 cups bing cherries
2 cups red raspberries
2 cups purple plums (pitted)
2 cups peaches (peeled, pitted
  and sliced)

2 cups apricots (pitted
  and sliced)
2 cups pears (peeled & sliced)
2 cups pineapple (fresh)
4 cups sugar
5 quarts rum
1 (fifth) brandy

Use only fresh fruit as it comes in season. Start with strawberries in June. Slice and stem fruit; add ½ cup sugar and 2 cups rum. Cover and let sit until cherries are ripe. Repeat by adding 2 cups cherries, ½ cup sugar and 2 cups rum. Repeat through summer as raspberries, plums, etc. are ripe. Use large crockery pot and keep covered. Add pineapple last in October. Let sit 2 weeks and add 2 cups rum; let sit one week and add 2 cups brandy. Start drinking after November 11th. Eat fruit as is or over ice cream. Make punch with 1 bottle champagne, 1 bottle white wine, 2 cups rumtopf.

**Jack L. Hill**
**(Long Grove, Iowa)**

*Recipe learned while working in Zweibrucken, Germany, a city very near Davenport's sister city of Kaiserslautern, Germany.*

11

# Dandelion Wine

1 gallon boiling water
2 quarts dandelion blossoms
   (packed tight)
Juice of 4 oranges

Juice of 4 lemons
1 yeast cake
2 to 4 pounds sugar

Add two quarts dandelion blossoms packed tight to 1 gallon boiling water. Let stand about 2 days. Strain. Add 2-4 pounds sugar to a gallon. Four pounds may be too sweet (see above ingredients). Add juice of 4 oranges, juice of 4 lemons, one yeast cake. Add to strained dandelion blossom water. After this ferments, strain 3 or 4 times, put in bottles and lightly cork. Takes about a week to ferment. (Better more oranges and lemons.)

**Dorothy O. Womack**
**(Lexington, N.C.)**
**(Formerly of Des Moines)**

*This recipe is from my Aunt Lucretia Owens Mitchell (Mrs. Frank), born 1881 in Tama County, Iowa and died 1985 in Ackley, Iowa (yes, she was 104 years old at her death). She lived on a farm near Iowa Falls, Iowa. Aunt Lu noted "recipe was from Mrs. Charles Archer who made wine for a medical doctor (Dr. Ashton) at Traer, Iowa." Aunt Lu made a home for her husband, her mother, two brothers, plus assorted relatives, from time to time. She probably used the wine for medicinal purposes.*

# Early Household Hints

*Submitted by: Dorothy Womack, Lexington, North Carolina, and James Owens, Mason City, Iowa, the notebooks of their grandmother Eloisa Jaqua Owens.*

*Eloisa was born in Ohio in 1856, a daughter of Gamaliel and Christina Jaqua who bought Iowa farmland that year and settled in the Traer-Buckingham area. Her parents had been teachers, and besides farming her dad was involved in politics, education and newspaper ownership. Both Gamaliel and Christina wrote columns used by Iowa weeklies, he on agriculture, she on women's interests.*

*Eloisa married Henry Owens, and her sister Florence Jaqua married Henry's brother John. The two couples had 23 children between them and farmed across the road from one another near Traer.*

### Household Hints

The kitchen work table is the right height when the palms can be laid flat on the table without stooping.

When making boiled starch add one-quarter teaspoon salt to each quart of starch to prevent clothes from sticking to your iron when ironing.

To semi, or dry scald chickens, immerse 28 seconds in water at 128°.

If you will rub vinegar on hands after washing them it will soften them and also is good to bleach them.

Put leftovers in fruit jars. When they are to be warmed set jar in warm water and heat. This is a good way to keep food warm for latecomers.

Bed bug killer: Beat the white of an egg to a froth, beat quicksilver into this and paint this mixture where the bugs live.

Take a cathartic the moment you find you are coming down with a cold. Castor oil is perhaps the best, though salts act more quickly.

*(Continued on Next Page)*

### (Early Household Hints - Continued)

A can of charcoal or coke will absorb odors if put in the icebox.

A good tonic for the feet is the salty glove. Take cool water and some coarse salt and thoroughly massage the feet with this moistened salt. Rinse the salt off with cold water, dry carefully and rub in cocoa butter.

When making hoecake some cooks prefer to sprinkle dry corn-meal in pan instead of greasing it.

# Appetizers

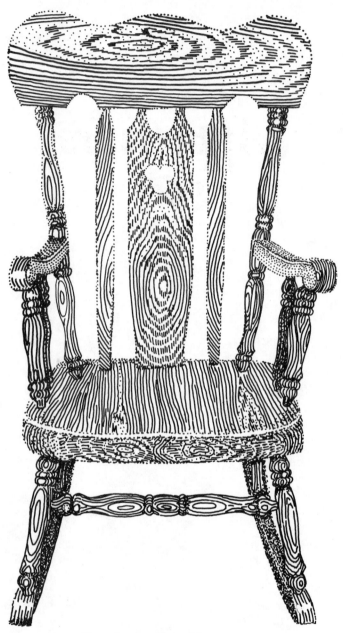

Drawing by Gary Nauman

16

# The Amana Colonies

## WILLKOMMEN

The Amana Colonies are composed of seven quaint and historic villages, each having its own charming characteristics. Amana is the largest village and home to the Woolen Mill and Furniture Factory. Middle Amana is famous for its beautiful Lily Lake, the Kitchen Museum, and Cooper Shop. Also here is the famous Amana Refrigeration Plant. One mile east of South Amana on Highway 6 is the furniture-making shop operated by Joanna and Norman Schanz. West Amana is home to the Broom and Basket Shop. Next door at the Schanz Outlet one of Iowa's largest solid walnut rocking chairs can be seen. Homestead was originally purchased for access to the railroad.

The establishment of the Amana Colonies in the 1850's and 60's originated from the desire for religious freedom. Of mostly German ancestry, people settled in Iowa, where they operated farms, woolen mills, meat shops, and wineries, among other businesses. A communal style of living was adopted in which everyone worked for the good of the community.

Meals were prepared in community kitchens where 30-40 people were served 3 times a day. More than 50 communal kitchens once existed, but only the one in Middle Amana still remains. Amana, the largest village, had 16 kitchen houses. Craftsmen such as the basketmaker, broommaker, tinsmith, blacksmith, cooper, and woodworker were very important. In 1932 people voted to drop their communal way of live. Religious and secular matters became separate. Today the family style of dining in restaurants such as Ronneburgs in Amana, Iowa, is reminiscent of communal style meals served in the big kitchen houses.

# APPETIZERS

**FRIENDSHIP CUP**
Friendship Cup . . . . . . . . . .19

**HORS D'OEUVRES**
Norwegian Kavring . . . . . .19
Cucumber Sandwiches . . .20
Hanky Panks . . . . . . . . . . . .20
Meatball Bites . . . . . . . . . .20
Olive Cheese Puffs . . . . . . .21
Cheese Straws . . . . . . . . . .21
Maytag Two-
    Cheese Tart . . . . . . . . . .22
Chicken Wings . . . . . . . . . .24
Cookies Meatballs . . . . . . .25
Ham Puffs . . . . . . . . . . . . . .25
Devilish Piggy Wings . . . .26
Burgundy Mushrooms . . .27
Stuffed Mushrooms . . . . . .27
Cheese Stuffed
    Mushrooms . . . . . . . . . .28
Parmesan Onion Canapes .28
Spinach Rolls . . . . . . . . . . . .29
Water Chestnut Wraps . . .29

**BREADS**
Cheese Stuffed Bread . . . .30
Cheese and Mushroom
    French Bread . . . . . . . . .30

**DIPS**
Creamy Bar "B"
    "Q" Beef Dip . . . . . . . . .31

Bean Dip . . . . . . . . . . . . . . .31
Caramel Dip . . . . . . . . . . . .32
Honey Caramel Dip . . . . . .32
Fruit Dip . . . . . . . . . . . . . . .32
Hawaiian Dip . . . . . . . . . . .33
Shrimp Dip . . . . . . . . . . . . .33
Stroganoff Dip . . . . . . . . . .34
Taco Dip . . . . . . . . . . . . . . .34
Vegetable Dip . . . . . . . . . .35

**SPREADS**
Cheese Ball . . . . . . . . . . . . .35
Cream Cheese Logs . . . . . .36
Cheese Spread . . . . . . . . . .36
Crab Cheese Spread . . . . .37
Crunchy Pork Spread . . . .38
Shrimp Mousse . . . . . . . . . .38

**SNACKS**
Baked Caramel Corn . . . . .39
No Fuss Caramel Corn . . .40
Peanut Butter Popcorn . . .40
Crunchy Peanut Butter
    Balls (Sugar Free) . . . . . .41
Southwestern Crunch . . . .41
Popcorn Balls . . . . . . . . . . .42
White Chocolate
    Party Mix . . . . . . . . . . . .42
Party Mix . . . . . . . . . . . . . .43

18

# Friendship Cup

| | |
|---|---|
| 1 (10½ ounces) can tomato soup | 2 cans water |
| 1 (10½ ounces) can beef consomme | ¼ teaspoon marjoram |
| | ¼ teaspoon thyme |
| | 6-8 lemon slices |

Combine soup and water; add marjoram and thyme. Simmer until seasonings are mixed well. Pour into cups. Thin slice of lemon can be floated on top. Serves 6 to 8.

**Shirely Weller**
**(Knoxville, Iowa)**

# Norwegian Kavring

| | |
|---|---|
| 1 cup graham flour | 1 teaspoon soda |
| 1 cup flour | ½ cup sugar |
| ½ teaspoon salt | ½ cup margarine |
| 2 rounded teaspoons baking powder | ⅔ cup buttermilk |

Mix together like pie crust and add milk. Roll out ½-inch cut with 2-inch cutter. Bake 10 minutes at 400° on cookie sheet. Remove from pan and split, then bake 40 minutes at 250°. Serve with Ghost cheese, a goat cheese from Norway, or use as a cracker with butter or peanut butter.

*This recipe was given to me by my*
*daughter Mary who lives in Emmetsburg.*

**Marilyn Ullestad**

# Cucumber Sandwiches

1 small loaf rye bread
1 package Good Season
  Italian dressing

1 package (8 ounce)
  Philadelphia cream cheese
1 cucumber (or more)
Dill weed

Mix softened cream cheese and good seasoning mix together. Spread on tiny bread. Slice the cucumber and place a slice on each piece of bread. Sprinkle with dill weed. Store in refrigerator until ready to serve.

**Mary Etta (Schneckloth) Thomsen**

# Hanky Panks

1 pound hamburger
1 pound Velveeta cheese

1 pound sausage
1 package Party Rye bread

Brown meat, drain. Add cheese, garlic powder, oregano. Serves 25 to 30 people. Bake at 350° for 4 to 6 minutes. Can freeze overnight or refrigerate before cooking. Serve hot.

**Linda (Schneckloth) Grimm**

# Meatball Bites

1¾ cup Bisquick
12 ounces Jimmy Dean
  "Spicy" Sausage

¾ cup shredded cheddar
  cheese

Mix and shape into walnut size balls. Bake at 350° for 20 to 23 minutes. Keep warm and spear with toothpicks.

**Carol Wenndt
(Ankeny, Iowa)**

# Olive Cheese Puffs

2 dozen green olives
¼ pound shredded cheddar
cheese
¼ cup margarine

¾ cup flour
¼ teaspoon salt
½ teaspoon paprika

Blend at room temperature cheese and margarine; add flour, salt and paprika, mix well to form dough. Drain and dry olives. Form about one teaspoon dough around each olive. Put on ungreased cookie sheet and bake at 400° for 10 to 15 minutes. Serve warm. (Can be refrigerated or frozen.)

**Suzy Ven Horst
(Bettendorf)**

# Cheese Straws

*This recipe is more than 75 years old.*

**SIFT INTO A BOWL:**
1 cup pastry flour
½ teaspoon salt
½ teaspoon paprika

½ teaspoon baking powder
1 cup grated cheese

Mix ingredients. Add ¼ cup butter and chop together until it is like meal. Mix to a paste with as little ice water as possible, and roll out on a pastry board into a sheet ¼-inch thick. Cut into narrow strips about 6-inches long. Bake to a pale yellow in a 425° oven.

**Alice Fischer
(Davenport)**

# Maytag Two-Cheese Tart

*For your pleasure, we offer an innovative way to make use of that burgeoning crop of zucchini. This savory tart combines the flavors of two favorite Maytag cheeses. The delicate blend of flavors complements simple grilled meats, as well as more elaborate dishes - perfect as an appetizer or accompaniment.*

1 unbaked tart shell in fluted 10-inch tart pan
2 or 3 medium sized zucchini
2 teaspoons salt
1 cup shredded Maytag White Cheddar Cheese
1 egg (beaten)

2 tablespoons finely chopped fresh or 2 tsp. dried parsley
¼ teaspoon black pepper
2 green onions sliced fine (tops and all)
Red bell pepper
Maytag Edam Cheese (about 2 ounces)

Grate the zucchini or shred in a food processor, measure 4 cups and toss in a colander with the salt and allow to drain for 30 minutes. Squeeze out as much moisture as possible. Mix the zucchini, egg, parsley, pepper and shredded Maytag White Cheddar and spread in the tart shell. Sprinkle green onion evenly over top, and arrange thin slices of red pepper in spokes, dividing the tart into 8 segments. Bake in a preheated 375⁰ oven for 30 minutes. Arrange ¼ -inch thick triangular slices of Maytag Edam between the red pepper spokes and return to the oven for 3 to 4 minutes, until the cheese just melts. Serves 8 as a first course or side dish.

**Maytag Dairy Farms**

# Maytag's Famous Blue Cheese
## Newton, Iowa

*(Special thanks to Mr. James Stevens, President and CEO)*

Maytag Dairy Farms was established in the early 1920's by E. H. Maytag. He was not only son of the founder of the Maytag washing machine company, but had developed a world-class herd of Holstein cattle in the 1920's.

On October 11, 1941 the first vat of Maytag Blue Cheese was made. Due to the combined efforts of Iowa State University's dairy department, which had just developed a blue cheese process, and the rich milk from the Maytag Dairy Farms, a cheese plant and curing caves were built in 1941.

Today Maytag Dairy Farms includes four farms totaling approximately 1,200 acres. The cheese is made exactly the same today as it was 50 years ago, with an aging process that takes from six months to a year. Mr. James Stevens has worked for the company for over 50 years and serves as President and CEO of Maytag Dairy Farms.

# Chicken Wings

**12 to 15 split wings (discard tips)**

**BUFFALO WING SAUCE:**

| | |
|---|---|
| 2 tablespoons Sue Bee Honey | 4 tablespoons margarine |
| 4 tablespoons hot sauce | (melted) |

**TIJUANA SAUCE:**

| | |
|---|---|
| Buffalo sauce + 1 tablespoon catsup | ¼ teaspoon cumin |
| ¼ teaspoon chili powder | 1/8 teaspoon garlic powder |

**ORIENTAL SAUCE:**

| | |
|---|---|
| 4 tablespoons soy sauce | 2 tablespoons Sue Bee Honey |
| 2 tablespoons hot sauce | ¼ teaspoon ginger |
| 2 tablespoons vegetable oil | 1/8 teaspoon garlic powder |

Dip wings in desired sauce and coat completely. Bake at 375⁰ for 1 hour on cookie sheet. Turn halfway through cooking time and baste with any remaining sauce.

**Sioux Honey Association**

## Sioux Honey Association
## Sioux City, Iowa

*(Thank you to Mary Mallett)*
*for the included recipes*

In 1921 five men in Sioux City collected $200.00 between them and 3,000 pounds of honey to create the Sioux Honey Association. Sue Bee Honey is the only nationally advertised brand of honey in the U.S.

24

# Cookies Meatballs

2 pounds ground beef          2 eggs
1 cup applesauce              Salt and pepper
1 cup bread crumbs

Mix well and make into balls. Put into a crock pot (brown first).
Cover with this sauce. 2 cups Cookies Bar-B-Q Sauce, 1 cup tomato
juice, 1 small onion chopped, and 1 green pepper. Cook until done
and serve.

**Cookies Food Products, Inc.**

# Ham Puffs

**PUFFS:**
½ cup boiling water          ½ cup flour
4 tablespoons margarine       Dash of salt
2 eggs                        ½ cup shredded Swiss cheese

**FILLING:**
¼ cup mayonnaise             2 cups ground ham
¼ cup finely chopped onion    ¼ cup finely chopped celery

In medium saucepan melt margarine in ½ cup boiling water. Add
flour and a dash of salt. Stir vigorously. Cook and stir until mixture forms a ball that doesn't separate. Remove from heat and cool
slightly. Add the eggs and beat well until smooth. Stir in cheese.
Drop dough onto greased baking sheet, using 1 teaspoon for each
puff. Bake at 400° for 20 minutes. Remove puffs from oven, cool and
split. Make the filling from the remaining ingredients and fill each
puff, or I sometimes use a prepared ham spread from the meat
counter, if pressed for time.

**Carol Schneider**
**(Le Mars, Iowa)**
**(Thanks also to the Plymouth County Extension Service)**

25

# Devilish Piggy Wings

1 pound ribs, cut into 1-rib
portions OR boneless ribs,
(skewered)
2 tablespoons butter (melted)
1 tablespoon hot pepper
sauce

4 tablespoons Cajun
seasonings (purchased)
2 tablespoons cracker crumbs
or cornflake crumbs

In small bowl mix together butter and hot pepper sauce. In shallow plate mix together Cajun seasoning and crumbs. Dip ribs in butter mixture and then roll in the seasoning mixture. Place ribs an inch apart on an ungreased cookie sheet or other shallow pan and bake in a preheated 350⁰ F. oven for 45 minutes, until golden. Serve with blue cheese dressing for dipping, if desired. Serves four as an entree or 6-8 as appetizers. Approximately, per entree serving: Calories: 232, Fat; 13 gram; Cholesterol: 82 milligrams. Serve with fresh grapes and dinner rolls.

**Iowa Pork Producers Association**

## Iowa Pork Producers Association
## Clive, Iowa

Pork production plays a very important role in Iowa's agricultural economy, generating more than one-fourth of total cash farm income. Iowa leads the nation in pork production, producing about 25 million hogs per year, over 25 percent of all hogs in the U.S. Special thanks to Joyce Hoppes, Iowa Pork Producers Association, for a number of delicious pork recipes scattered throughout the different categories.

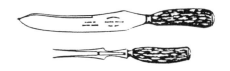

# Burgundy Mushrooms

*Delicious butter flavored mushrooms are simmered all day. They can be frozen in small containers and heated when friends drop in.*

| | |
|---|---|
| 1 cup butter | 1 teaspoon garlic powder |
| 1 quart red wine (cheap burgundy) | 2 cups boiling water |
| | 3 beef bouillon cubes |
| 2 tablespoons Worcestershire sauce | 3 chicken bouillon cubes |
| | 4 pounds fresh mushrooms |
| 1 teaspoon dill seed | Salt |
| 1 teaspoon pepper | |

Rinse mushrooms well and drain on paper towels. In a very large pot, combine butter, wine, Worcestershire, dill, pepper, garlic, water and bouillon. Bring to boil. Add mushrooms to liquid and reduce heat to simmer. Cover and cook 5 to 6 hours. Remove lid and cook 4 more hours. When ready, liquid should just cover mushrooms. Salt and pepper to taste. Serve hot. Yields: 12 to 16 servings.

**Bruce and Brenda Eckel**

# Stuffed Mushrooms

| | |
|---|---|
| 1 pound bulk pork sausage | 2 eggs |
| 1 pound white mushrooms | ¼ cup onions |
| 3 slices bread (wet and wrung out) | ½ teaspoon garlic powder |
| | 1 tablespoon parsley |

Fry sausage loose and drain. Add onions and mushroom stems. Cook 10 minutes, then add other ingredients. Fill mushrooms. Bake at 350⁰ for 30 minutes.

**Dorothy Willet**
**(Davenport, Iowa)**

27

# Cheese Stuffed Mushrooms

8 ounces fresh mushrooms
  (18-20)
6 slices bacon (cooked and
  crumbled)
2 tablespoons bacon drippings

1 small onion (chopped)
3 tablespoons mayonnaise
½ cup shredded cheese
  (cheddar)

Wash mushrooms, and remove stems. Chop stems and onion, and saute' in bacon drippings. Stir in mayonnaise, cheese, and bacon. Mix well, then stuff mushroom caps. Place on ungreased baking pan. Bake at 350° for 15 to 20 minutes. May cook for 10 minutes, cool, and freeze for later date.

**Donna Millhollin**
*Also thanks to: Carol R. Smith, Guthrie County Extension Service Center, Guthrie Center*

# Parmesan Onion Canapes

1 cup mayonnaise
1 cup grated Parmesan cheese
½ cup chopped onion

1 tablespoon milk
1 loaf cocktail rye (lightly
  toasted)

Mix first 4 ingredients. Spread on toast. Place on baking sheets. Broil 4 inches from source of heat for 2 to 3 minutes or until bubbly. Makes 36.

**Suzy Ven Horst
(Bettendorf, Iowa)**

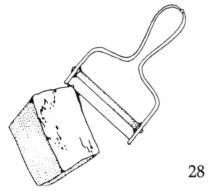

28

# Spinach Rolls

2 (10 ounce) packages
  chopped frozen spinach
  (thawed and drained)
1 cup sour cream
½ cup mayonnaise
8 ounces cream cheese
  (softened)

1 package Hidden Valley
  Ranch Dressing
1 bunch green onions
  (chopped)
½ package bacon bits
  (optional)

Mix all ingredients. Spread on tortillas, roll and refrigerate several hours. Slice and serve.

**Beulah Spaulding**

# Water Chestnut Wraps

2 cans whole water chestnuts    1 pound bacon

Cut bacon strips in half. Wrap around water chestnuts and secure with toothpick. Broil until brown. Drain grease. Cover with sauce and bake at 250⁰ for 1 hour.

**SAUCE:**
¾ cup brown sugar
1 small bottle catsup

1 tablespoon Worcestershire
  sauce

**Carol Wenndt
(Ankeny, Iowa)**

29

## Cheese Stuffed Bread

1½-2 pound bread loaf
 (preferably round)
2 cups cheddar cheese
8 ounces cream cheese
 (cubed)
1½ cups sour cream

1 cup diced ham/bacon
 (cooked)
1 can chopped green chilies
½ cup green onions
1 teaspoon Worcestershire
 sauce

Preheat oven to 350°, scoop out bread. Cut top off first, combine cheese, and sour cream in a bowl. Add ham, onions, green chilies and Worcestershire sauce. Stuff bread and place lid on top. Wrap in foil (2 layers of thin foil). Bake 1 hour and 10 minutes. Stir before serving.

Tina Vernon
(Davenport, Iowa)

## Cheese And Mushroom French Bread

2 loaves of French Bread
2 sticks of melted margarine
2 tablespoons of poppy seed
2 tablespoons of minced
 onions (instant is fine)
1 teaspoon dry mustard
1 teaspoon Lawry seasoned
 salt

1 teaspoon lemon juice
1 (8 ounce) package shredded
 Swiss cheese or use 1
 (16 ounce) package of
 sliced Swiss cheese (cut
 into pieces)
1 (8 ounce) can mushroom
 pieces

Mix all ingredients with melted margarine, except for the cheese and mushrooms. Preheat oven to 325°. Slice the French bread into about 1-inch slices. Spread butter and seasonings on each slice and add cheese and mushroom pieces. Wrap the bread in foil, but leave the top open (not sealed). Bake at 325° for about 30 minutes.

Robin Linville

# Creamy Bar "B" "Q" Beef Dip

1 (3 ounces) package dried
  chipped beef
2 teaspoons vinegar
2 teaspoons Cookies Bar-B-Q
  Sauce

1 (8 ounces) cream cheese
  (softened)
½ teaspoon onion or garlic
  powder
½ cup mayonnaise
Salt (to taste)

Tear or cut beef into small pieces and mix ingredients with electric mixer. Serve with chips, crackers or vegetables. This can be served hot or as firm cheese spread when chilled.

**Cookies Food Products, Inc.**

# Bean Dip

1 pound hamburger
1 bottle salsa
1 can refried beans

1 package taco seasoning
2 (8 ounce) packages cream
  cheese
16 ounces shredded cheddar
  cheese

Spread cream cheese on bottom of 9x13 inch pan. Cook hamburger and drain. Add salsa, beans, and taco seasoning. Pour over cream cheese. Add cheddar cheese over top. Bake at 350⁰ for 20 minutes or until cheese melts.

**Mary Noack
(Le Claire, Iowa)**

# Caramel Dip

1 (8 ounce) package cream
   cheese
¾ cup brown sugar

¼ cup white sugar
1 teaspoon real vanilla

Blend and serve with apples.

Melissa Gray
(Le Claire, Iowa)

# Honey Caramel Dip

½ cup Sue Bee Honey
1 (14 ounce) package caramels

½ cup evaporated milk
5 or 6 unpeeled, cored apples
   sliced into thin wedges

Combine first 3 ingredients in heavy saucepan. Heat over low, stir-ring constantly until caramels are melted and mixture is smooth. For a thinner sauce, heat with additional evaporated milk. Cool to room temperature and use as a dip for apple wedges. Also good as an ice cream topping or drizzled over unfrosted cake squares. Keep refrigerated for weeks.

**Sioux Honey Association**

# Fruit Dip

1 (7 ounce) jar marshmallow
   cream
1 (8 ounce) package cream
   cheese

⅓ cup Sue Bee Honey
Fresh fruit cut into slices

Whip marshmallow cream, cream cheese and Sue Bee Honey until smooth and creamy. Good with slices of apples, bananas, peaches, strawberries or oranges.

**Sioux Honey Association**

32

# Hawaiian Dip

1 (8 ounce) package cream
  cheese
1 (8 ounce) package sour
  cream
½ cup mayonnaise
2 tablespoons lemon juice
1 teaspoon salt

1-2 bunches green onions
1 package chopped Buddig
  Beef
1 (10 ounce) package frozen
  chopped spinach
1 round loaf Hawaiian bread

Mix cream cheese until soft, add sour cream and blend well. Add mayonnaise and lemon juice and mix well. Add 1 tsp. salt. Add finely chopped green onions and chopped Buddig Beef. Squeeze out the water in the spinach and chop it. Add to the mixture. Hollow out the Hawaiian Bread and save the inside, tear up the inside, and put the dip in the bread.

**Joni Lange**
**(Davenport)**

# Shrimp Dip

1 (3 ounce) package cream
  cheese
½ cup mayonnaise

1 teaspoon Tabasco sauce or
  hot sauce
1 small can small shrimp
1 teaspoon green onion

Mix and serve with chips.

**Carol Wenndt**
**(Ankeny, Iowa)**

# Stroganoff Dip

1 clove garlic
2 pounds Jimmy Dean
  Sausage
4 tablespoons flour
2 cups beef broth
2 onions (medium) chopped
1 cup sliced fresh mushrooms
½ stick butter

2 teaspoons soy sauce
2 tablespoons Worcestershire
  sauce
1 teaspoon dry mustard
Salt, pepper, paprika
Dash of Tabasco
2 cups sour cream

Rub large skillet with garlic; heat and brown sausage. Crumble sausage with a fork. Sprinkle sausage with flour; add beef broth. Simmer until slightly thickened and set aside. Saute' onions and mushrooms in butter until onions are tender. Add onions, mushrooms and seasonings to sausage mixture. Cook until mixture bubbles; remove from heat and add sour cream. Keep hot in chafing dish. Serve with toasted party rye or party size pumpernickel bread. (Freezes well before adding sour cream.)

**Mrs. Chris Branstad**
**(Terrace Hill)**

# Taco Dip

1 ripe avocado
1 (8 ounce) package cream
  cheese
1 cup cottage cheese
2 tablespoons lemon juice

Chopped onion
Shredded lettuce
1 chopped tomato
Shredded cheddar cheese

Cube avocado; add cheese, cottage cheese and lemon juice. Blend in blender. Spread in 9-inch glass pie plate. Layer on top: diced onion, shredded lettuce, chopped tomato and shredded cheese. Serve with taco chips.

**Carol Wenndt**
**(Ankeny)**

# Vegetable Dip

1 cup sour cream
1 cup mayonnaise
2 tablespoons parsley flakes

2 teaspoons Bon Appetit
  spice
2 teaspoons dill weed
2 teaspoons minced onion

Mix all ingredients. Store in the refrigerator.

**Donna Dudley**
**(Le Claire)**

# Cheese Ball

*Here is a recipe having to do with the Maytag Blue Cheese.*

2 packages (8 ounces each)
  cream cheese
1 package (4 ounces) Blue
  cheese

1 roll of hickory smoked
  cheese
½ pound butter

Mix the above with electric mixer until creamy. Then add the following:

2 cans (small) chopped ripe
  olives
1 bottle green stuffed olives
  (chopped)

1 tablespoon finely chopped
  onion

Continue beating until all ingredients are mixed. Chill until firm, then form into log or ball and roll in nuts. Return to the refrigerator until firm. The longer it sets (up to two weeks) the stronger the flavor. I also add nuts to the ball as well as rolling the ball in them.

**Charlotte Smith**
**(Jasper County Extension Service, Newton, Iowa)**

# Cream Cheese Logs

1 (8 ounce) cream cheese (softened)
2 to 3 T. ground black olives
1 tablespoon mayonnaise

1½ teaspoons Worcestershire sauce
1 teaspoon hot sauce
1½ teaspoons minced onion

Mix together. Butter hands and form into 2 logs. Roll in chopped dried beef. Refrigerate. Spread on Ritz Crackers.

**LeAnne Schneckloth (Wayne)**

# Cheese Spread

2 (8 ounce) packages Philadelphia cream cheese (softened)
1 (16 ounce) carton sour cream

2 (2.5 ounce) package Buddig Dried Beef
1 green onion
Celery
Green pepper
Olives

To softened cream cheese, add dried beef that has been cut up into fine pieces. Fold in sour cream. Last add 1 green onion, celery, green pepper and olives; all finely chopped. Use desired amounts to your taste. Mix together, then place in casserole and bake for 30 minutes at 350°. Cool before serving. Serve with crackers.

**Helen J. Kasparek**
**(Des Moines, Iowa)**

# Crab Cheese Spread

**LAYER I:**

1 (12 ounce) cream cheese
   (softened)
2 tablespoons Worcestershire
   sauce

1 tablespoon lemon juice
2 tablespoons salad dressing
Dash of garlic salt

**LAYER II:**
½ bottle chili sauce

**LAYER III:**
1 (16 ounce) crab meat
   (drained)

**LAYER IV:**
Parsley

Layer I: Mix well and spread on 9-inch plate.

Layer II: Spread chili sauce over Layer I.

Layer III: Flake crabmeat and put on top of Layer II.

Layer IV: Sprinkle generously with parsley. Wrap securely in Saran Wrap and refrigerate overnight. Serve with sesame crackers.

NOTE: Great Christmas Hors D'oeuvres

**Debra Brendeland**
**(Thanks also to: Story County Extension Service, Ames, Iowa)**

# Crunchy Pork Spread

½ pound ground pork
8 slices cooked bacon
1 (8 ounce) package cream
  cheese
½ cup Thousand Island
  dressing

¼ cup chopped green onion
¼ cup chopped bacon
2 cups shredded cheddar or
  mozzarella cheese

Brown ground pork; drain and set aside. Crumble cooked bacon. Combine ground pork; bacon and remaining ingredients. Blend and chill. Serve on crackers or cocktail rye bread.

Suzy Ven Horst
(Bettendorf)

# Shrimp Mousse

1 cup tomato soup

1 (8 ounce) package cream
  cheese

Simmer over low flame until melted.

1 package Knox gelatin

¼ cup water

Mix and add to soup mixture. Put in refrigerator and cool. While this is cooling, finely chop ½ cup celery and ½ cup green onions.

1 cup mayonnaise

2 cans (medium) shrimp
  (drained & broken up into
  pieces)

Add this to the cooled ingredients and mix. Put in mold and chill. Serve with crackers.

Kay Youngers
(Princeton, Iowa)

# Baked Caramel Corn

6 quarts popped JOLLY TIME Pop Corn
1 cup (2 sticks) butter or margarine
2 cups firmly packed brown sugar

½ cup light or dark corn syrup
1 teaspoon salt
½ teaspoon baking soda
1 teaspoon vanilla

Preheat oven to 250ºF. Coat the bottom and sides of a large roasting pan with a nonstick vegetable spray. Place popped popcorn in roasting pan. In a heavy pan, slowly melt butter, stir in brown sugar, corn syrup and salt. Bring to a boil, stirring constantly; boil without stirring for 5 minutes. Remove from heat; stir in baking soda and vanilla. Gradually pour over popcorn, mixing well. Bake for 1 hour, stirring every 15 minutes. Remove from oven; cool completely. Break apart. Makes about 6 quarts.

CHOCOLATE COATED CARAMEL CORN: Melt 6 ounces of any type of semi-sweet or milk chocolate used for baking. Pour the melted chocolate over 1½ quarts of Baked Caramel Corn. Stir until evenly coated. Chill in the refrigerator. Break into clusters. Store in refrigerator.

**JOLLY TIME Popcorn**
**American Pop Corn Company**

## JOLLY TIME Pop Corn
## American Pop Corn Company
## Sioux City, Iowa

The American Pop Corn Company in Sioux City goes back to 1914 when Cloid H. Smith founded it and created JOLLY TIME, America's first brand name popcorn. Today third and fourth generations of the Smith family continue to carry on their grandfather's and great-grandfather's legacy. The recipe for Baked Caramel Corn is a Smith family favorite and has been handed down from generation to generation.

Special thanks to Tom Elsen for sharing JOLLY TIME recipes.

# No Fuss Caramel Corn

3 quarts popped popcorn
1½ cups peanuts
1 cup brown sugar
½ cup butter

¼ cup light corn syrup
½ teaspoon salt
½ teaspoon baking soda

After popping 3 quarts of popcorn, put in a brown paper bag. Add peanuts with popcorn in brown paper bag. Combine brown sugar, butter, light corn syrup, and salt in 2 quart glass bowl that is microwave safe. Microwave the above ingredients for 3-4 minutes on high, then stir. Continue microwaving 2 more minutes, and stir again. Then put in baking soda and microwave 2 more minutes. When it begins to bubble, you are ready to take out. Pour syrup over popped corn. Close bag and shake well. Place brown bag with contents into microwave on high for 1½ minutes. Then shake again. Microwave 1½ minutes more, then pour popcorn into bowls and let set 30 minutes to cool.

NOTE: Shake well and watch closely so corn doesn't burn. Microwaves vary.

**Mrs. Carla Gerot**
**(Clive, Iowa)**

# Peanut Butter Popcorn

1 cup unpopped popcorn
½ cup Karo syrup
½ cup sugar

½ cup peanut butter
½ teaspoon vanilla

Pop popcorn. Bring syrup and sugar to full rolling boil. Remove from heat. Add peanut butter and vanilla. Pour mixture over popcorn and toss.

**Lea Henderson**
**(Thanks also to: Story County Extension Service, Ames, Iowa)**

# Crunchy Peanut Butter Balls
# (Sugar Free)

½ cup raisins
¼ cup apple juice concentrate
¼ cup peanut butter
¼ cup low fat dry milk

1 teaspoon vanilla
1 teaspoon cinnamon
1 cup Grape Nuts

Heat raisins and apple juice concentrate in a saucepan. Boil about 2 minutes. Pour raisins in a blender and puree. Mix raisin puree and remainder of ingredients in a bowl. If dry, add a few drops of water. Let children help you shape the mixture into small balls. Great to eat as is or even better if refrigerated overnight. Makes approximately 30 small balls.

**Bonnie Maguire**

# Southwestern Crunch

1 pop and serve bag
   (3.5 ounce) JOLLY TIME
   Light Microwave Pop
   Corn, Butter Flavored or
   Natural Flavor, popped
3 tablespoons butter or
   margarine

1 teaspoon chili powder
¼ teaspoon oregano
   (crumbled)
¼ teaspoon cumin
Dash cayenne pepper

Place popped popcorn in large bowl. Melt butter in small pan; add chili powder, oregano, cumin and cayenne pepper. Drizzle over popcorn and toss lightly. Makes about 2 quarts.

**American Pop Corn Company**
**(Sioux City, Iowa)**

41

# Popcorn Balls

2½ cups sorghum
½ cup water
½ teaspoon salt

½ teaspoon vinegar
1 teaspoon vanilla
5 quarts popped popcorn

Mix sorghum, water, salt and vinegar and bring to a hard ball, 250°.
Add vanilla, pour over popcorn and mix evenly. Let cool until sticky.
Butter hands and form popcorn mixture into balls. Wrap in plastic
to keep fresh.

**Neal Smith**
**(Former US Representative from Iowa)**

# White Chocolate Party Mix

1 (10 ounce) package mini
   pretzels
5 cups Cheerios
5 cups Corn Chex
2 cups salted peanuts

1 pound M&M's
2 packages (12 ounces each)
   vanilla chips
3 tablespoons vegetable oil

In a large bowl, combine first five ingredients; set aside. In a
microwave-safe bowl, microwave chips and oil on medium high for
2 minutes, stirring once. Microwave on high for 10 seconds; stir until
smooth. Pour over cereal mixture and mix well. Spread onto three
waxed paper-lined baking sheets. Cool; break apart. Store in an airtight container. Makes 5 quarts. (700 watt microwave was used)

**Lea Henderson**

# Party Mix

½ cup margarine
½ cup oil
2 teaspoons Worcestershire
   sauce
½ teaspoon garlic salt
1 teaspoon onion salt
½ teaspoon celery salt

4 cups Cheerios cereal
4 cups Wheat Chex cereal
4 cups Rice Chex cereal
4 cups Corn Chex cereal
2 cups broken pretzel pieces
1 package salted peanuts or
   mixed nuts

Melt margarine and oil in a large roaster on top of stove. Add and stir in all the spices. Add Worcestershire sauce. Take off heat and add cereals, pretzels, and nuts. Mix thoroughly until oil and spice mixture coats the cereal. Bake, uncovered, one full hour at 250⁰, stirring every 15 minutes.

**Sandy Cammack**
**(Thanks also to: Bertha Shaw, Hamilton County Extension**
**Service, Webster City, Iowa)**

43

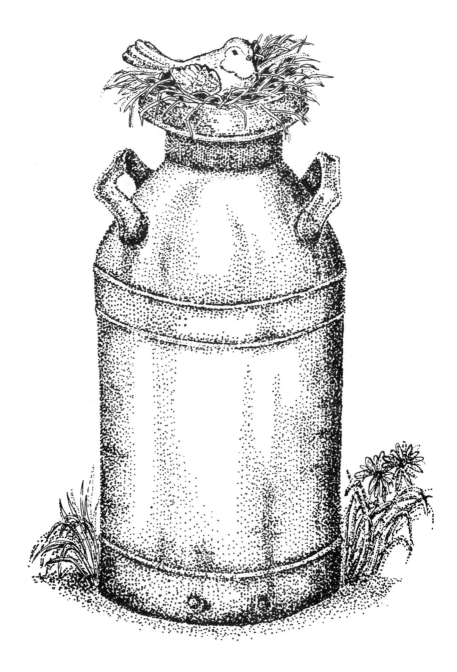

Carol Love

44

# Brunch

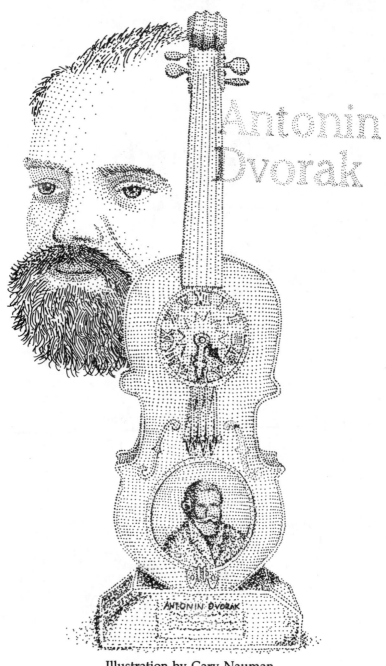

ANTONIN DVORAK

Illustration by Gary Nauman

# The Bily Clock Museum/Dvorak Exhibit
## Spillville, Iowa

Spillville, a town of a little over 400, is located in northeastern Iowa, on the south side of the Turkey River. Predominantly a Czech village, it combines Old World traditions with more modern ways.

The historic building, now the famous Bily Clock Museum/Dvorak Exhibit, was built in 1859 by Jacob Schmitt, a tinsmith. Clocks, throughout the museum, range in size from 8 inches to almost 11 feet, each with a different theme. Almost everyone has figural movement and musical discs that are played during tours.

The Bily Brothers, Joseph C. and Frank L., were born of Czech ancestry. Joseph was born at Calmar September 5, 1880, and his brother Frank was born on their home farm 4 miles north of Spillville on October 1, 1884. By trade they were farmers and carpenters. Carving was really just a hobby. They divided their work. Their tools were simple, many homemade. In 1947 they arranged for the entire clock collection to become property of the town of Spillville, after their death, never to be broken up; and to always remain at its present location, in the building once occupied by Composer Antonin Dvorak during his visit to Spillville in 1893.

Dvorak was born in Bohemia September, 1841. He came to Spillville upon encouragement from Joseph J. Kovarik, who as a young man, studied music in Prague. Later Kovarik became Dvorak's American secretary. After spending time in New York City Dvorak became homesick for his native country and Kovarik suggested he come to Spillville for his summer vacation. Dvorak's most recognized composition is the "New World Symphony".

When Dvorak was in Spillville, he often walked through Riverside Park. The Dvorak Memorial marks his favorite spot for composing music.

Spillville has a great deal to offer its tourist population. When a person leaves town, there is one more attraction to experience, and that is one of its famous kolaches!

**BRUNCH**

Apple-Bacon-
  Cheddar-Bake .........49
Apple Sausage
  Breakfast Ring.........49
Country Brunch .........50
Breakfast Baked Eggs ....50
Breakfast Egg Casserole ..51
Christmas Breakfast
  Casserole .............51
Company Breakfast ......52
Bed and Breakfast
  Tortillas ..............52
Aebleskivers (Danish
  Pancake) (Recipe used
  for Tivoli Fest) ........54
Aebleskivers ............54
Iowa Corn Pancakes .....55
Norwegian Sour
  Cream Waffles ......56,57
Coffee Cake ..........58,59

Butterscotch Coffee Cake .58
Cherry Coffee Cake ......59
Bundt Coffee Cake.......60
Good Morning
  Coffee Cake ..........61
Cinnamon Puffs .........61
Oatmeal Coffee Cake.....62
Sour Cream Coffee Cake .62
Easy Breakfast
  Cheese Danish ........63
Pfotrchen (Fudgens)......63
Ferden..................64
Svestkove' Knedli´ky .....64
Ferden..................65
Groton Hans..........65,66
Danish Kringle ..........67
Pigs In A Blanket .....68-69
Speck-Dicken
  (Old Year Cakes) ......70
Frozen Fruit.............71

# Apple-Bacon-Cheddar-Bake

1 pound bacon (fried crisp)
3 cups sliced apples
2 tablespoons sugar
2 cups shredded Cheddar
cheese

2 cups biscuit mix (or 2 cups
flour + 3 teaspoons baking
powder + ½ teaspoon
salt
2 cups milk
4-5 eggs

Mix apples and sugar. Spread in a 9x13-inch pan. Cover apples with cheese. Sprinkle with crumbled bacon. Beat remaining ingredients together and pour evenly over apples, cheese and bacon. Bake at 375⁰ for 30 to 35 minutes until lightly browned. Serves 12.

**LeAnne Schneckloth (Wayne)**

# Apple Sausage Breakfast Ring

2 pounds lean pork sausage
2 large eggs (slightly beaten)
1½ cups crushed Ritz
crackers

1 cup grated apple (peeled)
½ cup minced onion
¼ cup milk

Line a 2½ quart ring mold with plastic wrap or wax paper. Combine all ingredients. Mix well and press firmly into mold. Chill several hours or overnight. Unmold, removing plastic onto a baking sheet with raised edges. Bake at 350⁰ for 1 hour. Transfer onto a serving platter, fill center of ring with scrambled eggs. Yield 8 servings.

**Malinda Burk**
**(Thanks also to: Bret Warnke, Ida County Extension Education Director, Ida Grove, Iowa)**

49

# Country Brunch

The flavor depends on the sausage. Make sure you use the kind you particularly like.

9 slices bread (cubed)
2½ pounds bulk sausage
   (sauteed and drained)
10 ounces Cheddar cheese
   (grated)

8 eggs
3 cups milk
1½ teaspoons dry mustard
½ teaspoon salt
½ teaspoon pepper

Place half of bread cubes in bottom of 13x9x2-inch pan. Put half of sausage on top, followed by half of cheese. Repeat layers. Beat eggs with milk, mustard, salt and pepper. Pour mixture over layers in pan. Cover and refrigerate overnight. Remove cover and bake in 350° oven 1 hour. Makes 12 to 14 servings.

**Mrs. Billie Ray**
**(Wife of former Iowa Governor Robert D. Ray)**

# Breakfast Baked Eggs

8 eggs
2 cups milk plus juice of
   mushrooms
4 slices white bread cubed
1 teaspoon dry mustard
1 can mushrooms

½ pound grated cheese
1 cup chopped ham
½ pepper
½ onion
¾ cup chopped celery

Grease a 9x13-inch pan, then spread; meat, bread, mushrooms, cheese, celery, onions, and pepper. Mix eggs, milk, and mustard together. Pour over meat and refrigerate overnight. This must be done. The next morning take out and bake 45 minutes uncovered at 350°. Let set for 5 minutes. Then serve. After baking you may freeze and reheat.

**Catherine Freund**
**(Davenport)**

## Breakfast Egg Casserole

| | |
|---|---|
| 8 slices whole wheat bread | ¾ teaspoon dry mustard |
| ½ pound American cheese | ¾ teaspoon salt |
| ½ pound cheddar cheese | Chopped ham, cooked bacon |
| 3 cups milk | or sausage (as much as you |
| 6 eggs (well beaten) | wish) |

Lightly butter and cube bread. Shred cheese. Mix milk, eggs, mustard and salt. Alternate layers of bread and cheese in greased 9x13-inch glass baking dish. Add ham, bacon or sausage. Pour milk and egg mixture over other ingredients. Let stand overnight, covered, in refrigerator. Bake one hour at 325° until set.

*Our daughter, Linda, brought me this recipe for Christmas shortly after she was married. After enjoying it the first time she added this note: Serves 8 Vandehaars. We have continued to use this casserole recipe for our Christmas breakfast. Since our family gathering is much larger, we now prepare a double recipe and serve it with muffins or quick breads, fruit juice and coffee. This recipe has served many families, men's groups, and women's clubs, as the recipe appears in a cookbook published by the United Methodist Church of Mitchellville, Iowa.*

**Bonnie Vandehaar**
**(Mitchellville, Iowa)**

## Christmas Breakfast Casserole

This recipe is similar to one above. One variation that may be used if desired is 1 can of mushrooms.

*My family enjoys this dish during the holidays. Nice to make the day before to allow extra family time in the morning on special days!*

**Donna Millhollin**
**(Thanks also to: Carol R. Smith,**
**Guthrie County Extension Service, Guthrie Center, Iowa)**

51

# Company Breakfast

12-16 slices bread (remove
  crusts)
6 eggs (well beaten)
3 cups milk
6 slices ham (thin)
1 teaspoon salt

1 teaspoon pepper
1 teaspoon dry mustard
6 thin slices Swiss cheese
1 chopped onion (½ cup)
1 chopped green pepper
  (½ cup)

Cover bottom of 9x13-inch buttered pan with slices of bread. Cover bread with slices of ham and cheese. Repeat a layer of bread. Over all pour a mixture of eggs, milk, salt, pepper, mustard, onion and green pepper. Can be refrigerated overnight. Bake at 350⁰ for one hour.

*We have a group of five couples that get together about three times a year: February, July, and September. They come from all over the state. We would have them all up to our place on the Mississippi in the fall so we could go the apple festivals. They'd be at our place for breakfast and supper on Saturday night. It was always nice to find something simple and easy to prepare, something which could be made ahead.*

**Lucille Richards
(Denver, Iowa)**

# Bed And Breakfast Tortillas

½ pound seasoned pork
  sausage
5 eggs

½ cup shredded cheddar
  cheese
6 flour tortillas
6 tablespoons picante sauce

Cook sausage, drain and set aside. Scramble eggs. When eggs are set add sausage and warm briefly. Remove from heat and add cheese. Warm tortillas and fill with egg mixture. Add picante sauce and roll. Serve warm with sour cream.

**Andrew Lansink
(Thanks also to: Bret Warnke,
County Extension Education Director, Ida Grove, Iowa)**

# Macksburg, Home of The National Skillet Throwing Championship

By: Georgina Breakenridge
Madison County Cookbook

The National Skillet Throwing Championship has brought a certain kind of fame to the Madison County town of Macksburg. The first contest held some 15 years ago, was the start of an annual media attraction which grew to national and then world-wide coverage. Georgina Breakenridge is the Mayor of Macksburg and President of the Macksburg Community Club that sponsors the National Skillet Championship.

The second year of the event was headlined by country music hall-of-famer Kitty Wells and attracted an estimated crowd of 5,000 plus. Considering Macksburg's total population of 130, this influx of humanity made for standing room only. Macksburg is located 18 miles southwest of Winterset.

Perhaps the most noteworthy contest was what has been commonly referred to as, "The Year Japan Was Here." A film crew from Tokyo journeyed to Macksburg to tape the event for National Japanese television. On the way from the Des Moines Airport, it was suggested that perhaps this film crew, actor, and directors, could get together as a team and compete. Instant approval was given by the Japanese and a team was formed. They won the World Championship that year and could boast that the World's Skillet Throwing Champs were from Japan!

Also there was the year the target dummy was kidnapped. Three fretful days passed before "Dumb-Dumb" was found, perched peacefully on the right-hand side of the two-holer in the city park.

Another year, much energy was expended as each team was required to throw a skillet by relays from Macksburg to Winterset. Teams left Macksburg at 8:00 in the morning throwing a skillet as they went. Some 6 hours later they were met at the Winterset city limits by County Sheriff Rex Rouse. The skillet thrown by the winning team now holds a place of honor in the Madison County Museum.

Since the first Skillet Throw in 1975, the championship has been reported on radio stations in 37 states and seen on television stations in 29 states, Japan, and the armed service network. Articles have appeared in scores of newspapers, and letters have been received from all over the world.

The Annual Skillet Throw is held the third Saturday of June!

53

# Aebleskivers (Danish Pancakes)
# (Recipe used for Tivoli Fest)

12 cups flour
1½ cups sugar
1 tablespoon salt
½ cup baking powder

2 tablespoons soda
24 eggs (separated)
3 quarts buttermilk

Mix flour, sugar, salt, baking powder and soda. Add egg yolks and buttermilk. Whip egg whites and add last. Heat aebleskiver pan until hot on medium heat. Fill aebleskiver pan cups ¼ full of oil before filling with dough. As batter cooks, turn with a fine knitting needle or an ice pick, so that it forms a round ball. Turn slowly and bake thoroughly. Recipe can be halved.

**Danish Windmill**
**(Elk Horn, Iowa)**

# Aebleskivers

Recipe above with a variation: Place an apple slice into each depression before baking. Or try powdered sugar on top.

**Vivian Anderson**
**(Soldier, Iowa)**

# Iowa Corn Pancakes

| | |
|---|---|
| 1½ cups sifted enriched flour | ½ cup yellow cornmeal |
| 2 tablespoons sugar | 2 slightly beaten eggs |
| 1 teaspoon soda | 2 cups buttermilk |
| 1 teaspoon salt | 2 tablespoons melted butter |
| 1 teaspoon baking powder | or bacon fat |
| (optional) | |

Mix all the dry ingredients together well. Beat the eggs lightly with a fork and then mix the eggs well with 1 cup buttermilk. Mix the dry mixture with the egg, buttermilk mixture. Mix well with a hand beater, not a machine mixer. I then add melted butter to the mixture and mix. Add buttermilk to the mixture until it is the proper thickness for cooking. The 2 cups of buttermilk called for in the recipe is not an absolute quantity. Add just enough buttermilk to get the desired thickness. One soon learns the right thickness for proper cooking of the pancakes. I fry in a teflon-lined skillet heated between medium high and high (about halfway). The skillet is ready for frying when drops of water bounce around and quickly evaporate. This you will learn by experience. It is a good idea to fry the cakes as soon as you have the batter prepared. It loses "rising power" as it stands. You can see the bubbles form as the mixture stands. Try it. You will like them!

Jack Van Pilsum
(Minneapolis, Minn., formerly Prairie City, Iowa)

# Norwegian Sour Cream Waffles

*My recipe is from Norway, and so is the special heart shaped iron. May be served hot as a breafast waffle, but I like to serve them whenever I would other small sandwiches.*

| | |
|---|---|
| 5 eggs | 1 teaspoon ground cardamon* |
| ½ cup sugar | 1 cup sour cream |
| 1 cup flour | 4 tablespoons melted butter |

Beat the eggs and sugar 5-10 minutes until light and fluffy. Fold in flour and sour cream, then the butter. Heat waffle iron until hot and pour on ¾ cup of batter. Turn and lightly brown the other side. Place on rack to cool. Makes 5 large waffles or 25 heart shaped waffles. Separate into heart shapes carefully. To serve, arrange on pretty glass or silver plate and have an assortment of jams and marmalades (strawberry jam is the favorite and very colorful) and either bowl of whipped cream or sour cream. Place a small teaspoon of jam and cream in middle and fold over both sides or leave flat and serve on a small plate with salad fork.

*\*Cardamon is a favorite Norwegian spice used in many cookies. Stores in Decorah carry this spice in either ground form or may be purchased in buds where you remove the outer shell and use mortar and pestle to fine grind, which makes a stronger and fresher aroma. I usually make a double batch of these as they freeze well.*

**Eunice C. Stoen**
**(Decorah, Iowa)**

*I am very aware of the Sesquicentennial as two people from the Smithsonian in Washington D.C. were here last fall interviewing me about Norwegian cooking, our roots, farm, etc. I was also interviewed locally by a lady who was doing some writing on this subject.*

*(Continued on Next Page)*

We live on a farm 13 miles N.E. of Decorah on Stoen-haugen Farm, (Stoen farm on the hill). I have written three Norwegian cookbooks: one in 1981, 1988, and the last one in 1994. I am sending the recipe for Kransekake or wedding cake, plus one for lefse, Norwegian Sour Cream Waffles, and Julekake, which is a Christmas bread, rich with butter, eggs, cardamon flavoring and mixed citron and light raisins, frosted and decorated with red and green cherries, etc.

My friend and I also make lefse for demonstrations at our museum during Nordic Fest; We sell and ship all over by U.P.S., I also, at the Nordic Fest in Decorah, put on programs with Lefse, Goro, Heart Shaped Waffles, etc. Our church ladies make 45 dozen lefse for the Big Canoe's annual Lutefisk and Meatball Dinner. Gary Legwold, who wrote the book, "The Last Word on Lefse," did a write up on me, Wilbur, my husband, and our farm. My husband Wilbur and I are both 100 percent Norwegian, and Wilbur's family was one of the first settlers in this area, buying a section of land in the early 1850's; so almost at the time Iowa was admitted as a state.

I am one of the 1,000 field editors of the new magazine "Taste of Home."

**Eunice C. Stoen**
**(Decorah, Iowa)**

# Coffee Cake
### (Ellen Steamboat Recipe)

2 packages yeast
1 cup milk
¼ cup lard or shortening
½ cup sugar
1 teaspoon salt

2 eggs (optional)
½ cup raisins
Sugar and cinnamon
About 4 cups flour

Scald milk. Take from heat. Add sugar, lard, and salt. Cool to lukewarm. Add yeast. Let sit a few minutes until yeast dissolves. Add the 2 eggs. Then gradually add the flour. Turn out on board and knead until elastic and no longer sticky. Let rise about 1 hour until double. Roll out and add raisins, sugar and cinnamon. Roll up, like a jelly roll. Place in circle on greased baking sheet. Press ends together. Slit top at 1-inch intervals. Brush with butter. Bake 35 to 40 minutes or until golden brown.

**Rose Peters, Cook - Ellen Steamboat
Submitted by: Lois Havenhill
(Princeton, Iowa)**

# Butterscotch Coffee Cake

1 package yellow cake mix
  (no pudding in mix)
2 eggs
1 (17½ ounce) can Thank You
  Butterscotch Pudding

1 package (6 ounce)
  butterscotch chips
½ cup nuts
¼ cup sugar

Beat cake mix, eggs and can of pudding for 4 minutes. Pour into greased, but not floured, 9x13-inch pan. Mix chips, nuts and sugar together. Sprinkle the mixture over the cake. Bake at 350⁰ for 40 minutes.

*(Melts in your mouth - yummy)!*

**Marilyn Mitchem
(Bettendorf, Iowa)**

# Coffee Cake

2 sticks butter
1 cup sugar
2 eggs
2 cups flour
1 teaspoon baking powder

1 teaspoon soda
½ teaspoon salt
1 cup sour cream
1 teaspoon vanilla

TOPPING:
⅓ cup brown sugar
¼ cup white sugar

1 cup nuts
1 teaspoon cinnamon

Cream butter and sugar, then beat in eggs, and vanilla. Alternate rest of dry ingredients and sour cream. Bake at 350⁰ for 35 minutes.

*This is a Christmas morning tradition at our house.*

**Dorothy Willet**
**(Davenport, Iowa)**

# Cherry Coffee Cake

1 cup sugar
4 eggs
1 cup salad oil

2 cups flour
1 teaspoon baking powder
1 large can cherry pie filling

Mix all the ingredients together, then take half the batter and put it in a 13x9-inch greased pan. Spread pie filling over that, put the other half of batter on top, then sprinkle cinnamon over top. Bake 40 minutes in 350⁰ oven. When warm, spread with powdered sugar.

**Catherine Freund**
**(Davenport, Iowa)**

# Bundt Coffee Cake

| | |
|---|---|
| 1 package yellow cake mix | ¾ cup water |
| 1 package (3 ounce) instant vanilla pudding | 4 eggs |
| | 1 teaspoon vanilla |
| ¾ cup oil | 1 teaspoon butter flavoring |

**TOPPING:**

| | |
|---|---|
| ¼ cup sugar | ½ cup chopped pecans |
| 2 teaspoons cinnamon | |

Grease and flour bundt cake pan or 9x13-inch cake pan. Sprinkle ¼-⅓ of the topping in the pan. Combine ingredients and pour half of the batter into the pan. Add a layer of the topping mixture (about half of what is left) followed by the rest of the batter and then the remaining topping mixture. Use a knife to swirl the cinnamon mixture through the batter. Bake at 350⁰ for 45 to 50 minutes. Cool approximately 10 minutes before removing from pan.

**GLAZE:**

| | |
|---|---|
| 1 cup powdered sugar | 2 tablespoons milk (or enough for glaze consistency) |
| ½ teaspoon vanilla | |
| ½ teaspoon butter flavoring | |

Drizzle glaze on cake while it is still warm. Garnish with pecans.

**Tammy Watson**

# Good Morning Coffee Cake

2 cups flour
½ teaspoon salt
½ teaspoon soda
1 teaspoon baking powder
1 cup white sugar

⅓ cup butter
1 cup buttermilk
2 eggs
1 teaspoon vanilla

FILLING:
¼ cup butter
1 cup brown sugar
½ cup flour

2 teaspoons cinnamon
½ cup chopped nuts

Sift flour, salt, soda, baking powder, and sugar into large bowl. Cut in butter. Beat together the buttermilk, egg and vanilla, add to dry ingredients. Pour ½ of the batter in a well-greased, floured 12x8-inch pan. Combine filling ingredients except nuts and pour filling over batter. Sprinkle with nuts. Cover with remaining batter. Bake at 350° for 35 to 40 minutes. Note: Batter may be kept, unbaked, in refrigerator overnight and baked and served warm for breakfast.

**Mary Etta (Schneckloth) Thomsen**

# Cinnamon Puffs

1½ cups flour
1½ teaspoons baking powder
½ cup sugar
½ teaspoon salt
⅓ cup oil

½ cup milk
1 egg
1 teaspoon vanilla
1 teaspoon lemon or orange
extract

Mix all ingredients well. Pour into very small muffin tins (greased). Bake at 350° for 10 minutes. Cool. Can be frozen now. Roll in ⅓ stick melted butter and 1½ cups sugar mixed with 1 teaspoon cinnamon. You may double the topping if needed. Makes 30 puffs.

*(Great for a fall brunch or anytime!)*

**Marilyn Mitchem
(Bettendorf, Iowa)**

# Oatmeal Coffee Cake

| | |
|---|---|
| 1 cup sugar | ½ cup oatmeal |
| ½ cup shortening | 1 teaspoon soda |
| 2 eggs | ½ teaspoon baking powder |
| 1 teaspoon vanilla | ½ teaspoon cinnamon |
| ½ cup chopped dates | ½ teaspoon salt |
| ½ cup walnuts | 1½ cups flour |
| ½ cup coconut | 1 cup buttermilk |

Cream shortening (I use oleo) and sugar. Add eggs, beating well. Stir in vanilla, dates, walnuts, coconut and oatmeal. Sift dry ingredients together and add to first mixture alternately with buttermilk. Mix well. Bake in greased loaf pan for 50 to 60 minutes in 350⁰ oven.

Marguerite Vens
(Davenport, Iowa)

# Sour Cream Coffee Cake

| | |
|---|---|
| 2 sticks butter or margarine | 1 teaspoon baking powder |
| 2 cups sugar | ¼ teaspoon salt |
| 1 tsp. vanilla | 1 teaspoon cinnamon |
| 2 eggs | (optional) |
| 2 cups flour | 1 cup chopped pecans |
| 1 carton sour cream | Some cinnamon and sugar |
| | (mixed) |

Cream butter and sugar well. Beat in eggs and vanilla. Sift dry ingredients together. Add creamed mixture along with sour cream. Pour in bundt pan, alternate layers with nuts, and cinnamon and sugar mixture. Bake at 325⁰ for 1 hour or until done. Leave in pan or cool before removing and sprinkle with more cinnamon and sugar.

Marvella Hans
(Ankeny, Iowa)

## Easy Breakfast Cheese Danish

2 cans Pillsbury Crescent
   Rolls
1 (8 ounce) package cream
   cheese

1 cup sugar
½ teaspoon vanilla
1 egg yolk (save the white)

Spread 1 can of rolls in bottom of an ungreased 13x9-inch pan. Press together perforations. Mix together cream cheese, sugar, vanilla, and egg yolk. Spread over rolls. Top with remaining package of rolls, not necessary to press perforations together. Brush with beaten egg white. Bake at 350° for 25 minutes. Glaze while warm with milk, almond extract, and powdered sugar mixed together. May add raisins on top of cream cheese or a can of pie sliced apples sprinkled with a little sugar prior to topping with remaining rolls. Filling and frosting may be made ahead of time, and rolls opened and Danish assembled just prior to baking. Very easy to fix and very fast.

**Bruce and Brenda Eckel**
**(Denton, Texas)**

## Pfotrchen (Fudgens)

4½ cups flour
2 cups milk
1 package yeast
Salt and sugar (to taste)

1 cup raisins
1 stick butter
4 eggs
1 teaspoon cardamom

Scald milk, add butter, salt, sugar and 1 cup of flour, let cool. Add yeast, eggs (slightly beaten), raisins and rest of flour. Add cardamom. Set in warm place to raise. Fry in lard until brown. Dip in sugar.

**Mary Etta (Schneckloth) Thomsen**

63

# Svestkove' Knedli'ky
*(Czech Recipe)*

| | |
|---|---|
| 1½ cups mashed potatoes | ¼ cup Cream of Wheat |
| 2 beaten eggs | 20 plums |
| 1½ cups flour | Cinnamon-sugar mixture |
| 1 teaspoon salt | Melted butter |

Mix together first 5 ingredients. Roll out on flour board to ¼-inch thick. Cut in squares to cover plums. Boil 12 minutes. Serve hot. Sprinkle with cinnamon, sugar and butter.

Joan Kupka
(Ladora, Iowa)

# Ferden

| | |
|---|---|
| 6 eggs | 2 teaspoons cardamom |
| 1 cup milk | 1 cup raisins |
| ¾ teaspoon salt | ¼ cup sugar |
| 1¾ cups flour | 1 cake yeast (softened) |
| Lemon rind | |

Beat eggs and milk; add milk mixture to salt, cardamom, sugar, lemon rind, softened yeast, and flour. Lastly add raisins. Let raise for 1 to 1½ hours. Fry in Ferden pan.

*From Vera Strunk whose husband owned and operated the "St. Louis House" in Davenport, Iowa.*

Frieda Storjohann
(Princeton, Iowa)

*I came to this country from Germany 38 years ago, from a town by the name of Kaltenckirchenn.*
*Bruno and I married in America and farmed near New Liberty where we raised our 2 children. I still enjoy my flowers, looking at my beautiful pictures from the old country, and entertaining my 3-year old grandson.*

# Ferden

*The following recipe was always served on either Christmas Eve or New Year's Eve and was Grandma's recipe as was Groton Hans.*

3 eggs (beaten)
½ cup sugar
3 tablespoons butter
2½ or 3 cups of flour
1 cup raisins, boiled until
   puffed up (may add
apricots,
   apples, currants, or other
fruit)

1 tsp. ground cardamom seed
2 cups of milk
3½ teaspoons baking powder
   (add last)

Place shortening in each cavity of Ferden pan. When hot, drop batter to about half full. Place desired fruit on top then turn with a fork. Roll ferdens in sugar and serve hot. Serve with syrup.

**Tib Stewart**
*(Submitted by: Penelope Miller, Princeton, Iowa)*

# Groton Hans

1½ slices of white bread
1 tablespoon of butter

1 tablespoon of white sugar
½ cup of milk

Heat these until bread is mushy and then cool. Beat 5 eggs and add to above mixture and add 1 teaspoon salt. Add 1 pint of milk, ¾ cup raisins, and about 1½ cups of flour. This should be like pancake batter. Place a clean dish towel or a clean white muslin square in boiling water. Remove and sprinkle with flour. Pour batter into towel and tie with a cord. Cook for 2½ hours, in boiling water covered with lid. Make sure it doesn't cook dry. Serve with following syrup.

*(Continued on Next Page)*

## (Groton Hans - Continued)

**SYRUP:**
**1 cup of white syrup**          **¼ pound butter**

Heat together over slow burner. This recipe should serve 4 persons.
The bread is used instead of baking powder.

**Tib Stewart**
*(Submitted by Penelope Miller, Princeton, Iowa)*


*Marx Kroeger came to Le Claire, Iowa in 1871. He lived with the Jurgen Holst family. Anna Ahmling (Kroeger) came in 1872. Both came from the Schlesweig Holstein, Germany area. Marx Kroeger was a farmhand, and Anna was employed by the same family in Germany as a baker and housekeeper.*

*American birthdays were big occasions in the Kroeger family, and they were celebrated with a "Groton Hans."*

*This is the recipe which Aunt Ella had from Grandma Kroeger, and was passed on to her daughter, Elva Smith, from whom I received it; I, being Elma (Tib) Peitsher Elliot Stewart. "Groton Hans" was served with a cooked ham. Syrup and butter were heated together to pour over it. It was very filling.*

**Tib Stewart**
*(Submitted by: Penelope Miller, Princeton, Iowa)*

# Danish Kringle

| | |
|---|---|
| 4 cups flour | 1 cup milk (scalded and |
| 3 tablespoons sugar |    cooled) |
| 1 teaspoon salt | 1 package granular yeast |
| 1 cup lard or butter flavor | 3 egg yolks (beaten) |
|    Crisco | ½ cup lukewarm water |

Combine flour, sugar, salt and lard as for pie crust. Dissolve yeast in the ½ cup of lukewarm water. Combine milk, yeast and egg yolks. Work into the flour mixture, making a soft dough. Cover and place in the refrigerator overnight. Next day divide the dough into 4 parts. Roll each part into strips about 9-inches wide. Spread with your favorite filling (cherry, prune, etc.) Fold third of dough over filling. Place on baking sheet, set in warm place, cover, allow to rise for 30 minutes. Bake in 350⁰ oven until light golden brown, frost.

**Peggy Hansen**
**(Danish Bed and Breakfast)**
**(Elk Horn, Iowa)**

# Pigs In A Blanket
### *(Saucijze Broodjes)*

**CRUST:**

4 cups flour
3 teaspoons baking powder
1 teaspoon salt
1 cup butter

½ to 1 cup milk
2 beaten eggs or ½ cup cream
   for glazing

**FILLING:**

2 pounds ground pork
½ pound ground beef
½ teaspoon allspice (optional)

1 teaspoon salt
¼ teaspoon pepper

To Make Crust: Sift flour, baking powder and salt. Cut in butter. Add enough milk to make a dough that can be rolled. Divide into 4 parts. Roll each part into a thin crust. Cut into 3x4-inch rectangles.

To Make Filling: Mix meats and seasonings. Roll into 3-inch long sausages. Wrap filling in the strips of dough. Seal well.

Cover baking sheet with 2 layers of brown paper to absorb fat during baking. Place "Pigs" 1 to 2-inches apart on baking sheet. Brush tops with beaten egg or cream. Bake at 350° F. for 1 hour. Serve warm. Pigs in Blankets freeze well both before and after baking. If they are frozen uncooked, remove from freezer and bake at 375° F. for 15 to 20 minutes. Reduce oven temperature to 325° F. and bake 45 to 50 minutes longer.

*(Continued on Next Page)*

## (Pigs In A Blanket - Continued)
### *(Saucijze/Broodjes)*

*Orange City is a very Dutch community. I have lived in Orange City for 50 years, and I have never tired of eating Saucijze Broodjes. They are simply delicious. Everyone likes them. For 35 years the Orange City Hospital Auxiliary has made and sold "Pigs In A Blanket" at its annual bazaar. Members meet before the bazaar and make and freeze over 5,000 of them. They are very tasty when served with any salad, especially gelatin or fruit salad, pickles and olives.*

*My husband, Robert, "retired two years ago after serving as Orange City's mayor for 30 years."*

**Dorothy Carr Dunlop**
**(Orange City, Iowa)**

(Similar Pigs in A Blanket recipes were submitted by Dottie DeVries and Mina (Baker) Roelofs, both of Pella, Iowa)

*My recipe is an old one from my great great aunt, which my mother used, and now I am using. Some 25 years ago I shared this recipe with the Central College Auxiliary and we make hundreds of them each year for our Annual Tulip Time Celebration and also our Central College International fair, which is held in the fall. It has been a good money maker.*

**Dottie DeVries**
**(Pella, Iowa)**

MINT

69

# Speck-Dicken (Old Year Cakes)
### *(German)*

2 pounds Italian sausage
2 pounds bacon
4 eggs (well beaten)
1½ cups white sugar
1 cup dark Karo syrup
1 teaspoon whole anise

1 teaspoon soda in 2 cups
   boiling water
2 teaspoons salt
3½ cups Rye Graham flour
2½ cups white flour

Combine all the above ingredients. Add more hot water if needed. I make it fairly thin, I also mix in the morning and let set to flavor through. Crumble and steam 2 pounds Italian sausage. Cut in pieces 2 pounds bacon and cook out some of the grease. I use a waffle iron to bake them. Put some bacon and sausage on waffle iron. Add batter and bake. Good hot or cold. Can also bake like pancakes.

**Frieda Storjohann**

# Frozen Fruit

**COOK:**

2 cups sugar                    1 cup water until dissolved

**ADD:**

1 bag frozen strawberries       4 bananas (chunked and
2 small square containers          dunked in lemon juice
   frozen raspberries              (very important to dunk
2 cans chunk pineapple             bananas)
   (drained)                    4 cups apricot nectar

Combine in large container and freeze. You can add as much of one kind of fruit as you'd like. Thaw to a slush consistency when serving. Delicious for a brunch or during the holidays.

LeAnne Schneckloth (Wayne)

71

# — JUST FOR NOTES —

# Breads

# Steam Threshing Machinery

**THE**
**FARM IMPLEMENT NEWS**

Chicago, Il.     January, 1889     Vol. X No. 1

# Midwest Old Threshers
## Mt. Pleasant, Iowa

The Midwest Old Settlers and Threshers Association in Mt. Pleasant, Iowa, began in 1950 with a gathering of fifteen steam engines and eight separators. After 40 years, the annual Old Threshers Reunion, held five days ending Labor Day, is an established celebration of our rich agricultural heritage that attracts visitors from across North America.

Midwest Old Threshers provides the traveling public with a variety of enjoyable experiences for the entire family. Attractions range from displays of steam engines and agricultural exhibits to interpretive historical exhibits, educational programs and tours, a facility capable of hosting bus tours and camping rallies from mid-spring to mid-fall, and the unique Museum of Repertoire Americana, containing memorabilia of early theatre.

Midwest Old Threshers and Mt. Pleasant are situated in picturesque southeast Iowa and are located 50 miles south of Iowa City and Interstate 80 at the intersection of U.S. Highways 218 and 34.

# BREADS

## QUICK BREADS
A-Z Bread . . . . . . . . . . . . . .77
Banana Bread . . . . . . . . .77,78
Blue Ribbon
  Banana Bread . . . . . . . . .79
Graham Bread
  (1860's Recipe) . . . . . . . .79
Bannock Bread . . . . . . . . . .80
Corn Bread . . . . . . . . . . .80,81
Carrot-Raisin Bread . . . . . .81
Never Fail Johnny Cake . .82
Pecan Bread . . . . . . . . . . . .82
Nut Bread . . . . . . . . . . . . .83
Cranberry Nut Bread . . . . .83
Fiesta Bread . . . . . . . . . . . .84
Mountain Bread . . . . . . . . .86
Date Nut Bread . . . . . . . .86
Grape Nut Bread . . . . . . . .87
Round Raisin
  Nut Bread . . . . . . . . . .87,88
Poppy Seed Bread . . . . .88,89
Lemon Poppy
  Seed Bread . . . . . . . . . . .89
Squaw Bread . . . . . . . . . . .89
Rhubarb Bread . . . . . . . . . .90
Chocolate
  Zucchini Bread . . . . . . . .90
Wendy's Spicy
  Zucchini Bread . . . . . . . .91
Zucchini Fritters . . . . . . . . .91

## YEAST BREADS
Gadsby's Tavern - Sally
  Lunn Bread Recipe . . . .93
Swedish Coffee Bread . . . .94
Homemade Light Bread . .94
Houska . . . . . . . . . . . . . . .95
Julekake . . . . . . . . . . . . . . .96
Oatmeal Bread . . . . . . . . .97
Potica
  (Slovenian Bread) . . .98,99

Light Pumpernickel
  Bread . . . . . . . . . . . . . . .99
Rye Bread . . . . . . . . . . . . .100
Danish Rye Bread . . . . . . .100
Whole Wheat Bread . 101,102

## BISCUITS
Angel Biscuits . . . . . . . . .103
Cheese Biscuits . . . . . . . .103

## DUTCH LETTERS
Dutch Letters . . . . . . . . . .104

## ROLLS
Butterhorn Rolls . . . . .108,109
Killer Rolls . . . . . . . . . . . .109
Jumer's Cinnamon Rolls .110
Frigidaire Rolls . . . . . . . . .111
Mom's Cinnamon Rolls . .111
Half-Time Spoon Rolls . .112
Kolaches . . . . . . . . . . . . . .113
How To Shape
  Kolaches . . . . . . . . . . . .114
Kolaches or Rolls . . . . . .114
Kolach Fillings . . . . . . . .115
Refrigerator Whole
  Wheat Rolls . . . . . . . . .116

## MUFFINS
Wholesome Apple
  Raisin Muffins . . . . . . .117
Blueberry Muffins . . . . . .118
Bran Muffins . . . . . . .118,119
Six-Week Bran Muffins . .119
Jim's Delicious Heart
  Healthy Muffins (from
  the kitchen of
  Nancy Lightfoot) . . . . .120
Oatmeal Muffins . . . . . . .120
Rhubarb Muffins . . . . . . .121
Sweet Potato Muffins . . .122

# A-Z Bread

**MIX TOGETHER IN A BOWL:**

3 cups flour
1 teaspoon salt
1 teaspoon soda
1 or 2 teaspoons cinnamon

½ teaspoon baking powder
¾ cup egg mix
2 cups sugar
¼ cup dry milk

**ADD:**

1 cup water
⅔ cup oil

2 teaspoons vanilla
1 cup chopped nuts

Blend until smooth. Add 2 cups of A to Z fruit or vegetable (see below). Put into two well greased bread pans. Bake at 350° about 1 hour or until a toothpick inserted in center comes out clean. Cool in pan about 10 minutes and then turn out on rack to cool. Wrap and store in refrigerator. Makes 2 loaves.

A to Z: Use one of the following, or a mixture of the following to equal 2 cups. Apples, applesauce, bananas, carrots, cherries, coconut, cranberries, dates, eggplant, grapes, honey, lemons, marmalade, mincemeat, oranges, peaches, pears, pineapple, prunes, pumpkin, raisins, raspberries, rhubarb, strawberries, sweet potato, tomatoes, yams, yogurt, and zucchini.

Francine Lemke
(Nutrition Educator ISU Extension Polk County)

# Banana Bread

1½ cups sugar
½ cup shortening
2 eggs
2-3 bananas (mashed)
2 cups flour

½ teaspoon salt
1 cup sour milk or buttermilk
1 teaspoon soda (mix in milk)
Nuts (optional)

Grease and flour two bread pans. Mix all ingredients together. (Use hand or electric mixer.) Bake at 350° for 1 hour. Makes 2 loaves.

Brittany Ward
(Le Claire, Iowa)

# Banana Bread

| | |
|---|---|
| 1 cup sugar | 2 cups flour |
| ½ cup shortening | 1 teaspoon baking powder |
| 2 eggs (separated) | 1 teaspoon soda |
| 2 mashed bananas | ¼ cup chopped nuts |
| ½ cup cold water | (walnuts) |

Cream sugar and shortening. Beat in egg yolks and mashed bananas. Add cold water then add sifted dry ingredients. Fold in stiffly beaten egg whites and nuts. Pour into loaf pan (9x5-inch) and bake at 350° for one hour. I use butter and unbleached flour.

*A few years back Reader's Digest wrote about children who were surprised at their babysitter knowing their favorite recipes. Their parents were away on a trip. The babysitter said it was easy because the cookbook with the dirty pages gave away the most used recipes!*

**Ruth Bahan**
**(Bettendorf, Iowa)**

*The page with the Banana Bread recipe in my cookbook is dirty!*

# Banana Bread

Similar Banana Bread recipes were submitted by Holly Johnson and Pam Gray. Aloha Banana Bread was submitted by Pam Gray of Le Claire, which included an optional cup of coconut.

# Blue Ribbon Banana Bread

⅔ cup sugar
⅓ cup shortening
½ teaspoon butter flavoring
2 eggs
3 tablespoons sour milk
  or buttermilk
½ teaspoon soda

½ cup walnuts, chopped
  (optional)
1 cup mashed bananas
1 teaspoon banana flavoring
2 cups flour
1 teaspoon baking powder
½ teaspoon salt

Cream the sugar, shortening, butter flavoring and eggs together thoroughly. Stir in the milk, bananas and banana flavoring. (If you do not have sour milk or buttermilk, add 1 teaspoon vinegar to enough sweet milk to make the 3 tablespoons needed). Sift the dry ingredients together and beat into the batter. Lastly fold in the nuts. Pour into a greased loaf pan. Let stand in the pan at room temperature for 30 minutes before baking. (This improves the texture of the bread). Bake at 350° for 50 minutes. Turn onto a rack to cool. For variations we add some peanut butter to the mixture and sometimes fold in some chocolate chips also.

Rachel Klingsheim
(Howard Center Stars 4-H Club, Lime Springs, Iowa)

# Graham Bread
*(1860's Recipe)*

FOR QUICK GRAHAM BREAD:
1 teacupful of buttermilk
2 teacupfuls of sweet
  skimmed milk

½ teacup of loaf sugar
1 teaspoon of salt
1 teaspoon soda

Thicken with graham flour and bake ¾ of an hour in a moderate oven. This makes an excellent preparation of graham.

Penelope Miller
(Princeton, Iowa)

79

# Bannock Bread

**MIX TOGETHER:**

3 cups flour

1 level teaspoon baking powder

4 heaping tablespoons honey

1 teaspoon salt

½ cup raisins

⅔ cup dry milk

Stir in 2 tablespoons of vegetable oil and then add enough water to knead into a pliable, rubbery dough. Smooth it into a disc about 10-inches across and place on a greased pan and bake at 350° until brown and crisp on top. Wrap in foil and freeze. At suppertime prop next to fire or lay in coals, or use it as a pot cover for heating the stew!

*This recipe for Bannock Bread is an enhanced version of the flour, salt, baking powder and water bread that the early settlers "enjoyed". Make it in advance of your next camping trip and serve it with stew or soup. I've dined on Bannock and stew during trips on the Wapsi and Maquoketa Rivers.*

**Jerry Neff**
**(Pleasant Valley, Iowa)**

# Corn Bread

8 cups flour

4 cups cornmeal

7 tablespoons baking powder

¾ cup sugar

3 teaspoons salt

6 eggs

7½ cups milk

12 tablespoons cooking oil

Beat eggs. Add milk and oil. Add sifted ingredients. Bake in 400° oven 30 minutes. Serves 54.

*This is a quantity recipe from our 1973 cookbook, representative of some of the good foods served at our reunions by church and other groups.*

**Wesley Methodist Chapel**
**(Mt. Pleasant, Iowa)**

# Corn Bread

4 eggs (lightly beaten)
12 ounces buttermilk
1 teaspoon baking soda
1 teaspoon salt
2 cups coarse cornmeal

2 cups canned creamed corn
2 ounces drained, diced
  jalapeno peppers
7 ounces grated Colby or
  Longhorn cheese
5 ounces corn oil

Combine the ingredients in a bowl in the order listed and stir just until blended. Pour the mixture into a well greased 7x10-inch baking dish. Bake at 375° for 30 to 35 minutes in the center of the oven. Cool and cut into fingers (so to speak). Yields: 18 "fingers".

**Deba Leach**
**(Wife of US Representative Jim Leach of Iowa)**

# Carrot-Raisin Bread

1 cup sugar
¼ teaspoon baking powder
1 teaspoon baking soda
½ teaspoon salt
½ teaspoon ground cloves
½ teaspoon cinnamon
½ teaspoon ground nutmeg

½ teaspoon allspice
1⅔ cup flour
½ cup vegetable oil
½ cup water
1 cup cooked, mashed carrots
2 eggs
½ cup raisins

Combine sugar, baking powder, baking soda, salt and spices. Add other ingredients in order given. Mix well. Place in 9x5-inch loaf pan, greased or sprayed with nonstick spray. Bake 1½ hours at 325° or until toothpick inserted in center comes out clean. I use canola oil and have baked this for one hour at 350°.

**Ruth Bahan**
**(Bettendorf, Iowa)**

81

# Never Fail Johnny Cake

| | |
|---|---|
| 1 scant cup white sugar | 1 cup yellow cornmeal |
| ½ cup butter or lard (scant) | 1½ cups flour |
| 3 eggs (separated) | ½ teaspoon salt |
| 1 cup sweet milk | 3 teaspoons (level) baking powder |

Sift cornmeal, baking powder, flour, and salt together. Cream shortening and add sugar and egg yolks alternately with the milk. Beat egg whites until stiff and gently fold into above batter. Bake in a 9x9-inch pan for 25 to 30 minutes at 350⁰. To serve, cut into squares and serve warm with butter. Maple syrup may also be put over the squares of cornbread. (Add first procedure to second before folding in egg whites.)

*This recipe was brought to this country by my Scotch Grandmother, and it became a staple in our family. We especially liked it on Sunday evenings when our supper was light because of having a large meal at noon. My father enjoyed eating leftover Johnny cake in a bowl of sweet milk with a touch of white sugar added.*

D. Iris Juckem
(Davenport, Iowa)

# Pecan Bread

| | |
|---|---|
| 1 box Betty Crocker Butter Pecan Mix | 4 eggs |
| | ¾ cup oil |
| 1 small Butter Pecan Instant Pudding Mix (3 ounce) | ¾ cup water |
| | 1 cup chopped pecans |

Place first five ingredients in large bowl and mix well. Add pecans and place in two loaf pans (9¼ x5¼ x2¾ -inches). Bake at 350⁰ for 30 to 40 minutes. Test for doneness.

Mrs. Eugene (Elda) Way
(Kalona, Iowa)

# Nut Bread
### *(An Ellen Steamboat Recipe)*

1 cup sugar
1 stick oleo
1 egg
½ cup milk
2 cups flour

1 cup apples (cut fine)
1 teaspoon cinnamon
1 teaspoon soda
½ cup chopped nuts (walnuts or pecans)

Sift together flour, soda and cinnamon. Set aside. Cream oleo and sugar. Add egg and apples. Stir in milk alternately with flour mixture. Add the nuts that have been lightly dusted with flour. Pour batter into well greased 9x5x3-inch loaf pan. Bake about 1 hour at 350°. Test with toothpick for doneness.

**Rose Peters, Cook - Ellen Steamboat**
**(Submitted by: Lois Havenhill, Princeton, Iowa)**

# Cranberry Nut Bread

2 tablespoons shortening
1 orange (juice and rind)
1 egg (well beaten)
1 cup pecans (chopped)
1 cup cranberries (cut in half)

2 cups flour
1 cup sugar
½ teaspoon soda
½ teaspoon salt
1½ teaspoons baking powder

To the orange juice add enough boiling water to make one cup. Add shortening to this and dissolve. Blend juice into dry ingredients just enough to mix thoroughly. Add beaten egg, pecans, and cranberries. Pour batter into greased and floured loaf pan (10½x3½x2½-inches). Let set 20 minutes before baking in moderate oven at 325°.

**Julianne Garrison**
**(Camarillo, California, formerly Eldora, Iowa)**

83

# Fiesta Bread

1 cup Quaker Oats (quick or old fashioned, uncooked)
1¼ cups all-purpose flour
2 teaspoons baking powder
¾ teaspoon baking soda
½ teaspoon ground cumin
½ teaspoon chili powder
½ teaspoon salt (optional)
2 tablespoons margarine, chilled

¼ cup thinly sliced green onion
1 medium jalapeno pepper, seeded, finely chopped or 1 tablespoon canned chopped green chilies
1 cup plain nonfat yogurt
2 egg whites, lightly beaten

SPREAD:
4 ounces fat-free cream cheese, softened
2 tablespoons salsa

1 tablespoon thinly sliced green onion

Heat oven to 425° F. Lightly spray 10-inch ovenproof skillet or cookie sheet with no-stick cooking spray. In large bowl, combine dry ingredients; mix well. Cut in margarine with pastry blender or two knives until mixture resembles coarse crumbs. Stir in onion, jalapeno pepper, yogurt and egg whites; mix just until dry ingredients are moistened. Turn out onto well-floured surface; knead gently 8 to 10 times. Pat dough evenly into prepared skillet or into 9-inch circle on prepared cookie sheet. Bake 13 to 16 minutes or until golden brown. For spread, combine all ingredients; mix well. Cut bread into wedges; serve warm with spread. 8 Servings. Nutrition Information (1/8 of recipe): Calories 170, Total Fat 4 gram, Saturated Fat 1 gram, Cholesterol 5 milligrams, Sodium 380 milligrams, Dietary Fiber 2 grams

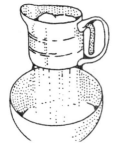

**Quaker Oats Company**

*(Continued on Next Page)*

# The Quaker Oats Company
## Cedar Rapids, Iowa

The roots of the Quaker Oats Company go back to 1873 with the building of the North Star Mill. Plant management was later expanded. Eventually the company joined and reorganized with a number of other companies until it became The Quaker Oats Company upon its incorporation in 1901. Through the years expansion continued and daily production of rolled oats steadily increased. The beginning of corn milling was in 1888. The round oatmeal box was introduced in 1917.

Quaker Oats in Cedar Rapids is today the world's largest cereal milling facility and has become the main producer of many nationally famous foods.

Thank you to Terry L. Osmanski for the Quaker Oats recipes used throughout the book.

85

# Mountain Bread

4 cups whole wheat flour
1 cup water
¾ cup packed brown sugar
½ cup honey
⅓ cup wheat germ
⅓ cup oil
¼ cup sesame seeds
¼ cup molasses
3 tablespoons nonfat dry
   milk powder
1½ teaspoons each of salt
   and baking powder

Mix all ingredients until smooth. Pour into well greased 8x8x2-inch pan and bake in preheated oven at 300⁰ for 1 hour or until bread starts to pull away from sides of pan. Let cool and cut into squares.

*I always take Mt. Bread on my mountaineering trips. It will keep for days even in hot weather. While climbing Mt. Elbert, Colorado's highest peak, I relied on Mt. Bread to give me the energy I needed to make the summit, 14,433 feet.*

**Jerry Neff**
**(Pleasant Valley, Iowa)**

# Date Nut Bread

1 cup sugar
1 egg
1 cup nutmeats (walnuts)
1 package dates (cut up, pour
   over dates 1½ cups boiling
   water with 1 tablespoon
   butter)
2¾ cups flour
½ teaspoon soda
2 teaspoons baking powder
½ teaspoon salt
1 teaspoon vanilla

Mix in order given. Bake slowly about 1 hour in a moderate oven at 350⁰. Double for 2 loaves.

*This recipe was from my Aunt and our girls used to take it to the Fair where it usually won a blue ribbon.*

**Gladys Lundquist**
**(Davenport, Iowa)**

# Grape Nut Bread

**COMBINE:**

2 cups sour milk (use 2 tablespoons vinegar to make sour milk, if none on hand)

1 cup Grape Nuts (pour into sour milk and let soak while mixing other ingredients)

**ADD:**

1½ C. sugar
2 eggs, pinch of salt (mix)
4 cups flour

1 teaspoon soda
2 teaspoons baking powder

Bake 1 hour at 350° in a loaf pan. I use grated orange peel, or lemon peel to add zest. This can be served with butter or cheeses, or as dainty sandwiches.

Margaret Lindsey
(Leon, Iowa)

# Round Raisin Nut Bread

2 cups raisins
2 cups water

2 teaspoons soda

Combine and bring to boil. When it begins to foam, remove from heat and cool. Add 1 cup chopped nuts and 1½ teaspoons vanilla.

2 eggs
1½ cups sugar

Dash salt
3 cups sifted flour

Beat eggs, sugar and salt and add to raisin mixture alternately with flour. Pour batter into No. 2 tin cans (save the ones with coated lining) two-thirds full, greased well. Bake at 350° one hour or less.

*(Continued on Next Page)*

### (Round Raisin Nut Bread - Continued)

*This can be served as bread, pudding with a sauce or spread with cheese mixtures. I usually triple this mixture. We are fond of raisins and more raisins can be used without altering this recipe.*

*I've included several very special family recipes. These are some of my favorite ones from The Leon Journal Reporter of which I am the editor and manager. It is a third generation family newspaper serving Decatur County. My two columns: "You Can Fix-It" and "It Now Occurs To Me" appear weekly in the newspaper.*

Margaret Lindsey
(Leon, Iowa)

# Poppy Seed Bread

3 cups flour
1½ teaspoons salt
1½ teaspoons baking powder
2¼ cups sugar
1½ tablespoons poppy seeds

3 eggs
1½ cups oil
1½ cups milk
1½ teaspoons each almond, butter flavored and vanilla extract

GLAZE:
½ cup orange juice
1½ cups powdered sugar

1 teaspoon each almond, butter flavored and vanilla extract

Mix ingredients for bread. Beat 1 to 2 minutes. Do not overbeat. Pour into greased and floured pans. This will make 2 (9x5-inch) loaf pans or 3 (8x3-inch) foil pans. Bake at 350⁰ for 1 to 1¼ hours. Cool slightly. The top will crack. Mix ingredients for glaze. Poke holes in bread and pour glaze slowly over top while bread is warm.

*(Continued on Next Page)*

### (Poppy Seed Bread - Continued)

*I like to make these in a foil pan at Christmas time, leave in the pan, wrap a pretty Christmas towel around it, and tie with a coordinating colored raffia bow! It makes a wonderful gift to give to friends at holiday time. Bread can be frozen and thawed. It still has great flavor from all the extracts and stays very moist!*

**Linda Klemp**
**(Hudson, Wisconsin, formerly Mitchellville, Iowa)**

## Lemon Poppy Seed Bread

1 lemon cake mix
1 box instant lemon pudding
4 eggs

1 cup hot water
½ cup oil
¼ cup poppy seeds

Beat cake mix, pudding, water, oil and eggs with electric mixer for 4 minutes. Fold in poppy seeds. Place batter in greased and floured pans. Bake at 350⁰ for 35 minutes. Recipe will make 2 large loaves or 4 small loaves.

**Trish O'Boyle**

## Squaw Bread

1 pint of sweet milk
2 tablespoons baking powder
1 tablespoon shortening
Flour to make a dough
  easily handled

1 teaspoon sugar
1 teaspoon salt

Mix all ingredients together. Roll out to any desired thickness. Cut into pieces. Perforate or slit these strips. Cook in a kettle of deep fat. Serve with syrup or fruit.

**Nancy Bettis**

# Rhubarb Bread

1½ cups brown sugar
⅔ cup oil
1 egg
1 cup sour or buttermilk
1½ cups chopped rhubarb, if
   using frozen, thaw just
   enough to break apart

2½ cups flour
1 teaspoon salt
1 teaspoon soda
1 teaspoon vanilla
½ cup nuts

Mix and pour batter in 2 bread pans that have been greased. Sprinkle top with ½ cup sugar mixed with 1 tablespoon butter. Bake at 325⁰ for 1 hour. It doesn't rise very high.

Mary Etta (Schneckloth) Thomsen

# Chocolate Zucchini Bread

3 eggs
1½ cups sugar
1 tablespoon vanilla
1 cup vegetable oil
2 cups zucchini (grated)
3 cups flour
1 teaspoon salt (optional)
1 teaspoon soda

½ teaspoon baking powder
1 tablespoon cinnamon
1 (3 ounce) box instant
   chocolate pudding
½ cup coconut
½ cup nuts (chopped)
½ cup chocolate chips

In a large mixing bowl, beat the eggs. Add sugar, vanilla and oil. Beat well. Fold in zucchini. Sift together flour, salt, soda, baking powder, cinnamon and dry pudding mix. Stir until combined. Fold in coconut, nuts and chocolate chips. Divide batter between 2 greased and floured 9x5-inch loaf pans. Bake at 350⁰ for 1 hour or until bread tests done. Cool on a rack 10 to 15 minutes before removing from pans. Complete cooling and sprinkle with powdered sugar if desired.

Barbara Schintler
(Master Gardener, Johnson County)

# Wendy's Spicy Zucchini Bread

3 eggs
1 cup oil
2 cups sugar
3 teaspoons vanilla
½ teaspoon baking powder
2 cups coarsely shredded and
   peeled zucchini
1 cup marmalade or jam or
   drained crushed pineapple

3 cups flour
2 teaspoons soda
1 teaspoon salt
2 teaspoons cinnamon
¾ teaspoon nutmeg
1/8 teaspoon cloves
1 cup chopped walnuts

Beat eggs, oil, sugar and vanilla with mixer until mixture is thick and foamy. Stir in zucchini, marmalade and flour which has been sifted with the soda, salt, etc. until just blended. Add nuts. Divide batter between 2 (9x5-inch) greased and floured loaf pans. (I put waxed paper in the bottom after greasing the pans and do not flour. Breads come right out by running a knife around the edge; waxed paper peels off easily.) Bake at 350º for 1 hour. Cool in pan 10 minutes before removing to cool on wire racks.

**Barbara Ann Grassley**
**(Wife of U.S. Senator Charles Grassley)**
**(Wendy is Their Daughter)**

# Zucchini Fritters

1½ cups grated whole
   zucchini
3 tablespoons chopped onion
⅓ cup Bisquick baking mix

4 tablespoons grated
   Parmesan cheese
Salt and pepper (to taste)

Mix well. Let stand 5 to 10 minutes. Mix again. Drop by spoonful in deep hot oil and fry until brown on both sides. Drain on paper towel.

*Zucchini is a prolific Iowa summer vegetable and can be used in various ways. I remember a country garden that provided more than I could use or give away.*

**Irma Plambeck Wilson**
**(Davenport, Iowa)**

91

# The Czech Village
## Cedar Rapids, Iowa

Many of the early immigrants who settled in the Cedar Rapids area came in the mid to late 1800's and early 1900's from what was once Czechoslovakia. Settling on the Cedar River, it served as a source of food, ice, and transportation. They began their own businesses, retaining many of their old crafts and trades. As many other ethnic groups have done, they also tried to preserve much of their culture from home.

The Czech Village is a very charming combination, in near downtown Cedar Rapids, of shops, businesses, and people who are a part of the area's ethnicity. The National Czech and Slovak Museum and Library has the largest collection of authentic national costumes outside the Czech Republic and Slovakia, over 40 of them.

*This special logo was designed by Marjorie K. Nejdl and used with permission of the National Czech and Slovak Museum and Library, Cedar Rapids, Iowa.*

# Gadsby's Tavern
# Sally Lunn Bread Recipe

*There are several old accounts of the origin of the name "Sally Lunn."
One of the more appealing is about an English girl who sold bread on the
streets, crying "Solet Lune!" to advertise the buns. The sun and the moon—
soleil-lune, as it is in French—were the images evoked to describe the golden
tops and white bottoms of the buns. By the time soleil-lune reached America
it had become Sally Lunn and, rather than a bun, was a baked bread in
a Turk's-head mold.*

3¼ cups flour
¼ ounce active dry yeast
½ cup (short) melted
  shortening
¾ cup sugar

¾ cup (plus) milk
½ teaspoon of salt
1 egg
4 tablespoons warm water

Makes one two pound loaf. Butter cookie sheet. Heat milk and
shortening to the temperature of a warm baby bottle. Mix flour, salt
and sugar in a separate bowl. Add water to the yeast in a separate
bowl. Mix the egg in a separate bowl. Add the warm milk and melted
shortening to the bowl of flour, salt and sugar. Add the eggs and
yeast and water. Beat the entire mixture until it comes off the side
of the bowl which should be clean. Cover, let rise in a warm (non-
air conditioned) place until double in size, about 1½ hours. Knead
the bread down in size and shape into a round loaf. Place on the
cookie sheet and let rise again to ½ again as big, about 45 minutes.
Bake bread at 300° F. for approximately 45 minutes. After 30 minutes
baste the top of the bread with butter and also again after it has
finished baking.

*This is a favorite from a Colonial Restaurant in Alexandria, Virginia.*

**Mrs. (Charles) Barbara Ann Grassley**

# Swedish Coffee Bread

| | |
|---|---|
| 7-8 cups flour | 1 egg |
| 2½ cups lukewarm milk | ½ tsp. salt |
| 2 packages dry yeast | ¾-1 cup melted margarine |
| 1 cup sugar | 1 teaspoon ground cardamon |

Dissolve yeast in ½ cup lukewarm milk. Mix remaining milk, sugar, egg, salt, margarine, and cardamon and small amount of flour; beat smooth. Add yeast and remaining flour, beating with wooden spoon until smooth and firm. Place in greased bowl and cover with towel. Let rise until doubled in size. Turn onto floured baking board and knead until smooth. Divide dough and make two rings. Sprinkle baking board with flour and roll out dough as thin as possible, about 15-inches in length. Spread with melted butter and sprinkle with sugar and cinnamon. (I also put raisins on top of sugar and cinnamon.) Roll dough jelly roll fashion, join ends to form circle. Place on buttered baking sheet. Cut slits on top with scissors and let rise. Bake at 375°, for 15 to 20 minutes. Frost with powdered sugar frosting. For the holidays decorate with pecans, red and green maraschino cherries.

**Dorothy Carlson**
**(Ankeny, Iowa)**

# Homemade Light Bread

| | |
|---|---|
| 1 quart lukewarm water | ¼ cup melted (or liquid) |
| 1 package dry yeast |    shortening |
| ¼ cup sugar | 1 tablespoon salt |
| | 12 cups flour (maybe more) |

Dissolve yeast in warm water, add sugar, shortening, salt and 6 cups flour. Mix well. Add remaining flour, a cup at a time; when unable to stir with spoon, knead with hands. Put in warm place, when double in size punch down and form into rolls or loaves. Put in warm place to double in size, bake in 350° oven for 35 to 45 minutes.

**Margaret Lindsey**
**(Leon, Iowa)**

# Houska

2 cups milk
½ pound butter
4 egg yolks
1 cup sugar
Approximately 6 cups flour
¼ teaspoon mace
2 cakes of yeast
½ cup golden raisins

½ cup rum or brandy
½ cup blanched almonds
½ cup red or green candied
   cherries
1 teaspoon salt
½ cup candied pineapple
½ lemon rind

Soak raisins in rum or brandy overnight. Mix milk, sugar, and yeast dissolved in water. Add eggs, mace, and 2 cups flour, and beat well. Then add salt, butter, and 2 more cups of flour followed by drained raisins, almonds, and candied fruit. Add enough flour to make soft dough, knead until smooth. Place in greased bowl and let rise until double. Mix down and rise again. This makes 2 Houskas. Divide each half portion of dough into 6 equal parts. Roll each in long ropes. Grease cookie sheet and braid 3 strands for bottom layer. Then braid 2 and twist a single strand for top layer. Place across sheet so both Houskas fit. Brush with melted lard and let rise. Before baking brush with beaten egg. Bake 45 minutes at 350° on a greased cookie sheet. When cool, frost with powdered sugar frosting and decorate with maraschino cherries and nuts.

**Joan Kupka**
**(Ladora, Iowa)**

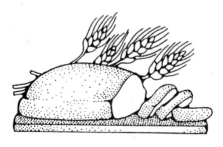

95

# Julekake

*This is a Norwegian Christmas Bread that is rich and slightly sweet, but I serve it most anytime. I have used this recipe most of my married life, and it makes excellent gifts when decorated with cherries, almonds etc. wrapped in colored Saran Wrap and tied with large bow. The cardamon and almond flavoring are typical Norwegian flavors.*

| | |
|---|---|
| 2 packages dry yeast | 1 teaspoon salt |
| ½ cup warm water | ¾ teaspoon cardamon |
| 1 cup milk (scalded) | ½ cup citron |
| ½ cup butter | ½ cup candied cherries |
| 1 egg (beaten) | ½ cup white raisins |
| ½ cup sugar | 5 cups flour, or more |

Dissolve yeast in warm water and a little sugar. Scald the milk and add butter; cool to lukewarm. Add egg and then yeast mixture. Add sugar, salt, and cardamon. Beat in 2 cups of the flour and mix well. Add small amount of the flour to candied fruit so it won't stick together and stir in the rest of the flour. Add candied fruit. Turn out dough on floured cloth and knead until smooth. Place in greased bowl; cover and let rise until doubled. Divide into 2 parts and form into round loaves and put on greased cookie sheets or in pie pans. Let rise until nearly double. Bake at 350⁰ for 30 to 40 minutes. While warm, brush with soft butter or decorate when cool with powdered sugar icing and almond flavoring, then sliced almonds and more candied cherries. To serve: cut slices in half on an angle and butter, or delicious toasted and buttered.

**POWDERED SUGAR ICING:**

| | |
|---|---|
| 2 cups powdered sugar | Almond flavoring |
| Water | |

Mix all together until consistency to spread. Let dry before wrapping.

**Eunice C. Stoen**
**(Decorah, Iowa)**

96

# Oatmeal Bread

| | |
|---|---|
| 1 package active dry yeast | 1 tablespoon salt |
| ¼ cup lukewarm water | 2 cups oatmeal |
| 1 teaspoon sugar | 1 cup boiling water |
| ¼ cup vegetable oil | 1 cup cold water |
| ¼ cup molasses | 5-5¼ cups sifted flour |
| ¼ cup brown sugar | |

Add the 1 teaspoon sugar to lukewarm water. Stir in the yeast and set in warm place until mixture is light and bubbly, about 15 minutes. In a large bowl combine the vegetable oil, molasses, brown sugar, salt and oatmeal. Add the 1 cup boiling water. Stir well. Add 1 cup cold water and stir. Add yeast and blend well. Mix in flour to make a soft dough. Knead on floured board until smooth. Grease top of dough, place in greased bowl. Cover; let rise until doubled in bulk. Shape into 2 loaves and place in greased 5½ x9½ -inch pans. Let rise until doubled in bulk. Bake at 425⁰ for 15 minutes. Reduce heat to 375⁰, bake 30 minutes more.

*Blue ribbon winner in 1960's at Grundy County Fair (4-H member then) and Iowa State Fair.*

**Sheryl Asmus**
*(Thank you also to Bertha Shaw,*
*Hamilton County Extension Service, Webster City)*

# Potica
### *(Slovenian Bread)*

**DOUGH:**

2 packages dry yeast
½ cup lukewarm water
2 cups milk (scalded)
2 teaspoons salt

½ cup sugar
2 sticks butter
2 eggs (well beaten)
8 or 9 cups flour

**FILLING:**

½ stick butter
½ cup each, brown sugar,
white sugar and cream
½ pound pitted, cooked
prunes (ground)

1 tablespoon or more of
cinnamon
½ pound ground nuts
1 teaspoon vanilla
2 cups raisins soaked in
warm water and drained)

DOUGH: Soften yeast in water. Combine hot milk, salt, sugar and butter. Blend thoroughly. Cool to lukewarm. Add eggs and softened yeast. Blend thoroughly. Add 5 cups of flour to mixture. Stir and then beat vigorously. Gradually add remaining flour or enough of it to make a medium soft dough. Place on well floured board. Knead 15 to 20 minutes. Place in a large greased bowl. Cover with a damp cloth. Let rise in a warm place until double in bulk. Punch down and let rise again. Cover a 38x48-inch table with a white cloth. Lightly flour cloth. Place raised dough on center of cloth. Roll dough out until it covers the cloth. Spread with filling and sprinkle with raisins. Form dough in a roll by lifting the end of the cloth. Roll evenly and tightly. Divide into 4 loaves and put into greased 6x9-inch pans to rise, at least 1 hour. Bake at 350⁰ for 1 hour. Cover bread with aluminum foil if it gets too brown before it's done baking. Leave in pan until bread is cool.

*(Continued on Next Page)*

### (Potica - Continued)

FILLING: Combine butter, sugar, cream, prunes, nuts and cinnamon. Cook over low heat about 5 minutes. Cool and add vanilla. Use as directed above.

*My grandparents and mother came from Germany and in their families no celebration was complete without Potica.*
*I am the third generation to carry on this tradition.*

**Virginia Boothroy**
**(Altoona, Iowa)**

# Light Pumpernickel Bread

| | |
|---|---|
| 3 packages active dry yeast | 2 tablespoons Crisco |
| 1½ cups warm water | 2 cups rye flour |
| (105°-115°) | 2 cups all-purpose flour |
| ½ cup light Karo corn syrup | Cornmeal |
| 4 teaspoons salt | 2 tablespoons caraway seed |

Dissolve yeast in warm water in large mixing bowl. Stir in Karo, salt, caraway seed, shortening, and rye flour. Beat until smooth. Stir in enough all-purpose flour to make dough easy to handle. Turn dough onto lightly floured surface. Cover, let rest 10 to 15 minutes. Knead until smooth, 5 to 10 minutes. Place in greased bowl, greased side up. Cover; let rise in a warm place until double, about 1 hour. Punch down and let rise until double, about 40 minutes. Grease baking sheet and sprinkle with cornmeal. Punch down dough and divide in half, shaping each half into a round, slightly flat loaf. Place loaves in opposite corners of baking sheet. Let rise about 1 hour. Heat oven to 375°. Bake 30 to 35 minutes. Remove from pan and cool on wire rack.

**Agnes Vrooman**
**(Davenport, Iowa)**

# Rye Bread

**IN SMALL BOWL MIX:**

½ cup warm water

2 packages dry yeast

1 teaspoon sugar

¼ teaspoon ginger

**IN A BIG BOWL PUT:**

1½ cups warm water

⅓ cup firmly packed brown sugar

1 tablespoon salt

3 teaspoons burnt sugar flavoring (or real burnt sugar)

1 teaspoon orange flavoring

¼ cup soft butter

Beat hard. Add first yeast mixture. Beat in 2 cups sifted rye flour. Add about 5 cups white flour (or enough to make good, firm dough). Turn out on board and knead well. Put in greased bowl and let rise until double (about 1 hour). Turn out and knead. Divide into two parts, shape into loaves and put in bread pans. Let rise until double (about 45 minutes). Bake at 350° about 45 minutes. Cool on racks. Butter crust for a soft crust.

Margaret Lindsey
(Leon, Iowa)

# Danish Rye Bread

2 packages yeast in ½ cup lukewarm water

8 cups warm water

½ cup lard

½ cup sugar or molasses

8 teaspoons salt

8 cups graham flour

8 cups rye flour

8 cups white flour, approximately

Combine water, lard, sugar and salt. Add yeast mixture, then graham flour and beat well. Add rye flour and as much white flour to make firm dough. Let rise until double in bulk. Knead down and form in loaves. Let loaves rise in greased bread pans. Bake at 350° for 1 hour. Makes 8 to 10 loaves depending on size.

**Minna Larsen**

100

# Whole Wheat Bread

| | |
|---|---|
| 4 cups boiling water | 3 teaspoons salt |
| ½ cup sugar | 1¼ cups whole wheat flour |
| 5 tablespoons lite molasses | 10 cups white flour |
| 2 tablespoons lard or margarine | 2 packages yeast |

Heat water. Add sugar, molasses, shortening, and salt. Cool and add yeast. After it dissolves, add whole wheat flour and mix. Add white flour 2 cups at a time and beat with mixer. Knead it well, grease top. Let rise once and punch down. Let it rise again, then shape into loaves. (I make 4 smaller ones and 1 large one). Bake at 350° for 30 minutes or until nicely browned and sounds hollow when tapped.

*Our three daughters made this recipe for 4-H and won blue ribbons on it. It is still their favorite bread when they come home for a visit. Up until two years ago we lived on a farm near Radcliffe, Iowa. Presently we are in Story City.*

**Myrtle Harper**
**(Story City, Iowa)**

101

# Whole Wheat Bread

1 cup milk
2 tablespoons sugar
1 tablespoon salt
¼ cup butter or margarine
½ cup honey or molasses
1½ cups warm water
 (105-115°F)

2 packages or 2 tablespoons
 active dry yeast
2½ cups all-purpose flour
4 cups whole wheat flour
1 cup wheat germ
½ cup sesame seeds
 (optional)

Heat milk until bubbles form around edge. Add sugar, salt, butter, and honey/molasses. Mix until butter melts and cool to lukewarm. Sprinkle yeast over water in large mixing bowl, stirring until dissolved. Stir in milk mixture. Add all-purpose flour, 2½ cups whole wheat flour, wheat germ, and sesame seeds. Beat with a wooden spoon until smooth. Gradually add remaining whole wheat flour until dough leaves side of bowl. Turn out dough onto lightly floured board, cover with bowl, and let rest 10 minutes. Knead until smooth and elastic, about 10 minutes. Place in lightly greased bowl and turn dough to bring up greased side. Cover with towel and let rise in warm place until double in bulk, about 1¼ hours. When fingers poked into dough leave an indentation, rising is sufficient. Punch down with fist and turn on to board or pastry cloth. Divide into halves and shape each half into a ball. Cover with a towel and let rest 10 minutes. Shape each ball into a loaf and place in lightly greased 9x5x3-inch pans (dough may be divided into 3 smaller loaves). Cover with a towel and let rise again until double in bulk, about 1¼ hours. Bake in 400° oven for 40 minutes. Tops should be well browned and sound hollow when rapped. Remove from pans immediately and cool on a wire rack.

Virginia Wadsley
Des Moines, Iowa

102

# Angel Biscuits

**MIX AND SET ASIDE:**
1 package dry yeast              2 tablespoons lukewarm water

**SIFT TOGETHER INTO MIXING BOWL:**
5 cups flour                        1 teaspoon soda
¼ cup sugar                        1 teaspoon salt
3 teaspoons baking powder

**CUT IN:**
1 cup shortening (until like coarse crumbs)

**MAKE A LARGE WELL IN FLOUR MIXTURE AND ADD:**
2 cups buttermilk

Stir yeast mixture into the buttermilk "in the well." Mix well. Knead on floured board or waxed paper. Roll and cut into biscuits. Bake on greased pans (touching each other) at 400° for 15 to 20 minutes. Yield approximately 50 biscuits.

**Mrs. (Charles) Barbara Ann Grassley**

*This is the recipe of our pastor's wife in Virginia.*

# Cheese Biscuits

1½ cups flour                     1 egg
¾ cup whole wheat flour        1 cup milk
1 tablespoon baking powder     1 cup grated cheese
½ teaspoon salt                    2 tablespoons margarine

Stir in ingredients together in a bowl. Add the cheese and margarine and work it into the flour. Blend together in a blender the milk and the egg and add it to the flour mixture. Drop by spoonfuls onto a greased cookie sheet or place in a greased pie pan. Brush with a little melted butter and sprinkle on some sesame seeds if you wish. Bake for 25 minutes at 350°. Serve warm. Variation: Add 1 tablespoon instant onions to the mix for an onion cheese biscuit.

**Bonnie Maguire**

# Dutch Letters

**DOUGH:**
1 pound butter
4 cups flour

1 cup water
2 egg whites (slightly beaten)

**FILLING:**
1 pound almond paste
2 cups sugar

3 eggs
1 teaspoon vanilla

DOUGH: Mix butter and flour. Stir in water and mix to form dough. Chill overnight or longer.

FILLING: Beat almond paste until smooth; add sugar, eggs, and vanilla; mix well. Chill overnight or longer.

ASSEMBLY: When ready to bake, divide dough and filling into 14 equal parts. Roll one (1) section of dough into a 14x4½-inch strip, then take a heaping tablespoon of filling and spread it down the center of the dough strip. Lap one side of dough over the filling, then the other side, and pinch ends shut. Shape letter or leave in one long strip and place on greased cookie sheet with seam on bottom. Brush tops with beaten egg whites and sprinkle sugar on top; prick with fork every 2-inches to allow steam to escape. Bake at 400° for 30 minutes. Makes 14 letters. These can be made and frozen either before or after baking.

*This recipe is an old recipe from my great, great aunt, which my mother used and now I am using. Some 25 years ago I shared this recipe with the Central College Auxiliary and we make hundreds of them each year for our Annual Tulip Time Celebration and also for our Central College International Fair, which is held in the fall.*

**Dottie DeVries**
**(Pella, Iowa)**

104

# Shenandoah's Famous Field Family

From a seed company business to building the radio station K.F.N.F., to starting "Mother's Hour Letter," and eventually "Kitchen Klatter News," the Field family has certainly contributed its share to Iowa history.

Henry Field was over 50 and had already developed a successful seed company, when he, with friends, decided to build K.F.N.F., the "Friendly Farmer Station." Leanna Field Driftmier, Henry's sister, is credited with having the first radio homemaker program. Ladies called in from surrounding states to share their recipes, household tips, and advice on raising children. Having 6 brothers and sisters, and having 7 children herself, Leanna enjoyed talking about these subjects with her listeners. Air time however, went by quickly, and many did not yet have a radio. A few months after the first broadcast in July, 1926, Leanna put out her first publication called "Mother's Hour Letter." The following story and picture appeared in the original July 1926 letter.

## Dish Washers

You mothers with several to cook for, know what a job it is to wash the dishes three times a day. I have 9 or 10 to cook for all the time and the dishwashing would be quite a job, were it not for my dishwasher.

The picture shows daughters Dorothy and Margery doing the dishes with our dishwasher. A couple of years ago my husband made this practical and inexpensive dishwasher for me, and the beauty of it is, it does the work as well as the high priced ones which are run by electricity. He made several before he finally got one made that was satisfactory.

*(Continued on Next Page)*

## (Shenandoah's Famous Field
## Family - Continued)

Upon seeing me use mine some of my friends wanted one too, so we had several made and they all proved a great help in the kitchen. Mr. Driftmier's sister, who lives on a farm, has one and says it is fine for washing cream separator parts, and is worth the price for that alone. Another friend in the country says that during threshing time the neighbors ask her to bring her dishwasher with her.

This dishwasher can also be used for canning fruit the cold pack method, and there are other ways it can be used conveniently. When I get the fire built I put the dishwasher on the back of the stove, and fill it about half full of water, putting in some soap chips or Gold Dust or any other soap easily dissolved.

By the time the meal is over the water is hot, and I scrape the dishes and put them into the inside pan, or container. This container has 2 handles which make it easy to plunge the dishes up and down in the hot water. This washes them quickly and easily.

When they are clean I raise the container out of the water, drop the handles over the edge of the large outside can, which holds the dish container in place above the water. I then rinse the dishes with scalding water. The bottom of the container is perforated, which allows the rinse water to run through. Now, isn't that easy? And it is even easier than it sounds.

I have made arrangements with a company to make these at a price which is within the reach of all. You ought to have one to use during the hot days this summer. Send me your order and I will send you one, transportation prepaid for $3.75.

**Leanna Field Driftmier**


In January of 1928 the publication became the "Kitchen Klatter News" after the well-known radio program, "Kitchen Klatter." The program and publications were truly a family project. It took the entire family to test recipes sent in before they were put in the paper. Following is one of the recipes sent in by a faithful listener:

*(Continued on Next Page)*

## Love Knot Cinnamon Rolls

Roll dough, either plain bread or Butter Scotch out in a sheet one inch thick, cut in one inch strips 6 inches long. Have two plates, one with milk in and the other with sugar and cinnamon mixed well. Take each strip and roll first in the milk and then in the sugar and cinnamon mixture and then tie in a knot. Put in greased pans and let raise. Bake 20 minutes. Butter Scotch rolls may be rolled in brown sugar, instead of in the cinnamon mixture.

Household tips like these were called, "Kitchen Klatter Kinks":

Put a piece of paper in empty fruit jars when putting them away to keep them fresh.

After boiling salt beef, leave two or three carrots in the liquid until cold—the carrots absorb the salt and the liquid can be used for soup.

In cooking vegetables, cover those that grow under the ground, as onions, etc., leave uncovered all those that grow above the ground.

To keep clothes pins new - To prevent new clothes pins from splitting, let them stand in cold water a few hours before using.

When weighing molasses for cooking purposes, if the scale is well floured first the syrup will run off quite smoothly, without leaving any stickiness behind.

Salt toughens meat, if added before it is done.

Several of Leanna's daughters and grandchildren gradually took over the work for her. Margery, the youngest daughter, retired from the radio program in 1976. She still lives in Shenandoah. 1976 also was the 50th anniversary of "Kitchen Klatter." 1986 marked the end of the radio program and the publications. After 60 memorable years "Kitchen Klatter" had become the longest sustained radio program in the country. An interesting sidelight: Of Henry Field and Leanna's siblings: Jessie Shambaugh founded the 4-H movement, Susan was a tremendous artist, Martha a poet, Helen a horticulturist, and brother Solomon was known for his boy scout work, especially for teaching mountain climbing survival. Grandma and Grandpa Field were definitely ahead of their time.

# Butterhorn Rolls

1 cup milk (scalded)
½ cup shortening
½ cup sugar
1 teaspoon salt

1 package dry yeast (fast rise preferable)
3 beaten eggs
4½-5½ cups flour

METHOD: Combine milk, shortening, sugar; add salt. Cool to lukewarm. Add yeast, dissolved in warm water (115⁰-120⁰). Stir well. Add eggs, then flour. Mix well to smooth, soft dough. Knead lightly on floured surface until dough doesn't stick to fingers. Add flour as needed. Place dough in greased bowl; cover with damp cloth, place in warm place and let rise until double in bulk. Divide dough in thirds; roll each third on lightly floured surface to 9-inch circle. Cut each circle into 12 wedges. Place on lightly greased cookie sheet and let rise until very light. Bake in (350⁰-375⁰) oven for 8 to 10 minutes, or until lightly brown. Remove from oven and brush with melted butter or margarine. Makes 3 dozen.

*My home town was Mitchellville, Iowa and I learned my breadmaking from my mother, Mrs. Robert Griffitts, lifelong resident of Mitchellville, Iowa.*

**Jo Elaine (Griffitts) Van Peursem**
**(Crystal Lake, Illinois, formerly Mitchellville, Iowa)**

# Butterhorn Rolls

**MIX THIS SPONGE AND LET STAND UNTIL BUBBLY**
1½ cups sifted flour          1 package moist yeast
1 cup milk (scalded)

**ADD:**
2½ cups flour               1 teaspoon salt
1 egg                       ¼ cup sugar
¼ cup melted shortening

Beat egg, add sugar, shortening and salt. Mix with the sponge mixture. Add flour, and mix thoroughly. Let stand 30 to 45 minutes. Turn out on floured board and knead thoroughly. Place in greased bowl and let rise until doubled in bulk. Divide into 2 parts. With rolling pin, roll dough until about ¼-inch thick. Cut into 12 pie-shaped pieces and spread with soft butter. Begin at large end and roll dough into butterhorn. Place on pan, point underneath. Let rise 15 to 20 minutes in warm room, bake at 350⁰ for 30 to 45 minutes.

Margaret Lindsey
(Leon, Iowa)

# Killer Rolls

18 frozen yeast rolls          1 cup brown sugar
½ small package butterscotch   1 cup chopped nuts
  pudding (not instant)        Cinnamon
1½ sticks margarine

Grease bundt pan and place rolls in pan. Sprinkle ½ package pudding on top. Melt margarine and brown sugar and pour mixture over rolls. Sprinkle cinnamon and chopped nuts. Cover pan with greased foil and dry tea towel. Place in warm spot. Let rise overnight. Bake at 350⁰ for 30 minutes. Let stand 5 minutes after taking out of oven and then turn over onto plate and enjoy. You can omit the butterscotch pudding for a caramel taste.

Nancy Meeker
(Davenport, Iowa)

# Jumer's Cinnamon Rolls

1 cup milk
⅔ cup shortening
⅔ cup sugar
1 tsp. salt
2 eggs (beaten)
4 cups white flour

1 package active dry yeast
½ cup warm water (110⁰)
½ cup butter (melted)
2½ tsp. cinnamon mixed into
    2½ teaspoons sugar

Scald the milk; add the shortening, the ⅔ cup sugar and salt. Cool to lukewarm. Add beaten eggs and half the flour to the milk mixture; mix until smooth. Sprinkle dry yeast granules over the warm water; stir until dissolved. Add the yeast mixture to the flour mixture; beat well. Add enough remaining flour to handle dough easily. Knead dough until smooth. Grease top of dough. Cover and allow to rise in a warm place until twice the size. Flatten dough. Place in refrigerator to chill. Cover until ready to use. TO BAKE: Turn dough out on floured board. Roll out 1/8-inch thick. Cut into strips 3-inches wide. Butter by brushing with melted butter; sprinkle with cinnamon sugar mixture. Cut into 1-inch pieces. Place on greased baking sheet. Bake for 30 minutes at 350⁰.

Renate Menzel, Executive Baker
(Jumer's Castle Lodge, Bettendorf, Iowa)

110

# Frigidaire Rolls
*(Very Special)*

| | |
|---|---|
| 1 cake compressed yeast | 7 cups flour |
| ½ cup sugar | 1 tablespoon salt |
| 2 cups lukewarm water | 2 tablespoons shortening |
| 1 egg | (melted) |

Crumble yeast into bowl. Add sugar, salt and water. Add well beaten egg. Sift flour once, before measuring. Add ½ flour and beat well. Add melted shortening and mix remainder flour. Let rise to double in bulk. Punch down. Cover tightly and place in refrigerator about an hour before baking, remove amount of dough. Shape into rolls. Mine are the size of a golf ball. I can put 24 in a large cake pan. Bake in a hot oven 425° for 20 minutes. I like them good and brown.

Margaret Lindsey
(Leon, Iowa)

# Mom's Cinnamon Rolls

| | |
|---|---|
| 1 cup milk | Cinnamon |
| ⅓ cup sugar | 1 tablespoon yeast |
| 1 egg | ¼ cup lukewarm water |
| ¼ cup butter | ½ teaspoon salt |
| Small amount butter (melted) | Approximately 3 cups flour |

Scald milk. Soften yeast in lukewarm water. Add butter, salt and sugar to milk. Cool mixture until lukewarm. Add beaten egg and yeast. Add enough flour to make a soft dough. Cover bowl and let rise in warm place for 45 minutes. Beat down and let rise again. Pat out on floured surface and top with melted butter, cinnamon. Roll up and slice rolls. Let rise in baking pan about 30 minutes. Bake at 325° to 350° for 10 minutes. Frost if desired.

*This is the recipe of Matilda Schoon, daughter of German immigrants. Her family has lived in Jones County since the turn of the 19th century.*

Thanks to: Sarah Schoon, Executive Director,
Anamosa Chamber of Commerce)

111

# Half-Time Spoon Rolls

| | |
|---|---|
| 1 package active dry yeast | ¾ cup scalded milk |
| ¼ cup lukewarm water | ½ cup cold water |
| ¼ cup sugar | 1 egg |
| ⅓ cup shortening | 3½ cups flour |
| 1 teaspoon salt | |

Dissolve yeast in the ¼ cup lukewarm water. Combine sugar, shortening, salt and scalded milk. Cool by adding the cold water. Blend in egg and yeast. Add 3½ cups of flour, mix until well blended. Place in greased bowl and cover. Let rise in warm place until double in bulk 45 to 60 minutes. Stir down dough. Spoon into well greased muffin tins, filling ½ full. Let rise in a warm place until batter has risen to edge of muffin tin and is rounded in center, about 45 minutes. Bake 15 to 20 minutes at 400⁰. Makes 1½ dozen rolls.

*The above is how the original recipe reads. This is how I do it: Put yeast and warm water in mixer bowl, add the sugar and salt. Heat the milk and shortening in microwave. While the milk is heating add the egg and cold water to the yeast. Add the warm milk and shortening. Beat this with the mixer, then add the flour and beat. This is a very soft dough so there is no kneading. I put the mixer bowl in a warm oven to rise. Watch the dough when it is double, stir it down and put in muffin tins. If your dough is nice and warm all the time, your rolls are out of the oven in 2 hours.*

**Kathryn Bredberg**

# Kolaches

| | |
|---|---|
| 1 cup evaporated milk | 1 cup boiling water |
| ½ cup sugar | 2 packages dry yeast |
| 2 teaspoons salt | ½ cup corn oil |
| 2 egg yolks | 4½ cups flour |
| 1 whole egg | |

Mix milk, sugar, salt, egg yolk and egg. Add boiling water, stir and cool. Add yeast and oil; fold in flour. Dough will be sticky. Do not add more flour. Let rise ½ hour, then stir down. Let rise until double in size. Butter hands, place walnut-size balls of dough on greased cookie sheet, brush with butter, and let rise until double. Indent center of each ball and add filling. Brush with butter. Bake 400° for 10 minutes or until brown. Brush with butter and let cool. Prune, apricot or poppy seed are good for fillings.

**Betty Stone**
**(Davenport, Iowa)**

## Warning

There is an art to making kolaches. It may take quite a while to master. Many ladies in our community claim they still haven't quite perfected it after 15 years of practicing, although most of the gentlemen would probably disagree.

**Kate Klimesh**
**(Spillville, Iowa)**

# How To Shape Kolaches

*(From our Church Cookbook in Spillville)*

*Pat out dough to about ½ to 5/8-inch thickness. Cut in strips about 3-inches. Cut in squares about 3-inches. Stretch out corners, put your desired filling in center, take corners cross ways and pinch together.*

**Mrs. Frank V. Klimesh**
**(Submitted by Kate Klimesh)**

# Kolaches or Rolls

2 cakes yeast, dry or
    compressed
2 teaspoons sugar

4 cups flour
2 cups milk (scalded and
    cooled)

Make a sponge of above ingredients. Beat until smooth. Set in warm place. Then add to sponge:

¾ cup sugar
1 cup butter or margarine
4 cups milk (scalded and
    cooled)

4 teaspoons salt
5 eggs (beaten)
12 cups flour (sifted)

Cream sugar and butter. Add eggs, salt and milk. Add the sponge and beat well. Add flour small amount at a time until dough is soft and knead until smooth. Cover with damp cloth. Let rise in warm place. Shape into rolls or kolaches. Place on greased pans, let rise. Bake at 375⁰ for 15 to 20 minutes.

**Mrs. A.A. Ira**
**(From Spillville Church Cookbook)**
**(Submitted by Kate Klimesh)**

# Kolach Fillings

**POPPY SEED FILLING:**

1 pound ground-up poppy seed

1 cup white sugar
½ cup white syrup

Cream or evaporated milk to make it stick together thick like fruit filling. Bring to a boil, stirring constantly to prevent scorching. Can store in refrigerator several weeks.

**PRUNE FILLING:**

1 pound dried prunes cooked until soft. Drain, remove pits, mash and add ½ cup sugar and ½ teaspoon cinnamon. Mix well.

**DATE FILLING:**

1 pound dates cooked with small amount of water until soft, stirring constantly, small amounts of water can be added while cooking keeping filling thick. When soft, add 2 tablespoons sugar. Cool.

**APRICOT FILLING:**

1 package dried apricots soaked overnight in water just to cover. Cook until soft, if any water remains drain well. Mash, add sugar to sweeten and taste. Cool. Makes 1 cup.

**COTTAGE CHEESE FILLING:**

1 lb. dry cottage cheese
½ cup white sugar, more if desired sweeter

½ teaspoon cinnamon
1 egg yolk
¾ cup cooked, drained white raisins

Mix well.

Mrs. Frank V. Klimesh
(From Spillville Church Cookbook)
(Submitted by Kate Klimesh)

# Refrigerator Whole Wheat Rolls

| | |
|---|---|
| 1 yeast cake (or 1 package) | 1 teaspoon salt |
| ⅔ cup melted shortening | 3 cups whole wheat flour |
| ⅔ cup sugar | 3 cups white flour |
| 2 eggs (beaten) | |

Dissolve yeast in ½ cup lukewarm water. While this is dissolving, mix melted shortening and sugar in 3 quart mixing bowl. Add 1 cup boiling water (stir to dissolve sugar) then add 1 cup cold water. Beat 2 eggs with fork, and add to liquid in mixing bowl. Add yeast, salt, and the 6 cups of flour as you stir with a spoon. (Stir until all flour is mixed in). It will be very sticky. Cover bowl with Saran Wrap and refrigerate. In 2 hours cut down with knife. Cut down once a day until used up. Fill non-stick muffin tin (¾ full of dough) using large spoon. Leave out of refrigerator about 4 hours before baking, (they should rise above tin about 1-inch). Bake at (400⁰-425⁰) for 10 to 15 minutes. Makes 3 dozen muffin tin rolls.

*The Trygve Olson family moved to Mitchellville, Iowa in about 1935. All nine children were born and raised in Iowa and all nine graduated from Mitchellville High School. Trygve came from Norway as a young man and settled near Thor, Iowa (near other Norwegians) and married my mother Edna (his English teacher). We had a good life in this small town of Mitchellville. Four of my six brothers served in the armed forces. We all played sports in school. We delivered milk for the local farmer to the residents of Mitchellville and earned 5 cents apiece (for two workers) every night. Trygve served in World War I for U.S.A. in France and received his citizenship this way. Iowa was a good place to raise a family. My mother baked bread about 3 times a week. Quite a few loaves at a time. She could stretch meals to feed 11 people 3 meals a day. We were very poor, but I didn't know it. The Lord brought us through it all and I praise Him for it.*

**Doris (Olson) Casperson**
**(Omaha, Nebraska formerly Mitchellville)**

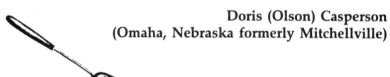

116

# Wholesome Apple Raisin Muffins
### *(Low-Fat)*

1½ cups Quaker Oats (quick or old fashioned, uncooked)
1 cup all-purpose flour
⅔ cup firmly packed brown sugar
1 teaspoon baking powder
½ teaspoon baking soda
½ teaspoon ground cinnamon
¼ teaspoon ground nutmeg

½ cup raisins
¾ cup applesauce
⅓ cup apple juice or skim milk
2 egg whites or 1 egg (lightly beaten)
2 tablespoons vegetable oil
¼ cup Quaker Oats (quick or old fashioned, uncooked)
¼ teaspoon salt (optional)

Heat oven to 400° F. Line 12 medium muffin cups with paper baking cups or spray bottoms only with no-stick cooking spray. Combine dry ingredients, including raisins; mix well. Add combined applesauce, apple juice, egg whites and oil; mix just until dry ingredients are moistened. Fill muffin cups almost full. Sprinkle with remaining ¼ cup oats, patting gently. Bake 20 to 22 minutes or until golden brown. Let muffins stand a few minutes; remove from pan. Serve warm. Makes 1 dozen.

Nutrition Information (1 muffin): Calories 180, Total Fat 3 grams, Saturated Fat 0 grams, Cholesterol 0 milligrams, Sodium 110 milligrams, Dietary Fiber 2 grams

**Quaker Oats Company**

# Blueberry Muffins

2 cups flour
1 cup plus 1 tablespoon sugar
2 teaspoons baking powder
½ teaspoon salt
½ cup milk
½ cup melted butter (cooled)

1 egg (lightly beaten)
1 teaspoon vanilla
2 cups fresh or frozen
  blueberries
½ cup walnut pieces
  (optional)

Preheat oven to 400⁰. Spray Pam in muffin tins or use muffin papers. In a large bowl mix all dry ingredients (except blueberries and 1 tablespoon sugar). In another bowl mix milk, egg, butter, vanilla until blended. Pour into dry ingredients and stir just to combine. Add blueberries and stir a little more (Just to mix in). Pour into muffin tins. Sprinkle 1 tablespoon of sugar on top of the muffins. Bake 20 to 25 minutes. Makes 12 muffins.

Joni Lange
(Davenport, Iowa)

# Bran Muffins

1 cup boiling water
½ cup 100 percent Bran
1¼ cups sugar
½ cup shortening
½ teaspoon butter flavoring
2 eggs

1 teaspoon salt
2⅔ cups flour, sifted with
  2½ teaspoons soda
2 cups buttermilk
2 cups additional Bran

Mix together water and Bran; let cool. Cream together well the sugar, shortening, butter flavoring, eggs and salt. Add flour/soda, buttermilk and Bran. Then add cooled Bran/water mixture and stir only about 20 strokes. Batter will be lumpy. Fill muffin cups about ⅔ full. Bake at 400⁰ for 20 minutes.

Nadine Johnson

# Six-Week Bran Muffins

| | |
|---|---|
| 3 cups sugar | 2 teaspoons salt |
| 5 cups Wondra flour | 4 eggs (beaten) |
| 1 (20 ounce box) Raisin Bran | 1 quart buttermilk |
| 5 teaspoons soda | 1 cup oil |

Bake at 350⁰ for 15 to 20 minutes. In LARGE mixing bowl, combine dry ingredients. Add rest of ingredients. Mix well. Store in refrigerator and use as needed. May be stored up to 6 weeks in refrigerator. Use as much batter as you want for muffins. Use paper lined muffin tins.

*We have an old family friend that always shows up when we have these. We swear he can smell those muffins baking for miles.*

**Nancy Billups
Princeton, Iowa)**

A similar six-week muffin recipe was submitted by Bruce and Brenda Eckel, Denton, Texas.

# Jim's Delicious Heart Healthy Muffins
*(from the kitchen of Nancy Lightfoot)*

2¼ cups oat-bran cereal
¼ cup brown sugar
2 teaspoons cinnamon
1 tablespoon baking powder
½ cup chopped black
   walnuts
¼ cup raisins
½ cup skim milk or
   evaporated skim milk

1 small can frozen apple juice
   concentrate (thawed)
2 egg whites
2 tablespoons white Karo
   syrup (vegetable oil may
   be substituted)
1 teaspoon Extra Touch black
   walnut flavoring
2 medium apples (peeled
   and grated)

Mix dry ingredients in large bowl. Add liquid ingredients in a bowl or blender. Add liquid ingredients to dry ingredients. Fold in grated apple. Line muffin pan with baking cups, fill with batter. Bake at 425° F. for 17 minutes. Store in plastic bags.

*Muffins taste even better when served with apple sauce or apple butter.*

**US Representative Jim Lightfoot of Iowa**

# Oatmeal Muffins

1 egg (beaten)
½ cup brown sugar
3 tablespoons each melted
   shortening, margarine
½ cup each rolled oats, coarse
   dry bread crumbs

1 cup sifted flour
1 teaspoon each salt, baking
   powder
½ teaspoon baking soda
1 cup buttermilk or sour milk

Mix egg, sugar, shortening, margarine. Combine oats and crumbs. Sift together; flour, salt, baking powder, and soda. Blend with oats mixture. Stir into shortening mixture alternately with milk, just until blended. Do not overmix. Fill greased muffin cups ⅔ full. Bake at 400° about 15 minutes, or until golden brown. YOU CAN FIX-IT! Makes 12 (3-inch) muffins.

**Margaret Lindsey**
**(Leon, Iowa)**

# Rhubarb Muffins

**COMBINE THE FOLLOWING:**

1½ cups packed brown sugar
⅔ cup oil
2 eggs

1 cup buttermilk or soured
  milk
2 teaspoons vanilla

**TO THIS MIXTURE ADD:**

3 cups flour
1 teaspoon salt

1 cup chopped nuts
2 cups chopped rhubarb

**TOPPING:**

½ cup brown sugar
1 teaspoon cinnamon

½ cup chopped nuts

Spoon into paper baking cups in a muffin tin. Fill only ⅔ full. Sprinkle with topping. Bake at 350⁰ for 30 minutes or until done. Makes 24 muffins.

**Betty Stone**

# Sweet Potato Muffins

⅔ cup canned or cooked
fresh sweet potatoes (well
drained)
4 tablespoons butter
½ cup sugar
1 egg
¾ cup all-purpose flour
2 teaspoons baking powder

½ teaspoon cinnamon
¼ teaspoon nutmeg
½ cup milk
4 tablespoons chopped pecans
or walnuts
4 tablespoons raisins,
chopped (optional)
½ teaspoon salt

Preheat oven to 400⁰. Grease muffin tins that are 1½-inches in diameter. Puree sweet potatoes with blender or food processor. Cream butter and sugar. Beat in egg and pureed sweet potatoes. Sift flour, baking powder, salt, cinnamon and nutmeg. Add dry ingredients by hand with milk, nuts, and raisins until just blended. Do not overmix. Spoon into muffin tins, filling each completely full. A little sugar and cinnamon may be sprinkled on top if desired. Bake at 400⁰ F. for 25 minutes.

Clorida Ferguson
(Des Moines, Iowa)

# Soups & Sandwiches

Illustration by Gary Nauman

# Sidney Iowa Championship Rodeo
## Sidney, Iowa
*(With Special Thanks to Donna Glenn)*

More than 300 top professional rodeo cowboys and cowgirls compete for top prize money each summer during the six performances of Iowa's largest and one of the nation's oldest and finest rodeos. Begun in 1923 as a two-man, $50 exhibition, this major American rodeo has grown and developed into a $250,000 annual production.

Owned and operated exclusively by the Williams-Jobe-Gibson Post #128 of the American Legion, the SIDNEY IOWA CHAMPIONSHIP RODEO, set in the Fremont County seat town of 1,250, is staged by more than 400 area men and women volunteers.

An old-fashioned July 4th-type parade around the town square, rodeo queen contest, modern carnival and midway, craft show and flea market, and down-home country cooking add to the charm of this "old west" celebration in the heartland.

For information on dates, lodging and tickets, telephone (712) 374-2695 (year round) or 1-800-845-2250 (summer months).


Publicity Contact:
Donna Glenn
(816) 931-0168 (Kansas City)

# SOUPS AND SANDWICHES

## SOUPS

Garbanzo Bean Soup
Chicken Wild
   Rice Soup . . . . . . . . . . . .127
French Market Soup . . . .128
Cheese Soup . . . . . . . . . . .128
Creamed
   Cabbage Soup . . . . . . . .129
Loess Hills
   Squash Soup . . . . . . . . .129
Blue Latin Soup . . . . . . . .130
Potato Soup . . . . . . . . . . .130
Spicy Salsa
   Chicken Soup . . . . . . . .131
"Klossle" (Dumplings) . .131
Spaghetti Soup . . . . . . . . .132
Spicy Tortilla Soup . . . . . .132
French Onion Soup . . . . .133
Lentil Soup . . . . . . . . . . . .134
Pumpkin Soup . . . . . . . . .134
Italian Sausage Soup . . . .135
Taco Soup . . . . . . . . . . . . .135
Garden Tomato Soup . . .136
Frozen Tomato Soup . . . .137
Dumpling Soup . . . . . . . .137
Vegetable Beef
   With Dumplings . . . . . .138

Homemade Chili . . . . . . .138
Hearty Corn Chowder . . .139
Ham and
   Potato Chowder . . . . . .139
Stew . . . . . . . . . . . . . . . . . .140
Uttsaputt . . . . . . . . . . . . . .140
Beef Stew . . . . . . . . . . . . .141
Easy But Hearty
   Beef Stew . . . . . . . . . . . .141
Elephant Stew . . . . . . . . . .142
5-Hour Stew . . . . . . . . . . .142
Wash Day Soup . . . . . . . .142
Britt's Mulligan Stew . . . .143
Wine Soup . . . . . . . . . . . .143
Valley Junction Stew . . . .144

## SANDWICHES

Deviled Hamburgers . . . .144
Beef Bar-B-Q
   Sandwiches . . . . . . . . . .145
Ham Salad
   (favorite sandwich) . . .145
Loosemeats . . . . . . . . . . . .148
Pork Au Jus
   Sandwiches . . . . . . . . . .148

# Garbanzo Bean Soup

*(From the Van and Bonnie Program...5:00-9:00 A.M...every weekday)*

2 cans El Paso garbanzo
  beans
1 (16 ounce) can of whole
  tomatoes or 6 of your own
  homegrown tomatoes
6-8 white potatoes cut bite
  size
1 green pepper cut bite size
1 Bermuda onion (chopped)

1 pound bacon cut bite size
2 cups chopped ham bite size
1 teaspoon oregano
1 teaspoon parsley
1 teaspoon sweet basil
½-¾ tablespoon chili powder
  or red pepper (to taste)
Throw in a few bay leaves
Salt and pepper (to taste)

Let all of this simmer in a big pot, perhaps a crock pot, for 4 to 5 hours. Water can be added if you feel it is not producing enough of its own juices. Remember, the longer it simmers, the better "DEW" it will have on it! Happy Eating!

*This is especially good in the fall after those crisp Friday night or Saturday afternoon football games!*

Van Harden
(WHO Radio, Des Moines)

# Chicken Wild Rice Soup

1 cup cooked wild rice
6 tablespoons margarine
1 tablespoon minced onion
½ cup flour
2½ cups chicken broth

2 cups cubed cooked chicken
½ cup finely shredded carrot
3 tablespoons slivered
  almonds
1 (12 ounce) can evaporated
  skim milk

Melt margarine and saute' onion. Blend in flour; gradually stir in broth, boil and stir 1 minute. Stir in wild rice, chicken, carrots and almonds. Simmer 5 minutes. Blend in milk and heat to serving temperature.

Lillian Duethman
(St. Paul, Minnesota, formerly Mitchellville, Iowa)
127

# French Market Soup

**1½ cups bean mix, washed***

Cover bean mix with water and 1 tablespoon salt. Soak overnight or at least 3 hours. Put beans in 3 quarts of water. Boil slowly for 2½ to 3 hours. Add diced summer sausage, ham bone, shrimp or chicken. Salt and pepper to taste.

**ADD THE FOLLOWING:**

**1 big onion (diced)**
**1 clove of garlic (diced)**

**¼ cup lemon juice**
**1 small can Rotel tomatoes with diced green chilies**

Cook for 30 minutes more. Serves 6.

*Mix made from combining white northern beans, kidney beans, black eye peas, lima beans, pinto beans, lentils, dry split peas, black beans.

**Bruce and Brenda A. Eckel**

# Cheese Soup

**1 cup celery**
**1 medium chopped onion**
**½ pound California mixed vegetables**
**2½ cups diced potatoes**

**2½ cups water (don't drain)**
**2 chicken bouillon cubes**
**2 tablespoons butter or oleo**
**2 cups milk**
**1 pound Velveeta cheese**

Cook first 6 ingredients until done. Add butter or oleo, milk and cheese, (cup up cheese) and stir into vegetables. Put in crock pot on low until ready to serve.

Variation: 2 cans of chicken soup may be used in place of 2 cups milk and 2 tablespoons butter or oleo.

**Mary Craig**
**(Mitchellville, Iowa)**

## Creamed Cabbage Soup

2 cans (14 ounce) chicken
  broth
2 celery ribs (chopped)
1 medium head cabbage
  (shredded)
1 medium onion
2 chopped carrots
¼ cup butter or margarine

3 tablespoons flour
1 teaspoon salt
¼ teaspoon pepper
3 cups half and half
2 cups cooked ham (cubed)
½ teaspoon thyme
Chopped fresh parsley

In a large soup kettle combine broth, celery, cabbage, onion and carrot; bring to a boil. Reduce heat, cover and simmer for 15 to 20 minutes. Meanwhile, melt butter in a medium saucepan. Add flour, salt and pepper, stir to form a smooth paste. Gradually add milk to flour mixture, stirring constantly. Cook and stir until thickened. Continue cooking 1 minute longer. Gradually stir into vegetable mixture. Add ham and thyme and heat through. Garnish with parsley.

**Linda Phillips**

## Loess Hills Squash Soup

1 can of cream of chicken
  soup (or use chicken broth)
Dash Tabasco (optional)
Chives or green onion tops
  (optional)

1 tablespoon peanut butter
½ cup cooked squash
  (whipped)

This is a recipe I created to look a little like loess, and it is also reminiscent of Nigerian soups. Heat the chicken soup or broth; if cream of chicken, be sure it's thoroughly mixed with the water as it heats. Add the rest, stir it well together, and top with chives, croutons, or whatever you like. Makes 2 big bowls.

*Absolutely the most warming soup you can make when the north wind is whistling down through the hills.*

**Phil Hey
(Sioux City, Iowa)**

129

# Blue Satin Soup

4 tablespoons butter
½ cup flour
¼ cup each finely minced
  green onion, green pepper
  and celery
1 can chicken broth (14
  ounces)

4 ounces Maytag Blue Cheese
1 cup light cream
1 cup milk
2 ounces dry sherry
Freshly ground pepper (to
  taste)

Melt butter in heavy saucepan, add vegetables, saute' very slowly until soft but not brown. Add flour and cook over low heat for a few minutes until flour is cooked but not brown. Add warm chicken broth, stirring constantly to prevent lumps and simmer two minutes. Add crumbled Maytag Blue Cheese and stir until smooth. Add cream and milk and heat to serving temperature (do not boil). Stir in sherry and freshly ground pepper to taste. Serve garnished with sour cream, chives, or croutons.

**Maytag Dairy Farms**

# Potato Soup
### *(With Noodles)*

6 medium potatoes, peeled
  diced

2 tablespoons butter

Cook potatoes in boiling, salted water until tender. Add 1 quart whole milk. Heat until steaming hot, ½ teaspoon onion salt or diced onion, pepper, added.

**NOODLES:**
1 cup flour
¼ teaspoon salt, pinch
  baking powder

1 egg

Place in small bowl, stir egg in flour mixture, with fork, making bite-size noodles, sprinkle noodles into soup and bring to boil. Turn off heat, cover, let stand until ready to serve.

*Very Special!*

**Margaret Lindsey
(Leon, Iowa)**

# Spicy Salsa Chicken Soup

1 cup water
1 cup chicken broth
2 potatoes (peeled and
 chunked)
2 carrots (peeled and
 chunked)
½ large yellow onion
 (chopped)

1½ cups frozen mixed
 vegetables
1 cup cooked, chopped
 chicken
¾ cup medium hot salsa
½ teaspoon salt
¼ teaspoon black pepper
1½ teaspoons parsley flakes

Mix water and chicken broth. Add potatoes, carrots and onion. Bring to boil. Reduce heat and cook 10 minutes. Add frozen vegetables, chicken, salsa and seasonings. Cook on low 15 minutes, or until vegetables reach the desired tenderness and flavors have blended. Serve with garlic bread; corn bread or crackers. Serves 4. Add a salad, and you have an Iowa winter supper that warms the soul.

*NOTES: This recipe was created when I discovered I didn't have any whole tomatoes in the house. And now I prefer the spicier version.*

**Clara M. Banks**
**(Des Moines, Iowa)**

# "Klossle" (Dumplings)

½ cup milk
½ cup flour
3 eggs

2 tablespoons butter
Pepper, salt and nutmeg
 (to taste)

Put milk, butter, and seasonings in saucepan and bring to boil. Add flour all at once, stirring until it leaves sides of pan; set aside to cool. Add well beaten eggs and beat well. Drop teaspoonfuls into any soup or stew.

**Lina Unglenk**
**(Amana, Iowa)**

131

# Spaghetti Soup

¾ cup chopped onion
sauteed' in 2 teaspoons
margarine
6 cups water
6 chicken bouillon cubes
8 ounces very thin spaghetti

1 (20 ounce) bag of chopped
broccoli
4 cups of milk
1¼ pounds Velveeta cheese
(cubed)

Saute' ¾ cup chopped onions in 2 teaspoons margarine in soup kettle or Dutch oven. When done, add 6 cups of water and 6 bouillon cubes. Bring to a boil and add 8 ounces very thin spaghetti and one (20 ounce) bag of chopped broccoli. Cook until boiling. Turn heat to simmer and add 4 cups of milk and 1¼ pounds of Velveeta cheese. Stir constantly until cheese has melted.

**Robin Linville**

# Spicy Tortilla Soup

½ pound lean ground pork
½ cup chopped onion
4 cups crushed canned
tomatoes
2 cups chicken broth
1 (8 ounce) jar salsa
(medium-hot)

1 teaspoon chili powder
½ teaspoon salt
½ teaspoon garlic powder
½ teaspoon ground black
pepper
4 corn tortillas (cut into thin
strips)

Brown pork and onions over medium-high heat in large saucepan, stirring occasionally. Add remaining ingredients except tortilla strips, cover and simmer 20 minutes. Stir tortilla strips into soup and simmer for 5-10 minutes more, until tortilla strips are softened. Serve hot.

**Iowa Pork Producers Association**

132

# French Onion Soup

6-8 medium onions (sweetest available), sliced thinly in rings
⅓ cup butter or margarine
1½ tablespoons flour
2 quarts beef or chicken broth
1½ teaspoons Worcestershire sauce
½ teaspoon Tabasco sauce
1½ teaspoons Kitchen Bouquet
Salt and pepper (to taste)
French bread, cut thick and toasted
Swiss or mozzarella cheese (grated)

Heat butter in large saucepan; add onion rings; cook slowly and gently over low heat. Stir almost constantly with wooden spoon until rings are golden. Sprinkle with flour and when well blended add remaining ingredients, except for bread and cheese. Stir soup until it begins to boil. Lower heat, cover pan and let simmer for 45 minutes. Toast French bread slices. Place one slice on bottom of individual oven-proof crock. Fill with soup and sprinkle 2-3 tablespoons cheese on top. Place crocks under broiler until cheese turns golden and bubbly. NOTE: May be frozen in ice cube trays for a quick and delicious supper.

Elaine Rosene Oles
(Bettendorf, Iowa)

133

# Lentil Soup

½ cup margarine
2 cups finely chopped carrots
(peeled)
2 cups finely chopped yellow
onions

2 cups finely chopped celery
7 cups chicken stock
¼ teaspoon white pepper
½ teaspoon garlic salt
1½ cups brown lentils

Saute' the carrots, onions and celery in margarine until tender, about 25 minutes. Add chicken stock, seasonings, and lentils. Bring to boil, reduce heat, and cover. Simmer until lentils are very tender, about 40 minutes. Add salt to taste. Yields 6-8 portions.

*The Green Gables Restaurant is famous for its homemade soups and sandwiches. Lentil soup is served on Saturdays and is always a popular choice.*

**Green Gables (Molly and Robert Seff)**
**(Sioux City, Iowa)**

# Pumpkin Soup

2 pounds pumpkin or winter
squash (peeled, seeded,
cubed; about 5 cups)
3 garlic cloves
2-3 bay leaves
¼ teaspoon marjoram
¼ teaspoon celery seeds
5 cups vegetable stock

2 fresh tomatoes (chopped) or
1 cup canned tomatoes
(chopped)
⅓ cup dry white wine
1 tablespoon honey
1 teaspoon cinnamon
Salt and freshly ground
pepper (to taste)
1 cup heavy cream

Place all ingredients, except the cream, in a large saucepan. Simmer until the pumpkin is soft. Remove the bay leaves. Puree' the mixture in a blender or food processor in several batches. Return the puree' to the saucepan on low heat and gradually stir in the cream. Heat through but do not let the soup come to a boil. Serves 6.

**Pat "Sam" Palmer**
**(Master Gardener '94, Johnson County)**

## Italian Sausage Soup

1 pound Italian sausage
1 cup chopped onion
2 garlic cloves (minced)
5 cups beef broth
½ cup dry red wine
1 (15 ounce) can stewed
  tomatoes
1 cup thinly sliced carrots
½ teaspoon basil

½ teaspoon oregano
1 (15 ounce) can tomato sauce
1½ cups sliced zucchini
8 ounces cheese tortellini
3 tablespoons parsley
1 medium green pepper
  (chopped)
Grated Parmesan cheese to
  garnish

Brown sausage with garlic and onion. Drain. Add the next 7 ingredients. Bring to a boil. Reduce heat and simmer 30 minutes. Stir in tortellini, zucchini, parsley and green pepper. Simmer 30 more minutes. Garnish with grated Parmesan cheese. Serve with garlic bread.

*This hearty soup is a meal itself. Perfect for a late fall or winter night to warm the soul and bones. A perfect football Saturday postgame favorite!*

**Mark Tippery**
**(Arlington Heights, Illinois)**

## Taco Soup

1 pound ground beef or
  turkey, browned (can use
  more meat)**
1 onion (finely chopped)
1 can green chilies (small
  size)
1 package taco seasoning mix

1 package Ranch dressing
  mix
1 can corn
1 can pinto beans
1 can kidney beans
1 can stewed tomatoes
6 cups of water
Salt and pepper (to taste)

**Can substitute 1½ cups textured vegetable protein along with 6-8 beef bouillon cubes instead of meat. Brown meat. Mix seasoning and dressing mix into meat. Add this and all other ingredients to large pot. Cook and simmer for a couple of hours or until of desired consistency.

**Bruce and Brenda Eckel**

135

# Garden Tomato Soup

*(Reprinted from "Recipes and Recollections From Terrace Hill", of which Mrs. Chris Branstad was editor-in-chief, and with permission of the Terrace Hill Society.)*

| | |
|---|---|
| 36 medium tomatoes (quartered) | 6 whole cloves |
| | ½ cup flour |
| 2 green peppers (cut in large strips) | ½-¾ cup packed brown sugar |
| | 1½ teaspoons salt |
| 2 medium onions (quartered) | ½ cup cold water |
| 2 celery stalks (chopped) | ¼ cup butter or margarine |
| 1 bay leaf | (optional) |

In a 6-quart kettle, combine tomatoes, green peppers, onions, celery, bay leaf, and cloves. Bring to boiling; reduce heat and simmer until tender. Remove bay leaf and cloves. Run mixture through a food mill to remove seeds. (If desired, divide between four 1-quart freezer containers. Freeze firm.) Return processed tomato mixture to kettle. Stir together flour, brown sugar, and salt. Stir in cold water and 2 to 3 cups of the tomato mixture. Return all to pot. Simmer, stirring occasionally, about ½ hour. Add butter. To prepare frozen soup, heat 1 container of the frozen tomato mixture in a covered 1½-quart saucepan over low heat until thawed. In a small bowl, stir together 2 tablespoons flour, 2 to 3 tablespoons brown sugar, and ¼ teaspoon salt. Stir in 2 tablespoons cold water to make a paste. Stir in about 1 cup of the tomato mixture. Return all to pot. Simmer as directed. Add 1 tablespoon butter or margarine. Makes 16 servings total.

*I've planted tomatoes every spring since Terry and I have been married.*

**Mrs. Chris Branstad**
**(Wife of Iowa Governor Terry Branstad)**

136

# Frozen Tomato Soup

4 quarts tomatoes (chopped)
4 pieces of celery (chopped)
2½ medium-sized onions (chopped)
4-5 sprigs of parsley

1 green onion (chopped)
2 teaspoons salt (we used other seasoning, no salt)
½ cup brown sugar
1 stick margarine
1 cup flour

Combine first 6 ingredients and cook until celery is soft, about 1 hour. Add ½ cup brown sugar. Melt 1 stick of margarine with 1 cup flour for thickening. In a large kettle when thickening is nice and smooth, add a little soup, then finally add to remaining soup and cook few minutes more. When it is cooled, put in containers to freeze. The following are modifications that we like: We use less flour for thickening. We wash tomatoes, take out core, cut in quarters or smaller, and then run them through a blender. We do not peel tomatoes.

Richard L. and Alice H. Stevens
(Le Claire, Iowa)

# Dumpling Soup

1 quart beef broth
3¾ cups soft bread crumbs
6 tablespoons butter
3 eggs (separated)

¾ teaspoon salt
3 teaspoons sugar
¼ teaspoon nutmeg
Diced parsley (optional)

Cream butter, add egg yolks, sugar, salt, nutmeg, (parsley if desired) and bread crumbs. Mix well. Beat egg whites stiff and add to crumb mixture. Form into small balls (about the size of a small walnut) and drop into boiling broth. Cook about 5 minutes uncovered.

Mrs. Alice Schmieder
(Amana, Iowa)

## Vegetable Beef With Dumplings

1½ pounds hamburger
½ cup chopped onion
26 ounce can vegetable beef
   soup (condensed)
1-2 potatoes (diced)

1½ cups water
½ cup celery, sliced (celery
   seed-1 tablespoon)
2 cups Bisquick
⅔ cup milk

Brown hamburger and onion, drain, stir in soup, potatoes, water, celery and heat to boiling. Reduce and simmer for 20 minutes. Stir Bisquick to soft dough with milk. Drop by giant spoonfuls on top of mixture, cook on low heat for 10 minutes, then cover and cook 10 minutes longer.

Susan Severs
(Princeton, Iowa)

## Homemade Chili

2 pounds ground beef
   (browned)
1 fried onion
2 (15 ounce) cans chili beans

Salt and pepper (to taste)
1 can tomatoes
1 can tomato juice or tomato
   paste

Mix all together and heat thoroughly to taste. Serve.

Richard Freund
(Davenport, Iowa)

SAGE

138

## Hearty Corn Chowder

½ pound sliced bacon
1 cup chopped celery
½ cup chopped onion
2 cups diced, peeled potatoes
1 cup water
2 cups frozen corn
1 can (14¾ ounce) cream style
  corn

1 can (12 ounce) evaporated
  milk
6 ounces smoked sausage
  links, cut into ¼-inch
  slices
1 teaspoon dill weed

In a large saucepan, cook bacon until crisp. Remove to paper towels; crumble and set aside. Drain all but 2 tablespoons of the drippings. Saute' celery and onion in drippings until onion is lightly browned. Add potatoes and water. Cover and cook over medium heat for 10 minutes. Stir in corn, milk, sausage, dill, and bacon. Cook about 30 minutes, until the potatoes are tender. This recipe makes 4-6 servings (1½ quarts).

**Ralph W. Held**
**(Sun City, Arizona)**
**(Formerly of Des Moines, Iowa)**

## Ham and Potato Chowder

1 medium onion
¾ cup ham
½ cup celery
1½ cups raw potatoes
½ cup carrots

¼ cup butter
1½ teaspoons salt
¼ teaspoon pepper
3 tablespoons flour
3 cups milk

Saute' onion, ham, celery, potatoes and carrots in butter, cooking until tender. Remove from heat and add salt, pepper and flour. Mix well. Add milk and stir. Return to heat and cook until thick.

**Holly Johnson**
**(Des Moines, Iowa)**

# Stew

1½ pounds stew beef (cut into 1-inch cubes)
6 medium potatoes cut into eighths
6 carrots (cut into ½-inch pieces)
3 stalks celery (cut into ½-inch pieces)

1 (1 pound 12 ounce) can tomatoes
½ cup quick cooking tapioca
1 large onion (cut into pieces)
¼ teaspoon pepper
2 bay leaves (crushed)
2 teaspoons salt
2½ cups water

Season and flour meat. Brown in separate pan. Put all ingredients in 3½ quart crock pot. Add meat. Mix thoroughly with large wooden spoon. Cover and cook on high 10 hours or low 20 hours. Makes 15 servings. I also use other types of meat.

**Nancy Bettis**

# Uttsaputt
### *(Belgium for "All In The Pot")*

1-2 pounds lean pork (preferably pork hocks)
1 small to medium head cabbage
2-4 potatoes

1 small onion (optional)
1 carrot (optional)
Pinch of paprika
Salt (to taste)
Pepper (to taste)

Cover meat with water in 4 quart pan. Cook until tender (approximately 2-4 hours), last hour add vegetables and spices.
NOTE: If meat is too fatty, cook day before and let cool. Skim off fat.

*HISTORY: My grandmother brought this recipe from Belgium in 1906.*

**Art Ahrens**
**(New Liberty, Iowa)**

# Beef Stew

1 tablespoon margarine
1 pound beef (cut in 1-inch
  cubes)
1 medium onion (diced)
4 cups water

1 cup diced carrots
1 cup diced celery
1 cup diced potatoes
Salt and pepper (to taste)

Melt the margarine in a heavy saucepan. Add cut-up beef and onion. Brown to a golden brown. Add water and simmer, covered for ½ hour. Add remaining ingredients and simmer for ½ hour longer, or until meat is tender.

Lina Unglenk
(Amana, Iowa)

# Easy But Hearty Beef Stew
### (Crock Pot)

1 pound stew meat (more if
  desired)
1 can Hunts Tomato Sauce
3-4 cups V-8 Juice
1 cup carrots
½ cup celery

5-6 potatoes small, peeled
  pieces
½ cup corn
Seasonings (Mrs. Dash)
Onions (if desired)
Stewed tomatoes (optional)

Roll stew meat in mixture of flour and seasonings (Mrs. Dash), cook in frying pan until meat is brown, put meat in crock pot. Prepare vegetables, put in crock pot with tomato sauce and V-8 Juice. Cook on "low setting" in crock pot for six hours or until vegetables are tender. Season to taste. The nice thing about this recipe is you really can't "ruin it," and it's fun to experiment with ingredients and spices each time you make it.

*We like to eat sweet Hawaiian bread with stew. It makes for an interesting contrast!*

Sue Danielson
(WHO Radio, Des Moines, Iowa)
141

# Elephant Stew

| | |
|---|---|
| 1 medium elephant | Salt and pepper (to taste) |
| 2 rabbits (optional) | |

Cut elephant into small pieces. Add enough brown gravy to cover. Cook about 4 weeks over kerosene fire. This will serve 3800 people. If more are expected, 2 or more rabbits may be added, but do this only in case of emergency...most people don't like hare in their stew.

**Nadine Johnson**

# 5-Hour Stew

| | |
|---|---|
| 1½ pounds cubed lean beef | 6 potatoes (quartered) |
| 6 medium carrots (quartered) | 1½ cups tomato juice |
| 1 large onion (diced) | 2 tablespoons tapioca |
| 1 cup celery (sliced) | Salt (to taste) |

Mix all ingredients together and put in large roaster (5-8 quart). Cover with lid and bake at 250⁰ for 5 hours. Yield: 6-9 servings. Can also be put in large crock pot. Delicious meal.

**Kay Barnes**
**(Mitchellville, Iowa)**

# Wash Day Soup
### *(Recipe from 1800's)*

WASH DAY SOUP: Boil the bones and scraps of meat from Sunday's dinner; four good sized potatoes, one onion, and season with salt and pepper. When nearly done slice several tomatoes and cook a little longer. Rub through a colander and add a little cream.

**Verlena Pelo**
**(Le Claire, Iowa)**

# Britt's Mulligan Stew

Twenty stew pots are used. They hold a total of:

| | |
|---|---|
| 450 pounds beef | 150 pounds tomatoes |
| 900 pounds potatoes | 20 pounds chili pepper |
| 250 pounds carrots | 25 pounds rice |
| 35 pounds green-red peppers | 60 pounds celery |
| 300 pounds cabbage | 1 pound bay leaves |
| 100 pounds turnips | 24 gallon mixed vegetables |
| 10 pounds parsnips | 10 pounds kitchen bouquet flavoring |

About 400 loaves of bread are served. A total of 5,000, 8 ounce cups ordered to serve the stew.

*1996 marks the 96th National Hobo Convention, a most unusual, but fun series of events held in Britt, Iowa, a community in northern Iowa. Britt welcomes all Hobos: retired Hobos, railroad workers, and any visitors with a Hobo heart. Saturday's fun includes a 5K Walk and 5 and 10K run, a huge parade, and serving 500 gallons of the famous Mulligan Stew; followed by the crowning of the Hobo King and Queen. In early August all roads definitely lead to Britt, Iowa.*

# Wine Soup
### (1800's Recipe)

WINE SOUP: Cut squares of white bread and fry them in butter until brown and add one quart of wine with a little water, one teaspoon sugar, a small pinch of mace and a pinch of saffron. Let this boil a short time and pour it over the yolks of two eggs (well beaten), stirring rapidly as it pours.

**Verlena Pelo**
**(Le Claire, Iowa)**

143

# Valley Junction Stew

*("This recipe is at least 80 years old, and still a favorite.")*
*(Reprinted with permission from "Recipes from Iowa...with love" by Peg Hein and Kathryn Cramer Lewis.)*

| | |
|---|---|
| 5 bacon slices (diced) | 1 tablespoon salt |
| 1 stewing chicken, 4-5 pounds | 6 medium onions (chopped) |
| 1 green pepper (chopped) | 1 cup sliced celery |
| 3 pounds canned tomatoes | 24 ounces corn |
| 3 pounds potatoes (peeled and sliced) | 3 cups water |
| | ¼ teaspoon pepper |

Fry bacon in a large kettle. Add remaining ingredients and simmer for 1 hour. Remove chicken and allow it to cool until it can be handled. Remove bones and skin, dice meat and return to kettle. Cover and let simmer for 3 hours. If necessary, add more liquid. Serves 8-10.

*At the turn of the century Valley Junction was a bustling railroad center. Today, located in West Des Moines, it is a shopper's delight, filled with antique and specialty shops managed by shopkeepers dedicated to preserving their heritage.*

# Deviled Hamburgers

| | |
|---|---|
| 1 pound ground beef | 1½ teaspoons Worcestershire sauce |
| ⅓ cup chili sauce | 1 teaspoon salt |
| 1½ tablespoons prepared mustard | Dash of pepper |
| 1½ tablespoons horseradish | 4 hamburger buns |
| 1 teaspoon minced onion | |

Combine all ingredients except buns. Cut buns in half and spread with meat mixture. Place on broiler rack 5-7-inches from heat. Brush with butter and broil about 10 minutes.

Neal and Marlene Schoepke
(Indianola, Iowa)

# Beef Bar-B-Q Sandwiches
*(Served at United Methodist Church stand, Sidney Rodeo)*

**COOK TOGETHER:**

| | |
|---|---|
| 10 pounds hamburger | 2 cups chopped onion |

**MIX:**

| | |
|---|---|
| 1 teaspoon salt | 1 cup brown sugar |
| ¾ teaspoon pepper | ¼ cup mustard |
| 3 cups tomato juice | ¼ cup vinegar |
| 3 cups catsup | 1½ tablespoons Worcestershire sauce |

Pour above mixture over meat and cook until well blended. Add 3 cups oatmeal. Cook a few minutes more. Serve on hamburger buns. Makes 40 to 50 sandwiches.

**United Methodist Church, Sidney Rodeo
(Sidney, Iowa)**

# Ham Salad (favorite sandwich)

| | |
|---|---|
| 1 pound chopped ham | 3 tablespoons salad dressing |
| 2 hard boiled eggs | 3 tablespoons Heinz pickle relish |
| 1 small onion | |

Grind ham, eggs, and onion through a food chopper. Add 3 heaping tablespoons of salad dressing and 3 tablespoons of Heinz pickle relish. Add slowly to check for consistency. A favorite in sandwiches or just on lettuce.

**Thelma Nopoulos
(Wilton Candy Kitchen)**

# Wilton Candy Kitchen

The history of the Candy Kitchen goes back to 1867 on Cedar Street. The building was constructed in 1856, one year after our town was platted (1855). We were named for Wilton, Maine, in turn named for Wilton, England.

Governor Terry E. Branstad is a frequent visitor. Actor Gregory Peck and wife Veronique, and producer Dennis Brown visited here September 16, 1995. Brooke Shields visited here September of 1991. They enjoyed their lunch and homemade ice cream. We are expecting a visit from Anthony Quinn before spring. My father-in-law Gus Nopoulos and a friend Nick Parros re-opened the Candy Kitchen June 10, 1910. The Nopoulos family will note 86 years open daily on Cedar Street on June 10, 1996. We have had a love affair with Coca Cola all these years via our soda fountain. This is considered the oldest soda fountain/Ice Cream Parlor/Confectionery in the U.S. (1867-1996). It is the oldest building in Wilton and is in the National Register.

Our Rock Island Depot is also listed in the National Register of Historic Places. My father, a Greek immigrant, was employed with the Rock Island Railroad here in Wilton all his life. My husband George's father, was also a Greek immigrant. Both of our fathers were associated with businesses listed in the National Register of Historic Places. They chose the right town for their American homes!

Thelma Nopoulos
(Wilton, Iowa)

# An En-Deere-ing Act of Kindness

I grew up on a farm bordering the Iowa River in Hardin County, Iowa. It was there that my father, William Eckel, and I unearthed Indian axes and numerous arrowheads.

My favorite pastime as a child was overseeing my own farming operation. It was complete with sheds and barns I made from scraps of wood, fences of sticks and store string, a toy Fordson tractor with a 2-bottom plow, and animals which were a Christmas present from my parents.

At the age of ten, my real farming career began with a team of horses and single-row cultivator. The stirrups on the cultivator beam were adjusted so that my feet could reach them. I remember well our first row crop tractor, a '36 John Deere "B" with steel wheels and a 2-row cultivator.

I was surprised beyond measure on Christmas Day in 1981 when our son-in-law, David Neff, drove on the farmyard near Mitchellville, Iowa with a '36 John Deere "B" wrapped in a giant red ribbon -a gift from my wife, Avis. Its original steel wheels had been replaced with rubber.

A year later, after having shopped in many antique lots around central Iowa, Avis surprised me with a set of front steel wheels like those on the original and like the ones I remembered from my youth.

Of course, the wheels never turned any Iowa soil and a few years later I retired after farming 55 years. The John Deere "B" was auctioned along with other farm equipment. We didn't know where we'd keep it in Annapolis, Maryland where sailboats are more common than tractors.

**Rudy Eckel**
**(Denton, Texas)**

# Loosemeats

1 cup water
1 small onion (chopped)
¾ cup catsup
¼ cup Sue Bee Honey
1 tablespoon chili powder

1 tablespoon paprika
1 pound hamburger
1 teaspoon salt
Pepper (to taste)
2 tablespoons prepared
   mustard

Mix all ingredients in a 2 quart saucepan and bring to a boil. Simmer over medium heat 15 to 20 minutes. Makes about 16 bun servings. Also good on hot dogs or chili dogs.

**Sioux Honey Association**

# Pork Au Jus Sandwiches

1 pound boneless pork roast
1 envelope (from a 2.6 ounce
   box) onion soup mix

16 mushrooms (thinly sliced)
1 teaspoon butter
4 crusty rolls (split)

Preheat oven to 350° F. Coat pork roast with the soup mix, place in a shallow pan and roast for 45 minutes, until meat thermometer inserted registers 155° F. Remove roast from oven and let rest for 5 minutes. Scrape any pan drippings into a microcook-safe measuring cup; add water to measure ⅓ cup. Cover and microcook on HIGH for 20-30 seconds, until boiling. Place mushrooms in microwave-safe container, top with butter and cover with plastic wrap. Microcook on HIGH for 45-60 seconds until mushrooms are tender. Slice roast and place in rolls; spoon over mushrooms and some of the pan juices. Serve immediately. Makes four sandwiches. Approximately, per serving: Calories: 360; Fat: 9 gram; Cholesterol: 71 milligrams
*Serve with coleslaw*

**Iowa Pork Producers Association**

148

# Salads & Dressings

SALADS AND DRESSINGS

Princeton, IA

Drawing by Rita Solter

# Princeton, Iowa
# On The River

Princeton is a small Mississippi River town located along Hwy. 67, halfway between Davenport and Clinton. At one time a large Indian village existed on a site now occupied by the town of Princeton. Indian burial mounds exist along the river. Particularly fascinating was the burial mound found in Princeton, and said to be over 5,000 years old. The mound was opened, and in 1940 its contents examined by scientists from the Davenport Putnam Museum.

Once named Elizabeth City, the area became known as Princeton after 1845, shortly before Iowa gained its statehood. Not until 1846 were there enough school age children and enough interest to set up a school. The first classes were held in a log house with Hannah Peaslee the teacher, earning a weekly salary of $1.75.

Railroads in the early 1900's allowed better transportation and brought electricity for home use and street lighting. The river also has played a very important part in the life of Princeton. Huge rafts of logs, at one time, floated down to the town's sawmills. The "Ellen", pictured, on the cover, began as a rafting boat. Steamboats would stop to unload passengers and pick up fuels and supplies.

Today people enjoy the river for many reasons. They have come to respect it, its power and its beauty. During Princeton Days, the last weekend in June, people come from surrounding areas to celebrate Princeton on the Mississippi.

# SALADS AND DRESSINGS

## SALADS

Wapsipinicon Salad .....153
Apple Salad ............154
Apricot Madonna Salad .154
Blue Cheese
   Artichoke Salad ......155
Avocado Salad
   (congealed)...........155
Stuffed Beet Salad ......156
Oriental Cabbage Salad..156
Cherry Salad ...........157
Chicken Salad .........157
Hot Chicken Salad ......158
Garden Crabmeat Salad .158
Oriental Chicken Salad ..159
Mustard Cole Slaw .....160
Cranberry Delight ......160
Cranberry Salad.....161-163
5-Cup Salad ............163
Crazy Salad ............164
Dandelions .............166
Frog Eye Salad .........167
Fruit Salad .........167,168
Fruit Casserole .........168
Gooseberry Salad .......169
Holiday Salad ..........169
Dutch Lettuce ..........170
Honeymoon Salad ......173
Layered Lettuce Salad ...173
Pink Arctic Freeze ......174

Pistachio Salad .........174
Make Ahead Salad......175
Pea Salad .............175
Raspberry Salad ........176
Red Top Salad..........176
Cold Rice Salad .......177
Sauerkraut Salad........177
Spaghetti Salad .........178
Spinach Salad ..........178
Strawberry-Banana
   Gelatin Salad.........179
Molded
   Strawberry Salad .....180
Strawberry Salad .......180
Strawberry
   Pretzel Salad .........181
Pretzel Surprise Salad ...181
Vegetable Pasta Salad ...182
Molded Waldorf Salad ..182

## DRESSINGS

Sweet Apple-
   Raisin Dressing.......183
Rosy Blue
   Cheese Dressing ......185
Cole Slaw Dressing .....185
Boiled Salad Dressing ...186
Pea Salad Dressing......186
Thousand Island
   Salad Dressing .......187

# Main Street - Princeton, Iowa
## (Early 1900's)

152A

152B

# Wapsipinicon Salad

*(Reprinted and with permission from "Recipes From Iowa...with love")*

¼ cup oil
2 tablespoons salad vinegar
1 teaspoon Worcestershire sauce
½ teaspoon salt
1 tablespoon parsley (chopped)

1 (15 ounce) can artichoke hearts (drained and sliced)
2 large pink grapefruit (sectioned)
6 cups salad greens, washed and crisped, (spinach, romaine, iceberg or leaf lettuce)

Combine all of the dressing ingredients, mix and pour over the artichoke hearts. Allow to stand several hours. Peel and section grapefruit with sharp knife so that membrane is removed. Combine with greens, artichokes and dressing; toss gently but thoroughly. Serves 6 to 8.

*In the early-mid 1800's many people acquired land in the northern part of Princeton Township on the bottoms of the Wapsi River. The Indian legend of the Wapsipinicon River tells that the river was named after Wapsi, an Indian maiden. She was wooed and won by Prinicon, son of Chief Black Feather. Wapsi and Pinicon floated down river in a canoe, planning their future together. Another Indian, also in love with Wapsi, and very jealous, shot Pinicon. As he lay dying in Wapsi's arms, the canoe overturned and both drowned. The waves murmured, "Wapsi, Wapsipinicon." Another explanation for the name, although not nearly as interesting, is that the Indian word refers to a type of artichoke grown along the river banks.*

**Peg Hein and Kathryn Cramer Lewis**

DILL

153

# Apple Salad

Apples, cored and cut into
  small chunks
Miniature marshmallows
Purple grapes (halved)

Walnuts (chopped)
Celery (diced)
Miracle Whip

Use only as much as you wish to make (varies according to how many you will be serving). Mix all ingredients with just enough Miracle Whip to hold salad together.

**Susan Severs**
**(Princeton, Iowa)**

# Apricot Madonna Salad

1 (3 oz.) package apricot Jello
¾ cup sugar
1 small flat can crushed
  pineapple (use juice)

1 (8 ounce) Philadelphia
  cream cheese (softened)
1 (6 ounce) jar junior baby
  food (apricot-tapioca)
1 (8 ounce) carton Cool Whip

Mix Jello, sugar, and pineapple juice together in sauce pan, and bring to a boil, cool. Then mix, 1 (8 ounce) softened package of cream cheese with a 6 ounce jar of junior apricot-tapioca baby food, usually Gerbers. After Jello has cooled, add to the cheese mixture. Last fold in 1 (8 ounce) carton of Cool Whip and refrigerate. This should be put in a pretty mold to look its best. Could be used as a salad or a dessert. Because of its sweetness some prefer it as a dessert.

**Helen Kasparek**
**(Des Moines, Iowa**

# Blue Cheese Artichoke Salad

⅓ cup olive or salad oil
2 tablespoons red wine vinegar and 4 tablespoons lemon juice (or you may use 6 tablespoons wine vinegar)
1½ teaspoons salt
¼ teaspoon pepper
1 teaspoon sugar
2½-3 quarts salad greens (head lettuce, leaf lettuce, parsley, spinach leaves, washed, dried, chilled and broken into bite sized pieces)

1 small jar marinated artichoke hearts, drained and cut into bite-size
1 small can water chestnuts (sliced)
2 tablespoons pimiento
¼ cup Maytag Blue Cheese (crumbled)

Mix first five ingredients. Toss well with remaining ingredients. Serves 10.

**Maytag Dairy Farms**

# Avocado Salad (congealed)

1 package lime gelatin
2 cups water
1 avocado (mashed)
1 package cream cheese (mashed)
½ cup mayonnaise

¼ cup celery (cut fine)
½ green pepper, chopped (can omit if wished)
1 pinch of salt
½ teaspoon onion juice (very important)

Dissolve gelatin in water. When nearly set, add remaining ingredients and place in a shallow 9-inch pan. Be sure all ingredients have been mixed until creamy and smooth textured. Can be poured into individual molds. If in pan, it can be cut into squares to serve.

**Mrs. Florence B. White**
**(Clarksdale, Mississippi, Formerly Des Moines)**

# Stuffed Beet Salad
*(Dated 1920)*

Boil several medium sized beets and remove skins. Hollow out center and in the center, place a mixture of peas, nutmeats, bread crumbs and mayonnaise (homemade). Serve on lettuce leaves with brown bread.

*This was in my Mother's recipe box and I remember her serving it. It is an attractive salad but a combination of beets and peas is not one we usually think of together. However, it works well.*

Phyllis Pfitzenmaier
(Bettendorf, Iowa)

# Oriental Cabbage Salad

(A). 1 head Napa cabbage (shred)

1 bunch green onions (chopped)

(B). 1 stick margarine
2 packages Ramon noodles (without seasoning)

1 ounce sesame seeds
1 package sliced almonds

(C). ½ cup sugar
¼ cup white vinegar

¾ cup oil (olive oil is nice)
1 tablespoon soy sauce

Mix the head of cabbage and, onions, and set aside. Saute' together margarine, noodles, sesame seeds and almonds. Cool and set aside. Boil together sugar, vinegar, oil and soy sauce. Let cool! Keep A,B and C separate until ready to serve. Toss together and serve. Doesn't store well mixed as noodles get soggy. Has a very unique and pleasant taste.

Sue Goddard-Gerrald
(Princeton, Iowa)

# Cherry Salad

1 can bing cherries
1 cup sugar
½ cup water
2 small packages cherry Jello

1 cup crushed pineapple
6 ounces Pepsi
1 package Dream Whip
1 small package cream cheese

In a pan put cherries, sugar and ½ cup water. Bring these ingredients to a boil. Remove and add 2 packages cherry Jello. Stir until dissolved and let cool. Add 1 cup crushed pineapple and 6 ounces Pepsi. Put in 9x12-inch dish and place in refrigerator. Before serving top with Dream Whip and 1 package cream cheese whipped together. Spread on top.

Beverly Havenhill
(Le Claire, Iowa)

# Chicken Salad

2 cups chicken (cut up,
  cooked and chilled)
1 cup of celery (cut up)
1 tablespoon lemon juice
Salt and pepper
  (to taste)

½ cup Hellmann's Lite
  Mayonnaise
1 cup seedless green grapes
  (halved)
1 cup pineapple tidbits
½ cup salted almonds

Combine all ingredients as given. Mix well, chill, and serve on lettuce.

Marguerite Vens
(Davenport, Iowa)

THYME

157

# Hot Chicken Salad

2 cups of cooked chicken (cut in small cubes)

1 can of mushroom soup (no water)

2 tablespoons onions (chopped)

1½ cups grated Swiss cheese

1 cup of fresh celery (cut in cubes)

1 cup of crushed potato chips

½ cup mayonnaise

½ teaspoon salt

2 tablespoons lemon juice

Mix all ingredients together and put in a 8x8-inch casserole dish. Bake in oven for 30 to 40 minutes at 350⁰. Serve on a lettuce leaf with toasted bread or small crescent rolls.

Wilma Howard
(Denton, Texas, formerly of Cedar Falls, Iowa)

# Garden Crabmeat Salad

1 (8 ounce) bag garden variety rotini noodles, cooked and drained

1 small can crabmeat (drained)

1 green pepper (chopped)

1 tomato (diced)

1 head broccoli flowerets (separated)

½ cup any Italian dressing

¼ cup Parmesan cheese

1 cup salad dressing

½ cup Sue Bee Honey

Pepper (to taste)

Mix Italian dressing, cheese, salad dressing, pepper and Sue Bee Honey. Blend mixture and remaining ingredients together and refrigerate.

Sioux Honey Association

# Oriental Chicken Salad

**DRESSING:**

3 tablespoons rice wine
vinegar
¼ cup salad oil
2 teaspoons soy sauce

2 tablespoons sugar
½ teaspoon dry mustard
1 teaspoon fresh shredded
ginger

**SALAD:**

Cubed uncooked chicken
Olive oil
Chopped garlic

Chopped celery, water chestnuts, shredded lettuce,
chopped green onions,
chopped cashew nuts,
green grapes, canned
oriental nooldes

Combine ingredients for dressing in glass jar with screwtop, shake vigorously. Saute' garlic in oil; add chicken and cook until no longer pink in middle. In bowl, put celery, water chestnuts, lettuce, green onions, nuts and grapes. Add dressing and toss. Add noodles right before serving and toss again. May add small amount of fresh cilantro.

**Bill Reichardt
(Des Moines, Iowa)**

159

# Mustard Coleslaw

4 cups purchased coleslaw mix
1 cup finely chopped celery
½ cup Kraft Fat Free Mayonnaise
1 tablespoon dried parsley flakes

1 tablespoon white vinegar
Sugar substitute to equal 2 tablespoons sugar
1 tablespoon Dijon Stick mustard
1/8 teaspoon black pepper

In a large bowl, combine coleslaw mix and celery. In a small bowl, combine mayonnaise, parsley flakes, vinegar, sugar substitute, Dijon mustard, and black pepper. Add mayonnaise mixture to vegetable mixture. Mix gently to combine. Cover and refrigerate at least 1 hour. Gently stir again just before serving. Makes 6 (¾ cup) servings.

Each serving equals: 45 calories, 1 gram fat, 1 gram protein, 8 grams carbohydrate, 228 milligrams sodium, 2 grams fiber. Diabetic: 1 vegetable, 1 free vegetable.

HINT: 3½ cups shredded cabbage and ½ cup shredded carrots can be used in place of purchased coleslaw mix.

JoAnna M. Lund
(DeWitt, Iowa)

# Cranberry Delight

**CHILL UNTIL SLIGHTLY THICKENED:**
1 package raspberry Jello

1 package lemon Jello
4 cups hot water

**COMBINE:**
2 cups ground cranberries
¾ cup crushed pineapple
1½ cups sugar

1 cup nutmeats
2 cups finely cut celery
1¼ cups seeded grapes

Fold combination into Jello and chill until firm. Serve with dressing.

**Bessie Sierk**
**(Bettendorf, Iowa)**

# Cranberry Salad

1 package cranberries
(chopped)

1½ cups white sugar

Stir sugar in berries and let stand overnight in refrigerator.

**NEXT DAY ADD:**

1 (16 ounce can crushed
pineapple)
2 cups small marshmallows
or more
¾ cup chopped English
walnuts

1 large package Dream Whip
or 1 container of whipping
cream or 1 can Milnot
whipped (lowfat)

Chill beaters and bowl thoroughly before beating Milnot, which has been thoroughly chilled in the can.

*A very good salad at Thanksgiving and Christmas, or any other time. A family favorite for many years, the salad can be made several days ahead - which we all love - right? It keeps beautifully, covered first with Saran Wrap and then foil. Leftovers may be frozen.*

Madeline R. Ryan
(Mitchellville, Iowa)

# Cranberry Salad

1 pound raw cranberries
1 pound small marshmallows
3-4 apples (cored and
quartered)

½ cup nuts
1 cup sugar
1 (12 ounce) carton whipped
topping

Grind together cranberries, marshmallows and apples. Add nuts and sugar, and place in refrigerator overnight. Fold in whipped topping. Pour into a 9x15-inch pan. Freeze.

Ann Pearson
(Mitchellville, Iowa)

# Cranberry Salad

1 cup ground raw cranberries
(squeeze lemon juice over
this mixture)
1 cup sugar
1 package lemon flavored
gelatin
1 cup hot water

1 cup pineapple syrup
1 cup crushed pineapple
(well drained)
½ cup nutmeats
1 cup chopped celery

Gelatin will not set if lemon juice is omitted. Combine cranberries and sugar. Dissolve gelatin in hot water; add syrup; chill until partially set. Add cranberry mixture, pineapple, walnuts and celery. I double the recipe and use a 9x13-inch pan.

Dorothy Overlin
(Mitchellville, Iowa)

# Cranberry Salad

2 apples (I use Jonathan)
2 oranges
1 (12 ounce) package raw
cranberrries
1 cup sugar
1 cup cut up walnuts

1 (3 ounce) package Lemon
Jello
1 (3 ounce) package
raspberry Jello
2 cups boiling water

Grind together: apples, oranges, and cranberries in large mixing bowl. Add sugar and walnuts. Stir well. Boil water and prepare Jello. Pour hot water over cranberry mixture. If the fruit is juicy enough, do not add cold water. Never more than 1 cup. Put salad in refrigerator and allow it to set.

*I serve it with Cool Whip. Miracle Whip can also be used if desired.*

Mary Park
(Panora, Iowa)

## Cranberry Salad

1 package cranberries
1 orange
2 small packages orange Jello
2 cups sugar

2 cups boiling water
1 cup cold water
Grind cranberries (and all of
    the orange)

Add sugar to Jello. Dissolve in boiling water and stir until completely dissolved. Add cold water, cranberries and orange. After it is partly set, stir to mix well.

*This old recipe belonged to Aunt Carrie Huyser.*

**Esther Van Houweling**
**(Pella, Iowa)**

## 5-Cup Salad

1 cup mandarin oranges
1 cup coconut
1 cup chunk pineapple

1 cup miniature marshmallow
1 cup sour cream

Mix all ingredients together. Drain juice off oranges and pineapple.

**Regina Portz**
**(Princeton, Iowa)**

163

# Crazy Salad

2 packages lemon Jello
3½ cups boiling water
8 marshmallows (cut in
  pieces)
2 bananas (sliced)
1 cup crushed pineapple
  (save juice)
½ cup sugar

2 eggs
Dash of salt
4 teaspoons flour
1 tablespoon lemon juice
1 tablespoon butter
1 cup whipped cream or
  Dream Whip
Nuts (if desired)

Dissolve Jello in hot water, cool and add marshmallows, drained pineapple, and bananas. Let stand until solid. Heat pineapple juice. Mix sugar, eggs, salt, flour, lemon juice, and butter. Add to the pineapple juice and cook until thick. Let it get cold, then add whipped cream and spread on top of Jello mixture. Sprinkle with nuts. I use miniature marshmallows. It depends on the size of the bananas as to how many I use: Serves 12. Use 9x13-inch pan.

*While living in Elkhart, our community had a card club that met one night each month. Mrs. Thompson forgot it was her turn to have the group in and she didn't feel that she had time to drive to the store. She looked through her cupboards and refrigerator, and this is what she came up with. We all liked it so well that we went home with the recipe, I've made it many times since. The card club named the recipe "Crazy Salad."*

**Mildred Stuart**
**(Mitchellville, Iowa)**

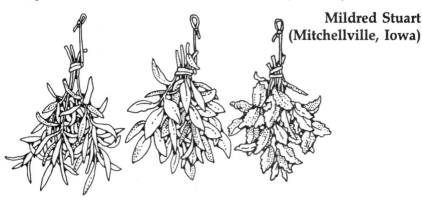

TARRAGON        SAGE        MINT

*I am submitting a poem titled "Will what we eat Today Make Our Ancestors Proud?" along with a recipe for dandelion greens. In early spring my family always went to our favorite secret spot to gather dandelions, lambs-quarter and wild mustard. We sometimes prepared them mixed together, either cooked or raw. They always added a nutritional supplement to our diet.*

## Will What We Eat Today
## Make Our Ancestors Proud?

Whether in Rome, Africa, Paris outer Tzar
We don't dine on pointed toast and caviar
We make our way to the salad bar

When out in the sticks
we search for our favorite salad mix
Wild mustard lambs-quarter dandelions
Throw in a bunch of wild nuts
that makes it mighty fine

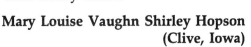

We breakfast at a quarter-to-eight
to fill our plates with light cuisine
Like Jack it makes us nice and lean
Rid our bodies of the toxic regime
This cuisine

When the sun is midway through the sky
it's time to chow-down cud food
Using our pearls to mix it well
our bellies fill for a healthy expel
We settle down to a snooze
Down time

Now it's six o'clock dusk time
We don't dine on the mighty bovine
Nor opulent swine
Tofu is our treat
Mixed with greens of the fibrous sort
We drank a mineral toast to these homily cohorts

**Mary Louise Vaughn Shirley Hopson**
**(Clive, Iowa)**

*(Continued on Next Page)*

# Dandelion Greens

Select dandelions early in the spring before they begin to blossom. Wash thoroughly, remove roots, drain and cook one hour or until tender in boiling, salted water. Allow two quarts of water to 1 peck of dandelion. Season with butter, margarine or olive oil, salt and pepper. Serve with vinegar, or serve it raw as a salad with salt, pepper and vinegar.

**Mary Louise Vaughn Shirley Hopson
(Clive, Iowa)**

# Frog Eye Salad

2 small cans mandarin
   oranges
1 large can pineapple chunks
¾ cup plus 2 tablespoons
   pineapple juice (drained
   from pineapple)
½ cup sugar
1 tablespoon flour

¼ teaspoon salt
1 slightly beaten egg
1 tablespoon lemon juice
¾ cup plus 2 tablespoons or
   ½ box Acini de Pepe Pasta
1 cup miniature
   marshmallows
1 cup or more Cool Whip

Drain juice from oranges and pineapple and reserve pineapple juice. Store drained juice for use later. Combine sugar, flour and salt in small pan. Slowly mix juice and egg into dry ingredients. Cook until thick. Add lemon juice. Cool. While mixture is cooling, cook pasta for 9 minutes as directed. When done cool quickly by draining through cold water in large sieve. Pour drained, cooled pasta in large storage bowl with tight lid. Pour cooled sugar mixture over and stir. Cover and refrigerate overnight. Next morning add miniature marshmallows, drained fruit and Cool Whip. Mix and refrigerate. Will stay good up to one week.

**Jo Ann Bittner**
**(Liscomb, Iowa)**

# Fruit Salad

1 can Eagle Brand milk
1 can cherry pie filling
1 (8 ounce) Cool Whip

1 cup miniature
   marshmallows
1 (20 ounce) can crushed
   pineapple

Mix altogether. Pour in a pretty bowl or a 9x13-inch pan and chill. This is easy to make. All you need is a can opener.

**Alyce Craig**
**(Mitchellville, Iowa)**

# Fruit Salad

1 large can pineapple chunks
  (well drained, reserve juice)
½ cup sugar
2 tablespoons flour
1 cup pecans (optional)
3 medium unpeeled apples

3 bananas (sliced)
1 egg (beaten)
2 (11 ounce) cans mandarin
  oranges (drained)
½ pound red seedless grapes
  (cut in half)

Drain pineapple. Put juice in a small saucepan. Add sugar, flour, and egg to juice. Cook over low heat, stirring constantly, until smooth and thickened. Let cool. Add fruits and nuts to dressing. Stir well. Chill before serving. Excellent!

Rachel Klingsheim
(Lime Springs, Iowa)

# Fruit Casserole

1 (21 ounce) can cherry pie
  filling
1 (21 ounce) can apple pie
  filling
1 pound can pear halves
  (drained)

1 pound can peach halves
  (drained)
1 (5¾ ounce) can pineapple
  chunks (drained)

Put into 2 quart casserole and bake at 350⁰ for 1 hour. I take this dish to a lot of potlucks. People always ask for the recipe. Sometimes it is darn right embarrasing to tell them how simple it is. I usually use a clear pyrex casserole because the fruit looks so pretty. Especially good with ham.

*I make this dish all through the year, but my family always asks for it at the holidays.*

Shirley Koester
(Dixon, Iowa)

# Gooseberry Salad

2 cups cooked gooseberries
with ¾ cup sugar
1 cup water
1 (3 ounce) package lemon or
pineapple Jello

1 cup chopped celery
½ cup chopped pecans
1 cup pineapple

Cook until berries are soft and add 1 (3 ounce) package Jello. Stir until dissolved; cool and add celery, pecans and pineapple. Optional frosting: 1 carton of sour cream, fold in 1 carton Cool Whip, one small marshmallow. Sprinkle with nuts.

*We lived at Elkhart, Iowa, retired and now spend our winters in Mission, Texas. I came from Marcus, Iowa.*

**Phyllis Volz**

# Holiday Salad
### (from Great-Grandma Kelly)

Grapes
Dates
Banana

Walnut meats
Whipped cream
Small amount Miracle Whip

Halve and seed grapes if necessary. Cut up dates. Slice bananas. Break up nutmeats. Mix with whipped cream and Miracle Whip. You will have to decide what amounts of each ingredient according to how much you want to make. Make same day you are going to use.

*This is always a delicious salad. We always have it at Christmas dinner.*

**Teresa and Patty Crossen**
**(Davenport, Iowa)**

# Dutch Lettuce

**SAUCE: (May be made ahead)**

| | |
|---|---|
| 1 tablespoon butter | 2 egg yolks or 1 egg |
| 1 tablespoon flour | ½ cup sugar |
| ½ cup water | ½ cup vinegar |

| | |
|---|---|
| 6 servings hot boiled potatoes | 2 teaspoons chopped onion (if desired) |
| 4 hard cooked eggs | 6 strips bacon |
| 6 servings coarsely cut lettuce | ⅓ cup vinegar |
| | ⅓ cup water |

Melt butter, add flour and when well blended, add water and bring to a boil, stirring constantly. Beat egg, add sugar and vinegar. Blend and stir into hot sauce. Let come to a boil. Have ready potatoes, eggs, lettuce, and onion. Dice bacon, fry in skillet until brown, add 3-4 tablespoons of sauce, vinegar, and water. Bring to boil and keep hot. Place a layer of hot potatoes (riced or mashed) in bowl; then a layer of lettuce, 2 sliced hard cooked eggs and several tablespoons of hot bacon dressing. Add remainder of potatoes, lettuce and sliced eggs. Pour rest of dressing over this and serve immediately. Serves 6.

Mina Baker-Roelofs
(Pella, Iowa)

170

# Iowa Celebrates Its 150th Birthday in 1996

Pella, founded in 1847 by Dominie (Rev.) Henrick Pieter Scholte, and a band of Dutch followers, will celebrate in 1997! The group, dressed as they did in The Netherlands, came bringing many of their food customs with them. These settlers ate "vet en stroep", bacon fat on bread with syrup or sorghum. This was probably eaten in rural Holland or was prairie food.

Pella is proud of its Dutch Heritage. Certain Dutch dishes continue, although most meal patterns are Americanized. In a recent study, made by the author of this essay, the current popularity of Dutch dishes was analyzed. Dutch Lettuce or Dutch "Mess" (recipe included) was most often made. "Erwten Soep" or Pea Soup, made with dried peas, sausage or ham, onions (sometimes potatoes and carrots) was next.

Dutch Letters are very popular but the pastry is difficult to make. Puff pastry, or a rich pie dough, surrounds a rope of almond paste with egg, sugar and flavoring added. It is then shaped into an initial. Letters, a Christmas treat in The Netherlands, are sold year round in Pella—thousands are sold during the Tulip Festival by Jaarsma and Vander Ploeg Bakeries.

Hutspot, similar to beef stew with meat separated, and potatoes, onions and carrots, mashed, rated high.

Stamppot, kale, cabbage, or kraut, mashed with potatoes was also popular.

The Pigs in the Blanket or Saucijze Broodjes are served with coffee or are a street food in The Netherlands. (Recipe included.)

Olie Bollen, raisin-filled yeast or baking powder leavened donut holes, are part of New Year's Eve Celebrations. Large platter-sized pancakes, often meat filled, are lunch treats. Cabbage salad or Cole Slaw originated in The Netherlands. Kool is the Dutch spelling for cabbage, Sla for salad. There is also the Koekjes—cookie connection.

A dinner menu at Pella's famous Dutch restaurant could include Spiced Beef (rolled rump with salt, pepper, cloves, and nutmeg or other spices inside) and cut green beans or Snijbonnen, cauliflower with nutmeg or sweet sour Red Cabbage (Recipe included). Strawtown Inn has colorful tiles, Dutch lace curtains and waitresses in Volendam's recognizable Dutch dress or costume.

The Dutch Koffie Tafel or Coffee Table is a tradition for easy entertaining during the year of Holidays in Pella. A collection of breads, including raisin bread which is "special," cold meats, assorted cheeses like Gouda or Edam and fresh fruits delight guests. The chosen drink is coffee. The coffee could be topped with real whipped cream if calorie counters approve.

*(Continued on Next Page)*

## (Iowa Celebrates Its 150th
## Birthday In 1996 - Continued)

During the May Tulip Time Festival Pella residents are more "Dutch than the Dutch." Letters, Pella Bologna and the Kiwanis Clubs' Poffertjes, mini pancakes with butter and powdered sugar, are worth "standing in line for"! Kermis, a summer carnival at the Historical village occurs in July as does a Dutch Elderhostel. Food experiences during Elderhostel include a Dutch dinner at Strawtown Inn, a Dutch lunch prepared by participants, and related lectures.

Sinter Klaas Day, officially December 6, is celebrated following Thanksgiving with a parade and Opera House Brunch. Dutch chocolate initials are given to each child. The Historical Society's Christmas Walk, featuring the decorated village, is fun and includes hot chocolate and Santa Claus cookies, spicy and shaped in molds, at the Old Fashioned Dutch Bakery.

Because of Holland's historical contacts with Indonesia, Oriental type foods are often incorporated into Dutch meal planning. Nasi Goreng Mix, similar to fried rice, is available at De Pelikaan Shop, 627 Franklin, in Pella. Some Pella Dutch like rice with butter, sugar and cinnamon. Americans, including Pellans, should eat meals more like the Dutch in Holland. Traditionally and nutritionally, popular pork, poultry and fish servings are smaller. Grains and cereals are featured in the two bread meals and more fruits and vegetables are served. Puddings and yogurts are common dinner desserts.

Pastries are used only for special occasions. The Dutch shop more frequently and enjoy meeting friends at the outdoor markets.

In Holland, and in Pella also, "Gezontheid" or "Proost," "to your health," is an often used toast. Pella is happy to share its authentic Dutch foods anytime during the year.

**Mina Baker-Roelofs**
**Associate Professor Emerita**
**of Home Economics**
**Central College**
**Pella, Iowa 50219**

**Co-Editor**
**"A Taste of the World"**
**Cookbook**
**Central College Auxiliary**
**Pella, Iowa 50219**

# Honeymoon Salad
*(For Beginners)*

**Head of Lettuce**

Just lettuce alone!

**Barbara Godlove**

# Layered Lettuce Salad

**1 head lettuce (chopped)**
**½ cup chopped celery**
**½ cup diced onion**
**1 (15 ounce) can of peas**
**(drained)**

**2 cups mayonnaise**
**½ cup grated cheddar cheese**
**8 slices crisp bacon**
**(crumbled)**

Using a 9x12-inch pan, start with a layer of the chopped lettuce and continue adding layers of celery, onion, peas, putting mayonnaise over each layer. Top with cheddar cheese, and bacon last. Cover and let set in refrigerator overnight. Serves 10.

*I got this recipe from a friend who lived in Davenport, years ago. When entertaining a large group of people, it can be made ahead. It stays crisp and fresh.*

**Lucille Richards**
**(Denver, Iowa)**

PARSLEY

# Pink Arctic Freeze

2 (3 ounce) packages cream
  cheese (softened)
2 tablespoons sugar
2 tablespoons mayonnaise
1 cup crushed pineapple
  (drained)

1 (1 pound) can jellied
  cranberry sauce
½ cup pecans (chopped)
½ cup whipped cream

Cream together cheese and sugar, stir in mayonnaise. Fold in
cranberry sauce, pineapple, nuts and whipped cream. Put into a
9x5x3-inch loaf pan and freeze until firm. Cut into slices and serve
on lettuce leaf. Serves 8.

Beverly Havenhill
(Le Claire, Iowa)

# Pistachio Salad

1 (No. 2) (15 or 16 ounce) can
  crushed pineapple
  (undrained)
1 (3 ounce) package of
  pistachio pudding (dry)

1 cup miniature
  marshmallows
1 (8 ounce) carton Cool Whip

Mix together and keep in refrigerator.

Catherine Freund
(Davenport, Iowa)

174

## Make Ahead Salad

| | |
|---|---|
| 1 cup Miracle Whip | 5-6 green onions (sliced) |
| ½ cup sugar | ½ cup diced cucumber |
| 3 tablespoons Tarragon vinegar | ½ cup green pepper |
| | 6-8 sliced radishes |
| 2 tablespoons prepared mustard | ¼ cup shredded cabbage |
| | ⅔ cup chopped green olives |
| ¼ cup milk | 4 hard boiled eggs (cut up) |

Combine all ingredients. Let stand in refrigerator at least 4 hours (overnight is okay). Break up lettuce and pour over. Serves 8 to 10. Very Good!

Jean Tannatt
(Des Moines, Iowa)

## Pea Salad

| | |
|---|---|
| 3 cans drained peas | 1½ cups diced celery |
| 1½ cups shredded cheese | 1 small onion diced fine |
| ¾ cup pepper relish or sweet relish | Approximately 1½ cups mayonnaise |

Mix together and refrigerate overnite. If so wished 3 chopped, cooked eggs may be added.

Gladys Biles

DILL

175

# Raspberry Salad

1 large package raspberry
   Jello
2 cups boiling water

1 package frozen raspberries
1½ cups sweetened
   applesauce
1 (8 ounce) carton Cool Whip

Dissolve Jello in boiling water. Stir in the frozen raspberries and applesauce. Chill until firm. Cover with Cool Whip before serving.

Sheryl Underwood
(Norfolk, Virginia)
(Formerly Princeton, Iowa)

# Red Top Salad

**MIX:**
1 (3 ounce) package lemon
   Jello
1 cup hot water

10 marshmallows, cut up, add
   to Jello and water but don't
   let it set

**ADD:**
1 (8 ounce) tub whipped
   topping
½ cup celery (diced)
¼ pound yellow cheese
   (shredded)

¼ cup Miracle Whip
½ cup nutmeats
1 (8 ounce) crushed pineapple

**TOPPING:**
1 (3 ounce) package red
   or green Jello

Put in oblong pyrex 9x13-inch. Let congeal, then dissolve 1 package of any red Jello (3 ounce) in 2 cups hot water. Chill, then pour over top of congealed mixture. Refrigerate. Cut in squares and serve. For green top, use lime Jello.

Thelma Smith
(Mitchellville, Iowa)

176

## Cold Rice Salad

1 package Rice-a-Roni Fried
    Rice with almonds
1 cup sliced water chestnuts
½ cup black olives (chopped)
1 jar marinated artichoke
    hearts

½ bell pepper, chopped
    finely
⅓ cup mayonnaise
1 package toasted sliced
    almonds

Prepare rice as directed on package. Cool in refrigerator. Drain water chestnuts and olives, but add juice of artichokes to rice. Cut artichoke hearts into thirds. Add all ingredients to rice. Mix well. Chill 2 hours or overnight.

NOTE: This salad transports well and is always a big hit at potlucks and picnics because it's different than the usual salads.

**Bert Brooke**
**(Bettendorf, Iowa)**

## Sauerkraut Salad

1 cup sauerkraut
2 tablespoons onion
1 section celery

½ cup green pepper
½ cup sugar
¼ cup vinegar

Mix all together. Chill and serve.

**Lila Maynard**
**(Princeton, Iowa)**

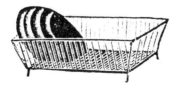

# Spaghetti Salad

8 ounces spaghetti (boiled)          1 small onion (finely cut)
1 small cucumber (finely cut)       1 small green pepper (finely
                                                  cut)

DRESSING:
1 tsp. salt                                    1 cup Mazola oil
1 cup sugar                               ⅓ cup ketchup

Beat 10 minutes. Add ⅓ cup vinegar.

Put spaghetti, vegetables and dressing in large bowl. Add dressing. Refrigerate overnight. Wonderful!

Bonny Dittmer
(Princeton, Iowa)

# Spinach Salad

2 packages lemon Jello            1 cup light 1 percent small
   (or 1 large one)                        curd cottage cheese
2 cups hot water                      2 tablespoons finely chopped
2 tablespoons vinegar                 onion
1 cup Light Hellmann's            1 package frozen chopped
   mayonnaise                             spinach (thawed)
¾ cup diced celery

Dissolve Jello in hot water, set aside to cool. When cool, add vinegar and mayonnaise. Mix well. Meanwhile put onions in food processor whirl a few seconds, add the celery until fine. Add spinach and cottage cheese separately with seconds of whirring between each. Add the Jello mixture with a wire whip. Chill. Mold in a small Tupperware gelatin mold or in a flat dish to be cut in squares. This may be topped with a dollop of dressing made from half light sour cream and half light mayonnaise and a dash of lemon juice.

Fran Lenton
(Newton, Iowa)

# Strawberry-Banana Gelatin Salad
### (Low Calorie)

1 (6 ounce) package
  strawberry-banana gelatin
1 cup hot water
1 cup small curd lowfat
  cottage cheese
¾ cup skim milk
1 tablespoon sugar

½ cup chopped pecans
  (optional)
Various fresh fruit pieces
  (approximately ½ cup each
  of strawberries, bananas,
  grapes, etc.)
1 (16 ounce) can crushed
  pineapple (optional)*

Mix gelatin with hot water until dissolved. Refrigerate gelatin mixture until it begins to congeal. Add all other ingredients and stir thoroughly by hand until evenly mixed. Let the mixture chill in the refrigerator until it is quite firm. This salad can be molded and turned out onto a plate when firm or can be mixed and served from a clear bowl as it is quite an attractive salad. *Only canned pineapple may be used. Fresh pineapple keeps the gelatin from congealing. Note: Other gelatin flavors may be used, lime, orange, etc.

*This salad was always part of our Easter Sunday dinner when I was growing up, thus reminds me of those beautiful spring days.*

**Mrs. Beth Millea**

THYME     PARSLEY     BASIL

179

# Molded Strawberry Salad

*(Reprinted from "Recipes and Recollections from Terrace Hill," of which Mrs. Chris Branstad was editor-in chief, and with permission of the Terrace Hill Society.)*

3 packages (3 ounces each)
  strawberry-or raspberry-
  flavored gelatin
2 cups boiling water
1 (16 ounce) package frozen
  sweetened strawberries or
  raspberries, thawed

1 can (20 ounces) juice-pack
  crushed pineapple
2 large ripe bananas (mashed)
1 (8 ounce) carton sour cream

Dissolve gelatin in boiling water. Stir in thawed berries, undrained pineapple, and bananas. Pour half the mixture into a 2-quart ring mold. Chill until set. (Leave remaining gelatin at room temperature.) When gelatin in ring mold is set, spread sour cream over surface. Carefully spoon unset gelatin mixture over sour cream. Refrigerate several hours until set. Unmold. Makes 12 servings.

Jacqueline Erbe
(Wife of Former Iowa Governor Norman Erbe)

*As First Lady, Jacqueline Erbe often shopped for the groceries for their dinner parties.*

A similar strawberry salad recipe was submitted by Anna Schmidt, Princeton, Iowa.

# Strawberry Pretzel Salad

| | |
|---|---|
| 2¾ cups crushed pretzels (not too fine) | 2 (10 ounce) packages frozen strawberries |
| 3 tablespoons sugar | 1 cup sugar |
| ¾ cup melted butter | 1 (9 ounce) Cool Whip |
| 1 (8 ounce) package cream cheese | 2 packages strawberry Jello |
| | 2 cups boiling water |

FIRST LAYER: Mix pretzels and 3 tablespoons sugar, pour butter over this. Pat into a 9x13-inch pan and bake at 350⁰ ten minutes.

SECOND LAYER: Cream softened cream cheese and 1 cup sugar. Fold in Cool Whip. Spread over cooled pretzel layer.

THIRD LAYER: Pour boiling water over Jello. Add frozen berries. When beginning to thicken, spoon over cheese mixture. May be made the night before. Unusual and delicious. Remember: Only two cups water.

**Charlotte Fliehler**
**(Secretary, Chamber of Commerce, Strawberry Point, Iowa)**

Strawberry Point, founded in 1853, is a town of almost 1,500 people, located 2½ miles northeast of Backbone State Park, Iowa's oldest and largest park.

Helen Kasparek, Des Moines, submitted a similar recipe, called Pretzel Surprise Salad, with this comment:

*This is our all time favorite, a must for Christmas. I received the recipe from Marie Colony in Coralville, Iowa.*

181

# Vegetable Pasta Salad

1½ cups vegetable oil
1½ cups apple cider vinegar
1½ cups sugar
2 tablespoons onion flakes
2 teaspoons prepared mustard
1 teaspoon Accent
1 teaspoon garlic powder

1 teaspoon parsley flakes
1 box or 1 pound cooked
  mostaccioli pasta noodles
1-2 purple onions (diced)
2 cucumbers (diced)
3-4 tomatoes (diced)
1 green pepper (diced)

Cook your box of mostaccioli pasta noodles until tender, drain and chill. Mix well oil, vinegar, sugar, onion flakes, mustard, Accent, garlic powder, parsley flakes, and salt and pepper to taste. Dice onion, cucumber, tomatoes, pepper. Dice in large pieces. Add vegetables to pasta, then stir in oil mixture over all. Refrigerate overnight before serving. Makes 4 quarts pasta salad. May be left in refrigerator up to 2 weeks! Very good! A sure hit with everyone!

Mary Serrano
(Bettendorf, Iowa)

# Molded Waldorf Salad

1 (3 ounce) package lemon
  flavored gelatin
1 cup boiling water
1/8 tsp. salt
½ cup mayonnaise

1 cup celery (sliced)
1½ cups red apple (diced)
½ cup nuts (chopped)
½ cup Cool Whip

Dissolve gelatin in water. Chill until slightly thickened, add salt, blend in mayonnaise. Fold in remaining ingredients. Place in 1 quart mold and chill. Unmold.

Shirely Weller
(Knoxville, Iowa)

## Comments About Mother and Her Cooking Skills

My mother, Mrs. Lydia Plambeck, was the wife of Scott County farmer, Herman Plambeck. Born in Switzerland, she came to America and to Iowa in 1894 at age 14. She married Herman in April, 1907, and became the mother of five children during the depression years, when monetary pleasures were practically non-existent.

Ingredients for her culinary art were chiefly supplied by a well-tended country garden, a small orchard, and a flock of chickens. We children were involved in all three of these projects.

She was, in my opinion, a gourmet cook—because she was able to make something delicious out of almost nothing.

All her children grew up strong and healthy—without the false comfort of "junk" food.

When Christmas Day, or other special days, came, we all looked forward to our special dinner. Our wonderful mother could make a tough old rooster, stuffed with Apple Raisin dressing, taste like "pheasant under glass."

Herb Plambeck
(Des Moines, Iowa)

*Herb Plambeck for many years was "the radio voice of rural Iowa."*

# Sweet Apple-Raisin Dressing

6 cups tart apples (peeled and cubed in ½-inch pieces)
1 cup sugar
½ teaspoon cinnamon

1½ cups dark raisins (soaked in boiling water for 15 minutes)
4 cups white bread (2 or 3 days old) cubed in ½-inch pieces

Mix cubed apples, sugar and cinnamon. Add well drained raisins and the cubed bread. Mix again. Stuff fowl and roast according to directions. If you have leftover dressing, put it in a buttered casserole, bake at 350⁰ for approximately 30 to 40 minutes and baste occasionally with drippings from roasting fowl.

**Herb Plambeck**

# Growing Up In Iowa

My birthplace was Davenport, Iowa. The date was February 29, 1908, so I have only had 22 birthdays. However, in this Sesquicentennial year, I do feel a bit older.

When I was three years of age, my parents and baby sister first moved to a rented 80 acre Lincoln Township farm. When I was about seven, we moved to a 156 acre rented farm in the same township, after which my father pooled all the family's savings and bought a 135 acre farm, also in Lincoln Township.

I grew up experiencing all the fun and the trials of boys and youths of that period. In rural school, it was "Andy, Andy Over," or baseball, or sledding, or tag games every noon, depending on the season. I had a pony and loved to ride.

When I was eight, I started to milk a few cows by hand and do all the other chores boys did in those days. By the time I was 18, I was milking more than 20 cows at times. When the Depression struck in 1921, land prices plummeted and losing the farm was a stark possibility, just as I was hoping to go to High School. However, there no longer was money to hire help so I became an unpaid "hired man" at age 13.

However, my father gave me the use of four acres of land on which I grew tomatoes, potatoes, sweet corn, and cucumbers, and with my four sisters' help, along with some cousins, made three trips a week to my Davenport vegetable routes, and did surprisingly well in selling my produce house to house. Incidentally, with the hard work and sacrifices by everyone in the family, the farm was saved.

Of course, as I matured, I did every farm task—plowing, planting, harvesting, threshing, husking corn, etc. I also became very active as a 4-H boy and later as a 4-H leader, and fell in love with every pretty girl in the county.

Eventually, I went to Ames to attend Iowa State College, then came back as Scott County 4-H leader to work with hundreds of great boys, after which I became farm editor of the Davenport Democrat, now the Quad City Times. In 1936, I was chosen to become Farm Director for Radio Station WHO, the first person in the nation to have such an assignment.

That, of course, ended my "growing up" in Scott County. However, I did return to marry lovely Frances Hahn, a Walcott farm family's daughter, and spent the next 60 years away, 34 of them with WHO in Des Moines, including stints as a WW II and Vietnam War correspondent overseas, and four years in Washington, D.C. as Assistant to two U.S. Secretaries of Agriculture, before returning to Iowa again for more broadcasting, the authoring of books, and writing for five magazines, including Wallaces Farmer. I am continuing in those capacities at the present time.

**Herb Plambeck**

184

## Rosy Blue Cheese Dressing

| | |
|---|---|
| 1 small onion | 2 tablespoons vinegar |
| 1 cup mayonnaise | ½ teaspoon salt |
| ⅓ cup salad oil | ½ teaspoon paprika |
| ¼ cup ketchup | ¼ teaspoon celery seed |
| 1 teaspoon prepared mustard | 1 (4 ounce) crumbled Maytag |
| 2 tablespoons sugar | Blue Cheese |

Blend all ingredients, except Maytag Blue Cheese, in food processor or blender until smooth. Stir in crumbled Maytag Blue and refrigerate until serving time.

**Maytag Dairy Farms**

## Cole Slaw Dressing

| | |
|---|---|
| 1 quart Miracle Whip | 2 tablespoons horseradish |
| 1 cup sugar | Seasonings: salt, pepper, |
| ⅓ cup oil | celery seed, garlic powder, |
| ¼ cup vinegar (scant) | seasoning salt and |
| 2 tablespoons catsup | sodium glutamate |

Mix together Miracle Whip and sugar. Then mix and heat oil and vinegar until they come to a boil, cool. To sugar mixture add: catsup, horseradish, and seasonings. Use your own discretion as to the amounts of the seasoning ingredients (sodium glutamate is a preservative which keeps the ingredients from spoiling). After it has cooled add liquid. Store in the refrigerator. This is handy to use as needed. No making it every time.

*I received this recipe from Harold Johnson, my brother, who now lives in Wittenburg, Arizona.*

**Helen J. Kasparek**
**(Des Moines, Iowa)**

185

# Boiled Salad Dressing

**COMBINE AND HEAT TO BOILING. SET ASIDE.**

½ cup cider vinegar                    ½ cup water

**COMBINE AND MIX THOROUGHLY:**

¼ cup sugar                              Dash pepper
1½ tablespoons flour                 1 whole egg or 2 egg yolks
¼ teaspoon salt

Cook in double boiler. Combine dry ingredients and egg. Add hot vinegar mixture. Cook until slightly thick, stirring constantly. Dressing will thicken as it cools.

**Wilma Davis**

# Pea Salad Dressing

1 cup sugar                              ⅓ cup vinegar
1½ tablespoons flour                 ⅓ cup water
1 egg (beaten)

Mix all together in saucepan until thick. When cool, put over peas or mixed vegetables.

**Catherine Freund
(Davenport, Iowa)**

# Thousand Island Salad Dressing

1 dill pickle
1 large onion
1 boiled egg
1 cup chili sauce

½ cup celery
½ cup green pepper
2 quarts mayonnaise

Boil eggs, dice vegetables, chop egg and blend. Stir in chili sauce and mayonnaise. Refrigerate.

Pat Underwood

## Iowa Fields

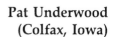

Like an honest face
with trusting eyes,
Iowa earth keeps giving.

Isn't it true within all nature
a miracle lives?

To feed the masses
is the voice of growth,
the song of prosperity.

Iowa is a fertile land
where homesteads house
the caretakers,
where the smile of rain and sun
meets a kernel of corn
like friends who work together.

As long as there is hunger,
as long as there is need.

Pat Underwood
(Colfax, Iowa)

187

# Underwood Memories

My husband, Steve, and I live four miles northwest of Colfax, Iowa in an area formerly called Oswalt. This was great Indian country: lots of wildlife; the height of hills contrasted with the depth of the South Skunk River valley. (Skunk is an Indian name, we've read, chosen because of the strong odor of wild onions growing along the river banks.)

Oswalt was named after Barny Oswalt and was platted in 1889. As the area was settled, this was a coal-mining town with two railroad lines, two general stores, a barber shop, a meat market, two boarding houses, a school house, a feed business, a Knights of Pythias hall, and a post office. 1,800 miners were employed.

Now we're a neighborhood of acreages and farmland. When we walk through our pastures and timbers, we can still see the ruts where the stagecoach ran, flint and stones of Indian campsites (mainly Sauk and Fox), indentations in the ground from coal shafts, and a few stove lids and remnants strewn about from miners' shacks. As our two sons were growing up, they loved hearing our local story of Indian lore—about a cache of gold never found, but buried in these hills "the depth of a log-cabin window with a cottonwood planted over top."

The land is an intimate part of my memory, having grown up on a farm and having lived in the country all these years. I've always been amazed at the fertility of our rich Iowa soil. I remember my father walking out to a field, grasping a handful of our good Tama loam, and letting it sift down through his fingers. He was checking it for moisture, I imagine, but I regarded it as a sacred experience—a blessing given us to feed the people of the world.

As we celebrate our sesquicentennial year, I think about how much we have to offer each other through our art, faith, livelihoods, families, and friendships, how fortunate we are to be chosen as guardians of this beautiful section of our nation, and what a grave responsibility it is.

I've been invited to share one of my poems with you. As a way of introducing myself and my writing, I will mention that I have been writing in a serious vein for the last twelve years and find poems about nature and the earth to be a source of joy. It's my pleasure to share this poem with you as a tribute to the State of Iowa and its people: a loving bond between those who will receive its passion.

Pat Underwood

188

# Memories of Oswalt
*By: Evelyn (Peggy) Gummert*

James A. Oswalt, the youngest son born to Barnett and Minerva Oswalt, was born March 3, 1880 in Oswalt, in a log cabin. In 1892 at the age of 12 James had to go to work in a coal mine, a mine called No.3. He worked in the mines for 50 years. Oswalt was a flourishing mining town of around 2,000 people at one time, located 4 miles northwest of Colfax, Iowa. James was my dad.

When he and mother married, they acquired some of the land my grandfather had owned. When I was a year old, they built a new home high on a hill which is still there. At the age of 5 I remember the coal mines in that area being not very good. So my parents moved to Des Moines. When I reached the junior high age, I walked to school, a distance of over a mile, twice a day. I graduated from East High School in 1931.

During the Depression my parents lost their home in Des Moines and moved back to the home in Oswalt. I married and moved to Marshalltown.

I never really knew my grandfather, and only saw him a few times, but I do know that he and his father fought in the Civil War.

Both my husband and I worked at Lennox Industries for 30 years and are now retired.

One interesting story that has been retold through the years is about buried gold. As stories are "handed down" they are usually altered, but this is the story as I remember it was told to me.

"Before his death at age 110, in Oklahoma, an old Indian doctor, son of a chief, sketched a crude map of Oswalt and told his story to a white man who had befriended him. His story according to the friendly "paleface," was that several Indian boys, including himself, had found the gold. The old chief, father of the Indian doctor, had wrapped the bullion in a blanket and buried it - "the depth of a cabin window" - on the brow of a hill. Over the "cache" he planted a Cottonwood tree. The gold was believed to have been stolen in a stage coach robbery. When Des Moines was but a fort, a stage trail ran through Oswalt. The old Indian doctor's crude map, handed down by his "palefaced" friend landed in the hands of an adventurous Indiana man. This man dug by a Cottonwood tree, but no gold was found."

Many people, including my father, have dug for the gold. All that was ever found were Indian relics.

**Evelyn (Peggy) Gummert**
**(Marshalltown, Iowa)**

189

# Casseroles

## The Little Brown Church in The Vale
### Nashua, Iowa

*Courtesy of Bill Dunn Photos*
*Charles City, Iowa*

192

# The Little Brown Church in the Vale
## Nashua, Iowa

*(With special thanks to present Pastors Bob and Linda Myren)*

Thanks to a young music teacher in 1857 by the name of William Pitts who was traveling, by stagecoach from Wisconsin, to visit his bride-to-be in Fredericksburg, Iowa, we have the beginnings of the song and church entitled, "The Little Brown Church in the Vale". When the stagecoach stopped in Bradford for a rest, young Pitts got out, walked around, and came upon one particular place he could not forget. His vision of a pastoral church set in the midst of the trees inspired the poem which he set to music in the song, "The Little Brown Church in the Vale".

Pitts married and returned to Bradford to teach music. He was stunned to see a small church being built at the same spot he had pictured in his hymn. The building was finished in 1864 and on dedication day Mr. Pitts' vocal class from Bradford Academy sang the song in public for the first time. People quickly fell in love with it. Pitts sold the song for $25.00 to a Chicago publisher.

When the railroad bypassed Bradford, and industry moved to nearby Nashua, the town slowly disappeared. Revival came about because of gospel groups which toured the U.S. singing about "The Church in the Wildwood". Its growing popularity and beauty of the church brought thousands of couples to be married in its lovely and rustic atmosphere.

Today an average of 600 weddings occur here every year. Altogether over 67,750 weddings have been held. In 1952 the First Annual Wedding Reunion was held in Nashua. It continues to be held the first Sunday in August, and the song is still sung in the small brown church in the wildwood.

# CASSEROLES

## CASSEROLES

Apple-Onion Casserole . . 195
Lima Bean Casserole . . . . 195
Barley Pilaf . . . . . . . . . . . 196
Broccoli Cheese
  Casserole . . . . . . . . . . . 196
Savory Beef Casserole . . . 197
Broccoli Casserole . . . . . . 197
Broccoli Rice Casserole . . 198
Creamy Broccoli
  Casserole . . . . . . . . . . . 198
Carrot Casserole . . . . . . . 199
Ambassador Chicken
  Casserole . . . . . . . . . . . 200
Baked Chicken
  Casserole . . . . . . . . . . . 201
Chicken Casserole . . . 201-202
Chicken Casserole
  and Dressing . . . . . . . . 203
Chicken Crunch
  Casserole . . . . . . . . . . . 203
Creamy Chicken
  Casserole . . . . . . . . . . . 204
Chicken Noodle
  Casserole . . . . . . . . . . . 204
King Ranch Chicken . . . . 205
Vel's Chicken
  Casserole . . . . . . . . . . . 206
Chicken and Rice
  Casserole . . . . . . . . . . . 206
Chicken and Wild
  Rice Casserole . . . . . . . 207
Wild Rice Chicken
  Casserole . . . . . . . . . . . 207

Chicken Chalupas . . . . . . 208
Chicken Klepto . . . . . . . . 208
Norwegian Chop Suey . . 209
Corn Casserole . . . . . . . . 209
Corn Bread Casserole . . . 210
Macaroni and Corn
  Casserole . . . . . . . . . . . 210
Scalloped Corn
  Casserole Supreme . . . . 211
Egg Casserole . . . . . . . . . 211
Dried Beef Casserole . . . . 212
Eggplant Casserole . . . . . 213
Hamburger Stroganoff . . . 213
Scalloped Pineapple . . . . 214
Aunt Dode's
  Potato Casserole . . . . . . 214
Tator Tot Casserole . . . . . 215
Reuben Bake . . . . . . . . . . 215
Rice Casserole . . . . . . . . . 216
Wild Rice Casserole . . . . . 217
Spaghetti Casserole . . . . . 217
Sweet Potato Casserole . . 218
Taco Twist . . . . . . . . . . . . 218
Tamale Pie (Featuring
  Iowa Corn and Beef) . . 219
Layered Tuna
  Casserole . . . . . . . . . . . 219
Turkey or Chicken
  Casserole . . . . . . . . . . . 220
Zucchini Casserole . . 220,222
"Jo Pohlman's
  Supper Dish . . . . . . . . . 222
Six Layer Dinner . . . . . . . 223
Swiss Veggie Casserole . . 223

## Apple-Onion Casserole

2-3 large onions (peeled &
    sliced)
2 tablespoons water
2 tablespoons butter
½ teaspoon salt and pepper

5 apples (sliced)
Cinnamon
Sugar
½ cup water

Cook the first four ingredients until half done. Grease a 2 quart casserole. Layer apples, then onions. Add cinnamon, and sugar (as much as you wish). I prefer just a sprinkling, so the apples and onions blend their flavors. Bake at 325⁰ uncovered for 20 minutes or at 350⁰ covered for 25 minutes.

*I've been told that this is an old German recipe. But my Irish friends and I really enjoy it!)*

Leona McCarville
(Fort Dodge, Iowa)

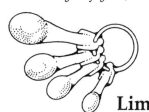

## Lima Bean Casserole

2 pounds dry lima beans
1 cup heavy cream

1 cup ketchup
1 cup brown sugar

Soak beans overnight or use frozen beans. Cook until almost done. Drain. Stir all in together. Bake at 350⁰ for 1½ hours.

*This is one of the recipes I can remember eating at my grandparents home, Earl and Gertrude May.*

**Betty Jane Shaw**
**(President and owner of Earl May Seed and Nursery)**
**(Granddaughter of Earl May, Shenandoah, Iowa)**

# Barley Pilaf

½ cup butter
1 large onion (chopped)
2 cups pearl barley

5 cups hot chicken broth
1½ teaspoons salt
½ teaspoon fresh green
  peppers

**STIR IN LATER:**
½ cup finely chopped green
  onions
¼ cup finely chopped parsley

1 cup lightly salted toasted
  cashews

Set oven to 350⁰. Heat butter in heavy skillet. Add onions and cook until soft and golden. Add barley and stir over low heat until coated with butter and lightly tan. Transfer to 2 quart buttered casserole and add ⅔ of boiling chicken broth or enough to generously cover. Season. Cover dish tightly and bake 25 to 30 minutes. Stir in green onions, parsley and rest of broth. Cook 15 minutes longer or until broth is absorbed and grains are puffed and tender. Adjust seasonings. Keep warm in low oven until ready to serve. Toss in cashews. Serves 12.

Pat Lujack

# Broccoli Cheese Casserole

2 packages frozen, chopped
  broccoli, cooked (1 package
  can be used)
⅓ stick butter, cut up, placed
  on top broccoli

Crush ¼ pound (1 roll) Ritz
  crackers, on top of cheese
½ stick of butter cut up on
  top of crackers
½ pound Velveeta Cheese
  (cut up, on top of butter)

Bake at 350⁰ for 20 to 30 minutes covered with tin foil.

Rachel Klingsheim
(Lime Springs, Iowa)

196

# Savory Beef Casserole

| | |
|---|---|
| 2 pounds round steak (cubed) | 1 tablespoon parsley flakes |
| ½ cup cooking oil | 2½ teaspoons salt |
| 1½ cups chopped onion | ¼ teaspoon pepper |
| 1 can tomatoes | 6 carrots (peeled) |
| 3 tablespoons tapioca | 3 medium potatoes (large |
| 1 (10½ ounce) can beef broth | cubes) |
| 1 clove garlic (minced) | ½ cup chopped celery |

Brown beef cubes in large skillet. Add onions, tomatoes, tapioca, beef broth, garlic, parsley, salt and pepper. Bring mixture to boil. Turn into 3 quart casserole. Cover. Bake at 350° for 1½ hours or until meat is tender. Add carrots, potatoes and celery. Continue baking covered for 1 hour or until vegetables are tender. Serves 6 to 8.

Jane Underwood
(Princeton, Iowa)

# Broccoli Casserole

| | |
|---|---|
| 1 pound package broccoli (chopped) | ⅔ cup celery (chopped) |
| 1 cup Minute rice | 1 can cream of chicken soup |
| 1 small jar Cheese Whiz | 1 can milk |
| ⅔ cup onion (chopped) | ½ cup water |

Saute' onions and celery with vegetable oil. Add broccoli, cook 10 minutes. Boil 1 can of cream of chicken soup, milk, water, Minute rice and Cheese Whiz. Add to first ingredients. Bake in a casserole dish at 350° for ½ hour.

Valerie Ward
(Le Claire, Iowa)

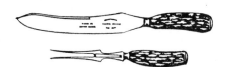

197

## Broccoli Rice Casserole

1 package frozen chopped
   broccoli
1½ cups cooked rice
   (½-¾ cup uncooked)
½ cup chopped celery

½ cup chopped onion
4 tablespoons butter
1 can cream of chicken soup
1 can cream of mushroom
   soup
1 cup grated cheese

Cook broccoli. Saute' onion and celery in butter. Combine the soups and cheese, making a sauce. Add the onion and celery. Mix well. Pour sauce over broccoli and rice. Put in buttered casserole dish and bake at 350° for 30 minutes.

Walt and Ruth Grimes
(Mitchellville, Iowa)

## Creamy Broccoli Casserole

2 eggs
1 (10¾ ounce) can condensed
   cream of mushroom soup
   undiluted
1 cup mayonnaise
¾ cup chopped pecans
1 medium onion (chopped)

2 packages (10 ounces each)
   frozen chopped broccoli,
   cooked and drained
1 (4 ounces) cup shredded
   cheddar cheese
1 tablespoon butter or
   margarine (melted)
¼ cup soft bread crumbs

In a bowl, beat eggs. Add soup, mayonnaise, pecans and onion. Stir in broccoli and pour into a greased 2 quart shallow baking dish. Sprinkle cheese over top. Combine butter and bread crumbs, then put on top. Bake uncovered at 350° for 30 minutes. Makes 8 to 10 servings.

Ralph W. Held
(Sun City, Arizona)

# Carrot Casserole
### *(Approximately 100 years old)*

| | |
|---|---|
| 2 cups cooked, mashed carrots | 1 teaspoon salt |
| ⅔ cup cracker crumbs | Dash of pepper |
| ¾ cup sharp cheddar cheese (grated) | ½ teaspoon onion flakes |
| 1 cup milk | 3 eggs |
| | ¾ stick butter |

Combine cracker crumbs, cheese, milk, salt, pepper and onion with well beaten eggs. Add cooked carrots and butter. Bake in greased casserole at 350° for 40 to 45 minutes.

**Joyce Brockhouse**
**(Princeton, Iowa)**


# Carrot Casserole

| | |
|---|---|
| 3 cups cooked carrots | ½ cup Carnation or evaporated milk (can substitute low fat) |
| 12 rolled soda crackers | |
| 2 tablespoons onions (minced) | 2 cups grated cheese |

Mash the carrots in the water in which they were cooked. Add remaining ingredients. Mix and pour into buttered casserole. Bake at 350° about 1 hour. Serves 6 to 8 people.

**Ida Weibel**
**(Long Grove, Iowa)**

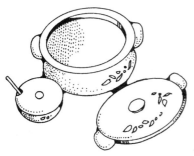

199

# Ambassador Chicken Casserole

*(Reprinted from "Recipes and Recollections from Terrace Hill," of which Mrs. Chris Branstad was editor-in-chief and with permission of the Terrace Hill Society.)*

1 green pepper (chopped)
1 onion (chopped)
1 stalk celery (sliced)
2 tablespoons butter or
  margarine
1 (6 ounces) package herb-
  seasoned stuffing cubes
½ cup hot water
4 cups diced, cooked chicken
1 (10 ounce) package frozen
  peas

2 (10½ ounces each)
  condensed cream of
  mushroom soup
5 eggs
1½ cups milk
1 teaspoon poultry seasoning
¼ cup grated Parmesan
  cheese
2 tablespoons butter or
  margarine (melted)

In a large saucepan, cook green pepper, onion, and celery in 2 tablespoons butter until tender. Add 3½ cups of the stuffing cubes; toss well. Continue to toss while gradually adding water. Spread in half of the stuffing mixture in the bottom of a 13x9-inch baking dish. Layer chicken and peas over stuffing. Cover with remaining stuffing mixture. Combine soup, eggs, milk, and poultry seasoning. Pour over layered mixture in baking dish. Crush remaining stuffing cubes; toss with Parmesan cheese and melted butter. Sprinkle over casserole. Bake in a 375° oven for 35 to 40 minutes or until center tests done with a knife. Makes 10 to 12 servings.

*When the British Ambassador dined with the family of Harold Hughes, former Iowa Governor, he said this homey Iowa casserole was the best meal he'd eaten during his stay in America.*

# Baked Chicken Casserole

| | |
|---|---|
| 3 cups diced, cooked chicken | 2 tablespoons lemon juice |
| 1 tablespoon minced onion | 1 cup mayonnaise |
| 1 cup diced celery | 2 ounce jar chopped pimentos |
| 8 ounce can water chestnuts (sliced) | ½ cup slivered almonds |
| 1 teaspoon salt | ½ of a 3 ounce can French fried onion rings |
| 1 teaspoon pepper | Cheddar cheese (shredded) |

Mix all ingredients except onion rings and cheddar cheese. Place in a greased 3 quart casserole. Cover with cheese and onion rings. Bake at 350⁰, covered, for 30 minutes. Do not overcook as it will dry out. Serves 4 to 6.

Luella Bishop Giles
(Panora, formerly West Des Moines, Iowa)

# Chicken Casserole

*(Served at Presbyterian Church Sidney Rodeo)*

| | |
|---|---|
| 1 cup uncooked macaroni | 2 chopped hard boiled eggs |
| 2 cans cream of chicken soup | ¼ cup shredded cheese |
| 1 cup milk | |
| 2 cups cooked, chopped chicken | |

Mix and let set overnight (or several hours) in a 2 quart casserole dish. Keep covered in refrigerator. Bake in 350⁰ oven for 1 hour. Let stand 10 minutes before serving. Serves 8 to 10.

Presbyterian Church
(Sidney, Iowa)

FINEST QUALITY CARVERS.

# Chicken Casserole

1 (about 6¼ ounce) package
   seasoned bread stuffing
1 stick melted margarine
2 cups chicken broth
2½ cups diced chicken
½ cup chopped celery
1 can mushroom soup

½ cup chopped onions
1 teaspoon salt
½ cup mayonnaise
Grated cheese
1½ cups milk
2 eggs (slightly beaten)

Mix together bread stuffing, margarine and chicken broth. Let soak 15 minutes, then put ½ mixture in 13x9-inch pan. Mix diced chicken, celery, onion, salt, and mayonnaise. Put this over the bread mixture. Mix eggs and milk; after putting remaining stuffing over meat, pour egg and milk mixture over the bread mixture. Cover with foil and refrigerate overnight. Take out 1 hour before baking. Spread 1 can mushroom soup over top. Bake uncovered at 325⁰ for 40 minutes, sprinkle with grated cheese and bake 10 more minutes.

**Virginia Thomas**
**(Mitchellville, Iowa)**

# Chicken Casserole

4 boneless, skinless chicken
   breasts (precooked)

2 (10 ounce) broccoli spears
   precooked crisp

Layer in a 9x13-inch glass pan. Top with 2 cans cream chicken soup, 1 cup mayonnaise and 1 can French fried onion rings. Stir together. Place over chicken and broccoli. Sprinkle with ½ cup grated cheddar cheese then crushed potato chips and 1 cup bread crumbs. Bake at 350⁰ for 30 minutes.

**Marilyn Erling**

# Chicken Casserole and Dressing

6 pound chicken or ½
   chicken breast per person
   (cooked and deboned)
¾ cup flour

6 eggs
½ cup lard
1½ quart chicken broth

Melt lard, add flour and chicken stock slowly. Cook 5 minutes after bringing to a boil. Add beaten eggs. Cook 2 minutes.

**DRESSING: Combine**
3 onions
½ teaspoon salt

¼ teaspoon sage
6 cups bread crumbs

Place in shallow well greased pan. Spread chicken on top. Pour the broth custard on top. Bake at 350° for 25 to 30 minutes. Cool and rebake 30 minutes. Serves 6 to 8.

**Fran Lenton**
**(Newton, Iowa)**

# Chicken Crunch Casserole

2½ cups cooked, diced
   chicken
1 can cream of mushroom
   soup
½ teaspoon salt

2 cups potato chips
1 cup milk
Paprika (as desired)
Cheese (as desired)

Mix chicken, soup, salt, and milk together. Heat on stove in pan until boiling point occurs, turn off so it won't stick and remove from stove. Take two cups of potato chips, put on bottom of casserole dish (grease dish). Then put in chicken mixture, and the rest of potato chips. On top of that put some cheeses if desired and paprika. Bake 350° for 30 minutes. Leave lid off casserole.

**Richard Freund**
**(Davenport, Iowa)**

203

# Creamy Chicken Casserole

12 slices dry wheat bread
  (cubed)
3 cups diced chicken
½ cup Miracle Whip salad
  dressing

1 cup diced onion
1 cup diced celery
½ cup margarine
4 beaten eggs
3 cups chicken broth

SAUCE:
1 can cream of mushroom
  soup

½ cup chicken broth
1 tablespoon butter or
  margarine

Mix bread, chicken and salad dressing. Saute' onion and celery in margarine. Drain off fat and mix vegetables with bread mixture, eggs and chicken broth. Put into a 9x13-inch casserole and cover with sauce. DO NOT STIR. This may be refrigerated overnight if desired. Bake at 350° for 1½ hours.

Reba Thompson
(Mitchellville, Iowa)

# Chicken Noodle Casserole

1 can cream of celery soup
½ cup milk
½ cup chopped onion
¼ cup green pepper

1 cup shredded cheddar
  cheese
1-2 cans mixin' chicken
1 (8 ounce) small bag egg
  noodles

Combine soup and milk in casserole dish, add onion, peppers, cheese and chicken. Cook noodles according to package directions, drain and rinse, add to casserole dish, stir well to coat. Bake at 350° for 30 minutes or until bubbly.

Susan Severs
(Princeton, Iowa)

# King Ranch Chicken

8 boneless, skinless chicken breasts

12 flour tortillas

1 can cream of mushroom soup

1 can cream of chicken soup

1 green bell pepper (finely chopped)

1 cup onion (finely chopped)

1 cup celery (finely chopped)

4-6 ounces fresh mushrooms, chopped (optional)

1 can Rotel tomatoes or 1 can diced tomatoes and 1 teaspoon chili powder more or less to control spiciness

Garlic salt (to taste)

¼ cup chicken broth

Spray a 9x13x2-inch baking pan with Pam. Simmer chicken until it's tender. (I add garlic salt to the water) and save the broth. Cool and dice the chicken into bite size pieces. Line the bottom and sides of the pan with 6 tortillas which have been cut into 1-inch strips. Sprinkle the tortillas with 2 or more tablespoons of chicken stock. Combine the soups, onion, green pepper, celery and mushrooms (if desired) until well blended. Pour half of this mixture and half the chicken over tortillas, and top with half the cheese. Make a second layer of tortillas and mixture and top with cheese. Pour Ro-tel tomatoes (or diced tomatoes plus chili powder) over all. Bake at 350° for 1 hour.

*We have enjoyed this recipe since we started wintering in Texas about 8 years ago. Our home is in Mitchellville, but we spend the winter in Rockport, Texas.*

**Mary Jane Reifschneider**
**(Rockport, Texas, formerly Mitchellville, Iowa)**

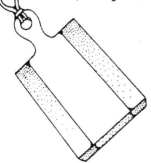

205

# Vel's Chicken Casserole

4 cups cooked, diced chicken
1 can cream of chicken soup
1 can cream of mushroom
soup
1 pound can chow mein
vegetables

1 pound chow mein noodles
3 tablespoons onion
1 cup diced celery
½ cup slivered almonds

Combine ingredients. Crush potato chips for top the last 10 minutes. Bake at 350⁰ for 1 hour.

Marvella Hans
(Ankeny, Iowa)

# Chicken and Rice Casserole

6 chicken breasts (skinned)
2 cups rice (white)
1 package French onion soup
Mushrooms (diced)
Salt

2 cans cream mushroom
soup
1 can cream celery soup
1 bag frozen broccoli
Garlic salt
Chives

Sear chicken in hot skillet. Put layer of cooked rice in bottom of casserole. Next, add cans of soup evenly over rice. Lay in chicken breasts. Next, put in layer of broccoli and add rest of rice. Next, lay in rest of broccoli. Pour cooked French onion soup over entire dish. Top off with garlic salt and chives to your taste. Cook in prewarmed oven at 350⁰ for 1 hour. Serve with warm garlic bread. NOTE: Pork chops can be substituted for chicken.

Bill Terry
(Master Gardener '94, Johnson County)

# Chicken and Wild Rice Casserole

1 (6 ounce) package Uncle
Ben's wild rice mix
2½ cups chicken broth (can
use Swansons low fat)
2 cups cubed cooked chicken
1 (16 ounce) can French-style
green beans (drained)
1 (10¾ ounce) can cream of
celery soup

½ cup mayonnaise (can use
light)
1 cup slivered toasted
almonds (optional)
1 (8 ounce) can sliced water
chestnuts
¼ cup chopped or grated
onion
1 (2 ounce) jar sliced
pimientos

Cook wild rice and mix in chicken broth. Combine with all remaining ingredients, pour into a 9x13-inch baking dish, and bake at 350° for 50 minutes. Serves 10 to 12. Doubles or triples with ease.

Jan Bailey
(Denton, Texas, formerly Colo, Iowa)

# Wild Rice Chicken Casserole

1 (6½ ounce) package Minute
Long Grain and Wild Rice
2 tablespoons butter
1 tablespoon flour
1 cup milk

½ cup grated cheddar cheese
2 tablespoons Chablis Wine
or 2 tablespoons lemon
juice
2 cups diced, cooked chicken

Prepare rice as directed on package. Spoon into greased 1½ quart casserole. Melt butter in saucepan, blend in flour, gradually add milk, and stir over low heat until thick and smooth. Add wine and cheese stirring until cheese is melted. Add chicken and sauce to rice in casserole. Mix well. Bake at 350° for 20 minutes until brown and bubbling. Serves 6. Enjoy!

Anna Schmidt
(Princeton, Iowa)

# Chicken Chalupas

2 cans cream of mushroom
  soup
1 (12 ounce) carton sour
  cream
1 onion (diced)
1 package soft flour tortillas

2-3 teaspoons hot peppers
  (diced)
1 pound cheddar cheese
  (shredded)
3 pounds chicken breasts

Cook and dice chicken. Mix soup, sour cream, onion and peppers. Heat for 5 minutes. Assemble, one at a time, tortillas filled with 2-3 tablespoons chicken, 2 tablespoons sauce and sprinkle with cheese. Roll up and use toothpicks to hold. Place assembled chalupas in greased baking pan and cover with remaining sauce. Bake at 350⁰ for 30 minutes. To make this dish more low-calorie and lowfat use no fat sour cream and lowfat mushroom soup. You can also use lowfat cheese.

**Sharon (DeRycke) Lenz**
**(KWQC-TV Channel 6, Davenport, Iowa)**

# Chicken Klepto

1 cut up cooked chicken
1 package cauliflower, carrots,
  water chestnuts—frozen
  (thaw and drain)

1 can cream of chicken soup
  (may add a little milk)
1 cup cheddar cheese
1 can French fried onion
rings

Combine all ingredients except onion rings. Place in baking dish. Put onion rings on top. Bake at 350⁰ for 1 hour.

**Syl Rex**
**(Le Claire, Iowa)**

208

# Norwegian Chop Suey

| | |
|---|---|
| 1 pound of hamburger | ½ cup uncooked rice |
| 2 onions (chopped) | 1 tablespoon soy sauce |
| 1 cup celery | ½ cup warm water |
| 1 cup cream of chicken soup | Chinese noodles |
| 1 cup cream of mushroom soup | |

Brown hamburger, onion, celery; then add soups, rice, water, soy sauce. Bake 2 hours in covered casserole. Moderate oven. Then add Chinese noodles and bake 15 minutes more.

*The Norwegian Chop Suey recipe story. My father really liked this casserole. My Mother did not have any Norwegian recipes so she dubbed this the Norwegian Chop Suey.*

**Jean Oxley**
**(Marion, Iowa)**

# Corn Casserole

| | |
|---|---|
| 1 can cream style corn | 3 tablespoons chopped onion |
| 1 can drained whole kernel corn | 1 cup melted butter or margarine |
| 2 eggs | 1 box Jiffy corn muffin mix |
| 1 cup sour cream | |

Mix all ingredients in a large bowl. Pour into greased pan(s). Bake at 350⁰ for 45 minutes. Makes a large casserole or 2 (2 quart) pans. Can freeze one uncooked for a later date.

**Donna Millhollin**

209

# Corn Bread Casserole

1 (10 ounce) can cream style corn
1 (10 ounce) can regular sweet corn
1 stick margarine or butter
1 (8 ounce) sour cream
2 eggs (slightly beaten)
1 package corn muffin mix

Heat cream style corn in small saucepan with one stick of margarine or butter. Add (drained) regular sweet corn to creamed mixture. Cool. Then add 8 ounces sour cream, slightly beaten eggs and 1 package of corn muffin mix. Blend completely and pour into a 8x12-inch oblong baking dish. Bake at 350⁰ uncovered for 45 minutes to 1 hour (until golden brown).

*This recipe was given to me by my very good friend, Jean Rossmiller. This is one of those dishes that is great for the holidays (or just about anytime!) The girls at the office have to take turns when it comes to making this dish for a potluck!*

**Lynn Mosier**

# Macaroni and Corn Casserole

1 can whole kernel corn and juice
1 can cream style corn
1 cup raw macaroni
1 cup Velveeta cheese (I use mild Mexican)
1 stick margarine

Mix and bake 45 minutes covered at 350⁰. Stir and bake uncovered for 15 minutes longer. This could require longer baking to thicken if corn is real juicy.

**Terry Swails**
**(KWQC-TV Channel 6, Davenport, Iowa)**

# Scalloped Corn Casserole Supreme

1 (1 pound) can golden
cream style corn
1 cup milk
1 egg (well beaten)
1 cup cracker crumbs

¼ cup minced onion
3 tablespoons chopped
pimiento
¾ teaspoon salt
½ cup butter cracker crumbs

Heat corn and milk. Gradually stir in eggs. Add next four ingredients and dash of pepper. Mix well. Pour into greased 8-inch round baking dish. Sprinkle buttered crumbs over all. Bake at 350° for 20 minutes. Serves 6.

**Catherine Freund
(Davenport, Iowa)**

# Egg Casserole

2 dozen eggs (beat well)
¼ pound oleo
½ cup milk
8 crisp strips bacon (crumble)
½ cup diced green peppers

¾ cup sliced fresh
mushrooms
2 cups cream of mushroom
soup (undiluted)
1 package shredded cheese

Beat eggs. Add ¼ pound oleo and milk. Mix well. Add bacon, green peppers, mushrooms, mushroom soup, to the above mixture. Sprinkle cheese on top, cover and refrigerate overnight. Bake uncovered in a greased 9x13 inch casserole dish at 250° for 50 to 75 minutes.

**Joni Lange
(Davenport, Iowa)**

211

# Dried Beef Casserole

1 cup dry macaroni
1½ cups milk
1 can cream of mushroom
  soup
1 tablespoon dry minced
  onion
1 tablespoon pimento
  (optional)

1 can mushrooms
8 ounces cubed Velveeta
1 or 2 sliced hard boiled eggs
1 small jar drief beef (or any
  other meat) chopped
½ teaspoon salt
¼ teaspoon pepper

Mix all together. Pour into greased 2 quart casserole. Sprinkle with crushed potato chips. Bake at 350°, covered, for 1 hour, then uncovered for 5 minutes.

*"My Little Anecdote"*

*When I was a young girl growing up on the farm, all of my older brothers and sisters got to do the "chores" outside. So I learned to cook at an early age for a big family. At the time, I thought that was so unfair. I wanted to milk cows! However, I learned to love to cook and still do. In "those days" we didn't always have the ingredients required and had to make do with what was in the house, no running to town for a bag of chocolate chips! And so I've always improvised, substituted, or invented new ways for old recipes. In the casserole above, I've used everything from Buddig meats, ham, turkey, beef and sliced polish sausage! Everything works. Be imaginative!*

**Judy Soenksen**
**(Princeton, Iowa)**

212

# Eggplant Casserole

Peel and cube eggplant. Cook in water until soft, then drain, and mash up well.

**ADD:**

| | |
|---|---|
| **1 tablespoon butter or margarine** | **2 beaten eggs** |
| **¼ cup milk** | **1 cup crushed crackers** |

Pour into baking dish that has been lined with butter and crushed cracker crumbs. Bake 30 to 45 minutes (or until done) in 350° oven. Test with toothpick. If it comes out clean, casserole is done. Can be cooked in microwave 10 to 15 minutes.

**Catherine Freund**
**(Davenport, Iowa)**

# Hamburger Stroganoff

| | |
|---|---|
| **½ cup minced onion** | **1 pound fresh mushrooms** |
| **1 clove minced garlic** | **(or 16 ounce can)** |
| **1 pound ground beef** | **1 can cream of mushroom** |
| **1 teaspoon salt** | **soup** |
| **¼ teaspoon pepper** | **1 cup sour cream** |

Brown hamburger. Add onion, garlic, salt and pepper. Stir well. Add soup and mushrooms. Just before serving add sour cream. Serve over warm noodles or rice.

**Tina Vernon**
**(Davenport, Iowa)**

213

# Scalloped Pineapple

½ cup margarine
½ cup sugar
3 eggs

1 (20 ounce) can crushed
   pineapple, undrained
1 quart soft bread cubes
2 tablespoons milk

In mixing bowl, soften margarine and cream with the sugar. Beat in the eggs, one at a time, beating well after each addition. Add remaining ingredients and stir to combine. Place in buttered 2 quart casserole. Bake, uncovered, at 350° for 1 hour. Excellent served with ham.

Carol Schneider
Le Mars, Iowa)
(Thanks also to the Plymouth County Extension Service)

# Aunt Dode's Potato Casserole

4-5 large baking potatoes
1 (8 ounce) sour cream

1 (8 ounce) cream cheese

Season to taste. Cook and mash potatoes. Blend in sour cream and cream cheese. Bake in buttered casserole at 350° for 30 minutes. This is great to make the day before. Then add time to baking or set out of refrigerator to room temperature.

Margaret Novosad
(Elmhurst, Illinois, formerly Stanwood, Iowa)

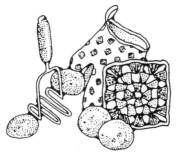

214

# Tator Tot Casserole

| | |
|---|---|
| 1 package tator tots | 1 can cream of chicken or |
| 1 pound hamburger | cream of celery soup |
| Mixed vegetables | ½ package onion soup |

Brown meat and pour off fat. Add vegetables and soups. Top with tator tots and bake at 400° for 1 hour.

**Bessie Sierk**
**(Bettendorf, Iowa)**

# Reuben Bake

| | |
|---|---|
| 1 (8 ounce) package egg noodles (cooked and drained) | ½ cup salad dressing |
| | ⅓ cup catsup |
| | 2 pound can tomatoes |
| 2 tablespoons butter | (chopped and drained) |
| 1 (1 pound) can sauerkraut | 2 cups shredded Swiss cheese |
| ¾ pound corned beef (chopped) | |

**TOPPING:**

| | |
|---|---|
| ¾ cup rye bread crumbs | 4 tablespoons butter (melted) |

Toss noodles with butter. Place in bottom of 9x12-inch baking pan. layer with sauerkraut, then corned beef.Combine catsup and salad dressing and spread over beef. Top with tomatoes and cover with cheese. Combine bread crumbs and melted butter and sprinkle over the top. Bake at 350° for about 35 minutes or until hot and bubbly. Serves 6 to 8.

*This has all the delicious ingredients of the Reuben Sandwich. May be assembled ahead of time, and it's great for serving a crowd. Also tastes great as a leftover.*

**Elsie Oehler**
**(Ronneburg Restaurant, Amana, Iowa)**

# Rice Casserole

1 box Uncle Ben's Long Grain
and wild rice
1 can mushrooms (not
drained)

½ stick butter or margarine
¾ can water
1 can French onion soup

Mix all together in a 2 quart casserole. Bake uncovered for 1 hour at 400°. Easy and good!

Donna Millhollin

# Rice Casserole

¼ pound butter (1 stick)        2 cups white rice

Melt butter and brown rice in skillet.

**ADD:**
1 can French onion soup
1 can beef bouillon soup

1 small can mushrooms and
juice

Mix together. Bake 1 hour at 350°. Wild rice can also be used, but must be pre-cooked.

**Marilyn Erling
(Le Claire, Iowa)**

TARRAGON

# Wild Rice Casserole

*(Reprinted with permission of the Terrace Hill Society)*

1 cup wild rice
1 (10½ ounce) can condensed
   consomme´
¾ cup chopped celery
¼ cup chopped onion

1 (3 ounce) can sliced
   mushrooms, drained
¼ cup butter or margarine
   (melted)
½ teaspoon salt
1/8 teaspoon pepper

Wash wild rice several times. Place in a buttered 1½ quart casserole; add remaining ingredients. Let stand for 3 hours or overnight. Bake, uncovered, in a 350º oven for 2 hours or until rice is tender. Stir once during cooking. Makes 6 servings.

*This recipe was reprinted from "Recipes and Recollections from Terrace Hill" of which Mrs. Chris Branstad was editor-in-chief. This recipe is one of Billie Ray's favorites from A Taste of Terrace Hill, the cookbook published during her time as First Lady. (Robert D. Ray was governor).It sold more than 22,000 copies.*

# Spaghetti Casserole

1½ pounds hamburger
1 large onion
1 green pepper
½ cup diced celery
2 tablespoons margarine
2 (15 ounce) cans tomato
   sauce
½ cup Bar-B-Que sauce

1 teaspoon mustard
2 tablespoons sugar
1 teaspoon salt
1 teaspoon pepper
1 can mushrooms
¼ cup pimento olives (cut)
1 (12 ounce) package
   spaghetti

Brown onions, celery in margarine. Add hamburger and brown well. Add other ingredients and simmer. Cook spaghetti until done. Run hot water over it and add to casserole. Bake at 350º for 30 minutes. Can put cheese on top if desired.

                        **Mona Justice**
                 **(Altoona, Iowa)**

# Sweet Potato Casserole

3 cups mashed sweet potatoes
½ cup brown sugar
¼ cup butter or margarine
¼ cup raisins
¼ pound marshmallows
¼ cup black walnuts
⅓ teaspoon salt
Dash of cinnamon or nutmeg

Mix all ingredients together and place in 1½ quart casserole. Bake 30 minutes at 350⁰. (If you like marshmallows, additional ones may be placed on top the last few minutes of baking. Also, this recipe is easily doubled for more servings.)

*This really is my good friend Jan Dusenberry's recipe, which she shared with me a number of years ago. We especially like it at Thanksgiving and Christmas.*

Elaine Langer
(Des Moines, Iowa)

# Taco Twist

1 pound ground beef
1 package taco seasoning mix
1 (15 ounce) can tomato sauce
3 cups corkscrew macaroni
cooked and drained (will
yield 6 cups when cooked)
¼ cup chopped green pepper
1½ cups shredded cheddar
cheese
½ cup sour cream

Brown ground beef and drain. Stir in seasoning mix, tomato sauce and green pepper. Bring to boil and remove from heat. Combine cooked macaroni, 1 cup cheese and sour cream. Place on bottom of 6x10-inch baking dish. Top with meat mixture and remaining cheese. Bake at 350⁰ for 30 minutes. Yields 6 servings.

Pat Speth
(Davenport, Iowa)

218

# Tamale Pie (Featuring Iowa Corn and Beef)

1 pound lean ground beef
1 medium onion (chopped)
1 (15 ounce) can tomato sauce
1 (10 ounce) can tomato soup
½ soup can water
1 (15 ounce) can corn
(drained)

1 cup chopped black olives
1½ teaspoons chili powder
1 teaspoon cumin
1 (8½ ounce) box corn muffin
mix
2 cups shredded cheddar
cheese

Brown hamburger and onion together. Drain off any fat. Add all other ingredients except muffin mix and cheese. Simmer about 15 minutes or until mixture is thickened. Stir in cheese. Grease a 3-quart casserole or 9x13-inch pan. Pour mixture in and top with prepared corn muffin mix. Bake at 400° for 20 to 25 minutes or until corn bread is done.

**Peggy Gerot**
**(Ainsworth, Iowa)**

# Layered Tuna Casserole

¼ cup butter
½ cup sliced onions
1 (8 ounce) package egg
noodles
⅔ cup crushed potato chips
or crushed corn flakes

1 teaspoon pepper
1 teaspoon salt
1 (10½ ounce) can cream of
mushroom soup
1 (No. 2) 7½ ounce can tuna
or bigger
1 cup cooked peas

Slice onions. Put in fry pan with butter or margarine. Fry until golden brown and crisp. Cook noodles in boiling salt water for 10 minutes or until tender. Drain off water. Mix with onions, salt, pepper, soup, peas, and tuna. Stir really well. Put in 2½ quart casserole. Put either potato chips or corn flakes over top. Bake in 400° oven for 25 to 30 minutes.

**Richard Freund**
**(Davenport, Iowa)**

## Turkey or Chicken Casserole

2 cups uncooked macaroni
2 cups cooked turkey or
   chicken
1 can cream of mushroom
   soup

1 can cream of chicken soup
3 cups milk
½ pound shredded cheddar
   cheese

Place all ingredients in a 9x13-inch pan. Stir until well blended, cover, and refrigerate overnite. Uncover and bake at 350° for 1 hour. Makes 6 servings.

**Lenore Mess**
**(Princeton, Iowa)**

## Zucchini Casserole

4 small zucchini (about
   5-6 inches long)
1 cup sliced fresh mushrooms
½ teaspoon garlic salt

1 (2.8 ounce) can French fried
   onions
⅔ cup sour cream
½ cup shredded cheddar
   cheese

Slice the zucchini, dust lightly with flour and saute' with mushrooms. When light brown and just tender, sprinkle with garlic salt. Mix sour cream and cheese in a saucepan and bring just to a boil. Toss with the zucchini and mushrooms. Place in a casserole and bake in a 350° oven for 15 minutes. Spread onions over all and return to oven until thoroughly heated through.

**Irma Plambeck Wilson**
**(Davenport, Iowa)**

## Mrs. Irma Plambeck Wilson's
## Comments On Growing Up

My three sisters and older brother (Herb), and I, all grew up on Lincoln Township farms in Scott County. I was born on one of those farms and did not leave until I married Clarence Wilson, a popular Davenport farm editor, and moved to the city.

Our growing up years included the Depression period in the early '20's when it was hard going on all farms, and especially so on our own farm. Our father had bought this farm at a high figure in 1920 just before land prices plunged drastically. The result was there was little money except for the bare essentials.

However, my sisters and I made the most of the trying times, attending our rural one-room school, enjoying both the studies and the games, joining the 4-H Club, attending our rural church where we joined Christian Endeavor and other youth groups, using an old Ford to go to high school, starting to date, and eventually, when the growing-up years were over, marrying the man of our dreams.

In time, my husband and I left Scott County for Des Moines for him to assume the editorship of the Iowa Farm Bureau Farmer, and then to Washington, D.C. where he became associated with the American Farm Bureau. This eventually took us to the New England states, and finally to Pennsylvania to our own farm and publication.

However, we never forgot our roots and on retirement in 1983, came back home to Scott County.

# Zucchini Casserole

2 pounds zucchini
(3 medium) diced, unpeeled
1 can cream of chicken soup
1 small or medium onion
(chopped)
1 can water chestnuts (sliced)

1 (8 ounce) carton sour cream
1 (8 ounce) package herb
seasoned croutons
¾ stick melted butter or
margarine

Steam zucchini until crisp/tender. Mix sour cream, soup, onion and
water chestnuts together. Add zucchini and stir until well combined. Pour melted butter over croutons and toss well. Line casserole
dish with ½ of croutons, spoon in zucchini mixture, and top with
rest of croutons. NOTE: Casserole can be frozen at this point. Bake
covered at 350⁰ for 30 to 40 minutes, then uncover for last 10 minutes.
NOTE: Deep dish type casserole will take longer to bake than flat
dishes. Serves 8 to 10.

**Pat Speth**
**(Davenport, Iowa)**

# "Jo Pohlman's" Supper Dish

1 pound veal cubes
1 pound pork cubes (or beef)
1 egg
1 can cream of mushroom
soup

Salt and pepper
1 cup bread cubes
Cracker crumbs
Butter

Brown meat. Add water to cover, and simmer until meat is tender.
Mix beaten egg, mushroom soup, salt, pepper and 1 cup broth from
meat. Mix in bread cubes. Put in casserole, top with cracker crumbs
and dot with butter. Bake at 350⁰ for 30 to 40 minutes. This is very
good!

**Teresa Crossen**
**(Davenport, Iowa)**

# Six Layer Dinner

Place a thick layer of sliced, raw carrots in a deep well greased, baking dish. Wash ⅓ cup rice and sprinkle it raw over the carrots. Cover rice with 1½ pounds ground beef, or steak, or leftover roast or ham. Add a thin layer of chopped onions. Add a thick layer of chopped celery (especially if onions are not used). Add a thick layer of sliced, raw potatoes. To 1 quart of canned (stewed) tomatoes, add 1 tablespoon each of salt and sugar and pour over potatoes, etc. Sprinkle a little pepper on top. Cover lightly and bake 2½ to 3 hours in 350⁰ oven. NOTE: If ham is used, use less salt.

*This is a recipe that my husband's Mother used often, especially in times of trouble which neighbors might have had. She received the recipe from her daughter-in-law's Mother and we usually refer to this as "Aunt Clara's Casserole." It would probably be a casserole recipe dated in the 30's.*

**Phyllis Pfitzenmaier**
**(Bettendorf, Iowa)**

# Swiss Veggie Casserole

1 (16 ounce) bag frozen broccoli, carrots and cauliflower combo (thawed and drained)
1 can cream of mushroom soup
1 cup shredded Swiss cheese (lowfat and low sodium)
⅓ cup milk
2 cans French fried onion rings

Combine vegetables, soup, ½ cup cheese, milk, and ½ can onion rings. Bake, covered, for 30 minutes at 350⁰ in a 1½ quart casserole. Top with remaining cheese and onions; bake, uncovered, 5 minutes longer. Microwave: Prepare as above. Cook, covered, on HIGH for 8 minutes, turn halfway through. Top with remaining cheese and onions. Cook, uncovered, on HIGH for 1 minute.

**Virginia Tabor**
**(Thank you also to Bertha Shaw, Hamilton County Extension Service Webster City, Iowa)**

Carol Love

# Meat Dishes

W. F. Cody, "Buffalo Bill," old time
U. S. Scout, and Showman.

With Permission from the Putnam Museum
of History and Natural Science
Davenport, Iowa

# Buffalo Bill Cody

*(Information from the Buffalo Bill Museum, Le Claire, Iowa)*

Iowa shares its 150th birthday with the legendary Buffalo Bill Cody, who was born on February 26, 1846 to Isaac and Mary Cody, on a farm, just outside Le Claire, Iowa. William Cody's longing for adventure and appreciation for the outdoors developed early, when he found he enjoyed riding horses and swimming in the Mississippi River more than doing his schoolwork. The Cody family moved several times within the Le Claire area. Eventually circumstances led the family out of Iowa and into Kansas Territory. At age 10 William's father was killed. To support his family, William became a Pony Express Rider. At 21 he became a government scout during the civil war for the U.S. Army. He earned his reputation for hunting by providing fresh buffalo meat to railroad workers and became Buffalo Bill when he won a contest in marksmanship killing 69 buffalo against a well-known scout and guide.

In the 1880's Buffalo Bill put together a Wild West Show touring America and Europe for 20 years. The show performed in Scott County several times with his last one being held in Davenport, Iowa, in 1915.

Buffalo Bill's farm (birthplace) and the surrounding area became known as Nap-Sin-Ekee, meaning "peaceful hollow". Composer and musician Cecil Fletcher, was born and still lives in the Homestead situated in Napsinekee Hollow. Mr. Fletcher's favorite musical contribution to the life of Buffalo Bill is "A Great Scout Named Buffalo Bill".

# A Great Scout Named Buffalo Bill

MUSIC AND LYRICS
by CECIL FLETCHER
arr. by PAUL F. CLARK

VERSE

1. You can talk about great heroes, they come and have gone. But the history of Bill Cody, still keeps moving on. He was born down at Le · Claire ground, Chief Blackhawk's trail did roam. Then moved on out to Mc Causland where they have his boyhood home.

2. His father moved them down to Kansas, an Indian trader be came, Un til they met with trouble, from the poli tician's game. Then Young Bill herded cattle, up on the mighty plains, grew up to be the Master, of a great wagon train.

CHORUS

He was a great scout, a chief and a brave scout

and he earned the pay for his family's way.

He took a man's place, only done by God's

grace was a great scout named Buf-fa-lo Bill.

227B

# The Famous Green Tree
# Le Claire, Iowa
*(Information from the Buffalo Bill Museum)*

Of simple beauty, and of exceptional interest was the famous elm tree that stood on the banks of the Upper Mississippi River Valley and was claimed by the old river town of Le Claire, Iowa. To residents of Le Claire and surrounding towns it was simply known as "The Green Tree."

In the ante-bellum river days Le Claire was an important river port because of its location at the head of the Upper Rapids. Most steamboats traveling on the Upper Mississippi stopped here. A short distance from the landing, on the water's edge, stood the famous elm tree. It became a gathering site for river men who came to Le Claire from all over looking for jobs as river hands. It was dubbed "The Green Tree Hotel" because some spread their blankets and stayed for weeks, eating their meals and sharing their river stories. One of many to visit the tree was Abraham Lincoln when he stayed in Le Claire while defending the railroad after the Ellie Afton incident.

One day during the summer of 1852, a young stranger by the name of William Cody, born in Le Claire, paid the tree a visit, and joined in on the fun by leaving his clothes under it and joining his friends for a swim.

The life of the tree was threatened several times; in 1899 by a new railroad being built along the river from Davenport northward. After much debate on which would give way, the track or the tree, the tree won and was spared.

Although the tree had to be taken down in 1964 because of Dutch Elm disease, the bottom slab of the tree is on display at the Buffalo Bill Museum in Le Claire.

# MEAT DISHES

**BEEF**

Stacked Enchiladas......231
Roast Beef with
Yorkshire Pudding....232
Yorkshire Pudding......233
Jim's State Fair Winning
Barbecued Beef
Brisket...............233
Beef Rolls German:
"Rinderroulader".....234
House-Warming
Pot Roast ...........234
Rouladen Recipe........235
Barbecue Steak In Oven .236
Frikadiller.............236
Stovetop Swiss Steak....237
Danish Meatballs .......237
Albert A La
Mountain Oysters*....238
Prime Rib Roast ........238
Steak With Mushrooms..240
Frikadeller* ...........240
Doppa i Gryta.........241
Kummelfleisch .........242
Majoran tokany.........242
Sauerbraten ...........243
Sweet Sour Spare Ribs ..244
1-Dish Meal ...........244
Beef Tenderloins and
Vegetables in
Herbed Oil..........245
Cookies ...............245
Sicilian Supper ........246
Peru Hamburgers.......246
Crustless Pizza ........247
Fluffy Meat Loaf.......247

Stir Fried Beef
and Vegetables .......248
Barbecued
Hamburger Sauce.....248
Healthy Jo's............249
Maidrites for 100 .......249
Prize Winning
Meat Loaf...........250
American Chow Mein ...251

**PORK**

Apricot-Glazed
Pork Kabobs .........251
Sauce for
Bar-B-Que Ribs .......252
Blue Cheese Stuffed
Pork Chops ..........252
Pork Chops ...........253
Pork Chops and
Potato Bake ..........253
Iowa Stuffed
Pork Chops ..........254
Senator Tom Harkin (D-IA)
Iowa Chops (Stuffed) .256
Peachy Pork Picante ....256
Chinese Pork Mignon ...257
Orange Country-
Style Ribs ...........258
Pork Chops with
Maple Syrup Glaze ...259
Barbecued Pork Lion with
Grilled Onions
and Oranges .........260
The Pioneer ...........261
Sweet-Sour Pork .......262

229

**(Pork - Continued)**
Pork Tenderloin with
  Raspberry Sauce
    Supreme ............263
Krautfleisch ............264
Reisfleisch .............265
Mustard-Bourbon
  Kabobs ..............266
Eggrolls...............267

**HAM**
Southern Ham Loaf .....268
Ham Loaf..............270
Hallies Ham Loaf
  or Balls .............271
Ham Balls .............271
Ham Balls Supreme .....272
Sekatina - Easter Loaf ...272
Schnitz Un Knepp ......273
Raisin Sauce for Ham ...273

**LAMB**
Kibbi .................274
Hashwitt al-Kibbi .......275
Kibbi bis-Sayniyyi ...275,276
Rack of Domestic
  Lamb Nichole ........277

**SEAFOOD**
Baked Catfish ..........278
Oven Fried
  Orange Roughy.......278
Cod in Mustard Sauce ..279

Grilled Salmon with
  Morel Mushroom
    Cream Sauce ........280
Shrimp in Lemon
  Garlic Sauce..........281
Fish Batter .............281
Snapper or Tuna Plaki ..282
French Tortillas ........282

**POULTRY**
Iowa Chicken Divan ....283
Mississippi River
  Boat Chicken ........284
Chicken Maytag Blue ...284
Stir-Fry Marinated
  Chicken Breasts ......285
Funky Chicken .........285
Turkish Chicken ........286
Chicken In A Hurry ....286
Cinnamon
  Honey Chicken .......287
Bread Dressing ........287
Chicken Souffle' ........288
Sweet 'N Sour
  Baked Chicken ......289
Holiday Crock
  Pot Stuffing ..........290

**GAME**
Lou Henry
  Hoover's Venison.....290
Grilled Tenderloin ......291
Indian Fry Bread .......292
Pheasant or
  Rabbit Stifatho .......293

# Stacked Enchiladas

1½ pounds ground beef
1 medium onion
1 medium green pepper
1 package flour tortilla shells
1 small carton sour cream

1 (10 ounce) can mild
  enchilada sauce
10 ripe olives (sliced)
1 pound sharp grated cheese
1 medium tomato (sliced and
  diced)

Brown beef, drain, add onion and pepper. Add ½ can enchilada sauce. Cook until absorbed into mixture. Place tortilla shells on greased baking sheets, 2 each. Spread with sour cream on each shell; ¼ container on each, top with meat, tomato, olives, cheese, and another shell. Repeat, then spoon over remaining sauce. Sprinkle cheese. Bake at 350⁰ for 20 minutes, cool 5 minutes. Remove with large spatula onto plate. Serves 4.

*I enjoyed looking up one of my favorite recipes. This is one that my mother, Linda shared with me a few years ago. I'm currently a senior at Cornell College in Mount Vernon, Iowa majoring in Communications and Marketing. I grew up on a farm along the Mississippi River in Louisa County and survived the "Flood of 1993." During my free time, I enjoy cooking, traveling, exercising, and singing. As Miss Iowa, I do a variety of appearances across the state. Anything from DARE Graduations, Schools, Nursing Homes, Recognition Dinners, Grand Openings, and representing the state of Iowa at the 75th Annual Miss America Pageant. My platform through the Miss America Scholarship Program is "An Approach for Helping America's Senior." I have learned a great deal from volunteering my time with the elderly for the past twelve years.*

**Jennifer Curry
(Miss Iowa 1995)**

231

# Roast Beef with Yorkshire Pudding

*(Taken from grandmother's cookbook, copyright of 1902)*

Roast upon a grating of several clean sticks (not pine) laid over the dripping pan. Dash a cup of boiling water over the beef when it goes into the oven; baste often, do not let the fat scorch. About three quarters of a hour before done:

**Mix pudding**
**1 pint of milk**
**4 eggs separated (beat yolks and whites separated)**

**1 teaspoon salt**
**2 cups flour (less flour if the batter grows too stiff)**

Pour fat from top of the gravy in the dripping pan leaving just enough to prevent the pudding from sticking to the bottom. Pour in the batter and continue to roast the beef, letting the dripping fall upon the pudding below. Have a brisk oven by this time, baste the meat with the gravy you have taken out to make room for the batter. In serving, cut the pudding into squares and lay about the meat in the serving dish.

*How blest we are to have modern cooking today.*

**Theo Ahrendsen
(Oxford Junction, Iowa)**

232

## Yorkshire Pudding

1 cup flour
1 teaspoon salt
1 dash pepper
2 eggs

1 cup milk
2 tablespoons butter or
   margarine

Mix flour, salt and pepper. Add to beaten eggs and milk. Put melted butter in 12 muffin tins or in a 9x9-inch baking dish. Bake at 425° for 25 to 30 minutes. Delicious served with roast beef gravy.

*This was a recipe belonging to my son-in-law's grandmother.*

Agnes Vrooman
(Davenport, Iowa)

## Jim's State Fair Winning
## Barbecued Beef Brisket

4-5 pounds beef brisket
1½ teaspoons salt
1 cup ketchup
¼ cup vinegar
½ cup chopped onion

½ teaspoon Liquid Smoke
¼ teaspoon pepper
1 tablespoon Worcestershire
   sauce

Rub the brisket with salt, place in baking dish. Mix remaining ingredients and pour over brisket. Cover tightly and bake at 350° for three hours. Slice brisket diagonally across grain.

**(US Representative and Mrs. Jim Lightfoot of Iowa)**

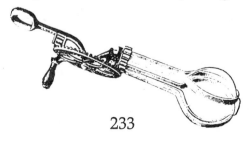

## Beef Rolls German: "Rinderroulader"

4 slices of beef (raw)
Salt and pepper (to taste)
4 slices of bacon
1 onion (julienned)
4 dill pickle spears
1 tablespoon chopped parsley

1 tablespoon Dijon mustard
1 tablespoon flour
2 tablespoons butter
½ cup water
2 tablespoons beef stock

Pound beef slices. Rub with salt and pepper. Spread equal parts mustard on each. Layer 1 pickle spear on each portion along with julienned onions. Roll tightly and place in shallow roasting pan. Add water and braise at 350° for 30 minutes. Remove rolls and set aside. Add salt, pepper, beef stock, pickle juice and pan drippings to make gravy. Return rolls to braising pan with gravy. Cover with film and foil and bake additional 30 minutes. Serve with mashed potatoes and rouladen gravy. Serves four.

Mike McClellan, Executive Chef
(Jumer's Castle Lodge, Bettendorf, Iowa)

## House-Warming Pot Roast

When a friend moves into a new house or a new neighbor arrives on the scene, it is always pleasant to take in a hot meal. The first step is to get out your best, covered roasting pan. Then go to your nearest fast food restaurant and buy a gift certificate for meals for the whole family. Put the certificates into the roaster, a smile on your face, and deliver to an appreciative newcomer.

C.J. Niles, Carroll, Iowa
Submitted by: Lila Jean Jensen, Audubon, Iowa

234

# Rouladen Recipe

| | |
|---|---|
| 2 pounds round steak | 1 bag stuffing |
| 8 ounces cooked, diced bacon | ½ cup sherry and white wine |
| 1 yellow diced onion | 1 cup water |
| 6 ounce capers | 2 tablespoons butter |
| 2 ounces chopped pickles | Salt and pepper |

Saute' onions until translucent, add bacon, cook a couple more minutes then add wine, reduce by half. Add water, and butter bring to a boil, then add capers, pickles and stuffing mix. Turn heat off, mix well, until all liquid is absorbed and stuffing is firm. Allow stuffing to cool, then lay steaks out on table, season with salt and pepper. Pipe stuffing through a tipless pastry bag onto one end of round steak, then roll steak so stuffing is inside of the steak, then place beef roll seam side down in a 2-inch long pan. Sprinkle tops of rolls with salt and pepper. Put steaks in a preheated 350⁰ oven for approximately 35 to 40 minutes, or until stuffing temperature reaches 150⁰. Pour hot raisin gravy over the rouladens.

**RAISIN GRAVY:**

| | |
|---|---|
| 1 cup raisins | 1 cup sherry |
| ½ cup diced onions | 1 cup water |
| 1 cup red wine vinegar | 2 cups brown gravy |
| 1 cup apple vinegar | ¼ cup chopped parsley |

Saute' onions until translucent, add sherrry, and both vinegars. Reduce by half, then add water, and gravy mix. Stir until sauce thickens. Add raisins and parsley. When raisins plump, gravy is ready. Hold at 140⁰ until ready to use.

**President Riverboat Casinos Inc.**

235

# Barbecue Steak In Oven

4 pounds round steak
1 cup catsup
½ cup water
¼ cup vinegar
1 tablespoon mustard
½ teaspoon salt

1/8 teaspoon pepper
¼ cup green pepper, onion
 (chopped)
1½ tablespoons
 Worcestershire sauce
2 tablespoons brown sugar

Combine all ingredients, bring to a hard boil; turn down and simmer for 5 minutes. Take off heat. Pound out round steak; cut in small pieces. Put in roasting pan. After sauce thickens, pour over meat. Put lid on pan and put in oven for 2 hours at 325⁰, or in crockpot, put on low heat half a day until done. Sauce won't be too thick when all done. You can slice a potato or 2 in pot if you want. Makes enough for 18 people.

**Richard Freund
(Davenport, Iowa)**

# Frikadiller

*(Danish Meatballs)*

3 pounds ground beef
4 tablespoons flour
4 tablespoons grated onion
3 teaspoons salt

4 eggs
1½ cups milk
2 cups bread crumbs,
 (6 slices)
¼ teaspoon pepper

Soak bread in milk. Combine all ingredients and mix thoroughly. Brown in skillet.

**Lisa Riggs**

236

## Stovetop Swiss Steak

2½-3 pound round steak
   (tenderized)
Flour (for dusting meat)
2 (16 ounce) cans whole
   tomatoes
1 (14½ ounce) can beef broth
   or 5-6 cubes beef bouillon
   dissolved in 1½ cups water

1 (8 ounce) can tomato sauce
3 tablespoons flour
1½ cups warm water
Salt and pepper (to taste)

Cut steak in serving sized pieces and generously coat with flour. In a frying pan, under medium heat, brown steak pieces in a small amount of oil. Season with salt and pepper to taste. Remove from pan. Drain oil off of the fried crumbles in the bottom of the pan and save. In a 6 quart pot, over medium heat, pour in tomatoes, beef broth and tomato sauce. Mash the tomatoes and remove any tough stem sections. Dissolve the flour in the water and add to the tomato and broth mixture while stirring. Add the steak pieces and fried crumbles. Cover and simmer over a low heat for 2 to 3 hours. Stir occasionally. Serve with mashed potatoes and a vegetable. Serves 4 to 6.

Teresa Behal
(Davenport, Iowa)

## Danish Meatballs

1¼ pounds lean ground beef
   (80-85 percent lean)
¼ cup flour
1 egg

½ cup evaporated milk
¼ cup chopped onion
1 teaspoon salt and pepper
   (to taste)

Mix all ingredients. Form into balls and fry in butter until brown.

Catherine Freund
(Davenport, Iowa)

## Albert A La Mountain Oysters*

| | |
|---|---|
| 1 pound ground chuck | 1 clove garlic (chopped or |
| 1 egg | garlic powder) |
| 1 tablespoon prepared | 1 cube or 1 teaspoon |
| mustard | granulated beef bouillon |
| 1 teaspoon salt | (dissolved in ½ cup hot |
| 1/8 teaspoon pepper | water) |
| 1 small onion (chopped) | |

Mix all together and make into patties. Broil in oven or outside on grill. Serves four. *A la means "prepared after the manner of."

John Sutcliffe, Audubon, Iowa
Submitted by: Lila Jean Jensen

## Prime Rib Roast

| | |
|---|---|
| 10 pound rib roast | Season with: garlic salt, |
| | pepper, lemon pepper, |
| | thyme |

Roast in slow cooking oven 2 hours at 250°. Then 4 hours at 140°.

*This is from Loren Hupp, manager at the T-Bone Club in Audubon. In an oven at home, roast at 350° for 34 minutes per pound for medium rare.*

Submitted by: Lila Jean Jensen
(Audubon, Iowa)

# Home of Albert The Bull
## Audubon, Iowa

*(Special thanks to Lila Jensen and the Audubon Chamber of Commerce)*

The story of Albert dates back to the early 1950's when local cattle shippers shipped large numbers of cattle, by railroad, into Chicago. Local shippers invited banker Albert (Al) Kruse to ride with them, but he declined after hearing how drafty and uncomfortable the caboose ride on a cold winter day could be. Arrangements were eventually made for a pullman car and soon a trainload of cattle and a car of shippers and businessmen had signed up for the Chicago trip. Thus, in 1951 the first Operation T-Bone took place.

The idea of "Albert" was conceived in 1961, and two years later a plan was organized to merge it with Operation T-Bone to promote Iowa's beef industry. Albert, named after Albert Kruse, became the largest bull in the world, a concrete and steel structure 30 feet high, having a horn span of 15 feet, and weighing 45 tons.

Illustration by Gary Nauman

239

# Steak With Mushrooms

3 T-Bone steaks (each
  serves 2)
1 tablespoon oil
7 tablespoons butter
1 cup dry white wine
1 pound mushrooms

Juice of lemon
Salt and pepper
1 small shallot (or 1 teaspoon
  onion) finely chopped
1 tablespoon chopped parsley

Sprinkle steaks with salt and pepper on both sides. Wash and quarter the mushrooms. Cook rapidly in 4 tablespoons butter with lemon juice. Add a sprinkle of salt and pepper and chopped onion (or shallot). Heat 2 tablespoons butter and 1 tablespoon oil in skillet: brown steaks. You may not be able to fry them all at one time. Place steaks on a warm platter. Remove fat from the skillet. Add wine and return to heat: stir well. Pour sauce over steak. Arrange the mushrooms around the steak. Serves 6.

Lila Jean Jensen
(Audubon, Iowa)

# Frikadeller*

1½ pounds ground round
  steak
½ pound ground pork
1 onion (finely chopped)
½ cup bread crumbs or
  cracker crumbs
¼ teaspoon pepper

1½ teaspoons salt
2 tablespoons flour
2 eggs
Milk or water
Shortening or bacon fat
  (for frying)

Mix together the beef and pork; add onion, crumbs, pepper, salt, flour and eggs. Add enough milk or water so you can form meat mixture into balls. Fry the meatballs in good shortening or bacon fat until brown. Cover and simmer slowly until meat is done. *This is a Danish meat dish.

Lila Jean Jensen
(Audubon, Iowa)

# Doppa i Gryta

Boil a 7 pound bone beef roast (and extra bones if you can get them) in 2 quarts of water, 2 teaspoons salt, 10 whole cloves and 4 bay leaves until tender (2 or more hours). Use the broth for dipping in the rye bread. Serve the broth in cups or small bowls. Cut the meat in serving pieces to have along with the broth.

*It wouldn't be Christmas Eve without having Doppa i Gryta. In Sweden this was served at noon preceding the big meal on Christmas Eve. This meal helped the mother in preparing the Christmas Day smorgasbord as well. This meal was not served at the table; the entire household helped themselves to a soup bowl, a spoon and a slice of bread. At the kettle each person, which may have included servants, hired farmhands etc., dipped a piece of bread and with a ladle also took some broth, a chunk of meat and some vegetables. The beauty of this meal is the simplicity, and the communion and fellowship it promoted. In our day, we sit around a dining room table and serve the broth in cups and dip small miniature loaves of rye bread into the broth. The meat is cut into small pieces and served along with peas, a cranberry sauce and celery. After this the Lutefisk is served with potatoes, salad, rye bread and relishes. Then comes the Ostakaka (cheese pudding) and Spritz cookies. The family enjoys this get together and would not miss it. Only at Christmas do you serve this menu, although (Ostakaka) has gotten to be served more and more for occasions during the year.*

*Lutefisk is cod fish and is shipped to the United States from Sweden. LUTEFISK: Drop fish into salted water. Cook about 5 to 7 minutes. Skin and remove bones. Cut up and set aside. Make a cream sauce made of ½ cup oleo, 3 tablespoons flour, 3 cups milk, salt and pepper to taste. Dissolve the oleo and stir in the flour, then add milk and seasonings and cook until thick. Pour over the fish and do not stir but enough to cover the fish. The sauce will be rather thick as the fish will thin it somewhat. Serve over boiled potatoes, topped with pepper. Serve very hot. It is delicious!*

**Dorothy Ossian**
**(Stanton, Iowa)**

241

# Kummelfleisch
*(Caraway Goulash)*

2 pounds boneless chuck, cut
   into ¾-inch cubes
1 onion (quartered)
½ teaspoon salt
Freshly ground black pepper

1 teaspoon crushed caraway
   seeds
½ teaspoon paprika
Pinch of ground cloves
2 teaspoons vinegar
Beef broth or water

Place the beef, onion, salt, pepper, caraway seeds, paprika, cloves and vinegar in a heavy casserole. Add beef broth or water to barely cover the ingredients, bring to a boil and skim the broth. Reduce heat, cover and simmer 2 hours until beef is tender. Serve with boiled potatoes or buttered noodles. Serves 4.

Wilma Howard
(Denton, Texas, formerly Cedar Falls, Iowa)

# Majoran tokany
*(Meat stew with sour cream)*

6 tablespoons butter
3 onions (chopped)
2 pounds rib steak or sirloin
   steak, cut into strips
1 teaspoon salt
Freshly ground black pepper

½ teaspoon marjoram
¾ cup white wine
¾ cup water
½ pound boiled ham, cut
   into strips
1 cup sour cream

Heat the butter in a large skillet. Add the onion and fry 4 to 5 minutes until golden. Add the beef and season with salt, pepper and marjoram. Saute' 3 to 4 minutes. Add the wine and water, bring to a boil and simmer, covered, for 1 hour. Add the ham and simmer for 30 minutes. Stir in the sour cream. Heat but do not boil and serve with noodles. Serves 6.

Wilma Howard
(Denton, Texas, formerly Cedar Falls, Iowa)

# Sauerbraten

1 (5 pound) boneless bottom round, chuck or rump pot roast
1 tablespoon salt
2 tablespoons sugar
6 peppercorns
1 tablespoon MSG
2 large onions (sliced)
2 carrots (sliced)
1 stalk celery (chopped)
6 whole cloves
1½ cups red wine vinegar (or dry red wine)
1½ cups water
2 tablespoons flour
4 tablespoons shortening
½ cup gingersnap crumbs (9 or 10 gingersnaps)
3 bay leaves

TO MARINATE: Place meat in earthenware, glass or enamel bowl. Add seasonings, vegetables, vinegar and water. Cover and marinate in refrigerator at least 2 days and preferably 4, turning once or twice a day so all sides of the meat became equally saturated.

TO COOK: Remove meat from marinade and pat dry. Strain marinade and reserve it and the vegetables. Roll meat in flour and brown in shortening until very deep brown. Add strained vegetables and 2 cups of the marinade to kettle. Cover tightly and cook over low heat 3½ to 4 hours or until meat is tender, adding small amount of more marinade when necessary. Remove meat to heated platter.

TO PREPARE GRAVY: Strain vegetables from marinade. If necessary, add enough reserved marinade to make 2 cups. Return to kettle and stir in gingersnap crumbs. Cook, stirring constantly until slightly thickened.

*This German classic is traditionally served with potato pancakes and red cabbage.*

**Barbara Davis (Davenport, Iowa)**

# Sweet Sour Spare Ribs

4 pounds ribs (small size
   cut up)
1 large onion (chopped)
Salt and pepper

6 bay leaves
¾ cup sugar
1 cup vinegar

In heavy pan, brown cut ribs in a small amount of fat, turning often to brown evenly. Add rest of ingredients and cook over low heat stirring often (2 hours approximately) add water as necessary. Ribs will be brown and coated with light glaze. Drippings can be used for gravy using potato water if desired.

*This recipe is an old one from my mother-in-law, Mrs. Henry Beuse, (deceased) of Germany.*

**Anna Schmidt**
**(Princeton, Iowa)**

# 1-Dish Meal

Brown 1 pound ground beef with 2 small onions. Cut up and par boil 3 medium potatoes and 5 large carrots. To this add 1 can of tomato soup and 1 can of water. Bake at 350° for 1 hour.

**Marguerite Vens**

# Beef Tenderloin and Vegetables In Herbed Oil

*(1st Place Recipe)*

1-2 pound beef tenderloin
1 large zucchini cut into
 ½-inch slices
1 large yellow onion cut into
 8 wedges
Olive oil for brushing on
 vegetables
2 teaspoons balsamic vinegar
½ teaspoon dried thyme
½ teaspoon salt

¼ teaspoon ground black
 pepper
4 cloves garlic pressed
2 teaspoons Worcestershire
 sauce
2 tablespoons finely chopped
 parsley
¼ cup olive oil
10-12 mushroom caps
1 red pepper cut into strips
½ cup Cookies Regular
 Bar-B-Q Sauce

Build medium fire for direct cooking. Sear tenderloin on all sides for 1-2 minutes each side. Tenderloin will cook 30 minutes for medium rare (150⁰). Baste with Cookies Bar-B-Q Sauce last 10 minutes. Remove tenderloin and cover with foil tent, let stand 10 minutes. Thread vegetables on skewers and brush with olive oil. Grill vegetables 10 minutes turning once. Place mushrooms on outer side of grill. In pan combine vinegar, thyme, salt, pepper, garlic, Worcestershire, parsley and olive oil. Wisk and warm on grill. Slice tenderloin on thin slices. Take vegetables off skewers and arrange around meat on platter. Drizzle with herbed oil.

**Cookies Food Products, Inc.**

### Cookies
*Wall Lake, Iowa*

The formation of Cookies Food Products, Inc. began in 1975 by a man named L.D. Cook, whose nickname was "Cookie." Operations have gone from beginning in the corner of the Wall Lake fire department garage, to a 1996 addition to the present location, taking the company to 65,000 square feet.

A special thanks to Cookies for sharing its many delicious recipes.

# Sicilian Supper

1 pound hamburger
½ cup chopped onion
1 (6 ounce) can tomato paste
¾ cup water
¼ teaspoon pepper
1 teaspoon salt
¾ cup milk

1 (8 ounce) cream cheese
   cubed)
½ cup grated Parmesan
   cheese
½ teaspoon garlic salt
½ cup chopped green pepper
2 cups cooked noodles

Brown meat, add onion, cook until tender. Add tomato paste, salt, pepper and water. Simmer 5 to 10 minutes. Heat milk and cream cheese. Blend well. Stir in ¼ cup Parmesan cheese, garlic salt, green pepper, and noodles. In 8-inch square casserole dish layer noodles, meat and top with noodles. Sprinkle on remaining Parmesan cheese. Bake at 350⁰ for 20 to 25 minutes. Great for potluck dinners and a great family favorite.

**Carol Wenndt**
**(Ankeny, Iowa)**

# Peru Hamburgers

1½ pounds ground beef
16 soda crackers (rolled fine)
5 tablespoons Parmesan
   cheese

Salt and pepper
2 eggs

Mix ground beef, salt and pepper to taste, half of cracker crumbs, eggs and Parmesan cheese. Shape into very flat patties. Coat with reserved crumbs and fry. Serve with rice and salad.

*This recipe came from Elba Equsquiza, a 4-H exchange student from Peru, who stayed on our farm in Ida County in 1969.*

**Catherine Noll Litwinow**
**(Davenport, Iowa)**

# Crustless Pizza
### (*Microwave Oven Recipe*)

½ pound ground beef
2 tablespoons onions
½ teaspoon Oregano
4 ounces mild cheese (any
  kind)

¼ teaspoon pepper
¼ teaspoon garlic powder
1/8 can tomato sauce

Cook ground beef and onion until brown in skillet, then pour off grease. Mix meat with garlic powder, pepper and oregano; then put in glass baking dish; then in 2 quart measuring bowl add tomato sauce. Put sauce in microwave on full power for 5 minutes until soft; then stir well. Put over ground beef. Then add cheese on top. Put back in microwave oven at full power for 3 minutes.

**Catherine Freund
(Davenport, Iowa)**

# Fluffy Meat Loaf

1⅓ pounds lean ground beef
3 slices soft bread in pieces
1 cup milk
1 egg (beaten)
¼ cup minced onion, or a
  little onion flakes

1 teaspoon salt (scant)
¼ teaspoon each pepper, dry
  mustard
¼ teaspoon each celery, salt
  and garlic salt
1 tablespoon Worcestershire
  sauce

Mix thoroughly. Shape in loaf in baking pan. Bake at 350° about 1½ hours.

**Agnes Vrooman
(Davenport, Iowa)**

# Stir Fried Beef and Vegetables

1 pound steak in 1/8-inch wide strips
1 large sweet onion sliced ¼-inch thick
2 cups or 8 ounces mushrooms ¼-inch thick
1 green pepper (cut in strips)
1 carrot (cut into thin strips)
1 celery (cut into thin strips)
¼ cup vegetable oil
1 (8 ounce) water chestnuts (drained)
Lots of fresh garlic (crushed)
2 teaspoons or 2 cubes beef bouillon
⅓ cup water
2½ teaspoons cornstarch
¼ cup soy sauce
1 teaspoon sugar

Dissolve bouillon; add soy sauce, cornstarch and sugar; set aside. In wok, heat 2 tablespoons oil on high. Add garlic, cook a few seconds; add meat and cook 2 minutes. Remove meat and juice. Wipe pan. Heat 1 tablespoon oil in wok, add vegetables and heat for 2 minutes on high. Add oil at edge of wok, then add meat with juice. Cook a minute or so. Add bouillon mixture, cover and cook 2-3 minutes. Serve over rice or noodles. Serves four.

**Paul Wallendal**

# Barbecued Hamburger Sauce

1 tablespoon butter
½ onion (chopped)
½ teaspoon salt
½ teaspoon pepper
4 teaspoons brown sugar
1 teaspoon dry mustard
4 teaspoons Worcestershire sauce
1 teaspoon paprika
½ cup catsup
¼ cup vinegar
¼ cup water
2 pounds hamburger

Melt butter and stir in onion, frying until brown. Add dry seasoning; stir well. Add catsup, vinegar and water; stir and bring to a hard boil. Brown hamburger and add to sauce; cook until it thickens. If too thin, add a little flour.

**Richard Freund**
**(Davenport, Iowa)**

# Healthy Jo's

16 ounces ground 90% lean
  turkey or beef
½ cup chopped onion
1 cup (8 ounce can) Hunt's
  Tomato sauce

½ cup chunky salsa
1 tablespoon Brown Sugar
  Twin
6 reduced-calorie hamburger
  buns

In a large skillet sprayed with olive-flavored cooking spray, brown meat and onion. Add tomato sauce, salsa, and Brown Sugar Twin. Lower heat and simmer 15 to 20 minutes. Serve on hamburger buns. Serves 6 (⅓ cup). Each serving equals: HE: 2 protein, 1 bread, 1 vegetable, 1 optional calorie: 207 calories, 7 grams fat, 17 grams protein, 19 grams carbohydrate, 417 milligrams sodium, 2 grams fiber DIABETIC: 2 meat, 1 bread, ½ vegetable. HINT: I leave the degree of 'hotness' of salsa to your personal choice.

JoAnna M. Lund
(Editor, Publisher, Healthy Exhanges Newsletter, DeWitt, Iowa)

# Maidrites for 100

20 pounds hamburger
10 cans tomato soup
1 can cheese soup
1 can nacho cheese soup

3 onions (chopped)
3 tablespoons prepared
  mustard
4 tablespoons salt
1 teaspoon pepper

Brown hamburger in roaster. Drain. Add remaining ingredients and stir well.

*The youth in our county have used this recipe many times for 4-H activities, farm sales, or other community service projects.*

Donna Millhollin
(Also thanks to: Carol R. Smith,
Guthrie County Extension Service Center)
249

# Prize Winning Meat Loaf

1½ pounds lean ground beef
1 cup tomato juice
¾ cup Quaker Oats (quick or old fashioned, uncooked)
1 egg or 2 egg whites, (lightly beaten)

¼ cup chopped onion
½ teaspoon salt (optional)
¼ teaspoon pepper

Heat oven to 350°F. Combine all ingredients; mix lightly but thoroughly. Pat into 8x4-inch loaf pan. Bake 1 hour, or until meat is no longer pink and juices run clear. Drain; let stand 5 minutes before serving. Servings 8.

NUTRITION INFORMATION: (1/8 of meat loaf without mix-ins or toppings): Calories 240, Fat 16 grams, Sodium 170 milligrams, Dietary Fiber 1 gram.

MIX INS: Customize meat loaf by adding one of the following mix-ins with meat loaf ingredients; proceed as directed above.

½ cup frozen (thawed) or canned corn (drained)
½ cup chopped green or red bell pepper
1 (2.5 ounce) jar sliced mushrooms (drained)

⅓ cup grated Parmesan cheese
2 tablespoons finely chopped parsley or cilantro

TOPPINGS: Sprinkle with 1 cup shredded cheese after removing meat loaf from oven and draining; let stand 5 minutes before serving. Spoon ready prepared spaghetti sauce, pizza sauce or salsa over each serving.

**Quaker Oats Company**

# American Chow Mein

1 pound hamburger
1 big onion (chopped)
1 cup chopped celery
½ cup raw rice

1 can chicken gumbo soup
1 can mushroom soup
1½ tablespoons soy sauce

Brown hamburger and onion. Stir in remaining ingredients and pour into medium size casserole. Bake 1 hour at 350⁰.

*I lived in Des Moines over 30 years, having originated in NW Iowa. During my working years, nursing, this recipe appeared in the Des Moines Register under "Cooking On the Run." It is a recipe one can mix in duplicate, one to eat now, the other for the freezer for the family to bake some evening when the "cook" is gone. We have lived in Colorado, having retired, eight years near our family and shall never forget our "roots" in Iowa.*

**Mrs. Arlene Shade**

# Apricot-Glazed Pork Kabobs

1 pound boneless pork loin,
    cut into 1-inch cubes
1 (10 ounce) jar apricot
    preserves

4 tablespoons orange juice
4 tablespoons butter

Stir together apricot preserves, orange juice and butter; simmer in a saucepan until butter melts. Place pork cubes in plastic bag. Pour ¾ cup apricot mixture over to coat. Marinate at least 30 minutes. Thread pork onto 4 to 6 skewers. Grill over hot coals 10 to 12 minutes, turning once. Baste with marinade. Warm remaining sauce and serve with finished kabobs.

**Suzy Ven Horst**
**(Bettendorf, Iowa)**

251

## Sauce for Bar-B-Que Ribs

¼ cup vinegar
⅔ cup water
2 tablespoons brown sugar
1 teaspoon onion salt
1 teaspoon pepper
¼ teaspoon garlic powder

¼ teaspoon cinnamon
2 tablespoons margarine
½ cup ketchup
2 tablespoons Liquid Smoke
1 tablespoon Worcestershire
  sauce

Combine the first eight ingredients and simmer for 20 minutes. Add the ketchup, Liquid Smoke and Worcestershire sauce. Yields 2 cups.

*The above sauce recipe is a Green Gables favorite. It's also a favorite of Sioux City born Ann Landers and her twin sister Abigail Van Buren. Robert Self, owner of Green Gables, is proud to say that his grandfather, a doctor, delivered both Ann and Abby.*

**Green Gables Restaurant
(Sioux City, Iowa)**

## Blue Cheese Stuffed Pork Chops

6 thick pork loin chops, with
  pocket cut
3 tablespoons butter
1 teaspoon minced onion
¼ cup finely sliced
  mushrooms

½ cup crumbled Maytag Blue
  Cheese (about 3-ounce)
¾ cup fine dry bread crumbs
Dash of salt

Melt butter in skillet, add onion and mushrooms, cook 5 minutes. Remove from heat and stir in Blue Cheese, bread crumbs, and salt. Stuff pockets with mixture. Secure with picks. Bake at 325⁰ for 1 hour.

**Maytag Dairy Farms
(Newton, Iowa)**

# Pork Chops

**Put chops in baking dish and add:**

½ cup orange juice
6 tablespoons honey
¼ teaspoon pepper

1 teaspoon salt
½ teaspoon dry mustard

Bake at 350⁰ for 1 hour and 30 minutes or until chops are done.

**Rachel Klingsheim**
**(Lime Springs, Iowa)**

# Pork Chops and Potato Bake

**Brown 6 pork chops. Use flour, salt and pepper. Set aside.**

**COMBINE:**

½ cup sour cream
1 can cream of celery soup

½ cup milk
1 cup shredded cheese
American

Line a 9x13-inch pan with package (24 ounces) of O'Brien frozen potatoes. Pour the above mixture on the potatoes. Arrange pork chops over the potatoes. Bake at 350⁰ for 40 minutes (covered), uncover, and arrange 1 can French fried onion rings over all. Bake 10 minutes more.

**Alice Hubbs**
**(Princeton, Iowa)**

ROSEMARY

253

# Iowa Stuffed Pork Chops

*(Reprinted from "Recipes and Recollections From Terrace Hill" of which Mrs. Chris Branstad was editor-in-chief, and with permission of the Terrace Hill Society.)*

⅓ cup chopped celery
¼ cup chopped onion
3 tablespoons butter or
  margarine
1 cup dry bread crumbs
2 tablespoons snipped parsley

1/8 teaspoon salt
1/8 teaspoon paprika
¼ to ⅓ cup milk
6 pork loin rib chops, cut
  1½-inches thick
Milk

In a 10-inch skillet, saute' celery and onion in butter until just tender. Remove skillet from heat. Use a slotted spoon to remove celery and onion to a large mixing bowl. Add bread crumbs, parsley, salt, and paprika to celery mixture. Toss until well mixed. Add ¼ to ⅓ cup milk to moisten. Trim excess fat and cut a pocket in the side of each chop. Fill the pocket with stuffing mixture. Close pockets with toothpicks. Brown chops, three at a time, in the 10-inch skillet. Arrange the browned chops in a 13x9-inch baking dish. Add additional milk to a depth of ½-inch. Cover and bake in a 350⁰ oven for 45 to 60 minutes. Remove toothpicks before serving. Makes 6 servings.

*A real Iowa specialty. I prepared stuffed chops often when we lived on the farm.*

**Mrs. Chris Branstad**

254

## The Old Dinner Bell

Its clear voice rang across the fields,
Oh, I can remember it well—
Calling us in at noonday,
The sound of the old dinner bell.

Come mealtime the countryside echoed,
With a deep and resonant tone;
Eager and hungry we hastened,
On the path that led toward home.

Now forgotten, rusty and mute,
It sits on its weathered mast,
Just one more silent relic
Of our long-gone, colorful past.

If I could have a wish today,
I would hear the rolling swell,
Echoing again across the valley . . .
The sound of the old dinner bell.

*My grandparents lived in Fairfield, Iowa, and my mother was born there. The poem "The Old Dinner Bell" has been published in my book called "A Patch of Blue".*

*Planning for the Iowa celebration is so exciting as well as a lot of hard work. Good luck and much success.*

**Dorothy Birdwell**
**(Waterford, Ohio)**

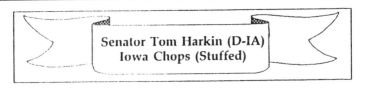

Senator Tom Harkin (D-IA)
Iowa Chops (Stuffed)

**INGREDIENTS:**

½ cup whole kernel corn
½ cup bread crumbs
Pinch of salt and pepper
¾ tablespoon parsley
Pinch of sage

½ tablespoon chopped onion
½ cup diced apple
1 tablespoon milk (whole)
2 Iowa pork chops (thick
cuts)

**BASTING SAUCE:**

¼ cup honey
¼ cup mustard
¼ teaspoon rosemary leaves

½ teaspoon salt
Pinch of pepper

In a bowl, combine the first eight ingredients until well mixed. Cut a slit in the side of chop and stuff with the mixture. In a separate bowl, combine the basting ingredients and blend until smooth. In frying pan, brown the stuffed chops and then bake in a 350° oven for about one hour, basting the chops often with sauce.

**US Senator Tom Harkin of Iowa**

# Peachy Pork Picante

1 pound boneless pork, cut
into ¾-inch cubes
1 package taco seasoning mix
or can (use only 1
tablespoon for lighter taste)

2 teaspoons vegetable oil
8 ounces picante sauce (I use
medium spicy)
½ cup peach preserves

Coat pork cubes with taco seasonings. Heat oil in large nonstick skillet over medium-high heat: add pork and cook to brown, stirring occasionally. Add picante and preserves to pan. Lower heat, cover, and simmer for 15-20 minutes. Serves 4. Per serving: Calories 263; Fat 10 grams; Cholesterol 66 milligrams; Serve over hot rice.

**Dr. Bruce Eckel**
**(Denton, Texas, formerly Mitchellville, Iowa)**

# Chinese Pork Mignon
*(Delicious Iowa Pork)*

½ cup soy sauce
2 tablespoons honey
½ teaspoon cinnamon
2 cloves crushed garlic
2 green onions (cut in half)
1 teaspoon ginger

½ pound bacon
2 whole pork loins
½ cup maple syrup (can add 2 teaspoons sesame seed oil)

Combine first 6 ingredients. Add pork tenderloins, stirring to coat completely, cover and marinate several hours. Drain and overlap bacon around loins. Cook on grill. Baste with maple syrup to 170° approximately 1 hour. Serves 6 to 8. Excellent served cold, too.

*I grew up in Algona. After college I moved to Wall Lake, but have been in Urbandale for 8 years.*

**Clarice Sarchet**
**(Urbandale, Iowa)**

## To Give A Lift To Your Day
*(Used with permission of Wichita Eagle & Beacon)*

Count your garden by the flowers,
Never by the leaves that fall.
Count your days by golden hours,
Don't remember clouds at all.
Count your nights by stars, not shadows;
Count your life by smiles, not tears,
And with joy on every Birthday—
Count your age by Friends, not years.

# Orange Country-Style Ribs

2 pounds country-style pork ribs
1 (6 ounce) can tomato paste
½ cup packed brown sugar
¼ cup frozen orange juice concentrate (thawed)

2 tablespoons red wine vinegar
1 tablespoon prepared mustard
1 tablespoon Worcestershire sauce
½ teaspoon pepper

Cut ribs into 1-rib portions. For sauce, combine remaining ingredients; mix well. Place a large piece of foil over coals beneath grill to catch drippings. Place ribs on grill, about 6-inches above slow coals. Close hood of grill and cook about 20 minutes; turn ribs and cook, covered, 20 minutes more. Brush ribs with sauce and cook, covered, 25-35 minutes more or until done, turning and brushing frequently with sauce. Serve hot. Serves 4. Approximately, per serving: Calories: 428; Fat 18 grams; Cholesterol: 85 milligrams. Serve with potato salad and sliced cucumbers and tomatoes.

**Iowa Pork Producers Association**

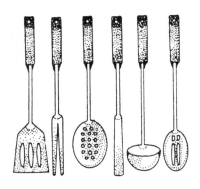

# Pork Chops with Maple Syrup Glaze

6 bone-in pork chops,
  1¼-inch thick
¼ cup maple syrup
3 tablespoons oil
2 tablespoons vinegar
4 bay leaves (finely chopped)
2 tablespoons juniper berries,
  coarsely chopped
1 tablespoon chopped fresh
  sage or 1 teaspoon dried

2 teaspoons minced garlic
1 teaspoon cracked black
  pepper
Salt
2 tablespoons maple syrup
1 tablespoon oil
1 tablespoon vinegar

FOR MARINADE: In a small bowl combine ¼ cup syrup, 3 tablespoons oil, 2 tablespoons vinegar, bay leaves, berries, sage, garlic and pepper. Rub all over chops. Place chops in shallow baking dish. Cover and marinate in the refrigerator for 6 to 8 hours or overnight. Drain chops, discarding marinade; sprinkle with salt. In a small bowl stir together remaining ingredients; set aside. Place chops on grill directly over medium-hot coals, and grill for 20 to 30 minutes, turning once, until chops are done, brushing frequently with sauce. Serves 6.

**Iowa Pork Producers Association**

259

# Barbecued Pork Loin with Grilled Onions and Oranges

1 pork loin (approximately 4 pounds)
2 tablespoons grated orange rind
8 ounces of Italian Salad Dressing (bottled or packaged and prepared according to directions)

3 large red onions, peeled and sliced ¼-inch thick
4 large navel oranges, peeled and sliced ¼-inch thick

Add grated orange rind to the Italian dressing. Place the pork loin, onion and orange slices in a container large enough to hold the ingredients. Pour dressing over and marinate for 1 to 2 hours, turning occasionally. Place pork loin in center of oiled rack over hot coals. Sear for a minute or two on all sides to seal in juices. Move the loin to side of rack where heat is less intense. Grill for 10 minutes on each of all four sides or a total of 40 minutes or until internal temperature reaches 145°-150° F. on a meat thermometer. Spoon marinade over loin each time you turn it. Remove from fire and let rest for 10 minutes before carving. While pork is resting, place the orange and onion slices in a grilling basket and grill over coals for about 3 minutes, pouring any remaining marinade over slices. Serve with the sliced pork. Serves 8.

**Mrs. Chris Branstad**
**(Terrace Hill)**
**(Des Moines, Iowa)**

CHIVES

260

# The Pioneer
*(Winner 1992 Iowa Pork Producer's "Taste of Elegance")*

| | |
|---|---|
| 1 tablespoon flour | 2 pounds homestyle egg |
| 1 tablespoon thyme | noodles (precooked) |
| ½ teaspoon salt | 4 tablespoons butter |
| 2 pounds peeled pork tender- | 1 tablespoon basil leaves |
| loins (cut into 1 ounce | ½ teaspoon Kitchen Bouquet |
| medallions)-silver skin | ½ teaspoon minced garlic |
| removed | 1 pint heavy cream |

Precook pork medallions in a large saucepan and remove. Add butter and garlic (minced) to pork drippings. Simmer for 1 minute. Add flour and blend well. Add all remaining ingredients and cook until reduced by ¼ volume. Place 6 ounce precooked egg noodles on a large plate, top noodles with 5 precooked medallions slightly overlapping each other. Top all with ¼ cup herb sauce. Garnish and serve. Makes 5 servings.

**The Machine Shed**
**(Davenport, Iowa)**

## The Machine Shed's Roots

We opened the original Iowa Machine Shed Restaurant in 1978 in rural Davenport, Iowa, with just over 100 seats. Our location wasn't great and much of the equipment was old (but clean) and broken too often. We all were pretty young and green. But we started with a powerful commitment; that commitment was a simple five word constitution - "Dedicated to the Iowa Farmer." That dedication meant that we worked to have a restaurant that wasn't just "farm" themed, but would be something that farmers could be proud of. That meant using only the best pork and beef, real whipped cream on the pies, hearty soups, and fresh baked goods made from scratch, and little things like genuine mashed potatoes and real butter. Although we still had a lot to learn, that dedication guided us through the early days, even though money was tight and going the cheaper route can be tempting.

*(Continued on Next Page)*

## (The Machine Shed's Roots - Continued)

Thankfully to you, folks liked The Machine Shed from the start. The original Machine Shed has been expanded and improved many times. And now, other Machine Sheds have sprung up in Des Moines, Iowa; Olathe, Kansas; Rockford, Illinois, and in early 1996, Pewaukee, Wisconsin. Along the way we have been delighted to have received a bushel basket full of honors from farm groups like the Pork Producers and The Beef Industry Council. We're constantly trying to live up to those honors in the food we prepare and in the way we bring it to you.

Thanks for your help.

Mike Whalen, Owner

# Sweet-Sour Pork

3½-4 pounds pork roast (boneless)
1 tablespoon shortening
¾ cup water
3 tablespoons brown sugar
¼ teaspoon ground ginger
1 large green pepper
1 medium onion
Hot fluffy rice

1½ cups undrained pineapple tidbits
½ cup pineapple juice
Another ¾ cup water
3 tablespoons cornstarch
¼ cup cider vinegar
2 tablespoons soy sauce
½ teaspoon salt

Trim excess fat from roast. Melt shortening in Dutch oven. Sprinkle on salt. Brown all sides of roast. Add ¾ cup water. Cook pork roast until tender. Remove from heat. Drain off liquid and reserve. Chill. In the meantime, drain pineapple. Combine pineapple juice and ¾ cup water. Add brown sugar, ginger, cornstarch, vinegar and soy sauce. Cut cooled meat into strips. Pour sauce over meat. Add pineapple tidbits and the green pepper and onion that have been cut into strips and sauteed lightly in 1 tablespoon oil. Bring all to a boil. Cook 5 minutes. Serve over hot fluffy rice.

*An Oriental dish that makes a meal special. This is one of my family's favorites.*

**Ethel M. Dobbins**
**(Wilton, Iowa)**

# Pork Tenderloin with Raspberry Sauce Supreme

1 pound pork tenderloin,
   cut into 8 crosswise pieces
Cayenne pepper, to taste
2 tablespoons margarine
2 kiwi fruit, peeled, thinly
   sliced
6 tablespoons red raspberry
   preserves

2 tablespoons red wine
   vinegar
1 tablespoon reduced-calorie
   ketchup
½ teaspoon horseradish
½ teaspoon soy sauce
1 clove garlic, minced
Fresh raspberries (optional)

Press each pork tenderloin slice to 1-inch thickness. Lightly sprinkle both sides of each slice with cayenne pepper. Heat margarine in large heavy skillet over medium-high heat. Add pork slices; cook 3-4 minutes on each side. Meanwhile combine preserves, vinegar, ketchup, horseradish, soy sauce, and garlic in small saucepan; simmer over low heat about 3 minutes, stirring occasionally. Keep warm. Place cooked pork slices on warm serving plate. Spoon sauce over; top each pork slice with a kiwi slice. Garnish serving plate with remaining kiwi slices and fresh raspberries, if desired. Servings: 4; Preparation time: 20 minutes; Nutrient information per serving: Calories: 300 protein: 25 grams; Fat: 10 grams Sodium: 164 milligrams Cholesterol: 79 milligrams

**Iowa Pork Producers Association**

# Krautfleisch
*(Pork and cabbage stew)*

2 pounds pork shoulder, cut
  into squares
1 teaspoon salt
Freshly ground black pepper
6 tablespoons butter
2 onions, chopped
1 clove garlic, crushed
1 tablespoon paprika

½ tablespoon wine vinegar
1 head white cabbage,
  shredded
2 cups chicken broth
6 tablespoons heavy cream,
  lightly beaten
1 tablespoon chopped chives

Season the pork with salt and pepper. Heat 3 tablespoons of the butter in a skillet. Brown the pork on all sides. Remove from the pan. Heat the remaining butter and fry the onions with the garlic until golden. Add the paprika and wine vinegar and simmer for 1 minute, stirring constantly. Place the pork, onion mixture and cabbage in a casserole. Add the chicken broth. Simmer gently for 1 hour. Transfer to a heated serving dish. Spoon the cream into the center of the dish and garnish with chives. Serve with boiled potatoes. Serves 6.

**Wilma Howard
(Denton, Texas, formerly Cedar Falls, Iowa)**

# Reisfleisch
*(Pork with rice)*

| | |
|---|---|
| 3 tablespoons butter | ½ teaspoon salt |
| 1 onion, finely chopped | Freshly ground black pepper |
| 1 clove garlic, crushed | 5 cups beef broth |
| 2 pounds pork shoulder, cut | 1½ cups rice |
| into ½-inch cubes | 4 tablespoons heavy cream |
| 1 tablespoon paprika | 12 thin strips pimiento |

Heat butter in a casserole and saute' the onions and garlic until softened. Add the pork and saute' until brown. Pour off the accumulated fat and add the paprika, salt, pepper and 2 cups broth. Cover and simmer 1 hour. Meanwhile, cook the rice in the remaining broth until all the liquid has been absorbed. Strain the pork and onions reserving the cooking liquid. Combine the rice with the strained pork and onions. Mold firmly into individual serving dishes. Stir the cream into the reserved cooking liquid and bring to a simmer. Pour a small amount of sauce over each serving. Garnish with 2 strips of pimiento and serve immediately. Serves 6.

**Wilma Howard**
**(Denton, Texas, formerly Cedar Falls, Iowa)**


# To Preserve Children
*Used with permission of Wichita Eagle and Beacon)*

Take:

| | |
|---|---|
| 1 large grassy field | 1 pinch of brook and |
| ½ dozen children | some pebbles |
| 2 or 3 small dogs | |

Mix children and dogs well together. Put them in the field, stirring constantly. Pour this brook over pebbles; sprinkle with flowers. Spread over all a deep blue sky and bake in hot sunshine. When brown, remove and set away to cool in bathtub. "Delicious."

# Mustard-Bourbon Kabobs

| | |
|---|---|
| 1 pound boneless pork, cut into ¾-inch cubes | 4 tablespoons brown sugar |
| 4 tablespoons Dijon-style mustard | 2 tablespoons bourbon |
| | 2 tablespoons soy sauce |

**Italian Seasoning**

| | |
|---|---|
| 1 teaspoon garlic powder | 1 tablespoon fennel seed, crushed |
| 1 teaspoon lemon pepper | |
| 2 teaspoons oregano, crushed | 1 tablespoon dill seed, crushed |
| 2 teaspoons basil, crushed | |

(Makes ¾ cup)

In self-sealing plastic bag, combine all ingredients and mix well. Refrigerate overnight (6-24 hours). Remove pork from marinade and thread pork cubes onto skewers. (Note: If using wooden skewers, soak skewers in water for an hour before using to prevent burning). Broil or grill kabobs about four inches from heat source, turning occasionally, for 8-10 minutes, until nicely browned. Serves four. Approximately, per serving: Calories: 234; Fat: 7 grams; Cholesterol: 66 milligrams

*Serve with broccoli vinaigrette and hard rolls.*

**Iowa Pork Producers Association**

266

# Eggrolls

| | |
|---|---|
| 1 pound sausage | 1 cup chopped green onion |
| 1 teaspoon pepper | ¼ cup Sue Bee Honey |
| 2 teaspoons garlic powder | 1 tablespoon cornstarch |
| 2 tablespoons soy sauce | |

Saute' all ingredients in fry pan until sausage is browned. Drain.

| | |
|---|---|
| 4 cups bean sprouts or shredded cabbage | 2 cups shredded carrots |

Stirfry bean sprouts and carrots with browned sausage several minutes until heated through. Empty into a bowl and set aside.

| | |
|---|---|
| 2 tablespoons cornstarch | 18 eggroll skins or 1 pound package |
| 2 tablespoons water | |
| 1 cup vegetable oil | |

Mix water and cornstarch in a small bowl. Place a heaping tablespoonful of stirfry mixture in center of each eggroll skin. Fold the four corners towards the center over the stirfry mixture, coating the outside edges with the cornstarch mixture as you go. This seals them shut. Don't make too many ahead as they may fall apart if they dry out. Heat the oil in a skillet until it is hot enough to smoke. Fry several eggrolls at a time, turning once after they brown on one side. Place on a paper towel lined plate. Serve hot with dipping sauce.

## DIPPING SAUCE:

| | |
|---|---|
| ¼ cup peach preserves | 2 tablespoons catsup |
| ¼ cup grape jelly | 2 tablespoons Sue Bee Honey |

Combine all ingredients and microwave on high for several minutes until mixture boils. Stir until blended. Microwave again if necessary.

**Sioux Honey Association**
**(Sioux City, Iowa)**

267

# Southern Ham Loaf

3 tablespoons butter
5 tablespoons brown sugar

3 slices canned pineapple, halved

Melt butter in loaf pan, add brown sugar, stirring until dissolved. Add pineapple and saute' a few minutes.

1 pound lean smoked ham, ground
½ pound fresh lean pork, ground
½ cup bread, or cracker crumbs, or corn flakes

¼ teaspoon pepper
2 eggs (unbeaten)
¼ cup milk

Mix and spread in pan, over pineapple and press down. Bake at 375⁰ for 50 to 60 minutes. Turn out with pineapple on top. Serves 6-8.

*This is one of the recipes I can remember eating at my grandparents home, Earl and Gertrude May.*

**Betty Jane Shaw
(President and owner of Earl May Seed
and Nursery and granddaughter of Earl May)**

SAGE

MINT

## Earl May Seed & Nursery
### Shenandoah, Iowa
*(With special thanks to Betty Jane Shaw)*

The May Seed & Nursery Company centered around its founder and namesake, Earl May. He was born in 1888 and raised on a farm in Nebraska. At an early age he developed a curiosity for learning and a tremendous desire for education. At college he met and later married Gertrude Welch from Shenandoah.

The May Seed and Nursery Company was organized in 1919. Mr. May's dynamic personality led largely to the company's growth and expansion. It became a very successful mail order and retail business.

In the early 1920's his ability to foresee the value of communicating to large groups of people led to building his own radio station. So in 1925 Radio Station KMA was opened. Radio caught on very quickly. In 1926 he was voted winner in the Radio Digest Poll for the World's Most Popular Radio Announcer by over 452,000 people in the U.S.

As of 1989 Betty Jane Shaw, the granddaughter of Earl May, has been president and owner of Earl May Seed & Nursery. Rather than catalogs, today the company concentrates on its profitable Nursery & Garden Centers. Presently retail outlets, known as Earl May Nursery & Garden Centers, have grown to include over 50 stores in Iowa, Nebraska, Missouri, and Kansas.

# Ham Loaf

2 eggs
1 cup milk
1 cup dry bread crumbs
¼ teaspoon pepper
1½ pounds ground fully
cooked ham

½ pound ground pork (can
use ground beef or ground
lamb if you desire a change
in taste.)

**GLAZE:**
⅓ cup packed brown sugar
¼ cup vinegar

½ teaspoon dry mustard
2 tablespoons water

In a large bowl, beat the eggs, add milk, bread crumbs, and pepper. Add ham and pork, mix well. In a shallow baking pan, shape meat mixture into a loaf, about 8x4x2½-inch. Insert a meat thermometer. Bake at 350° for 30 minutes. Meanwhile combine glaze ingredients. Spoon over loaf. Continue baking until the thermometer reaches 170°, about 40 minutes longer, basting occasionally with glaze. Yield: 8 servings. If cooking for two, wrap individual slices in foil and freeze.

**Glenn Maynard**
**(Princeton, Iowa)**

# Ham Loaf

Similar "Ham Loaf" recipes were submitted by Marguerite Vens of Davenport and Margaret Lindsey, Leon.

PARSLEY

# Hallies Ham Loaf or Balls

2 pounds ham (ground)          4 cups graham cracker
2 pounds beef (ground)            crumbs
2 pounds pork (ground)        2½ cups milk
4 eggs (beaten)               No salt or pepper

Mix all ingredients; meat and eggs, crumbs and milk. Shape into one large loaf, or smaller loaves or balls. Bake large loaf 2½ to 3 hours. Bake smaller loaves and/or balls for 1 hour at 325⁰.

**SAUCE FOR POURING OVER TOP, WHEN HALF DONE:**
1 (10¾ ounce) tomato soup      1 cup brown sugar
⅓ cup vinegar                  1 teaspoon dry mustard

Combine all ingredients, mix well. Baste occasionally, during the baking time. I use various sizes of pans. I usually make 50 to 54 balls, and I use an ice cream dipper 2¼ -inches for this. Then from what is left of the meat mixture I make a small loaf, pan size 4x7-inches. For the balls I use 2 pyrex oblong baking dishes 9x13-inches and 2 pyrex 7x10-inches. These will hold the balls. It really can be worked out most any way you wish. I try to use pans that I can get in my oven all at the same time. This recipe freezes well, as I have done it many times.

**Thelma Smith**
**(Mitchellville, Iowa)**

# Ham Balls

Similar recipes were submitted by Evalyn E. Fritz, Ackley and Leann Longfellow (Taylor County Extension Office, Bedford, Iowa)

271

# Ham Balls Supreme

**HAVE BUTCHER GRIND 3 TIMES:**
2½ pounds cured ham
2 pounds lean pork

1 pound lean beef

**MIX WITH:**
3 eggs
1½ cups crushed soda
  crackers

1½ cups crushed graham
  crackers

Form into balls ⅓ cup each.

**COVER WITH FOLLOWING MIXTURE:**
2 (15 ounce) cans tomato
  sauce
¾ cup vinegar

1 pound box brown sugar
2 teaspoons dry mustard

Bake at 350⁰ for 1 hour uncovered. These may be frozen without liquid and then add liquid later. The secret is to be sure to grind meat mixture 3 times. This will serve 40 people.

Lola Tjelmeland Anderson
(Nevada, Iowa)

# Sekatina - Easter Loaf
*(Czech)*

4 cups veal
3 cups ham
21 eggs
2 level teaspoons salt

1 teaspoon pepper
1 tablespoon onions or chives
  (chopped)

Boil meats separately. Chop meat into small cubes. Beat eggs thoroughly, combine all ingredients. You may wish to add 1 tablespoon of veal broth for each egg added. Pour it all into a greased 9x13-inch pan and bake at 300⁰ for 1 hour.

Mrs. Caroline Sobolik, Mrs. Rosalyn Poshusta
(Submitted by Kate Klimesh, Spillville, Iowa)

# Schnitz Un Knepp

"It's wonderful good."

3 pounds ham         1 quart schnitz (dried apples)
2 tablespoons brown sugar

DUMPLINGS:
2 cups flour         4 teaspoons baking powder
1 teaspoon salt       3 tablespoons melted butter
1 egg (beaten)       1 cup milk

Wash the dried apples, cover with water and soak overnight. Cover ham with cold water, bring to a boil and simmer 2 hours. Add apples and water (in which they have soaked). Boil another hour. Add the brown sugar.

FOR DUMPLINGS: Sift together flour, salt and baking powder. Stir in the beaten egg, melted butter and milk. Drop from spoon over the boiling ham and apples. Cover tightly and boil gently for 20 minutes. Serve hot on a large platter.

**Mrs. Melvin Dobbins
(Wilton, Iowa)**

# Raisin Sauce for Ham
*(Special)*

2 cups raisins         3 cups water

Cook until tender. Add: 2 tablespoons butter and 3 tablespoons vinegar. Mix 3 tablespoons flour with 2 cups sugar, pinch of salt. Stir into raisins and cook until thick. Cool or serve hot with ham.

**Margaret Lindsey
(Leon, Iowa)**

273

# Kibba (The national dish of Lebanon)

*A familiar saying by Arabic speaking peoples upon completing a meal is "Sahtayn"...which literally means "two healths to you."May you enjoy many happy hours of cooking and "Sahtayn."*

Twenty five years ago when I first got married, and if I had been asked my favorite recipe, I would have said: "Buy any frozen pizza on sale and pop that baby into the oven until it looks done!"

Today, having married an American man, with a Lebanese background, I couldn't understand why his cultural dishes that I made didn't taste as good as the ones the elderly ladies made at church. Finally, a dear relative from Cedar Rapids, Iowa, told me that some will deliberately leave out one ingredient so that their dishes will always taste better. AHEM!

Here is my husband's favorite dish with all the ingredients and our "secret ingredient" added:

## Kibbi
*(Basic recipe)*

2⅔ cups burghul (additional ½ cup when using lamb)
1 large onion (grated)
2 tablespoons salt
¼ teaspoon pepper

1/8 teaspoon cinnamon
1/8 teaspoon allspice
2 pounds ground lean lamb
   or beef (4 cups)

Burghul is partially cooked cracked wheat. It is available in three sizes. The fine or medium is usually used in the salad tabbouleh and the large for dishes in which it replaces rice. Cover burghul with cold water, soak for 10 minutes. Drain and press between palms of hand to remove excess water. Work onions and spices together with fingers. Knead meat and spices thoroughly; add crushed wheat and continue kneading. Dip hands in ice water while kneading in order to soften kibbi. (Ingredients must be kept cold). Run the kneaded mixture through a meat grinder one to three times for a finer consistency. NOTE: When using beef, a ¼ teaspoon of ground sweet basil may be added.

*(Continued on Next Page)*

## Hashwit al-Kibbi حشوة الكبّة
*(Basic Kibbi Stuffing)*

¼ cup pine nuts
2 tablespoons butter
½ pound ground lamb
 shoulder

1 medium onion (finely
 chopped)
1/8 teaspoon cinnamon
1/8 teaspoon allspice
Salt and pepper (to taste)

Brown pine nuts in butter until golden. Then add meat and saute'
for 10-12 minutes. Add chopped onions and spices and cook until
onions are limp. Remove from fire.

## Kibbi bis-Sayniyyi كبّة بالصينيّة
*(Baked Kibbi)*

1 basic Kibbi recipe
1 basic Kibbi stuffing
½ cup melted butter or
 margarine

Our secret ingredient
 8 ounces spreadable cream
 cheese

Generously butter a 9x12-inch glass pan. Spread a half inch layer of
kibbi on the bottom of the pan. The next layer should be a thin layer
of the spreadable cream cheese. (My husband likes a thin layer; I
like a thick layer.) (It is easier to take several large balls, pat them flat,
place in the pan, piecing kibbi to form an even layer on bottom of
pan.) Then go over kibbi with hand and smooth evenly. Spread the
stuffing evenly over the kibbi layer. Then spread the remaining kibbi
mixture on top. (The top layer should be thicker than the bottom.)
Use the same method as bottom layer, dipping hands in cold water so
kibbi will not stick to the hands. Smooth well. Score the top layer
½ -inch deep in a diamond shaped design 1-inch apart. Pour melted
butter across top. Bake in a 400⁰ oven for 25 minutes, lower heat
to 300⁰ and bake for 20-30 minutes more. It should be golden brown.
When serving, cut along diamond shaped wedges. Serves 8-10.

**Pam Abdo**
**(Davenport, Iowa)**

275

## Preserving A Husband
*(Used with permission of Wichita Eagle & Beacon)*

Be careful in your selection. Do not choose too young, and take only such varieties as have been reared in a good moral atmosphere. When once decided upon and selected, let that part remain forever settled and give your entire attention to preparation for domestic use. Some insist on keeping them in a pickle, while others are constantly getting them into hot water. Even poor varieties may be made sweet, tender and good by garnishing them with patience, well sweetened by smiles and flavored to taste with kisses. Then wrap well in the mantle of charity and keep warm with a steady fire of domestic devotion and serve with peaches and cream. When thus prepared they will keep for years.

# Rack of Domestic Lamb Nichole

**2 lamb racks (domestic,
8-bone, chime bone removed)**

**MARINADE:**

| | |
|---|---|
| **3 cups water** | **1 teaspoon cracked black** |
| **½ cup olive oil** | **pepper** |
| **½ cup Cabernet Sauvignon** | **1 teaspoon salt** |
| **Wine** | |
| **1 teaspoon crushed thyme** | |
| **leaf** | |

**NICHOLE SAUCE:**

| | |
|---|---|
| **2 ounces brandy** | **1 teaspoon shallots** |
| **1 teaspoon cracked black** | **½ teaspoon fresh mint** |
| **pepper** | **(minced)** |
| **½ cup mango chutney** | |

Marinate lamb several hours or overnight. Sear meat in pan to seal in juices during roasting. Heat at 300° for 20 minutes or until internal temperature is 135°. Remove from oven and let stand for 15 minutes. Serve with Nichole sauce (which is also good with pork tenderloin.) Makes 4 servings.

*John Economos was born in the United States, but went to Greece with his parents when he was 5. After W.W. II, and after spending time in New York City, John came to Des Moines to live with an uncle. As a sophomore at Roosevelt High School in Des Moines, he learned English from a language tutor. He started out in the coney business, a business his son now operates. He is today retired and enjoying more of a "gourmet style". He has mastered bread baking, the making of pastas, and the preparing of fish, pork, beef, chops and leg of lamb. Also pheasant and rabbit when he can get them.*

**John Economos
(West Des Moines, Iowa)**

# Baked Catfish
### *(low calorie and low fat)*

Catfish fillets
¼ cup cornmeal
¼ cup flour
¼ cup Parmesan cheese
1 teaspoon paprika
Catfish fillets

½ teaspoon salt
½ teaspoon pepper
1 egg white
2 tablespoons skim milk

Mix together all dry ingredients. Beat egg white and mix with milk. Dip fillet in egg white and milk, and then in flour mixture. Place on Pam sprayed cookie sheet. Spray each fillet with Pam. Bake at 350⁰ for 30 minutes.

**Doris Haesemeyer**
**(Elmhurst, Illinois, formerly Stanwood, Iowa)**

# Oven Fried Orange Roughy
### *(low calorie and low fat)*

Orange roughy fillets
1 tablespoon salt
1 cup milk (2% is okay)

1 cup dried bread crumbs
Melted butter

Cut fish fillets into serving size portions. In a shallow bowl, mix salt and milk. Dip fish in milk (let it soak for a few minutes), and then dip in the bread crumbs. Place in well greased baking pan (not Pyrex or glass) (I line a pan with foil for easy clean up). Spoon a little melted butter over fish. Bake on shelf near top of the oven for 12 minutes at 500⁰.

**Doris Haesemeyer**
**(Elmhurst, Illinois, formerly Stanwood, Iowa)**

# Cod In Mustard Sauce

| | |
|---|---|
| 1 package frozen cod (1 pound) | 1⅓ cups of milk |
| 1 tablespoon lemon juice | ½ teaspoon salt |
| 3 tablespoons butter | ¼ teaspoon pepper |
| 2½ tablespoons flour | 1 tablespoon Dijon mustard |

Defrost the cod, wash and drain the fish, put on a plate, sprinkle lemon juice over it and let stand for 15 minutes. Pat it dry, and put in greased baking dish. Sprinkle a little salt over it. Preheat oven to 350⁰. Melt 3 tablespoons butter in a pan, add to this 2½ tablespoons flour, mix well for 5 minutes over low heat. Pour in slowly 1⅓ cups of milk, and mix with whisk until smooth and thickened. Add ½ teaspoon salt and ¼ teaspoon pepper, and 1 tablespoon Dijon mustard. Pour the mixture over the fish. Bake uncovered for 30 minutes. And of course...serve with boiled potatoes and carrots.

*I was born and raised in Rotterdam, the Netherlands, and came to the United States with my American husband. There are a number of dishes that I remember from my youth, and subsequent return visits to my family. I recall quite well that a fisherwoman from Scheveningen, in her traditional costume, would come to our door with a big basket of fresh fish. I don't know if my mother would buy the "stokvis" from her that we would eat from time to time. "Stokvis" means literally "stick fish," but it was cod dried on a stick (I believe in Norway). My mother would soak this fish for about two days, after which she took off skin and bones and boiled the fish for more than an hour. The fish was always served with a thickened mustard sauce. Not having "stokvis" readily at hand in Iowa, I have to rely on frozen cod.*

**Cornelia (Nella) B. Kennedy
(Orange City, Iowa)**

279

# Grilled Salmon With Morel Mushroom Cream Sauce

*(Reprinted from "Recipes and Recollections from Terrace Hill," of which Mrs. Chris Branstad was editor-in-chief, and with permission of the Terrace Hill Society.)*

6 whole fresh dill sprigs
Salt
4 salmon steaks about
¾-inch thick
2 tablespoons butter or
margarine (melted)
½ teaspoon fresh lemon juice
Freshly ground pepper
6 ounces fresh morel
mushrooms
2 tablespoons butter or
margarine

½ cup dry white wine or
chicken broth
1 tablespoon snipped parsley
1 tablespoon snipped
fresh dill
1 tablespoon snipped fresh
chives
⅓ cup whipping cream
½ cup sour cream
Freshly ground white pepper
Milk (optional)
Fresh dill sprigs (optional)
Lemon slices (optional)

Arrange the 6 whole dill sprigs on a foil-lined broiler pan. Sprinkle lightly with salt. Cover dill sprigs with salmon. Combine the 2 tablespoons melted butter and lemon juice; brush half the mixture over salmon. Sprinkle with salt and pepper. Broil about 6 inches from heat for 8 minutes. Carefully turn salmon steaks so dill sprigs remain underneath. Brush with remaining butter mixture. Broil 8 minutes more or until steaks flake easily with a fork. Meanwhile, prepare sauce. Wash mushrooms and pat dry; cut into bite-sized pieces. Cook mushrooms in remaining butter until they begin to water (4 minutes). Add wine, snipped parsley, dill, and chives. Cook, covered, about 5 minutes. Remove from heat. Just before serving, whisk whipping cream and sour cream into mushrooms, until mixture is smooth; heat through, but do not boil. Season with salt and white pepper to taste. (If needed, add milk 1 teaspoonful at a time to make a pourable sauce.) To serve, place steaks on serving platter. Spoon sauce over. Garnish with additional dill sprigs and lemon slices, if desired. Makes 4 servings.

*This recipe was from the family of Governor Fulton who served briefly when Governor Hughes left office early to become Iowa Senator.*

# Shrimp in Lemon Garlic Sauce

| | |
|---|---|
| 1 pound large shrimp (peeled and deveined) | ½ teaspoon salt |
| | ½ teaspoon dry mustard |
| About 1½ cups milk | 1/8 teaspoon ground red pepper |
| 2 egg yolks | |
| 1½ tablespoons lemon juice | ½ cup butter (melted) |
| 1 tablespoon finely chopped fresh parsley | 1 cup vegetable oil |
| | 2 cups all purpose flour |
| 2-3 cloves garlic (crushed) | ½ teaspoon salt |
| 2 teaspoons chopped chives | 1/8 teaspoon pepper |

Place shrimp in shallow pan; cover with milk. Let stand in refrigerator for at least 20 minutes. Combine next 8 ingredients in bowl of food processor. Process 30 seconds or until well mixed. With processor running, add butter through food chute; process 1 minute or
until sauce is thickened. Set aside. Heat oil in a large skillet to 375⁰. Combine flour, salt, and pepper. Drain shrimp, and dredge in flour mixture. Fry shrimp in hot oil until golden brown, turning once; drain on paper towels. Arrange shrimp in 4 or 5 individual baking dishes, and top with the sauce. Broil shrimp 30 to 45 seconds. Yield: 4 to 5 servings.

Bruce and Brenda Eckel
(Denton, Texas)

# Fish Batter

| | |
|---|---|
| ½ cup flour | 1 egg |
| ¼ teaspoon sugar | ½ cup ice water (cold) |
| ¼ teaspoon salt | 1½ tablespoons oil |

Beat with hand mixer until smooth. Dip fish in batter and cook until golden brown. Grease should be 375⁰.

Rachel Klingsheim
(Lime Springs, Iowa)

# Snapper or Tuna Plaki

1 green pepper (sliced
  lengthwise)
2 stalks celery (chopped in
  diamond shapes)
1 carrot (sliced)
2 bunches green onion
  (chopped)

1 (16 ounce) can tomatoes
  with juice
3 tablespoons chopped
  parsley
½ cup olive oil
1 teaspoon tomato paste
3 pounds red snapper or tuna
Salt and pepper (to taste)

Saute' vegetables with seasonings in olive oil. Add tomatoes and
tomato paste and bring to boil. Pour over fish in oblong baking dish.
Season to taste. Bake at 350º for 35 minutes. Makes 4 servings.

**John Economos**
**(West Des Moines, Iowa)**

# French Tortillas

2 cans of tuna
6 medium potatoes (sliced
  and cooked)

3 eggs
½ cup thinly diced pickles
  (sweet)

Mix tuna, cooked and sliced potatoes, eggs, and pickles in a bowl and
mix thoroughly. Put in a skillet (12-inch) with 3 tablespoons of oil.
When oil is hot, pour in mixture. Keep skillet in motion so mixture
won't stick and will brown like hashbrowns. When nice and brown,
put plate over skillet and turn over. Then slide uncooked side back in
skillet and brown. When done, slide onto plate and slice as you
would a pie.

*I got this recipe while visiting in Guiana Bissau, Africa.*

**Norma Tilghman**
**(Colfax, Iowa)**

# Iowa Chicken Divan

1 (32 ounce) package frozen broccoli (thawed)
6 chicken breast fillets (can also use turkey)
1 (10 ounce) can cream of chicken soup

2 cups shredded cheddar cheese
Pepper
1 (3 ounce) can French-fried onions
¼ cup grated Parmesan cheese

Arrange broccoli in microwave-safe dish, arrange chicken fillet evenly over broccoli. Combine soup, cheese and pepper in a bowl; mix well. Spoon over chicken. Microwave Instructions: Cover and microwave for 20-25 minutes at 80%. Add onions and Parmesan cheese and microwave for 3 minutes longer. Oven Instructions: Assemble as for in the microwave, cover with foil and bake at 350° for 1 hour. Add onions and cheese and bake 10 minutes longer. Crock Pot: Assemble casserole as before, add soup-cheese mixture and cook for 3-4 hours on low. Ten minutes before serving remove the cover and add onions and cheese.

**John Borchers**
**(Thanks also to Bret Warnke, Ida County Extension Education**
**Director, Ida Grove, Iowa)**

## Friendship Recipe
*Used with permission of Wichita Eagle & Beacon)*

One cup of tolerance and one of trust,
Two cups of loyalty and never a thrust.
Blend in true understanding and good measure;
Mix faith, and good sportsmanship in all pleasure.
Add for seasoning a pinch of humor and wit,
A few grains of kindness won't hurt a bit.
Use confidence and courage, let none go to waste;
Mix in a bowl of oil of love to taste.
This above all: To thine own self be true.

# Mississippi River Boat Chicken

6 chicken breasts (halved)
12 strips bacon
½ pound chipped beef

1 (10¾ ounce) can mushroom
 soup
1 cup sour cream
Sliced almonds

Wrap each breast with bacon strip diagonally. Cover bottom of 9x12-inch pan with chipped beef. Place chicken on the beef. Cover with a mixture of soup and sour cream. Sprinkle top with almonds. Do not salt, as the chipped beef seasons it. Bake at 250⁰ for 3½ hours. Cover the last hour. If it starts getting dry, add a bit more sour cream. 12 servings.

# Chicken Maytag Blue

6 boneless skinless chicken
 breast halves
1 (10 ounce) package frozen
 chopped spinach
1½ cups rice, cooked according to package directions

1 tablespoon olive oil
2 ounces Maytag Blue Cheese
Dried parsley, ground pepper,
 dry bread crumbs and
 soy sauce
1 clove garlic

Thaw spinach and squeeze nearly dry, cook rice, flatten chicken breasts between two sheets of waxed paper. Heat oil in non-stick skillet and add crushed garlic clove, spinach and Maytag Blue Cheese. Season with pepper to taste. Cook over medium heat, stirring constantly until well mixed and cheese is melted (2-3 minutes). Divide spinach mixture among chicken pieces, folding chicken around filling, tucking ends under. Season cooked rice with chopped parsley and place in oiled oven-proof dish. Place chicken roll seamside down on rice. Brush tops of chicken lightly with soy sauce, sprinkle with bread crumbs, cover dish wtih foil, and bake at 375⁰ for 20 to 25 minutes, until chicken is tender. Serves 6.

**Maytag Dairy Farms**

# Stir-Fry Marinated Chicken Breasts

6 tablespoons soy sauce
6 tablespoons red wine
6 tablespoons brown sugar
1 tablespoon ginger
Lots of crushed garlic
1 large onion (finely sliced)
2½ pounds chicken (chunked)
4 carrots, cut thin and long
3 tablespoons peanut oil
1 (8 ounce) can bamboo shoots

1 (8 ounce) can water
   chestnuts
1 package frozen pea pods
1 (8 ounce) package fresh
   mushrooms
1 tablespoon corn starch
1 tablespoon or 1 cube
   chicken bouillon
½ can beer

Combine: Soy sauce, wine, beer, ginger, brown sugar, garlic, onion, chicken, carrots and toss. Place in refrigerator for several hours, or overnight. Heat oil and drained bamboo shoots. Fry 2 mintues. Drain and save chicken mixture. Stir fry uncovered chicken in med./hot wok 5 minutes. Cook covered 20 minutes more. In measuring cup: Combine cornstarch, then bouillon, remaining soy-wine liquid mixture, microwave to warm and stir until smooth. Add to chicken in wok and cook until thick. Last 2 minutes add (in order) sliced mushrooms, warmed pea pods, stir. Add water chestnuts. Stir. Add bamboo shoots, stir and heat quickly on high. Serves 4-6 over white rice or noodles.

**Paul Wallendal**

# Funky Chicken

Sprinkle 6 boneless skinless chicken breasts with garlic salt and bake 15 minutes at 350⁰.

1 cup apricot preserves
½ cup barbeque sauce

½ cup onion (optional)
2 tablespoons soy sauce

Mix together and pour over top of chicken and bake until done at least 1 hour at 350⁰.

**JoAnn Bittner**

This recipe was also submitted by Margaret Eckel, Huxley.

285

# Turkish Chicken

| | |
|---|---|
| 1 frying chicken (cut up) | ⅓ cup dry white wine or |
| ½ teaspoon ginger | white cooking wine |
| 1 can cream of mushroom | 2 teaspoons freeze dried |
| soup | coffee crystals |
| ⅓ cup grated cheddar cheese | 2 tablespoons lemon juice |
| | (optional) |

Brown chicken until golden. Sprinkle with ginger, salt and pepper. Place in baking dish. Mix rest of ingredients in saucepan and melt. Bake 1 hour at 325⁰. Serve with rice or noodles.

*This is a recipe of our Sunday School teacher's wife in the Mt. Vernon area of Alexandria, Virginia.*

**Mrs. (Charles) Barbara Ann Grassley**

# Chicken In A Hurry

*(Reprinted from "Recipes and Recollections from Terrace Hill," of which Mrs. Chris Branstad was editor-in-chief and with permission of the Terrace Hill Society. Mary Lou Hoegh related that the excitement of her young family moving into the Governor's Mansion is as clear today as it was in 1955.)*

| | |
|---|---|
| 2 tablespoons flour | 1 jar (6 ounces) marinated |
| 1 teaspoon salt | artichoke hearts |
| ½ teaspoon paprika | 2 tablespoons butter or |
| Dash pepper | margarine |
| 1 large (2½-3 pounds) frying | ½ cup dry white wine or |
| chicken, cut up or meaty | chicken broth |
| chicken pieces | Hot cooked noodles or rice |
| | (optional) |

In a paper bag, combine flour, salt, paprika, and pepper. Add chicken and shake to coat. Drain marinade from artichoke hearts and place in a large heavy skillet or Dutch oven. Add butter to marinade and heat until melted. Brown chicken in marinade mixture. Add wine to skillet and cover. Cook over low heat until chicken is tender (50 minutes). Add artichoke hearts and continue cooking for 10 minutes. Serve with noodles or rice, if desired. Makes 6 servings.

## Cinnamon Honey Chicken

1½ cups dry sherry
2 tablespoons cinnamon
1 cup honey
⅓ cup lime juice
2 large cloves garlic (crushed)
Salt and pepper, freshly
    ground (to taste)

3 to 3½ pound chickens (cut
    in serving pieces)
I use 3 (2 to 2½ pounds)
    chickens, not including the
    backs (save for other use)

Mix together sherry, cinnamon, honey, lime juice, garlic, salt and pepper. Arrange chicken pieces in single layer in shallow oven-proof pans; Pour over marinade, turn pieces to coat well. Refrigerate overnight, longer if desired; turn pieces occasionally. Drain marinade and reserve. Bake at 350⁰ for 40 to 50 minutes, depending on the size of the pieces, basting with marinade, and turning once or twice. In warmer months chicken can be grilled on outdoor barbecue. Yield: 12 servings.

Dorothy W. Edelen

## Bread Dressing

6 quarts bread (cubes)
1 cup fat, chicken, butter or
    oleo
1 tablespoon salt

1 cup chopped onion
1 cup chopped celery
1½ tablespoons poultry
    seasoning
Broth

Saute' onions and celery in fat until tender. Mix lightly with bread and seasoning. Add broth until moist. Bake in large pan at 350⁰ for 45 minutes. Makes 24 servings.

*This is a quantity recipe from our 1973 cookbook, and an excellent example of the good foods served at our reunions by church and other groups.*

First United Methodist Church
(Mt. Pleasant, Iowa)

287

# Chicken Souffle´

| | |
|---|---|
| 1 stewing chicken | Broth and milk |
| 1 loaf of bread | Poultry seasoning |
| 3 beaten eggs | Salt and pepper |

Cook a stewing chicken until tender, take meat from bones. Mix meat with 1 loaf of bread broken in small pieces. Add 3 beaten eggs, enough broth and milk combined to moisten well. Season with poultry seasoning, salt and pepper. Place in baking dish about 1 hour at 350⁰.

*This recipe was handed down by my grandmother who came to the United States from Denmark.*

**Dorla Schroder**
**(Princeton, Iowa)**

## A Good Friend

David Neff's mother, Caroline, and I were very close friends. We shared many things together - our church activities - traveling and raising chickens. Caroline would come out to our farm in Princeton and help me pick and clean chickens. I learned one important thing about cleaning a chicken. When you clean a chicken, you leave it whole. There is a special way to cut open the chicken, around the rectum. I can never thank Caroline enough for the helpful instructions. I still continue to use this technique when I clean them. I really treasure all the sharing we did while we picked and cleaned chickens.

A Friend,
Dorla J. Schroder
Princeton, Iowa

288

# Sweet 'N Sour Baked Chicken

| | |
|---|---|
| ¼ cup margarine | 1 tablespoon soy sauce |
| ½ cup chopped onion | ½ teaspoon garlic salt |
| ½ cup chopped green pepper | ½ teaspoon salt |
| ½ cup chopped carrots | ¼ teaspoon pepper |
| ¾ cup catsup | Dash ground red pepper |
| 1 cup pineapple juice | Dash ground ginger |
| 2 tablespoons vinegar | 1 cup drained pineapple |
| ¼ cup brown sugar | chunks |
| | 1 (3 pound) broiler chicken |

Melt margarine in fry pan, add onion, green pepper and carrots and cook 5 minutes. Stir in other ingredients (except pineapple and chicken) and bring to a boil. Add pineapple. Arrange chicken pieces in 9x13-inch pan, and pour sauce over all. Bake covered 45 minutes at 400⁰. Uncover and bake 30 minutes longer or until chicken tests done.

**Evelyn McMullen
(Cresco, Iowa)**

## Recipe For Happiness
*(Used with permission of Wichita Eagle & Beacon)*

Take 12 full months and see that they are thoroughly free from all memories of bitterness, rancor, hate and jealousy. Cleanse them complete from every clinging spite; pick off all specks of pettiness and littleness.

Divide each of these months into 28, 30, and 31 parts. Do not try to make up the year's batch all at one time, but prepare one day at a time, as follows:

Into each day put 12 parts of faith, 11 parts of patience, 10 parts of courage, 9 of work (some omit this ingredient and so spoil the rest), 8 of hope, 7 of loyalty, 6 of liberality, 5 of kindness, 4 of rest (leaving this out is like leaving the oil out of the salad), 3 of prayer, 2 of meditation, and one well-sprinkled resolution. To this add a dash of fun, a sprinkle of play, and a cupful of good humor.

Pour into the whole mixture lots of love and mix with vim. Cook thoroughly with fervent heat, garnish with smiles and a sprig of joy. Serve with quietness, unselfishness, and cheerfulness. Happiness is sure to be the result.

# Holiday Crock Pot Stuffing

| | |
|---|---|
| 1 cup butter | 1½ teaspoons salt |
| 2 cups chopped onion | 1½ teaspoons sage |
| 2 cups chopped celery | 1 teaspoon thyme (dried) |
| ¼ cup parsley sprigs | ½ teaspoon pepper |
| 2 (4 ounce) cans sliced mushrooms (drained) | ½ teaspoon marjoram |
| | 2-2½ cups chicken broth |
| 12-13 cups slightly dry bread cubes | 2 well-beaten eggs |
| 1 teaspoon poultry seasoning | |

Melt butter in skillet and saute' onion, celery, parsley, and mushrooms. Pour over bread crumbs in a very large mixing bowl. Add all seasonings and toss together well. Pour in enough broth to moisten. Add beaten eggs and mix together well. Pack lightly into a crock pot. Cover and cook on high for 45 minutes. Reduce heat to low and cook 4 to 8 hours.

**Jackie Sampson**
**(Atlantic, Iowa)**

# Lou Henry Hoover's Venison

*(Reprinted with permission, from "Dining With The Hoover Family: A Collection of Reminiscences and Recipes," By Dale C. Mayer).*

Moose, elk, reindeer, bear meat, or any tough or dry meat (As frequently cooked by mountain folk). Fashion into small cutlets; dip in olive oil; fry in deep fat exactly like doughnuts until done as you like (perhaps 5 minutes, but you had better experiment with a small bit first.) Sprinkle with salt and pepper. Serve instantly. (The cutlet may first be rolled in bread crumbs, cornmeal or batter. But this makes them much greasier.)

**Mrs. Lou Henry Hoover**

*Lou Henry Hoover was born in Waterloo, Iowa and wife of the 31st President of the U.S., also the first President born west of the Mississippi River.*

290

# Grilled Tenderloin
(*A'* La Terrace Hill)

*(Reprinted from "Recipes and Recollections from Terrace Hill," of which Mrs. Chris Branstad was editor-in-chief, and with permission of the Terrace Hill Society.)*

**Hickory or oak chips**
**1 venison tenderloin, beef**
   **tenderloin, or boneless**
**pork**
   **loin (2½ to 3 pounds)**

**Salt**
**Fresh cracked pepper**

About 1 hour before cooking time, soak hickory chips in enough water to cover. Drain. To prepare meat, season with salt and press pepper into meat. In a hooded barbecue grill, sprinkle damp chips on hot coals. Place meat on rack. Close cover and cook until meat thermometer registers 135° for venison or rare beef; 155° for pork (about 1¼ to 1½ hours). Let meat stand about 10 minutes before slicing to allow beef temperature to rise to 140° and pork to 160°. Makes 8 to 10 servings.

*We use Iowa meats, smoked with native wood, to produce one of Terry's favorite entrees.*

**Mrs. Chris Branstad**

# Indian Fry Bread Tacos
### *(Fry Bread Dough for Tacos)*

**INDIAN FRY BREAD TACOS:**

2 pounds deer meat
½ pound wild mushrooms
½ teaspoon black pepper
½ teaspoon red chilies

⅓ cup green pepper (finely chopped)
1 teaspoon onions

**FRY BREAD DOUGH FOR TACOS:**

4 cups flour
1 tablespoon baking powder
1 teaspoon salt

1 tablespoon melted butter
2 cups milk

Cook meat and vegetable mixture until meat is brown. Make small circle. Fill meat mixture into dough. Seal into ball and deep fry. Enjoy!

## Time For Thanks

Grandpa's deer hanging on the porch.
Grandma's apron with yellow roses.
The fire's bright orange torch.

The weeping willow's blowing breeze.
Brother's yelling tag and freeze.
Dinners ready, spread the blanket now.
Give thanks to Wakan Tanka.
Our heads we bow.

**Betsy Logan
(Mitchellville, Iowa)**

*(Continued on Next Page)*

**(Memories - Continued)**

After I wrote my recipe for "Indian Fry Bread Tacos" I jotted down some thoughts of some fond memories I had while growing up in Iowa. My grandmother was born in Montour on the edge of the Tama settlement, but my grandparents spent most of their married life in Gilman. They had a huge weeping willow tree in their front yard. I used to swing on a vine over my brother's head, one of my five brothers that is. I remember my grandmother spreading out her trade blanket to eat from. "Wakan Tanka," mentioned in the above poem/prayer, is Sioux for God. I have a strong appreciation today for my heritage, and am thankful for so many good and lasting memories.

Betsy Logan
(Mitchellville, Iowa)

## Pheasant or Rabbit Stifatho

2 pheasants (about 4 pounds),
    cut in serving pieces
Butter for browning
Salt and pepper (to taste)
1 medium onion (chopped
    fine)
½ cup olive oil
1 (16 ounce) can tomatoes
    (undrained)
2 tablespoons tomato paste

5 garlic cloves (chopped)
¼ cup wine vinegar
¼ cup chopped parsley
3 tablespoons whole pickling
    spices (tie in cheesecloth or
    place in a tea infuser)
3 pounds whole baby onions
    (peeled)
1 bay leaf
½ teaspoon oregano

Brown pheasant pieces with chopped onion in butter in large Dutch oven. Season with salt and pepper. Add rest of ingredients. Cover and bring to boil. Reduce heat; cook slowly for 1½ hours until meat is tender. Rabbit can be substituted for pheasant. Makes 4 servings.

John Economos
(West Des Moines, Iowa)

# Vegetables, Rice, & Potatoes

*4-H Building*

# Iowa State Fair

*Drawings By: William H. McNarney, Des Moines, Iowa*

*Grandstand*

296

# Iowa State Fair

No other State Fair in the country compares with that of Iowa. The State Fair is Iowa's largest event and tourist attraction, and one of the oldest and largest agricultural expositions in the U.S.

The first State Fair was held in Fairfield in 1854. The weather was superb, and visitors came from all directions. Fairgoing families traveled by covered wagon for the 3-day attraction. The daily admission price was 25 cents. The first event was the presentation of a 360 pound cheese made at Denmark, in Lee County, to James W. Grimes, the Governor-elect. The event making the greatest impression was the exhibition of women riding horseback.

In 1879 the Fair moved to Des Moines. Money was appropriated in 1884 to purchase grounds on the east side and 2 years later the Fair was first held on its permanent home site.

The 4-H building is now home to award winning displays of 4-H members throughout Iowa. Located on the Grand Concourse, the Grandstand, built in 1909, has been a focal point for large public gatherings, ranging from truck and tractor pulls to top entertainers. It seats 12,000.

The Fair is home to a 20-acre Farm Machinery show and the largest arts show in Iowa. Its annual livestock show, with competitive judging of beef and dairy cattle, sheep, hogs, horses, poultry and more, is one of the world's largest.

For 11 days in August people come to see over 600 exhibitors, enjoy the music, eat their corn dogs "on a stick", and ride their way through Midway. For 50 years Bill Riley's talent shows have provided energy, excitement, and opportunity for young people. The Iowa State Fair is a celebration of excellence and personal achievement, of which all Iowans can be proud.

# VEGETABLES, RICE, AND POTATOES

## VEGETABLES

Haricot Beans . . . . . . . . . . 299
Baked Beans . . . . . . . 299,300
Aunt Glotha's
   Baked Beans . . . . . . . . 300
Burlone Baked Beans . . . . 301
Calico Beans . . . . . . . 301,302
Cooked Red Cabbage . . . 302
Jazzy Green Beans . . . . . 305
Cabbage Mix . . . . . . . . . . 306
Cabbage Rolls . . . . . . . . . 307
Kysele' Zele
   (sauerkraut) . . . . . . . . . 307
Stuffed Cabbage Rolls . . . 308
Zelniky . . . . . . . . . . . . . . 308
"Roode Kool" -
   Red Cabbage . . . . . . . . 309
Sweet 'N Sour Red
   Cabbage (Roode Kool) 310
Glazed Carrots . . . . . . . . 310
The King's Carrots . . . . . 311
Scalloped Carrots . . . . . . 311
Escalloped Corn . . . . . . . 312
Scalloped Corn . . . . . . . . 312
King-Style
   Scalloped Corn . . . . . . 313
Whole Kernel Corn . . . . . 313
Harvest Corn Pudding . . 314
Corn Souffle' . . . . . . . . . . 314
Deep-Dish Veggie Pie . . . 315

Egg Plant . . . . . . . . . . . . . 316
Stir-Fry Vegetables . . . . . . 316
Spinach Pizza . . . . . . . . . . 317
Black-eyed Peas
   and Red Beans . . . . . . . 318
Parsnip Puffs with
   Walnuts (optional) . . . . 319
Spinach Souffle' . . . . . . . . 320
Vegetable Pizza . . . . . . . . 320
Zucchini . . . . . . . . . . . . . . 321
Zucchini and Tomatoes . . 321

## RICE

Chinese Rice . . . . . . . . . . 323
Rice Pizza . . . . . . . . . . . . . 324

## POTATOES

Potatoes William . . . . . . 325
Bramborova' Kase
   Knedlik (Czech
   Potato Dumplings) . . . . 325
Lefse . . . . . . . . . . . . . . . . 326
Company Hash Browns . 327
Easy Potatoes . . . . . . . . . 327
Oven-Baked
   Potato Cake . . . . . . . . . 328
Party Potatoes . . . . . . . . . 328
Potato Puff . . . . . . . . . . . . 329
Twice Baked Potatoes . . . 329

# Haricot Beans

*(1840's)*

Soak half a pint of small white beans overnight in just enough cold water to cover them. The next day boil two hours, strain and put in a pie-dish with one-half ounce of butter, a teaspoonful of finely chopped parsley, previously fried, cover with slices of raw bacon, and bake for a quarter of an hour.

*Found pasted in a 1846 periodical. "Medical Truth Teller" a monthly family journal of health.*

**Penelope Miller**
**(Princeton, Iowa)**

# Baked Beans

2 cans of beans
½ cup brown sugar
½ cup diced onion
½ cup diced green pepper
1 cup diced, cooked bacon

½ cups (1 can) diced
  pimentos
½ cup BBQ sauce
¼ cup Worcestershire
  sauce
**Salt and pepper (to taste)**

NOTE: Saute' onions, green peppers, bacon, and pimentos until onion turns transparent (approximately 4-5 minutes). Add remaining ingredients. Bake at 350º for 1 hour.

**President Riverboat Casinos, Inc.**
**(Davenport, Iowa)**

# Baked Beans

3 pound 5 ounce can beans
1 onion (chopped)
5-6 strips bacon

½ cup brown sugar
½ cup dark corn syrup

Brown bacon and onion in skillet. Mix other ingredients in casserole dish. Drain bacon, onion, add to casserole dish, mix well and bake at 350° for 1 hour (longer if necessary).

*These were always good for a big family get together, and my aunt was usually the one to bring these.*

**Susan Severs**
**(Princeton, Iowa)**

# Aunt Glotha's Baked Beans

1 (No. 2) can pork and beans,
   rinsed with water

**ADD APPROXIMATELY:**
4 tablespoons catsup
2 tablespoons molasses
2 tablespoons brown sugar

2 tablespoons bacon
   drippings
Minced onion, celery
   green pepper and salt

**OPTIONAL:** 3 drops Tabasco or few grains, red pepper or ½ of a jalapeno pepper

Place beans in a greased shallow oven dish. Cover top with thin strips of salt pork or sliced franks. Bake in moderate oven at 375° for 30 minutes.

*Take these baked beans to any gathering and you will always take home an empty dish. My Aunt Glotha takes these to church dinners. There may be other baked beans, but everybody waits for this recipe. When my husband heard that, we had to have the recipe, and have been making them since! This is an award winner in my book.*

**Jackie E. Ragsdale**

300

## Burlone Baked Beans

Bacon
½ cup chopped onion
2 cups brown sugar
2 (16 ounce) cans pork and
beans

½ cup chili sauce or
barbecue sauce

Preheat oven to 400°. Fry bacon; drain and crumble. Fry onion in bacon drippings until brown. Remove onion to 1-quart baking dish. Add beans, brown sugar, chili sauce or barbecue sauce. Stir well. Top with crumbled bacon. Bake for 1 hour.

Richard Freund
(Davenport, Iowa)

## Calico Beans

1 (16 ounce) can kidney beans
1 (16 ounce) can pork
and beans
1 (16 ounce) can lima beans
or add another can of pork
and beans
½-1 pound ground beef or
turkey

½ pound bacon (cut up)
½ cup onion (chopped)
¾ cup brown sugar
2 tablespoons vinegar
½ teaspoon mustard
½ C. catsup
2 cups cooked macaroni

Brown bacon and ground beef. Drain grease. Mix all ingredients together. For the crock pot add 2 cups water and use ½ cup raw macaroni. You can bake this at 325° for 1 hour or cook it on the stove. Make a double batch and freeze it.

*Every pot of Calico Beans is different. So is every quilt. like making a quilt you can adjust Calico Beans to please your taste.*

Darlene Neff
(Pleasant Valley, Iowa, Quilt Instructor)

301

# Calico Beans

| | |
|---|---|
| 1 can dark red kidney beans | 1 cup onion |
| 1 can butter beans | ¼ cup vinegar |
| 1 can lima beans | ½ cup brown sugar |
| 1 can pork and beans | 1 teaspoon dry mustard |
| 2-4 slices bacon (optional) | ½ teaspoon garlic salt (optional) |

Drain kidney, butter and lima beans. Cook, drain and crumble bacon. Saute' onion in small amount of oil. Combine vinegar, brown sugar, dry mustard and garlic salt. Fold ingredients together. Bake at 325⁰ for 1 hour.

*We were served Calico Beans when we first moved to Des Moines in the late sixties. It's been a favorite all through the years. I have cut the amount of bacon and sugar in the original recipe and it still tastes great! We now live in Maryland and Florida.*

**Kathleen Bell**
**(Formerly Des Moines, Iowa)**

# Cooked Red Cabbage

| | |
|---|---|
| 6 cups shredded red cabbage | 2 tablespoons sugar |
| 1 small onion (diced) | 2 teaspoons salt |
| 1 tablespoon Crisco | 1 small apple peeled and diced (optional) |
| ½ cup water | 1 tablespoon flour |
| ¼ cup vinegar | |

Melt Crisco, add cabbage, water, onion, diced apple and cook covered over medium heat until tender. Mix flour and vinegar and add to cooked cabbage. Add seasonings and bring to a boil.

**Mrs. Alice Schmieder**
**(Amana, Iowa)**

Illustration by William H. McNarney

## Agriculture Building
*(Iowa State Fairgrounds)*

Built in 1904, the Agriculture Building is one of the best remaining examples of exposition-style architecture anywhere in the world. Typifying turn-of-the-century construction with its wide oak balcony and airy, open design the Agriculture Building is a versatile hall ideal for its many displays during the Iowa State Fair.

# State Fair Champion!

Vincent Pemble first started showing his garden vegetables at the Iowa State Fair back in 1927, almost 70 years ago. He was 14 years old when he won his first blue ribbon.

Born on a Dallas County farm, Vincent and his parents moved to Indianola, a community south of Des Moines, in 1915. By the mid-1920's he was an active 4-H member, growing a variety of garden vegetables. In 1932 he enrolled at Iowa State College where he studied and received his degree in horticulture. After working on the east coast Vincent returned to Indianola where he married Marian Hoppe, his college sweetheart, and obviously the "apple of his eye." His studies certainly helped throughout the years in not only furthering his favorite hobby, but in helping to beautify the entire community. His magnificent garden has covered sections of 3 city lots next to the Pemble home.

Vincent is the third of 5 generations of state fair exhibitors. He has entered potatoes, tomatoes; and with the help of the children, was still entering exhibits at the ripe young age of 81. It wasn't all that long ago that Vincent was busy caring for 250 tomato plants, 10 varieties of potatoes, squash, melons, pumpkins, strawberries, large squares of sweet corn; not to mention the grapevines, peaches, blue plums, and apple trees. Add to this the gorgeous beds of flowers, and you have a green thumb that anyone would envy.

# Jazzy Green Beans

*("with corn on the cob and crusty bread, you have a meal")*
*(Reprinted with permission from "From Iowa..with love" by Peg Hein and*
*Kathryn Cramer Lewis)*

**1 pound fresh green beans,**　　**1 (12 ounce) package smoke-**
　**washed and snapped in**　　　**flavored link sausages**
　**bite-size pieces**

Put beans in a large kettle. Cut sausages into bite-size pieces and add
to beans. Cover with water, bring to a boil, turn heat to simmer,
and cook covered until beans are fork-tender. Do not overcook. This
can be done early in the day, refrigerated after cooling and reheated
when ready to serve. This allows the flavors to blend. Serves 4.

*The most famous river-centered summer festival is Davenport, Iowa's
Bix Beiderbecke Jazz Festival. The festival is named after the jazz musician who grew up in Davenport and died at the young age of 28. His cor-
net playing stunned his listeners. The Bix Festival combines four days of
listening and dancing, on the riverfront, to some of the country's best jazz,
with the Quad-City Times Bix 7 Run, a 7-mile race that some call the
"Boston Marathon" of the Midwest." It attracts thousands upon thousands
from across the world and continues to grow.*

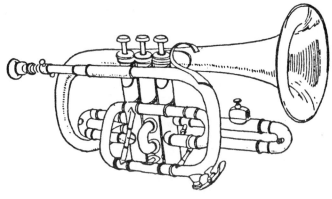

305

# Cabbage Mix

1 small cabbage
2-3 cups celery
1 green pepper
A few carrots
¾ cup white vinegar

⅓ cup water
1 cup sugar
¼ teaspoon salt
Dash pepper

Cut up vegetables. Boil liquids with sugar, salt and pepper. Let mixture cool, then add to vegetables. Store in a glass jar with a tight lid. Keeps one month in refrigerator.

*I am delighted to be included in this project for the Iowa Sesquicentennial. Although my family moved to Texas when I was 9 (1959), my roots are in Pella and I have fond memories of visits to this fascinating Dutch town. My grandfather, Gerrit VanDerWal, settled in Iowa when he came to the states from Holland. The recipe above is the only one I have from my grandmother, Jennie. She loved the outdoors and growing things. In the Dutch tradition, she never wasted anything and even had a bowl in the sink to catch unused water which she poured on her plants. I suspect this is because when she and Gerrit lived on a farm, they had to pump water by hand. Their farm has long since become a part of the Fifield area of Red Rock Lake. Jennie grew beautiful flowers and delicious vegetables and often ate raw onions. Since she lived to be 102, I guess vegetables must be good for you like we have always been told.*

**Shirley (VanDerWal) Sisk
(Denton, Texas, formerly Pella, Iowa)**

# Cabbage Rolls

½ pound each ground pork
  and ground beef
¼ cup finely chopped onions
½ cup chopped green pepper
1 (8 ounce) can tomato sauce

2 tablespoons uncooked
  regular rice
2 teaspoons salt
¼ teaspoon dried leaf thyme
1 large head cabbage

In large bowl, mix pork, beef, onion, green pepper, tomato sauce, rice, salt, pepper and thyme. Place whole cabbage in large kettle of boiling water and cook for 10 minutes. Remove from water, carefully peel off leaves and cut out tough core. Place two table-spoons meat filling on center of each leaf, fold sides over filling and roll up. Repeat with remaining leaves. Place a rack in a large skillet, and add water to the depth of the rack, about one inch. Place cabbage rolls on rack, seam side down; cover and steam for 1½ hours. Keep the water simmering; if it evaporates, add additional water. (Makes 28 rolls)

**Betty E. Bunten**
**(Carlisle, Iowa)**

# Kysele' Zele (sauerkraut)

2 quarts undrained sauerkraut
1 onion (diced)
¼ cup diced green pepper
1 cup duck grease

½ cup sugar
2 tablespoons caraway seed
1 tablespoon parsley
Cut up pieces of duck

Cut up as many duck pieces as desired. Bring all ingredients to a boil over medium heat for 20 minutes. This can either be the main or side dish. We like to use wild duck. The more the better.

**Joan Kupka**
**(Ladora, Iowa)**

# Stuffed Cabbage Rolls

1 head cabbage (not a tight
  head)
2 pounds ground beef or
  turkey (browned)

1 chopped onion (browned)
¾ cup rice
⅓ cup barley

Cook cabbage in 4 quarts of boiling salted water. Drain and separate leaves. Brown meat and onion. Start barley boiling in pan of water first (about 15 minutes). Add rice and cook until almost done. Put through a sieve. Remove thick cores of leaves. Then add cooked rice and barley to beef and onion. Put spoonful on each leaf and roll up loosely. Either fasten with toothpicks or tie loosely.

**SAUCE:**
1 can tomato soup
1 can Hunts tomato sauce

2 cups tomato juice

Bring sauce ingredients to boil and pour over rolls in the casserole. Bake 1 hour at 375⁰.

*This is a Polish recipe which belonged to my mother-in-law.*

Pat Lujack

# Zelniky

1 can sauerkraut, canned or
  leftover cooked, drained
  well

1 to 2 cups cracklings
2 cups flour (about)

Mix together well, roll out to ¼-inch thick. Cut into squares if you desire and place in pan. Bake at 375⁰ for 20 to 25 minutes until lightly brown. If cooked sauerkraut is used, add 1 teaspoon salt.

**Mrs. Charles Andera, Mrs. A.A. Ira**
**(Submitted by Kate Klimesh, Spillville, Iowa)**

# "Roode Kool"- Red Cabbage

*(Red cabbage is very familiar in Orange City*
*and used at special Dutch dinners).*

3 quarts shredded red
  cabbage
1 quart sliced apples
½ cup sugar
½ teaspoon salt

1 tablespoon butter
¼ cup vinegar
Enough water to cover
  cabbage and apples

Cover cabbage and apples with water and vinegar.Boil until tender, add sugar, salt, and butter. Serve hot. Can be canned to use later. This is an old recipe from a grandmother of a friend of mine. She used to cook this in her summer kitchen. You will find that red cabbage is surprisingly very tasty.

**Dorothy Carr Dunlop**
**(Orange City, Iowa)**

*This vegetable is believed to cause disharmony in a home when served on Monday, because it is too heavy a dish to serve following Sunday's dinner. It is especially delicious served with pork.*

## A rhyme to remember:

Don't eat red cabbage on Monday, my friend;
A quarrel will throw you off the deep end.
Pots and pans will be hurled at your head,
and for days your poor face will be red.

# Sweet 'N Sour Red Cabbage (Rode Kool)

¾ cup water
1 small head red cabbage
   sliced fine (5 cups packed)
3 tart apples, cored, peeled or
   not, cut in eighths
¼ cup firmly packed brown
   sugar

¼ cup vinegar
½ teaspoon allspice
¼ teaspoon cinnamon
¼ teaspoon ground cloves
2 tablespoons butter or
   margarine

In a large saucepan, bring all ingredients except butter to a boil. Reduce heat and cover. Stir occasionally and simmer 35-45 minutes or until tender yet crisp. Stir in butter. Serve hot.
FOR MICROWAVE: Combine all ingredients except water in 3 quart casserole. Cover and cook on high, stirring once, for 12-15 minutes or until cabbage is crisp-tender. Let stand for 3 minutes. Serves 6 to 8.

Mina Baker-Roelofs
(Pella, Iowa)

# Glazed Carrots

1 to 2 pounds whole
   carrots
3 tablespoons brown sugar
Grated rind of one orange

1 tablespoon each orange
   juice, honey, butter
½ teaspoon salt

Drain cooked carrots, saving ⅓ cup juice. Mix juice with rest of ingredients. Pour over carrots in shallow 1½ quarts baking pan. Bake at 350⁰ about 20 minutes, or until heated through.

Margaret Lindsey
(Leon, Iowa)

# The King's Carrots

Up to 1¼ pound carrots
½ teaspoon salt
2 teaspoons sugar

2 tablespoons water
2 tablespoons butter (cut in
  small pieces)
Parsley

Peel up to 1¼ pounds carrots and cut diagonally into pieces about 1½-inch long. Place in 1 quart casserole, ungreased. Top with salt, sugar, water, butter and small amount of parsley. Mix lightly and cover tightly with aluminum foil as it must steam. Bake at 350° for 40 to 50 minutes depending on how many carrots were used.

Marguerite Vens
(Davenport, Iowa)

# Scalloped Carrots

8-10 carrots (sliced)
1 small onion (minced)
2 tablespoons butter
2 tablespoons flour
½ teaspoon salt

¼ teaspoon mustard

Dash of pepper
1 cup milk
3-4 slices processed cheddar
  cheese
3 tablespoons bread crumbs
or
  cracker crumbs

Cook carrots in small amount of water until tender. Saute' onions in butter. Add flour and make your white sauce. Arrange carrots and cheese in layers in a 2 quart casserole dish. Melt butter, add crumbs and put on top of casserole. Bake for 25 minutes at 350°.

*A one-room schoolhouse by the name of Prairie Bell School was located on our farm. Both of my parents, my brother, and I attended. The building was sold many years ago and eventually became a home on Main Street entering Mitchellville. Our farm is now called Prairie View Farm.*

Peggy Crusan
(Mitchellville, Iowa)

# Escalloped Corn

1 (No. 303) can cream style
  corn
2 eggs (beaten)
½ cup milk
2 tablespoons butter or
  margarine

½ cup onion finely chopped
  or use flakes
½ cup soda cracker crumbs
  (12-14 crackers)

Beat eggs. Add other ingredients, then mix and pour into greased casserole. Place in shallow pan of water. Bake at 350⁰ for 45 minutes. Serves 6.

**Agnes Vrooman**

# Escalloped Corn

1 can creamed corn
1 can corn (undrained)
1 (8 ounce) carton sour cream
3 eggs (beaten)

Salt and pepper (to taste)
4 tablespoons melted butter
1 (8½ ounce) box Jiffy corn
  muffin mix

Mix first 6 ingredients together. Add Jiffy corn muffin mix. Bake in a 3 quart casserole, which has been greased. Bake at 350⁰ until golden brown (45-50 minutes). Serves 12-15.

**LaVonne Ankeney**
**(Denton, Texas, formerly from Bloomfield, Iowa)**

# Scalloped Corn

Similar to Escalloped Corn by LaVonne Ankeney

*This is a good recipe for potlucks or big family reunions. I've been asked for the recipe after serving it, so others must like it, too.*

**Mrs. Dean Davison**
**(Eldora, Iowa)**

## King-Style Scalloped Corn

1 (16 ounce) can cream-style
  corn
1 cup crushed cracker crumbs
½ cup chopped celery
¼ cup chopped onion
⅔ cup American cheese
  (shredded)

1 teaspoon salt
2 eggs (beaten)
2 tablespoons melted butter
¼ teaspoon paprika
1 cup milk

Combine ingredients. Pour into greased 1½ quart casserole. Bake for one hour at 350⁰. I often double recipe for family gatherings and bake in crockpot for 3 hours on low setting. Of course, homegrown IOWA corn is best!

Faithe Walters
(Eldora, Iowa)

## Whole Kernel Corn

18 cups corn
1 pint half and half

2 sticks butter
2 teaspoons salt (or less)

Stir together in roaster. Bake at 350⁰ for 1 hour. Stir often, 3-4 times. Cool and freeze.

Rachel Klingsheim
(Lime Springs, Iowa)

313

# Harvest Corn Pudding

1 cup hot milk
1 tablespoon butter
1 chicken bouillon
2 eggs (beaten)
1 pound can white corn
  (drained)
1 pound can yellow whole
  corn (drained)
¼ cup chopped ham

1 tablespoon each chopped
  pimiento, chopped onion,
  chopped green pepper
2 ounce can sliced
  mushrooms (drained)
2 tablespoons soft bread
  crumbs
¼ teaspoon salt
Pinch of pepper

Heat milk, butter, bouillon cube to scalding. Mix rest of ingredients in 1½ quart baking pan. Blend in milk mixture. Bake at 325⁰ for about 1 hour. Makes 6 to 8 servings.

Margaret Lindsey
(Leon, Iowa)

# Corn Souffle´

2 cans cream style corn
1 cup milk
2 eggs

4 tablespoons flour
6 tablespoons melted
  margarine
6 tablespoons sugar

Mix all ingredients together and pour into greased baking dish. Bake 1 hour at 350⁰, or until knife inserted in center comes out clean. Serves 6.

Carolyn Jones
(Eldridge, Iowa)

# Deep-Dish Veggie Pie

**FILLING:**

⅓ of a small cauliflower
1 cup canned garbanzo beans
  (drained)
3 ribs celery (sliced thin)
1 medium onion (chopped)
2 carrots (sliced thin)

1 cup fresh mushrooms
  (sliced)
1 cup shredded cheese (mild
  Cheddar, brick or any
  favorite)
⅓ cup whole wheat flour

**THICK SAUCE:**

3 tablespoons butter or
  margarine
2 medium onions (chopped)
⅓ cup whole wheat flour

Milk
1 teaspoon pepper
¼ cup soy sauce

**BISCUIT TOPPING:**

2 cups whole wheat flour
  (pastry flour if available,
  otherwise use ½ whole
  wheat and ½ white flour)
¾ teaspoon salt

1 tablespoon baking powder
¼ cup butter or margarine
1½-2 cups milk

Mix together filling ingredients, sprinkling whole wheat flour through.

FOR THICK SAUCE: Combine butter or margarine, onions, whole wheat flour and enough milk to make a very thick sauce. When sauce is thick, add pepper and soy sauce.

FOR BISCUIT TOPPING: Combine all biscuit ingredients adding milk to make a thin dough.

Add sauce to filling, combining well; make sure sauce is thick. Place in a 9x13-inch pan or large casserole dish. Spread topping over pie and sprinkle with ¼ cup sesame seeds. Bake at 350⁰ until crust is brown and pulls away slightly from sides of pan. Makes about 10 large servings.

*This was a favorite, at the now closed Blue Parrot Vegetarian Restaurant in Iowa City.*

**Lila Bailey**
**(Master Gardener - '94, Johnson County)**
315

# Egg Plant
*(Around 100 years old)*

1 good size egg plant (cut into small pieces and cook until tender 5-10 minutes. Drain.

**MIX WITH EGG PLANT:**

| | |
|---|---|
| ¼ cup cracker crumbs | 2 tablespoons butter |
| ¼ cup milk | 1 can mushrooms |

Cover with cornflake crumbs and bake about 30 minutes or until thick.

Joyce Brockhouse
(Princeton, Iowa)

# Stir-Fry Vegetables
*(A wok is not necessary to stir-fry, a skillet will do.)*

| | |
|---|---|
| 2 tablespoons oil | 1 teaspoon cornstarch |
| 2 cups chopped fresh broccoli | ½ teaspoon garlic powder |
| 1 cup carrots, peeled and sliced thin | 1 teaspoon soy sauce |
| ½ cup sliced onion | ⅓ cup water |

Heat the oil in a large skillet or saucepan. Add vegetables. Stir and cook over moderate heat for 3-5 minutes or until vegetables are crisp tender. (If you like them more tender, add 2-3 tablespoons water, cover lightly and cook a little longer.) In a small bowl mix cornstarch, garlic powder, soy sauce, and water. Add this mixture to the vegetables. Stir and cook 1 minute. Serve with rice. Serves 4.

Francine Lemke
(Nutrition Educator, ISU Extension, Polk County)

# Spinach Pizza

**DOUGH:**
1 recipe for 12-inch deep dish pan or 1 package hot roll mix.

**STUFFING:**

¼ pound fresh spinach

2 cups (8 ounce) mozzarella cheese

**TOMATO SAUCE:**

3 pounds fresh or canned tomatoes (drained and chopped)

2 tablespoons olive oil

1 teaspoon dried oregano

2 teaspoons fresh basil (chopped) or 1 teaspoon dry basil

1 teaspoon salt

1 clove garlic (minced)

Make your favorite recipe to fit a 12-inch deep dish or use packaged hot roll mix (this is my usual choice.) Thoroughly wash and dry spinach. Remove and discard stems; chop the leaves. Combine with mozzarella cheese which has been chopped into ¼-inch cubes. Without cooking, combine tomato sauce ingredients; set aside. Makes 2 cups. Place the stuffing mixture into the deep dish crust. Cover with tomato sauce. Bake at 500⁰ for 25 to 30 minutes. Let stand 10 minutes before serving. Serves 4.

**Joanne Leach**
**(Master Gardener '94, Johnson County)**

*The record for the tallest cornstalk in the world at any time goes to Donald Radda, a farmer northwest of Washington, Iowa. In the 1940's Mr. Radda grew one stalk that measured an unbelievable 31 feet 5/8-inches.*

# Black-eyed Peas and Red Beans

½ cup dry red beans
½ cup dry black-eyed peas
1 bay leaf
½ teaspoon salt
3 slices crisp bacon
1 cup chopped red, yellow,
   and/or green sweet pepper

1 large white onion, chopped
   (1 cup)
3 cloves garlic (minced)
1 teaspoon dried thyme
   (crushed)
1/8 tsp. ground red pepper
Dash ground black pepper

Rinse red beans; drain. In a large saucepan combine red beans and 3 cups water. Cover and let stand overnight, (or bring to boiling; reduce heat, simmer, uncovered, for 2 minutes, remove from heat, cover and let stand for 1 hour.) Drain the red beans, discarding the soaking liquid. Rinse the beans and return them to the saucepan. Add 3 cups fresh water, black-eyed peas, bay leaf and salt. Bring to boiling, reduce heat. Cover and simmer for 45 to 60 minutes or until peas and beans are tender. Drain, discarding the bay leaf. Meanwhile, in a large skillet cook bacon until crisp. Drain on paper towels, reserving 1 tablespoon drippings in skillet. Crumble bacon, set aside. Add sweet pepper, onion, garlic, thyme, red pepper and black pepper to skillet. Cook until vegetables are tender. Stir in beans, peas and bacon. Heat through. Makes 6 side dish or 3 main dish servings. Per serving: 154 calories, 2 grams total fat (1 gram saturated fat), 4 grams fiber, 246 milligrams sodium

**Evelyn McGrath**
**(Davenport, Iowa)**

# Parsnip Puffs with Walnuts (optional)

8 small, tender parsnips
2 beaten eggs
3 tablespoons flour
½ teaspoon salt

8 whole California walnut
   meats (optional)
Parsley
Crisco for frying

Wash parsnips: steam or boil until tender, 20-30 minutes. Remove skins and mash. Stir in eggs, flour and seasonings. Form into balls, placing a walnut meat in each. Pan fry in deep fat or just enough to cover the puffs a light brown. Garnish with parsley. Makes 8 puffs. Serve immediately while thick and puffy. NOTE: Keep the puffs a secret and serve them last while they are hot and puffy.

*As an Air Force wife in W.W.2 I did a lot of entertaining and this parsnip recipe was a big surprise on the dinner table as one of the officers was telling us of his dislikes in food. He mentioned so many vegetables. I began to wonder if I dare bring the parsnips to the table. I decided to make up a story about this vegetable, then bring it to the table. The story started by telling one has to wait until late fall before digging. They are a pretty light yellow after they are cooked. Very good without the walnuts.*

*P.S. My heart was in my mouth, when this officer asked for seconds. He had never heard of "Parsnips!"*

**Ruth Dollerhide**
**(Davenport, Iowa)**

# Spinach Souffle′

1 or 2 packages frozen
  chopped spinach
2 pints cottage cheese (small
  curd)
6 tablespoons flour
½ pound Longhorn cheese

¼ pound butter or margarine
6 eggs
Salt and pepper
1 teaspoon onion powder
  (optional)

Thaw and drain spinach. Beat eggs, then add cottage cheese and flour. Shred cheese and butter; add to egg mixture. Fold in spinach. Bake 1 hour at 350⁰. May be made 24 hours before baking and refrigerated. Leftovers can be reheated in microwave. Tastes great!

*This is a real family favorite for special events.*

Mrs. Rainsford A. Brown, Jr.
(Bettendorf, Iowa)

# Vegetable Pizza

2 (8 ounce) Crescent dinner rolls

Roll out and place in jelly roll pan. Pinch together to make a crust. Bake according to directions until lightly browned.

TOPPING:
2 (8 ounce) cream cheese
1 cup mayonnaise
Dill weed (to taste)

Garlic salt (to taste)
Minced onion (to taste)

Add any combinations of vegetables, such as cauliflower, green onions, radishes, celery, carrots. Chill topping to blend flavors. Don't put topping on crust until just before serving as crust may get soggy. Then put shredded cheese, (cheddar) over all.

Mary Etta (Schneckloth) Thomsen

## Zucchini

Sometime in the 1950's Americans were re-introduced to this vegetable which came originally from Italy. Various myths and legends say it is protected by the gods, and others say it was brought to us through Christopher Columbus. Its name means "sweetest." It comes in a rainbow of colors now besides the speckled green and most varieties take only 40-55 days to mature. Huge, bushy leaves hide the fruit and without daily inspection some of the squash escapes detection and grows, and grows, and grows! Six plants will yield fifty pounds of fruit a summer. What to do with it all? It is said that in some parts of the country—Iowa included—people are told to carefully lock their cars in midsummer as overloaded zucchini growers desperately take to dumping loads of it in the back seats! To cope with this prolific, explosive vegetable, recipe for omelets, cakes, cookies, quiches, pickles, breads, dips and spreads have come into existence. Zucchini is eaten baked, fried, steamed, poached, boiled, mixed with chocolate, coconut, lemon, honey, and is stuffed, shredded and skewered!

**Judy Terry**
**(Master Gardener, Johnson County)**

## Zucchini and Tomatoes

½ cup water
2 zucchini (sliced)
15 cherry tomatoes (halved)
¼ cup lemon juice

1 teaspoon fresh thyme
1 teaspoon dry mustard
4-5 green onions
¼ teaspoon salt and pepper

Stir together, cover and simmer until just tender.

**Cathie Moore**
**(Master Gardener, Johnson County)**

321

# Master Gardeners

*(Special thanks to Judy Terry, Johnson County, Master Gardener)*

The Master Gardener Program is designed to educate volunteers in the field of horticulture in return for their service in the community. It is part of the Iowa State University Extension Service. For a small fee they receive 40 hours of intensive training in soils, plant pathology, flowers, weed control, houseplants, vegetables, entomology, etc. After the training, 40 hours of volunteer service must be given back to the community.

# Chinese Rice

*(Reprinted with permission, from "Dining with The Hoover Family: A Collection of Reminiscences and Recipes," by Dale C. Mayer.)*

The combination of flavors is delicious and must be tasted to be appreciated. Try it next time you have a little leftover ham.

**1 cup ground, cooked ham**      **2 eggs**
**1 cup cooked rice**             **Salt and pepper**

Fry ground ham slightly in skillet. Break eggs into skillet and scramble slightly. Add cooked rice, salt and pepper. Mix and heat through. I add odds and ends like a small can of mushrooms, a tablespoon of parsley or some chopped spinach. In fact, look in the refrigerator and see what needs using up in the way of vegetables.

*Mrs. Lou Henry (Herbert) Hoover learned of this dish in China where the Hoovers were from approximately 1899-1901. It has remained in the Hoover family ever since.*

**Mrs. Lou Henry (Herbert) Hoover**

ROSEMARY

# Rice Pizza

**CRUST:**

3 cups cooked rice (1 cup rice cooked in 2 cups water)
½ cup dry egg mix or 2 eggs
½ cup water

1 cup grated Mozzarella cheese

**TOPPINGS:** 1 (15 ounce) can pizza sauce or 2 (8 ounce) cans tomato sauce with ½ teaspoon each oregano, basil, and garlic salt; 1 cup canned beef or pork, drained, and fat removed; 1 cup grated Mozzarella cheese and 2 tablespoons Parmesan cheese.

In a 3 quart saucepan with a tight fitting lid, combine rice and water. Add ½ teaspoon salt, if desired. Heat to boiling and stir once or twice. Reduce heat to simmer and cover pan. Cook 20-25 minutes without removing lid or stirring. Remove from heat and fluff with fork. The water will be absorbed. Beat together the dry egg mix and water. Combine beaten eggs with cooked rice and 1 cup Mozzarella cheese. Press firmly into a greased 12-inch pizza pan or two 9-inch pie pans, spreading evenly. Bake at 450° for 20 minutes. Spread pizza sauce evenly over rice crust. Top with canned beef or pork, 1 cup Mozzarella cheese, and Parmesan cheese. Bake 10 minutes longer. Cut into wedges. Makes 8 servings.

Francine Lemke

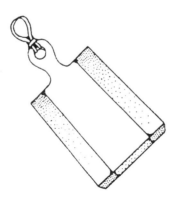

# Potatoes William

| | |
|---|---|
| 3½ cups water | 1⅔ cups sour cream |
| 2 teaspoons salt | 3½ cups Country Store |
| 6 tablespoons butter or | Mashed Potato Flakes |
| margarine | Slivered almonds |

In a large saucepan, measure water, salt and butter; bring to a boil. Remove from heat; add sour cream immediately. Mix well. Add potato flakes and stir gently until flakes are soft and moist. Beat briskly with fork or wire whip. Place potatoes in pastry bag with star tube. Pipe ½ cup servings onto greased baking sheets, about 2-inches apart. Garnish with almonds. Bake at 350⁰ for 30 to 35 minutes. Makes 12 servings (½ cup).

*From the essay: "EASTERN Iowa," by Bill Wundram, Quad-City Times, IOWA Celebrating the Sesquicentennial.*

*While flying cross-country, my New York City seat mate seemed puzzled by my love affair with Iowa. His questioning opened large answers, and I could best reply: "Alabama is the South, and the North is the North, and California is California, but Iowa is America."*

**Mr. and Mrs. Bill Wundram**

# Bramborova´ Kase Knedlik
## (Czech Potato Dumplings)

| | |
|---|---|
| 4 cups mashed potatoes | 2 cups flour |
| 2 eggs (beaten) | 1 teaspoon salt |

Boil potatoes and skins. Peel while hot and mash with fork. Mix well with eggs and salt. Roll mixture in flour to make 1½-inch roll. Spoon into small round balls and roll. Put in 2-inches of boiling water. Cook 20 minutes with lid on. Add caraway seed if you wish (optional).

**Joan Kupka**
**(Ladora, Iowa)**

# Lefse

*This potato lefse is a Norwegian specialty, especially at Christmas, but also served during the year for special occasions. A simple recipe, but it takes a little practice to roll them out very thin. They should be almost translucent and rolled into 18-inch rounds to fit the lefse grill. If you start with a perfectly round ball of dough, it will be easier to maintain that round shape. Beginners sometime say their lefse looks like the map of Texas!*

**5 cups riced potatoes (packed)**　**2 cups flour**
**½ cup melted butter**　　　　　　**½ teaspoon salt**
**3 tablespoons powdered sugar**

Use Idaho Russet potatoes, they are drier. Peel and boil until done but not mushy. Drain well and let cool uncovered so steam may escape. Rice potatoes before entirely cool and then cool completely. Measure out 5 cups of potatoes and mix in melted butter. Add remainder of ingredients and mix very well using your hands. Knead on floured cloth until smooth. To roll out, use ⅓ cup of dough for each round, shaping with your hands into a smooth round ball as you would for buns. Place on floured cloth rolling surface and roll into a large round, turning over at least once. Use flour sparingly; if dough is of the right consistency not much will be needed and you won't have to wipe off the grill after each use. Fry on hot grill, a few seconds on each side until a few brown (not dark) spots appear. Remove and place between two kitchen towels to cool. You don't want them to dry out. Cut into desired size and use butter, brown sugar or whatever you like.

HINTS: Use a special round, rubber-footed, canvas covered board that is made for rolling lefse. Also, use a cotton stocking on the rolling pin.

OPTION: You can substitute instant potatoes for about ⅓ of the potatoes, but I wouldn't recommend using all instant. If using leftover, mashed potatoes, you may have to increase the amount of flour.

If a beginner, start with a smaller amount of dough and roll out to 10-inch or pie crust size; this will be easier to handle.

**Eunice C. Stoen**
**(Decorah, Iowa)**

326

# Company Hash Browns

2 pound package hash brown
  potatoes
½ cup butter or oleo
1 (10 ounce) can cream of
  mushroom soup

1 cup sour cream
½ teaspoon salt
1 cup grated cheddar cheese
1 cup cornflakes
½ cup onion (chopped fine)

Thaw hash browns completely. Melt butter and add soup, onion, sour cream and seasoning. Mix with hash browns and put into a 3 quart casserole. Top with grated cheese, then cornflakes. Bake 1 hour at 350⁰.

*Easy cooking: delicious with any kind of meats! (From a lazy 74-year old cook.)*

**Donna A. Slick**
**(Cedar Rapids, Iowa)**


# Easy Potatoes

Betty Crocker Potato Buds
3 ounces cream cheese

1 cup sour cream

Follow the amount on the back of box; do step 1 and step 2. For step 3; add 3 ounces cream cheese and 1 cup sour cream. Whip until desired. Consistency: Serve at once or can be made up ahead and warmed in oven. Serves 4-6.

**Velma E. Skola**
**(Kalona, Iowa)**

# Oven-Baked Potato Cake

About 3 pounds potatoes
1 large onion
6 slices bacon
Bacon drippings

3 eggs
2 tablespoons flour
1 teaspoon salt
Freshly ground pepper

Peel and grate potatoes and onion. Fry bacon until crisp. Crumble and add, with bacon drippings, to potatoes and onion. Beat eggs and add, then sprinkle in salt and pepper, and flour. Mix to blend. Put potato mixture in shallow baking dish that has been well-greased with bacon fat. Bake uncovered at 325° for 1 hour or until potatoes are tender and nicely browned. Makes 8 or more servings. YOU CAN FIX-IT!

Margaret Lindsey
(Leon, Iowa)

# Party Potatoes

9 large potatoes
6 ounces cream cheese
1 cup sour cream
2 teaspoons onion salt

¼ teaspoon pepper
2 tablespoons butter
Paprika (garnish)

Peel, cook, and mash potatoes. Blend in remaining ingredients. Store in refrigerator until needed, up to 10 days. Heat 35-40 minutes before serving.

Bessie Sierk
(Bettendorf, Iowa)

PARSLEY

# Potato Puff

| | |
|---|---|
| 2 cups cold boiled potatoes (riced) | ½ cup grated cheddar cheese |
| 2 tablespoons melted butter or margarine | ½ teaspoon salt |
| ⅓ cup hot milk | ¼ teaspoon pepper |
| | 2 eggs (slightly beaten) |

Boil red potatoes with skins on. When done, peel skins and then cool potatoes. Force enough cold boiled potatoes through ricer to make 2 cups. (Potatoes can be shredded if ricer not available). Add remaining ingredients in order given. Pour into greased one quart casserole. Bake in 350⁰ oven for 30 minutes or until set. Makes 4 servings. I always doubled the recipe for family dinners. Casserole can be prepared ahead and then refrigerated until ready to bake for mealtime.

**Rose Tippery**
**(Bradenton, Florida, formerly Des Moines, Iowa)**

# Twice Baked Potatoes

| | |
|---|---|
| 8-10 large baking potatoes | ¼ pound margarine |
| 1 (8 ounce) sour cream | Salt and pepper |
| 1 (12 ounce) cottage cheese (small curd) | ¼ teaspoon garlic salt |
| | Cheddar cheese slices |

Bake potatoes until done, then cut potatoes in half. Scrape out inside into large bowl. Set potato shells aside. Add to potatoes; sour cream, cottage cheese, margarine, garlic and salt and pepper. Mash the potatoes and mix well. Refill the shells, sprinkle tops with paprika (optional). Place slice of cheese on top, place potatoes on cookie sheet, heat in oven at 350⁰ for 25 to 30 minutes. Or can freeze, then rebake.

**Thelma Smith**
**(Mitchellville, Iowa)**

329

# — JUST FOR NOTES —

# Pasta

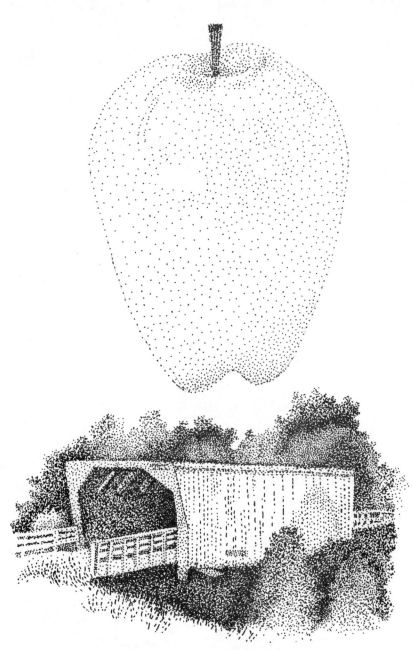

Illustration by Gary Nauman
Bridge Photography by Gene Crawford

# C.H.I.R.C.H.

## The Bridges of Scenic Madison County
## By: Dave Braga, Winterset Madisonian Editor

*(Reprinted with permission from the Winterset Madisonian Newspaper)*

Madison County's six remaining covered bridges have a storied history with tales ranging from those of awe and horror to those of love and romance.

While Madison County's covered bridges carry with them a sense of local pride and treasure, most local folks would have a difficult time remembering the names of all the bridges. Here's a quick little trick which might help, however. It's "C.H.I.R.C.H." - each letter in the make-believe word can be used to quickly reference the names of all the remaining bridges: Cedar Covered Bridge; Hogback Covered Bridge; Imes Covered Bridge; Roseman Covered Bridge; Cutler-Donahue Covered Bridge, and Holliwell Covered Bridge.

# PASTA

**PASTA**

Divine Macaroni
and Cheese .........335

Macaroni Corn
Casserole ...........335

Lasagne...............336

Meat Sauce
for Spaghetti ........336

Mediterranean
Fettuccine...........337

Spaghetti with
Meat Sauce .........337

Spaghetti Pizza ........338

Spaghetti-In-A-Pie .....339

# Divine Macaroni and Cheese

2 cups elbow macaroni (8 ounces)
3 teaspoons butter
¼ cup chopped onion
3 teaspoons flour
½ teaspoon pepper
½ teaspoon salt
1 cup heavy cream
½ cup dry white wine
2 cups (8 ounces) grated sharp cheddar cheese

Cook macaroni, drain. Brown onion in butter, stir in flour, salt and pepper. Slowly add cream and wine. Stir constantly over low flame until thickened. Then add cheese, stir until it melts. Mix macaroni and this sauce. Put in 1½ quart casserole, bake at 350° for 15 minutes.

**US Representative Jim Leach of Iowa**

# Macaroni Corn Casserole

1 can creamed corn
1 can corn
1 stick margarine or butter
1 cup macaroni noodles (uncooked)
1 cup Velveeta cheese (cubed)

Combine corn, creamed corn, margarine and macaroni noodles in large microwave safe bowl. Cook on high for 5 minutes. Stir. Cook until noodles are almost soft. Add Velveeta cheese and microwave on high 5 minutes. Do not drain corn or cover bowl during cooking. Let set for 5 minutes.

**Leann Longfellow**
**(Taylor County Extension Office, Bedford, Iowa)**

# Lasagne

1½ pounds ground beef
1 pound pork sausage
1 (15 ounce) can spaghetti
  sauce
2 (15 ounce) cans tomato
  sauce
10 ounce lasagna noodles
2 eggs

1 (15 ounce) container Ricotta
  cheese
1 (15 ounce) jar Romano
  cheese
3 cups shredded Mozzarella
  cheese
1 teaspoon pepper
1 teaspoon Italian seasonings
2 tablespoons minced onions

Brown all meat with pepper, seasonings and onions. Drain meat. Add the spaghetti sauce and tomato sauce. Simmer for 30 minutes. Cook noodles, drain and rinse. Beat eggs. Add Ricotta and Romano cheeses and mix thoroughly. Layer ½ the noodles in a 13x9-inch pan. Spread ½ of the egg mixture over noodles. Add 1¼ cups mozzarella spread over the egg mixture. Top with ½ of the meat sauce. Repeat. Top with ½ cup mozzarella cheese. Bake at 375° for about 30 minutes (or until the middle is hot). Let stand 5 minutes before serving. Serves 6-8.

**Deborah Collins**

# Meat Sauce For Spaghetti

1 pound hamburger
½ cup chopped onion
2 tablespoons shortening
½ teaspoon garlic powder

1 (15 ounce) can tomato sauce
¼ teaspoon pepper
½ teaspoon salt
½ teaspoon sugar

Brown meat and onion in skillet, drain. Add remaining ingredients and simmer for 20 minutes. Ladle over spaghetti noodles.

**Susan Severs**
**(Princeton, Iowa)**

# Mediterranean Fettuccine

| | |
|---|---|
| 1 medium green pepper (cut in strips) | Salt, pepper and oregano (to taste) |
| ½ medium red pepper (cut in strips) | 1 (16 ounce) can diced tomatoes in juice |
| 1 large onion | 1 pound frozen artichoke hearts |
| 1 stalk celery (chopped) | hearts |
| 2 tablespoons parsley | ¼ pound butter |
| 2 cloves garlic (minced) | ½ cup Parmesan cheese |
| ¼ cup olive oil | 1 pound fettuccine |

In large frying pan saute' all ingredients except cheese and fettuccine in olive oil until soft, adding artichokes last. Melt butter separately. Cook fettuccine in boiling, salted water according to package directions. Drain pasta and mix in melted butter and Parmesan cheese. Blend and arrange pasta on large platter. Pour sauce over pasta. Makes four servings.

John Economos
(West Des Moines, Iowa)

# Spaghetti with Meat Sauce

| | |
|---|---|
| 1 onion (chopped) | ½ teaspoon pepper |
| 3 tablespoons fat | 1 bay leaf |
| 2½ cups tomatoes | 1 pound ground beef |
| 2 (6 ounce) cans tomato paste | Salt and pepper |
| 2 cups water | 1 (8 ounce) package long spaghetti |
| 1 tablespoon sugar | spaghetti |
| 1 teaspoon salt | |

Cook onion in hot fat until golden; add tomatoes, tomato paste, water, sugar, salt, pepper and bay leaf. Brown ground beef and add salt and pepper if desired. Add to tomato mixture. Cook slowly for 1 hour. Serve over cooked spaghetti. Makes 6 servings.

Carol Hunter
(Thanks to Bertha Shaw, Hamilton County Extension Service)

# Spaghetti Pizza

**CRUST:**

1 small package spaghetti
2 eggs
½ cup milk

1 cup mozzarella cheese
   (shredded)
¾ teaspoon garlic salt
½ teaspoon salt

**TOPPING:**

32 ounces spaghetti sauce
1 package sliced pepperoni or
   1 pound sausage (browned)

3 cups Mozzarella cheese
   (shredded)
1½ teaspoons oregano leaves

Cook spaghetti as directed on package, drain and cool. Preheat oven to 400°. Beat eggs slightly; stir in milk and 1 cup cheese. Add to cooked spaghetti, stir. Grease a 9x13-inch glass baking dish (I use PAM). Pour spaghetti mixture in. Bake 15 minutes. Remove from oven, reduce heat to 350°. Spread sauce on spaghetti. Sprinkle with oregano, then 3 cups cheese (I use some cheddar cheese). Add topping; pepperoni or browned, drained sausage. Bake 30 minutes. Set at room temperature at least 5 minutes before serving. This is a great "do ahead" dish. Prepare, but do not bake. Store in refrigerator. Remove and bake (add about 10 minutes to allow for the cold ingredients). Works great for potlucks as it needs to set anyway. For potluck; remove from oven. Cover with foil. Wrap in towel and transport. Will stay hot for some time.

Donna Furrow
(Eldridge, Iowa)

338

# Spaghetti-In-A-Pie

1 ounce spaghetti noodles
  (cooked)
½ cup grated Parmesan
  cheese

2 eggs (beaten)
2 tablespoons butter

Combine and put in pie pan as the crust.

1 pound ground beef
½ cup onions (chopped)

15 ounces tomato sauce

Mushrooms, Italian seasonings, green peppers (optional). Brown beef and onions. Drain grease and add sauce. Layer ingredients on top of noodle crust in the following order; 1 cup cottage cheese, ½ cup Mozzarella cheese and meat sauce. Bake at 350⁰ for 30 minutes. Top with Mozzarella cheese and bake 5 more minutes or until cheese is melted. Let stand 5-10 minutes before serving.

**Wendy Butcher**
**(Thanks also to: Bret Warnke)**
**(Ida County Extension Education Director, Ida Grove, Iowa)**

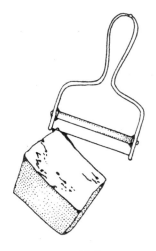

# — JUST FOR NOTES —

# Desserts

# The Music Man

Seventy Six Trombones

Lida Rose

342

# Mason City's Famous Willson Family

Meredith Willson, the youngest of three children, was born to John and Rosalie Willson in 1902 in Mason City, Iowa. Meredith's father was the son of a well-to-do landowner and graduated in 1885 in the first graduating class of Notre Dame's law school. Meredith's mother Rosalie was an extremely religious person. Not only was she the primary department school superintendent of the Congregational Church, but she was responsible for introducing the idea of kindergarten to Mason City in the early 1890's. Preceding Meredith were brother Cedric and sister Dixie, the oldest of the three.

While Meredith was busy writing his music, Dixie was busy with her own career. Meredith, of course, is best remembered for having written "The Music Man", a musical that continues to be performed. Remember the song "Lida Rose"? Meredith's mother Rosalie had a sister named Lida. Meredith also wrote both the music and words for the "Iowa Fight Song" in 1951.

Dixie L. (for Lucille) Willson Lampbert, older than Meredith by 12 years, was as well-known for writing in her own time as Meredith was for his music. She wrote 32 books, mostly for children and over 150 short stories and poems that have been published. The poems, "Pancake Batter", "Cats 'n Kittens", and "Interim", were among her works.

*The following recipes were handwritten and are believed to have been in the handwriting of Meredith's mother Rosalie, for her daughter Dixie.*

343

# Valuable
# Recipes

*Dixie L. W. Lampert.*
*Christmas 1915—*

**Price Thirty-five Cents**

"Prove all things; hold fast that which is good."—
1st Thessalonians v:25.

# —— THESE ——

# Valuable Recipes

## were Collected by the Ladies Aid Society
## of the First Congregational Church
## of Mason, City, Iowa,
## in 1896.

————— —————

REVSED AND ENLARGED BY

## THE WOMAN'S UNION
October, 1908.

/

"We may live without poetry, music or art;
 We may live without conscience and live without
      heart;
We may live without friends, we may live without books;
 But civilized man cannot live without cooks."

—— ◆ ——

The Times-Herald Co. Printers,
Mason City, Iowa.

One qut. flour.
1 teaspoon salt.
2 tablespoons butter.
2 tablespoons baking powder or { 1 cup sour milk or cream. + 1 tsp soda

Rub the butter into the flour,
then add the salt, baking powder +
enough milk or water to make a
soft dough. Mix quickly —
Divide into two equal lumps —
Roll out about one & 1/2 in. thick —
butter — place one on top of
the other + bake — When
done — open. spread again
lightly with butter, — & then
spread with fruit mashed with sugar,
both between + on top.

Cold Water cake - Miss Bonnie
Anna Laurie
Sanborn.

1 cup Sugar
1/2 " butter
2 eggs.
1/2 cup cold water. 2 cups flour,
1 cups raisins, add flour.
1 teaspoon baking powder.
Cinnamon - nutmeg - Vanilla.

Devils' Food cake - Mrs. Glanville.

1 1/2 cup 2 granulated Sugar
1/2 cup butter. 3 eggs. 1 cup Sour Cream.
1/2 cup hot water. 1/2 cup grated Chocolate.
1 teaspoon Soda.
2 1/2 cups flour, Scant, & Sifted
Flavor — 3 times.

Cream butter and Sugar, add Yolks
eggs. Chocolate dissolved in hot
water. & most of the flour, then add
sour cream, Soda, beaten whites
and remainder of flour.
over tins with two or three papers
bake in moderate oven.

347

Fritters,— Never stick a fork
into anything frying in hot lard, as
doing so — allows it to absorb fat.

Plain Fritters. from White book.

Two eggs, 1 cup milk,
Pind Salt. one + one half cups
flour, 1 teaspoon baking-
powder.
Serve with powdered sugar
        Mable Syrup or
fruit pudding sauce.

White Cake frosting { To Lucile, from
                      Mrs. George Brown

White Cake frosting
2 cups Sugar — (rolled.)
1 cup Water.
1 tablespoon vinegar
Boil till it strings — then
pour slowly, over the
beaten whites of two eggs.

# DESSERTS

## CAKES

Apple Cake . . . . . . . . 351,352
Applesauce Cake . . . . 352,356
Banana Cake . . . . . . . . . . 356
Caramel-Fudge Cake . . . . 357
Carrot Cake . . . . . . . . . . . 357
Chocolate Cake . . . . . . . . 358
Nancy Lightfoot's
    Chocolate Cake . . . . . . . 359
Crazy Chocolate Cake . . . 359
Buttermilk
    Chocolate Cake . . . . . . 360
Chocolate Chiffon Cake . 361
Chocolate
    Mayonnaise Cake . . . . . 361
Deadly Chocolate Cake . . 362
Chocolate Eclair Cake . . . 362
Chocolate Sheet Cake . . . 363
Fruit Cake . . . . . . . . . . . . 364
Wacky Cocoa Cake . . . . . 364
Little Chocolate Cakes . . . 365
Italian Coconut Cake . . . . 366
Cranberry Cake . . . . . . . . 366
Devils Food Cake . . . . . . 367
E's Crazy Cake . . . . . . . . 367
Drop Cake or
    "Stir-Up" Cake . . . . . . . 368
Gugelhupf . . . . . . . . . . . . 369
Jello Cake . . . . . . . . . . . . 369
"Kransekake" Norwegian
    Wedding Cake . . . . 370,371
Lemon "Cake" Dessert . . 371
Lemon Cake . . . . . . . . . . 372
Molasses Cake . . . . . . . . . 372
Gables Lemon
    Cheesecake . . . . . . . . . . 373
Nut Cake . . . . . . . . . . . . . 373
Mississippi Mud . . . . . . . 374
Orange Cake Recipe . . . . 374
Nun's Oatmeal Cake . . . . 375

Pineapple Nut Cake . . . . . 376
Pear Cake . . . . . . . . . . . . . 376
Pineapple Upside
    Down Cake . . . . . . . . . . 377
Poppy Seed Cake . . . 377,378
Holiday Pound Cake . . . . 378
Prune Cake . . . . . . . . . . . 379
Hot Fudge
    Pudding Cake . . . . . . . . 379
300 Dollar or Red Cake . 380
Momma's Rhubarb
    Shortcake . . . . . . . . . . . 381
Skinny Cake . . . . . . . . . . . 382
Hot Milk Sponge Cake . . 387
Tin Wedding Cake . . . . . 387
Surprise Cake . . . . . . . . . 388
War Cake . . . . . . . . . . . . . 389
Grandma's War Cake . . . 389
Mrs. Hubbell's
    Cupcakes . . . . . . . . . . . 390

## PIES

Dutch Apple Pie . . . . . . . 391
Cheesecake Pie . . . . . . . . 391
French Apple Pie . . . . . . 392
Chocolate Pie . . . . . . . . . 393
Easy Coconut Pie . . . . . . 393
Custard Pie . . . . . . . . . . . 394
Graham Pie . . . . . . . . . . . 394
French Silk Pie . . . . . . . . 395
Dreamy Ice
    Cream Pie . . . . . . . . . . . 396
Lemon Pie . . . . . . . . . . . . 396
Mincemeat for Pies . . . . . 397
Green Tomato
    Mincemeat . . . . . . . . . . 398
Never Fail Meringue . . . . 398
Party Pie . . . . . . . . . . . . . 399
Peanut Butter
    Cream Pie . . . . . . . . . . . 399

# DESSERTS

## (Pies - Continued)

Peach Custard Pie . . . . . . 400
Pilgrim Pie . . . . . . . . . . . . 401
Prune Pie . . . . . . . . . . . . . 401
Heavenly Pumpkin Pie . . 402
Rhubarb Cream Pie . . . . . 403
Mother's Fresh
  Rhubarb Pie . . . . . . . . . 403
Rhubarb Meringue Pie . . 404
Fresh Strawberry Pie . . . . 404
Sweet Potato Pie . . . . . . . 405
Baily Vinegar Pie . . . . . . . 405
Strawberry Pie . . . . . . . . . 406
My Grandmother's
  Shoofly Pie . . . . . . . 407,408
Triple Layer Party Pie . . . 409
Pie Crust . . . . . . . . . . . . . 410
Oil Pie Crust . . . . . . . . . . 410
Press In Pie Crust . . . . . . 410

## PUDDINGS

Christmas Plum
  Pudding . . . . . . . . . . . . 411
Once-A-Year
  Plum Pudding . . . . . . . . 412
Chocolate Pudding . . . . . . 412
Sophia's Brazil Pudding . 413
Mom's Bread Pudding . . 414
Hot Fudge Pudding . . . . . 414
Norwegian Rommegrot
  (Cream Pudding) . . 415,416
Ostakaka
  (Swedish Pudding) . . . . 416
Rice Pudding . . . . . . . . . . 417
Almond Rice Pudding . . . 417
Yummy Pudding . . . . . . . 418

## PASTRIES

Butterscotch Nut Torte . . 419
Kolacki (Polish) . . . . . . . . 419
Sour Cream Twists . . . . . . 420

## TOPPINGS

Carrot Cake Frosting . . . . 420
Coconut Pecan
  Frosting . . . . . . . . . . . . 421
White Frosting . . . . . . . . 421
Hot Fudge Sauce/
  Butterscotch Variation . 422
Yellow Sauce for the
  X-mas Pudding . . . . . . 422
Chocolate Dip . . . . . . . . . 423
Extra Special
  Chocolate Sauce . . . . . . 423

## FURTHER DELIGHTS

Apple Crisp . . . . . . . . . . . 424
Caramel Dumplings . . . . . 424
Blueberry Cobbler . . . . . . 425
Fruit Soup-Danish . . . . . . 425
4 Layer Cherry Dessert . . 426
Chocolate Roll . . . . . . . . . 427
Death By Chocolate . . . . . 428
Norwegian Sweet Soup . . 428
Gingerbread . . . . . . . . . . . 432
Grandmother's
  Gingerbread . . . . . . . . . 433
Graham Cracker
  Dessert . . . . . . . . . . . . . 433
Hefenklosse mit
  Zimmetsoske . . . . . . . . 434
Banana Ice Cream . . . . . . 436
Old Fashioned
  Ice Cream . . . . . . . . . . . 436
Marvelous Maple-
  Nut Ice Cream . . . . . . . 437
Oreo Dessert . . . . . . . . . . 438
Peppermint Dessert . . . . . 438
Pineapple Delight . . . . . . 439
Rhubarb Crunch . . . . . . . . 439
Raspberry Dessert . . . . . . 440
Rhubarb Delight . . . . . . . . 441
Strawberry Mousse . . . . . 442
Yogurt Delight . . . . . . . . . 443

# Apple Cake

| | |
|---|---|
| 1 cup sugar | 1 teaspoon cinnamon |
| ½ cup margarine | 1 teaspoon baking soda |
| ½ cup cold coffee | ½ teaspoon baking powder |
| 1 egg | ¼ teaspoon salt |
| 2 cups chopped apples | 1½ cups flour |

Cream shortening and sugar, add egg and coffee. Add dry ingredients. Stir in apples. Pour into 9x13-inch greased pan. Sprinkle with topping and bake at 350° for 30 minutes.

**TOPPING:**

| | |
|---|---|
| 2 tablespoons white sugar | ½ cup walnuts |
| 2 tablespoons brown sugar | |

Bertha Wenndt
(Lowden, Iowa)

# Apple Cake

Similar Apple Cake recipe submitted by Stephanie Gray, (Le Claire, Iowa).

# Apple Cake

| | |
|---|---|
| 4 cups apples (diced) | 1 cup chopped walnuts |
| 2 eggs (break over apples and stir) | 2 teaspoons cinnamon |
| | 2½ cups flour |
| 2 cups sugar | 2 teaspoons soda |
| ½ cup salad oil | Dash of salt |

Mix apples and eggs. Combine remainder of ingredients and add to apple mixture. Mixture will be very thick. Spread in 9x13-inch greased pan. Bake 50-55 minutes in 350° pre-heated oven.

**BUTTER SAUCE:**

| | |
|---|---|
| ½ cup butter (melted) | 1 cup condensed milk |
| 1½ cups sugar | ½ teaspoon vanilla or rum |

Mix and boil 1 minute. Serve warm sauce over cake serving.

Lois L. Stillman
(Emmetsburg, Iowa)

# Applesauce Cake

| | |
|---|---|
| 1 cup white sugar | 1 cup nuts |
| ½ cup butter | 2 cups flour |
| 1 egg | 2 teaspoons soda |
| 1 cup stewed raisins | 1 teaspoon cinnamon |
| 1½ cups sweetened applesauce | ½ teaspoon vanilla |

Combine first 5 ingredients. Sift flour, soda, and cinnamon; add. Last put in vanilla and nuts. Bake in moderate oven (350°) in 9x13-inch pan for approximately 40 minutes or until tests done.

Irenee Tracy
(Madison County, Iowa)

# Discoverer and Discovery of the Delicious Apple
## By: Henry Miller

*(Reprinted from the Madison County Cookbook with permission from the Madison County Historical Society)*

Many Iowans probably have seen the original Delicious apple tree which grew on a farm two miles north of Peru, Iowa, 12 miles southeast of Winterset. However, few may know that we have those red Delicious apples only by the merest chance. The world is full of chances. Perhaps it was only one chance in a million that the Delicious tree sprouted and still less of a chance that it fell into the hands of a man who would know it and fight for it.

Jesse Hiatt was the youngest of twelve children and had ten of his own. He was born February 19, 1826, in Randolph County Indiana, of Quaker parents. His father, William Hiatt, owned a farm and orchard and was known among his neighbors as an authority on fruit. He had developed some apple varieties of his own. So Jesse early on learned the art of planting and pruning and grafting and acquired an enduring life for it.

Hiatt was a slow-moving, slow-talking Quaker, known as a kindly man. All who knew him remember and were impressed by his kindness. He was a man "whose honesty could not be doubted." As was often true of Quakers, his religion molded his life in a vital way.

One day in the spring of 1872, Hiatt found that a Bellflower seedling in his orchard had died, but from the root had sprung a healthy shoot. He resolved to watch that apple sprout and see if it was worthwhile. He would give it a chance in the world. The sprout continued to grow, developing a round bushy top.

A few years later, the Bellflower reached the producing point. The first crop was meager. Upon tasting one of the apples, Hiatt decided then and there it was the best apple in the world. The flavor, like the aroma, was unlike any other apple. The shape was different. Each apple had a quintet of rounded knobs, well defined. This precluded it being a Bellflower apple, in the opinion of Jesse Hiatt—a new apple altogether.

Thus it came about that, in honor of his adopted state, Hiatt gave his new apple the name "Hawkeye," Iowa's nickname.

The tree produced every year afterward, until it was filling a barrel. But the top had blown over and the bark was sunburned, cracked, and peeling, he was taking no chances. He put a heavy cover about the trunk, tying it securely. When a freeze killed three-fourths of his orchard, it did not harm his Hawkeye.

*(Continued on Next Page)*

353

# (Discoverer and Discovery
## of the Delicious Apple - Continued)

It is one thing to be convinced you have the best apple in the world, but quite another to convince the world of it. Hiatt sent apples to the Iowa fairs. They got little notice. He tried to persuade his friends to promote the sale of his Hawkeye, but they could see no future in the apple.

Hiatt began carrying some of the prized apples with him and let people taste them. Nobody appeared to be interested, feeling that the apple was just ordinary. But Jesse Hiatt was stubborn. Nobody could convince him that he did not have the world's best apple.

At last, after 11 years of trying, in 1893, Hiatt sent four apples to a fruit show in Louisiana, Missouri. There they fell into the hands of a man who was looking for just such an apple. He was C.M. Stark, senior member of the Stark Brother's Nursery, who staged the annual show.

Stark always carried a little red book in his pocket. In it he was continually jotting down appropriate names for new fruit varieties as they occurred to him. So when he discovered a new variety, he usually had a name all ready in his little book.

For years, the book had retained the name Delicious. He was waiting for a fruit worthy of it. When he bit into the first apple in the lot from Madison County, Iowa, he had a sensation he never forgot. Here was the Delicious apple.

Stark would have written to Hiatt at once but in the confusion of the show, his name and address had been lost. Nobody knew where the apples had come from. He could do nothing but wait for another show on the bare chance that the unknown exhibitor would enter again.

There was one thing Jesse Hiatt had learned and that was patience. He forwarded apples to the Missouri show again in 1894. Stark went through the exhibits anxiously. He knew the apples with their streaked strawberry color the moment he unwrapped them. Now, he wrote to Hiatt and later made a trip to the orchard and secured permission to propagate the tree. Henceforth, the Hawkeye became the Delicious and eventually the nation's leading apple.

At the time of his death in 1898, the Delicious was still unrecognized and was not mentioned in his obituary. His death was not noticed by the state horticultural society.

In 1922, however, when the fiftieth anniversary of the Delicious was observed, Hiatt became very well known for his achievement.

*(Continued on Next Page)*

## (Discoverer and Discovery
## of the Delicious Apple - Continued)

The first Delicious tree lived and produced fruit until 1940 when it succumbed to the Armistice Day storm as did many other apple trees in the state of Iowa. From its roots have sprung two sizable trees with the same luscious apples as the original. These trees along with the exact place of the old tree, are enclosed in a triangular fenced plot on what is now (1972) the Raymond Tracy farm.

Madison County, Iowa, is indeed proud to be the site of the origin of all Delicious apple trees in the world and is indebted to Jesse Hiatt for his alertness in discovering the fine qualities of this strange new apple, which became so valuable and useful to mankind.

*Elma Tracy, her sister Irenee, and their brother Dick still own this farm. Over the years, they and other family members have been visited by many a stranger wanting to see this historical site. Elma says that in 1992 they got nearly two bushels of pretty nice apples from the trees on the site.*

# Applesauce Cake

| | |
|---|---|
| 1 cup brown sugar | 2 teaspoons soda |
| ½ cup shortening | ½ teaspoon salt |
| 1 egg | ½ cup nuts (chopped) |
| 2 cups flour | ½ cup raisins |
| 1 teaspoon cinnamon | 1½ cups thick applesauce |
| ½ teaspoon cloves | 1 teaspoon vanilla |

Cream sugar and shortening. Add egg and beat thoroughly. Sift together flour, cinnamon, cloves, soda, and salt. Add to creamed mixture. Add nuts, raisins, applesauce, and vanilla. Stir until blended. Bake in 8x8-inch or 9x9-inch greased pan 40-45 minutes at 350⁰.

*This recipe was used frequently by my mother since we always had applesauce on hand. It was a forerunner to the carrot cake.*

Beverly W. Allphin
(Bay Village, Ohio, formerly Mitchellville, Iowa)

# Banana Cake

| | |
|---|---|
| ½ cup margarine | 1 teaspoon vanilla |
| 1½ cups white sugar | ¼ teaspoon lemon extract |
| ½ cup sour milk (add lemon juice to milk) | ½ cup nuts (optional) |
| | 2 cups flour |
| 2 eggs | 1 teaspoon baking powder |
| 1 cup mashed bananas (those brown soft ones are best) | ½ teaspoon soda |
| | ¼ teaspoon salt |

Cream margarine and sugar. Add remaining ingredients and beat 2 minutes. Pour into greased 9x13-inch cake pan. Bake 25-30 minutes at 325⁰. Serve plain or top with whipped cream or frosting. We prefer it with powdered sugar frosting while still warm.

*This is from the '48 Delmar, Iowa Cookbook - great use of over ripe bananas - with the lemon extract giving a very different taste.*

Donna Furrow
(Eldridge, Iowa)

# Caramel-Fudge Cake

German Chocolate cake mix
1 can Eagle brand milk
Mrs. Richardson butterscotch
  caramel, fudge mix

Cool Whip
Crushed Heath bar

Bake cake mix as directed. While still warm, not hot, poke holes with wooden spoon. Pour in milk and topping. Top with whipped cream and sprinkle Heath bars on top.

**Dorothy Willet**
**(Davenport, Iowa)**

# Carrot Cake

2 cups sugar
1½ cups vegetable oil
3 eggs
2½ cups flour
2 teaspoons cinnamon
½ teaspoon salt
1 teaspoon soda

1½ teaspoons vanilla
2 cups grated carrots
1 cup chopped nuts (optional)
1 (13 ounce) can crushed
  pineapple, drained (save 1
  tablespoon for frosting)

Mix oil, sugar, and eggs. Add dry ingredients. Batter will be thick. Add carrots, nuts and pineapple. Bake in 9x13-inch greased and floured pan, at 325° for 1 hour.

**Betty (Schneckloth) Nelson**
**(Davenport, Iowa)**

357

# Chocolate Cake

2 cups sugar
¼ pound margarine
2 eggs
3 rounded tablespoons
  cocoa

2 teaspoons baking soda
1 cup boiling water
1 cup sour milk
2 cups flour
2 teaspoons vanilla

Beat first 4 ingredients together until smooth. Add the baking soda to the boiling water and add to first mixture along with the other remaining ingredients. Stir until well mixed. Pour into a greased 9x13-inch pan and bake at 325° for 25 to 30 minutes. May be frozen. Makes 12 servings.

**Bea Smith (Wife of former US Representative Neal Smith of Iowa)**
**(Altoona, Iowa)**

# Chocolate Cake

2 cups sugar
5 tablespoons cocoa
1 cup butter
2 eggs
2 teaspoons vanilla

3 cups cake flour
½ teaspoon salt
2 teaspoons soda
1 cup commercial buttermilk
1 cup boiling water

Combine sugar, cocoa and butter, and beat well. Add eggs and vanilla. Sift dry ingredients and add alternately with buttermilk. Lastly add boiling water. Batter is thin. Bake at 325° for 1 hour, in 9x13-inch pan. Mine is done in 50 minutes.

*I have used this recipe for 47 years. It was from an old school teacher.*

**Mary Boatwright**
**(Runnells, Iowa)**

# Nancy Lightfoot's Chocolate Cake

3 blocks Hershey's
  semi-sweet chocolate
¼ cup butter or margarine
1 cup boiling water
2 cups light brown sugar
  (firmly packed)
1½ teaspoons baking soda
2 cups flour
1 teaspoon salt
1 teaspoon vanilla
½ cup sour cream
2 eggs

Combine the chocolate squares, butter and boiling water and stir until chocolate is melted. In a large bowl combine the sugar, flour, soda and salt. Make a well and gradually add the chocolate mixture, then the eggs one at a time, beating with each addition. Add sour cream and vanilla and beat at medium speed with electric mixer for one minute. Bake at 350° for 35 to 40 minutes or until it tests done. Use a 9x13-inch pan.

Nancy Lightfoot
(Wife of US Representative Jim Lightfoot)

# Crazy Chocolate Cake

2 cups sugar
1 cup whole wheat flour
2 cups enriched white flour
⅓ cup cocoa
½ teaspoon salt
2 teaspoons baking soda
1 teaspoon vanilla
2 tablespoons vinegar
⅔ cup oil
2 cups cold water

In a 9x13-inch pan stir sugar, flours, cocoa, salt and soda. Blend well. Make three holes or indentations in the dry mixture. Put the vanilla in one hole, the vinegar in a second hole, and the oil in the third hole. Pour the water over all and stir the mixture until well mixed. Bake at 350° for 30-35 minutes. Serves 24.

Francine Lemke

# Buttermilk Chocolate Cake

**MELT IN DOUBLE BOILER:**
1 stick oleo
2 cups sugar

2 squares unsweetened
  chocolate
1 cup boiling water

Let mixture cool.

**BEAT TOGETHER:**
2 beaten eggs
½ cup buttermilk

1 teaspoon vanilla

**MIX TOGETHER:**
2 cups sifted flour
1½ teaspoons baking soda

½ teaspoon salt

Alternate mixing cooled chocolate mixture and dry ingredients to the beaten egg and buttermilk mixture. Pour into greased 9x13-inch pan. Bake at 350° for 30 minutes or until toothpick is clean when inserted to center of cake. This cake is better as a pan cake, not a layer cake.

ICING: MELT TOGETHER IN DOUBLE BOILER:
1 square chocolate
½ stick oleo

¼ cup boiling water

ADD: 1 teaspoon vanilla and enough powdered sugar to make fudge-like consistency. Cover cooled cake.

*This cake has been a favorite of our family for 50 years. My mother received this recipe from a bridge club friend when she was first married.*

**Ann Suiter**
**(Princeton, Iowa)**

# Chocolate Chiffon Cake

| | |
|---|---|
| 1¼ cups white corn syrup | 4 level tablespoons cocoa |
| ⅔ cup shortening | 2 unbeaten eggs |
| 2 cups sifted flour | 1 teaspoon vanilla |
| 1 teaspoon soda | ½ cup sour milk |
| ¼ teaspoon salt | ¼ cup water |

Cream the shortening well. Add the 1 cup syrup beating well as it is added. Sift all the dry ingredients together. Add ⅓ of sifted ingredients to syrup and shortening mixture; blend well. Then add eggs, one at a time, beating well after each egg has been added. Add 1 teaspoon vanilla, next add remaining dry ingredients and sour milk; mix well. When well blended, heat the combined ¼ cup of syrup and ¼ cup of water to boiling and add to the batter. Mix until blended. Pour into a greased and floured pan. Bake in moderate (325⁰-350⁰) oven. Test with toothpick for doneness.

*This is an excellent "World War II" recipe, well worth a try. I still make one now and then. It was in the days of sugar rationing that this was "famous." The beating was done by hand and rotary egg beater. Try it, you'll love it!*

Mrs. Melvin Dobbins
(Wilton, Iowa)

# Chocolate Mayonnaise Cake

| | |
|---|---|
| 1 cup sugar | 2 teaspoons baking soda |
| 1 cup mayonnaise | 1 cup cold water (for moister |
| 2 cups flour | cake ¼ cup more) |
| 4 tablespoons cocoa | 1 teaspoon vanilla |

Blend first two ingredients, add remaining alternately. Mix well. Pour into greased and floured 9x13-inch pan, bake at 350⁰ for 35 minutes or until done.

Susan Severs
(Princeton, Iowa)

# Deadly Chocolate Cake

Duncan Hines Swiss
  Chocolate Cake Mix
1 can Eagle brand condensed
  milk

1 bottle Kraft Caramel ice
  cream topping
6 Heath candy bars
Cool Whip

Mix and bake cake per package instructions. While hot, make holes
all over the top of the cake and pour the condensed milk and caramel
topping over it so that it soaks into the cake. Then sprinkle on top
three of the Heath Candy Bars that have been crushed. Refrigerate.
Before serving, top with Cool Whip and the remaining three crushed Heath Bars.

Doris Haesemeyer
(Elmhurst, Illinois, formerly Stanwood, Iowa)

# Chocolate Eclair Cake

1 pound box graham crackers
  (Keebler's work well)
2 packages (3¾ ounce)
  (instant French vanilla
  pudding)

3 cups milk
8 ounces Cool Whip (thawed)

FROSTING:
2 ounces Baker's liquid
  chocolate
3 tablespoons soft butter
3 tablespoons milk

2 tablespoons white syrup
1 teaspoon vanilla
1½ cups powdered sugar

Layer bottom with whole graham crackers. Beat pudding and milk
until thick. Add Cool Whip and mix well. Pour half of pudding over
crackers, add another layer of crackers, then remaining pudding,
add third layer of crackers. FROSTING: Mix and beat well. Pour
over top layer of crackers. Spread. Refrigerate 24 hours before serving. NOTE: You can make liquid chocolate by using 6 tablespoons
cocoa and 2 tablespoons oil for this recipe.

Linda (Schneckloth) Grimm

# Chocolate Sheet Cake

2 cups sifted all-purpose
  flour
2 cups white sugar
1 teaspoon baking soda
¼ teaspoon salt
1 cup butter or margarine

4 tablespoons cocoa
1 cup water
½ cup buttermilk
2 beaten eggs
1 teaspoon vanilla

Sift together all dry ingredients. Heat water and butter until butter is melted. Stir in cocoa until well blended. Pour into dry ingredients and mix well. Stir in eggs, buttermilk and vanilla. Pour into a greased 10x15x1-inch pan. Bake at 375⁰ for 17 to 20 minutes. Frost.

CHOCOLATE FROSTING: Put ½ cup butter or margarine and 6 tablespoons buttermilk or sweet milk in a saucepan. Bring to boil and stir constantly so it will not curdle. Stir in 3 tablespoons cocoa, 1 pound confectioners sugar and 1 teaspoon vanilla. Spread on cooled cake. 1 cup of chopped walnuts can be added with the vanilla.

*This is a thin cake batter but even so bakes into a very moist cake and will keep moist for 4 or 5 days. Very good.*

**Maurine Coe (Mrs. Floyd)**
**(Des Moines, Iowa)**

363

# Fruit Cake

1½ cups sugar
1 cup sour cream
1 cup raw apples
1 cup raisins
1 cup dates
1 cup nuts
1 cup mixed fruit (use own judgment)

½ cup butter
2½ cups flour
2 eggs
2 teaspoons soda
1 teaspoon each cloves, cinnamon and nutmeg

Put in bread pans and bake 1 hour.

**Marguerite Vens**
**(Davenport, Iowa)**

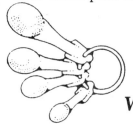

# Wacky Cocoa Cake

3 cups unsifted all-purpose flour
2 cups sugar
½ cup cocoa
2 teaspoons baking soda

1 teaspoon salt
2 cups water
¾ cup vegetable oil
2 tablespoons vinegar
2 teaspoons vanilla

Combine all dry ingredients. Add water, oil, vinegar and vanilla - beat 3 minutes at medium speed until blended. Pour batter into greased and floured 9x13-inch pan. Bake at 350° for 35-40 minutes. Cool and frost.

*This is the only chocolate cake my mom ever made, and I've loved it all my life. Once you try it, you'll never go back to a box mix! We never knew why it's called "Wacky" cake, but it's given me a wacked-out addiction to chocolate!*

**Paula Sands**
**(KWQC-TV Channel 6, Davenport, Iowa)**

# Little Chocolate Cakes

| | |
|---|---|
| 1 cup sugar | 1½ cups flour |
| 2 tablespoons butter | Flavor |
| Yolks of 2 eggs | Nuts (if desired) |
| ½ cup water | Add whites of 2 eggs (well |
| 2 squares chocolate, melted | beaten) |
| over hot water - cool a | |
| little before adding | |

Bake in gem tins in moderate oven. Fudge frosting if desired.

*This is a recipe from my Mother's recipe box with the name of Mrs. Roadman on the card, along with the date of February 7, 1917. Mrs. Roadman's husband was the minister who married my parents and February 7, 1917 was the date of their marriage in the town of Bristow, Iowa. Perhaps that was the custom in those days for the minister's wife to share her favorite recipe with the new bride. Evidently it meant a lot to my Mother for she kept the recipe in Mrs. Roadman's handwriting and signature. The card is yellowed with age, but, still legible. We would call this recipe "cupcakes" nowadays, no doubt.*

**Phyllis Pfitzenmaier
(Bettendorf, Iowa)**

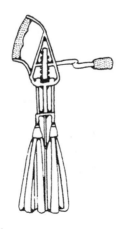

# Italian Coconut Cake

2 cups sugar
½ cup salad oil
½ cup oleo
5 egg yolks
2 cups flour
2 teaspoons vanilla

1 teaspoon soda
2 cups flaked coconut
1 cup buttermilk
1 cup nutmeats
2 egg whites (beaten)

Beat first 4 ingredients. Add rest of ingredients except egg whites; stir well. Fold in beaten egg whites. Makes three layers (9-inch). Bake at 350⁰ for 25-30 minutes. FROSTING: 8 ounces cream cheese (softened), 1 pound powdered sugar, ½ cup oleo, and 2 teaspoons vanilla. Beat well.

Beulah Findley
(Mitchellville, Iowa)

# Cranberry Cake

3 tablespoons butter
2 cups flour
1 cup sugar
½ teaspoon salt

1 cup milk
1 teaspoon vanilla
3 teaspoons baking powder
2 cups whole cranberries

SAUCE:
½ cup butter
1 cup sugar

1 teaspoon vanilla
¾ cup whipping cream

Mix cake ingredients together, folding in cranberries. Bake in 9x9-inch pan at 350⁰ for 30-40 minutes. Mix sauce ingredients together in saucepan and bring to a boil. Boil 4 minutes. Serve hot. This cake freezes very well.

Vivian M. Cook
(Davenport, Iowa)

# Devils Food Cake

| | |
|---|---|
| 3 tablespoons cocoa | 1½ cups flour |
| 1 teaspoon baking soda | 1 teaspoon vanilla |
| ½ cup hot coffee | ½ cup buttermilk |
| 1½ cups sugar | 2 eggs |
| ½ cup butter or oleo | Pinch of salt |

Mix cocoa, baking soda and hot coffee; stir and set aside. Cream sugar and butter; add the cocoa mixture to the creamed mixture and beat well. Add flour, salt and buttermilk; then beaten eggs and vanilla. Bake at 350⁰ for 25-30 minutes in 9x13-inch greased and floured pan.

**Gus Null**
**(Submitted by and thanks also to: Sarah Schoon,**
**Executive Director, Anamosa Chamber of Commerce)**

# E's Crazy Cake

| | |
|---|---|
| 4½ cups flour | 3 tablespoons vinegar |
| 3 cups sugar | 7 ounces melted butter or |
| 6 tablespoons cocoa | Crisco oil |
| 3 teaspoons soda | 3 teaspoons vanilla |
| 3 pinches salt | 3 cups cold water |

Mix the dry ingredients together and sift twice. Mix the liquids in well. Cook 25-30 minutes at 350⁰ in a 9x13-inch cake pan (actually next bigger size is better).

*My Mom came up with this recipe when she was a little girl. She's kind of crazy (in a good sense) so I think she named this kind of after herself.*

**Billie Hoover**
**(Atlantic, Iowa)**

367

# Drop Cake or "Stir-Up" Cake

| | |
|---|---|
| 2 eggs | 2 cups flour |
| Cream (see directions) | 2 teaspoons baking powder |
| Salt (a dash) | 1 teaspoon vanilla |

Beat two eggs in a teacup. Fill the cup with cream. Add a dash of salt and vanilla. Sift (or otherwise mix) flour and baking powder together. Add gradually to egg mixture, beating until mixture is smooth and creamy. Bake in moderate (350º-375º) oven until done.

*This recipe was a favorite of my mother's, she got it from an MPA cookbook—MPA standing for Mutual Protective Association of a community just east of Des Moines known as Rising Sun. I think it's vintage must have been in the 1920's, and it had been a fundraising project of the neighborhood families who joined together as much for social reasons as for "protection." (It was NOT a vigilante group.) In the depression days we often had this "stir-up" cake, nearly always without icing, and once or twice during the summer with home-made ice cream. Living on the farm, we had our own milk and cream, even when other commodities were not so plentiful. I've also included a poem that relates in part to cake-baking.*

## Ah! Sweet Perfume!

Watching Mother pour a capful
of flavoring into the creamy cake batter,
I begged to taste the delicious sweetness
the dark brown liquid promised.
The aroma of vanilla enticed me then
as Jontue and Enjoli would in later years.

Against her warnings my furtive finger
probed the bottle and touched my tongue.
The bitter sting brought tears to my eyes.

Now bottles in my own cupboard
are silent reminders
of the bittersweetness of many discoveries
and the Jontue bottle's contents
have evaporated to a dark brown stain.

**Editor-Lyrical Iowa: Lucille Morgan Wilson**
**(Des Moines, Iowa)**

# Gugelhupf
*(Marmor cake)*

½ cup butter
¾ cup sugar
4 eggs
2½ cups flour
¼ teaspoon salt
2½ teaspoons baking powder

Grated rind of 1 lemon
6 tablespoons light cream
3 squares (3 ounces) semi-
    sweet chocolate (grated)
¼ cup ground almonds
½ cup powdered sugar

Beat altogether the butter and sugar until light and creamy. Beat in the eggs, 1 at a time. Fold in the flour, salt and baking powder. Divide the batter into 2 bowls. Add the grated lemon rind and 3 tablespoons cream to one bowl. Add the grated chocolate and remaining cream to the second half. Butter a fluted ring pan (Gugelhupf pan) and sprinkle evenly with ground almonds, pressing them gently into the flutes. Fill the pan with ⅓ of the lemon mixture, add all of the chocolate mixture and finally the remaining lemon batter. Bake in a preheated 350⁰ oven for 40 to 45 minutes. Unmold, coat with powdered sugar while still warm, and allow to cool. Serves 10.

**Wilma Howard**
**(Denton, Texas, formerly Cedar Falls, Iowa)**

# Jello Cake

1 white cake mix
1 (3 ounce) package Jello (1
    cup boiling water, ½ cup
    cold water)

1 box vanilla instant pudding
1½ cups milk
Cool Whip

Bake cake as directed. Cool 15 minutes. Prick cake with meat fork at ½-inch intervals. Meanwhile prepare Jello. Carefully pour over warm cake. Let cool and firm. Prepare pudding with milk. Whip in Cool Whip. Frost cake. Refrigerate.

**Submitted by Rachel Klingsheim**
**(Lime Springs, Iowa)**

369

# "Kransekake" Norwegian Wedding Cake

**1 pound almond paste***
**1 pound powdered sugar**
**(sifted)**

**2 egg whites (unbeaten)**
**¼ cup powdered sugar for**
**kneading**

**FROSTING:**
**1½ cups powdered sugar**
**(sifted)**

**1 egg white (unbeaten)**
**1 teaspoon vinegar**

*Most bakeries will sell you the almond paste in bulk. Norwegians have a special nut grinder with a very fine sieve and grind their own almonds to make this special treat. It's a tradition for weddings, anniversaries, Christmas, Confirmation, etc. It is made in 18 concentric ring mold pans sold in Scandinavian shops, or you can make these on foil covered cardboard squares with the circles drawn on. My molds are non-stick so no greasing is necessary. There are 6 molds with three graduated rings in each. Mix almond paste and powdered sugar. Add egg whites, mix well. Place bowl in another bowl of hot water and knead dough until it is lukewarm. Turn out on baking cloth sprinkled with ¼ cup powdered sugar. Let rest 10 minutes. Knead 2-3 minutes. Butter molds or use cooking spray. Either press dough through cookie press into ring forms, or roll into rope width of little finger. Place in molds pressing ends together. Bake 12 minutes at 350°, watch! Remove from oven and place at once in deep freeze for 5 minutes. Remove carefully with plastic utensil and pry loose. Cool before frosting.

FROSTING: Mix ingredients and use the writing tip of your cookie press. Place largest ring on bottom and making "V" shapes go back and forth around ring. Continue stacking and frosting rest of rings. If freezing for later use, I place 6 rings in 3 Tupperware containers. To decorate, use small Norwegian flags in attractive pattern or sometimes small packages are wrapped in colored foil and placed on rings and on top.

*(Continued on Next Page)*

**("Kransekake" Norwegian Wedding Cake - Continued)**

TO SERVE: Instruct whoever serves the cake to use 2 spatulas to lift top 17 rings together and carefully remove the bottom ring, and this way cake still retains original shape. If you don't wish to serve the cake but save for later, then make one batch with a cookie press into a flat shape on cookie sheet and cut these strips into 2-3-inch lengths and serve as cookies on attractive plate or tray.

*This cake should be chewy almost like a macaroon made with coconut. If dries out, store in metal tins or add apple slice or slice of bread for moisture in container or even carefully cover ring cake with a damp kitchen towel. As with many of Norwegian treats made with special irons, you should practice this one before making to serve. Have patience. It helps to have the correct equipment. Freezing and then thawing makes for a chewier cake too.*

*HINT: When taking in sections and then setting up later, I take some frosting in the press to touch up if necessary, or if some layers seem too loose. Few ingredients, but lots of directions!*

Eunice Stoen
(Decorah, Iowa)

## Lemon "Cake" Dessert

¼ cup flour
1 cup sugar
½ teaspoon salt
3 egg yolks (well beaten)

¼ cup lemon juice
1½ cups milk
1 tablespoon grated lemon rind
3 egg whites (stiffly beaten)

Sift together flour, sugar, and salt. Blend together egg yolks, juice, milk, and rind. Combine liquid and dry ingredients; beat until smooth. Fold in egg whites. Pour into greased 8x8x2-inch pan; place in larger pan with hot water. Bake in slow oven (325⁰) for 45 minutes. Serve warm or cold; cut in squares. Makes 6 servings.

Mrs. Sharon Boyle
(Long Grove, Iowa)

# Lemon Cake

| | |
|---|---|
| 1 (3 ounce) package lemon Jello | 1 tablespoon lemon juice (fresh) |
| 1 cup boiling water | 4 eggs |
| Lemon cake mix | 1 cup powdered sugar |
| ¾ cup oil | 4 tablespoons fresh lemon juice |

Dissolve 1 (3 ounce) package of lemon Jello in 1 cup boiling water. Set aside. Mix lemon cake mix with the oil and lemon juice and eggs (one at a time). Fold in the lemon Jello mixture. Pour into a 13x9-inch cake pan, bake at 350⁰ for 35 to 40 minutes. Make a glaze of 1 cup powdered sugar and 4 tablespoons lemon juice and spread on top of hot cake. You can punch holes in top of cake with a toothpick so glaze will seep into cake.

Vern McCurnin
**(Overland Park, Kansas, formerly Mitchellville, Iowa)**

# Molasses Cake

*(This is a Dutch coffee cake which Aunt Gesiena Van Pilsum always made at Christmas.)*

| | |
|---|---|
| 2 cups brown sugar | 2 teaspoons cinnamon |
| 1 cup butter | 2 teaspoons cloves |
| 1 cup molasses | 1 teaspoon grated nutmeg |
| 1 cup strong coffee | 1 pound raisins |
| 4 eggs | 1 pound currants |
| 1 teaspoon soda | 4 cups flour |

Mix all ingredients, first the sugar, butter and molasses. Add coffee and eggs, then spices, raisins and currants and flour. Can use all raisins or all currants if desired. Bake at 350⁰ about 50 minutes or 325⁰ about an hour and 10 minutes. Test center. Bake in 8x12-inch dish or pan.

Laurie Van Dyke
**(Mequon, Wisconsin, formerly Mitchellville, Iowa)**

# Gables Lemon Cheesecake

*(An everyday favorite)*

**CRUST:**

1¾ cups graham cracker
    crumbs
¼ cup granulated sugar

¼ teaspoon lemon peel
⅓ cup melted butter

Mix cracker crumbs, sugar and lemon peel. Mix in margarine. Press crumbs on bottom and sides of 9-inch springform pan.

24 ounces cream cheese
1 tablespoon lemon juice
1½ cups granulated sugar
4 eggs

1 cup sour cream
1 teaspoon vanilla
1 teaspoon lemon peel

Beat lemon juice into the cream cheese to soften. Add the sugar and beat well. Add the eggs, one at a time, beating at medium speed. At low speed, add sour cream, vanilla, and lemon peel. Pour into crust. Bake at 350⁰ for 50 minutes. Cool. Refrigerate at least 4 hours. Top with your favorite topping, if desired. Yields 12 servings.

**Green Gables, Molly and Robert Seff**
**(Sioux City, Iowa)**

# Nut Cake

*(Around 100 years old)*

2 cups sugar
¾ cup butter
2 teaspoons baking powder
1 teaspoon vanilla

4 egg whites (beaten stiff)
3 cups (regular) flour
1 cup milk
½ cup black walnuts

Cream butter and sugar, sift dry ingredients, add 1 cup milk, nuts, and vanilla. Fold in egg whites. Bake at 350⁰ until done.

**Joyce Brockhouse**
**(Princeton, Iowa)**

# Mississippi Mud

| | |
|---|---|
| 2 cups sugar | 1½ cups flour |
| 1 cup butter | 1½ cups coconut |
| 2 tablespoons cocoa | 1 cup nuts (chopped) |
| 4 beaten eggs | 1 (7 ounce) jar marshmallow |
| 1 teaspoon vanilla | creme |

FROSTING:

| | |
|---|---|
| 4¾ cups powdered sugar | ⅓ cup cocoa |
| ½ cup butter | 1 teapoon vanilla |
| ½ cup evaporated milk | |

Cream sugar, butter and cocoa. Add eggs and vanilla. Slowly mix in flour, coconut and nuts. Pour into 9x13-inch pan. Bake at 350⁰ for 30 to 40 minutes. Spread marshmallow creme immediately after taking from oven. Frost after completely cooled.

Bryan's favorite
Mary Etta (Schneckloth) Thomsen

# Orange Cake Recipe
*(1860's)*

BEAT TOGETHER:

| | |
|---|---|
| Two cupfuls of sugar | A little salt |
| ½ cupful of water | The juice and grated rind of |
| Yolks of 5 eggs | 1 orange |
| The whites of 5 eggs | |

ADD LAST: 2 cupfuls of flour, a teaspoonful of baking powder.

Bake in 4 jelly pans. Put the layers together with icing made with whites of 2 eggs, the grated rind and juice of an orange and a sufficient quantity of powdered sugar to make icing stiff enough.

Penelope Miller
(Princeton, Iowa)

# Nun's Oatmeal Cake

1½ cups boiling water
1 cup quick oatmeal
  (uncooked)
½ cup dates (finely cut)
½ cup margarine
1 cup brown sugar
1 cup white sugar

2 eggs
1 teaspoon vanilla
1½ cups flour
½ teaspoon salt
1 teaspoon soda
½ cup nuts

Place dates, oatmeal and boiling water in a bowl and let stand 20 minutes. Cream margarine and sugar. Add eggs and vanilla and beat well. Alternately add to this the dry ingredients and cooled date and oatmeal mixture. Pour batter into a greased and floured 9x13-inch pan. Bake at 375⁰ for about 30 minutes or until done. Let cool and frost.

FROSTING:
½ cup butter or margarine
½ cup brown sugar
½ cup milk or half and half

1 teaspoon vanilla
1 cup coconut
1 cup black walnuts

Cook together the sugar, butter and half and half until it starts to thicken. It will get thicker as it cools. Add the rest of ingredients and beat well. This recipe was printed in the LeMars Globe Post and is from the Sisters of Sacred Heart Hospital at LeMars, Iowa.

**Carol Schneider**
**(LeMars, Iowa)**
**(Thanks also to the Plymouth County Extension Service.)**

# Pineapple Nut Cake

2 cups sugar
2 eggs
1 teaspoon vanilla
2 cups flour

1 (20 ounce) can crushed
   pineapple (not drained)
2 teaspoons soda
1 cup nuts

Beat together sugar, eggs and vanilla. Add the rest of the ingredients and bake in a 9x13-inch greased pan for 40 minutes at 350º. Cool and frost.

FROSTING: Cream
1 (8 ounce) package cream
   cheese

1 stick margarine

ADD:
1 teaspoon vanilla

1½ cups powdered sugar

*An easy recipe. Easy to take to school, church, etc. Everyone loves it. Also gets better as it ages!*

**Margaret Novosad**
**(Elmhurst, Illinois, formerly Stanwood, Iowa)**

# Pear Cake
*(Around 100 years old)*

½ cup soft butter
1 cup sugar
1 egg
1½ cups flour
¼ teaspoon salt

1 teaspoon baking soda
½ teaspoon cinnamon
1 teaspoon vanilla
2 cups grated raw pears
½ cup chopped pecans

Mix butter, sugar and egg. Sift flour, salt, soda and cinnamon. Add to butter, sugar and egg mixture. Add vanilla, pears and nuts. Mix well. Pour into greased and floured 8 or 9-inch square pan. Bake at 300º for 1 hour. Serve with whipped cream.

**Joyce Brockhouse**
**(Princeton, Iowa)**

# Pineapple Upside Down Cake

½ cup butter
8 slices canned pineapple

1 cup brown sugar
8 maraschino cherries

Melt butter in cake pan and add brown sugar. Spread evenly. Place pineapple slices over brown sugar mixture and put cherries in the hole in the middle of the pineapple.

4 eggs (separated)
⅔ cup sugar
⅔ cup flour

½ teaspoon salt
½ teaspoon lemon extract
1 teaspoon baking powder

Sift flour, baking powder and salt 3 times. Beat egg whites until stiff. Beat egg yolks until thick and light in color. Add the extract and the sugar, which has been sifted. Fold in half of the beaten egg whites; then fold in the flour mixture. Fold in the rest of the beaten egg whites. Pour over fruit and brown sugar mixture and bake at 350⁰ until light brown and top springs back when touched lightly, about 30-35 minutes. Invert at once onto serving plate or cookie sheet.

*This is a recipe from Mrs. Grassley's mother, Mrs. Verla Speicher, from the 1930's.*

**Mrs. Charles Grassley**

# Poppy Seed Cake

1 white cake mix
1 tablespoon vanilla
1 tablespoon almond
   flavoring

1 can lemon pie filling
Cool Whip
⅓ cup poppy seeds

Mix cake according to directions on box. Add vanilla, poppyseeds and almond flavoring. Bake as directed on box. Cool completely. Frost top with lemon pie filling and the Cool Whip mixed with a little powdered sugar to keep firmer. Refrigerate.

**Submitted by Rachel Klingsheim
(Lime Springs, Iowa)**

# Poppy Seed Cake

¾ cup butter
1½ cups sugar
½ cup water
½ cup milk
½ cup poppy seed

2¼ cups cake flour
2 teaspoons baking powder
4 egg whites (whipped)
1 teaspoon vanilla

Soak poppy seed for 3 hours in milk and water which have been heated through. Cream butter and sugar, add liquid and poppy seed alternately with dry ingredients, fold in whipped egg whites and vanilla. Bake at 350° until done (30-35 minutes).

**Mrs. Louie Hageman**
**(Submitted by Kate Klimesh, Spillville, Iowa)**

# Holiday Pound Cake

3 cups sugar
½ pound oleo
6 whole eggs
3 cups flour (sifted)
¼ teaspoon soda
½ teaspoon salt
1 cup sour cream
½ tablespoon rum flavoring

1 tablespoon orange flavoring
¼ tablespoon almond
  flavoring
½ tablespoon vanilla
  flavoring
½ tablespoon lemon
  flavoring
½ cup apricot brandy

Cream oleo and sugar. Add eggs one at a time beating well with each addition. Add other ingredients in order listed above, alternately with flour and sour cream. Pour into a greased and floured tube cake pan. Bake at 325° for 1 to 1¼ hours. Serve plain or with a glaze.

*I have given this recipe along with a tube pan and the various flavorings called for as a shower gift to a new bride. It is an easy cake to bake and makes a hit whenever served. Does not need an icing. But sometimes I use a thin orange glaze.*

**Alverta Hatch**
**(Bettendorf, Iowa)**

# Prune Cake

| | |
|---|---|
| 1 cup vegetable oil | 1½ cups sugar |
| 3 eggs | 2 cups flour |
| 1 teaspoon cinnamon | 1 teaspoon nutmeg |
| 1 teaspoon allspice | 1½ teaspoons soda |
| 1 cup buttermilk | 1 teaspoon vanilla |
| 1 cup cooked prunes (cut up) | |

Blend oil and sugar. Add eggs and blend well. Add sifted dry ingredients alternately with buttermilk; add vanilla and prunes and beat well. Pour into large loaf cake pan or 2 (9-inch) cake pans. Bake at 300⁰ for 45 minutes to 1 hour. Let cool in pan.

Marguerite Vens
(Davenport, Iowa)

# Hot Fudge Pudding Cake

| | |
|---|---|
| 1¼ cups granulated sugar | ½ cup milk |
| 1 cup all-purpose flour | ¼ cup margarine (melted) |
| 4 tablespoons cocoa powder | 1½ teaspoons vanilla extract |
| 2 teaspoons baking powder | ½ cup brown sugar (packed) |
| ¼ teaspoon salt | 1¼ cups hot water |

Heat oven to 350⁰. Stir together ¾ cup of the granulated sugar, flour, baking powder and salt. Blend in milk, margarine, and vanilla. Beat to smooth. Pour batter into greased 8 or 9-inch square baking pan. In separate bowl, stir together remaining sugar (granulated), brown sugar, and 4 tablespoons of cocoa. Sprinkle mixture evenly over batter. Pour hot water over top, do not stir. Bake 35 to 40 minutes or until center is almost set. Garnish with whipped topping. Makes about 8 servings. May add ⅓ cup chopped pecans.

*This was my mother-in-law's tried and true recipe.*

Betty Hainstock
(Lost Nation, Iowa)

# 300 Dollar or Red Cake

**CREAM:**

½ cup shortening

1½ cups sugar

2 eggs (one at a time)

Mix and then add coloring:

2 tablespoons cocoa

1 teaspoon vanilla

2 bottles or 2 ounces red
food coloring

1 teaspoon salt

1 cup buttermilk

2 tablespoons vinegar

1 teaspoon soda

2½ cups sifted cake flour

Add flour and liquid alternately.

**ICING:**

1 cup milk

5 tablespoons flour

1 cup sugar

1 teaspoon vanilla

1 cup shortening

Dash of salt

Bake in layers (two 9-inch or three 8-inch pans). Bake at 350⁰ for 30 to 35 minutes. ICING: Cook the milk and flour until thick. Beat until bubbles are gone. Cool and add the remaining ingredients. Beat to look like whipped cream.

**Submitted by Rachel Klingsheim
(Lime Springs, Iowa)**

# Momma's Rhubarb Shortcake

| | |
|---|---|
| 1½ pounds strawberry rhubarb | 1 cup white sugar |
| 4 tablespoons butter | 1 egg (beaten) |
| 1 cup milk | 2 cups flour |
| 2 teaspoons baking powder | 2 cups brown sugar |

Cut rhubarb into 1-inch pieces. Divide evenly and put in bottom of 2 loaf pans. Pour 1 cup of brown sugar over each layer of rhubarb. Make shortcake batter out of remaining ingredients: Cream butter, sugar, and beaten egg. Add: flour, milk, and baking powder. Pour batter (divided evenly) over rhubarb and brown sugar. Bake one hour at 350°. Turn pans upside down to cool. Serve in upside down position so that rhubarb is on top.

**This is the story that Andy told of his boyhood in Wall Lake:**

*When Andy was four years old in Wall Lake, he once accompanied his dad on the early morning mail run. Because the train did not stop at Wall Lake on its return trip, his father bundled the little boy into a mailbag, had the locomotive engineer slow to five miles an hour entering Wall Lake and hung the bag—boy and all—from the side of the train on a swing out bar. A hook at the depot neatly snatched the bag from the bar and Andy was back home. His mother upon hearing the train whistle would walk down the hill to the depot and retrieve the little boy from the mailbag.*

**Andy Williams**
**(Submitted by Betty Brotherton, Wall Lake, Iowa)**

381

# Skinny Cake

*(Not Fat Brownies)-Named by my family and friends*

| | |
|---|---|
| 2 cups sugar | 2 eggs |
| 2 cups flour | ½ cup sour milk or |
| Pinch of salt |    buttermilk |
| 2 sticks oleo | 1 teaspoon soda |
| 3 heaping tablespoons cocoa | 1 teaspoon vanilla |
| 1 cup water | |

Sift together first three ingredients in mixing bowl. Melt oleo, add cocoa and water and bring to a boil. Then pour over dry mixture and mix well. Then add beaten eggs, soda dissolved in milk, and vanilla. Pour in sheet cake pan, 12x18 or 2 smaller ones. Bake 20 minutes at 400⁰ and if not done, reduce heat to 350⁰. Frost with 1 stick oleo, 6 tablespoons milk, 2 heaping tablespoons cocoa. Bring to a boil and add to 1 teaspoon vanilla, 1 cup nuts and powdered sugar with enough consistency to spread. A quick cake to make when rushed for time.

*I asked some friends and my family which recipe I should send, and they all said "your skinny" cake. I never knew a name for it, but it was sheet cake and my children and their friends always asked if it was a skinny cake or fat brownies, so hence the name.*

**Esther Brunotte**
**(Mitchellville, Iowa)**

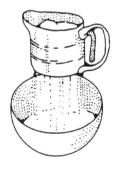

# Grocer On Main Street

Back in the days when a grocery store
enticed as a grocery store could,
The aroma of coffee beans just ground,
made the atmosphere homey and good,
And the vinegary tang of the pickle barrel
co-mingled with freshly cut cheese,
you could help yourself to crackers near by
for the grocer was anxious to please.
The old wood stove was encircled with those
who came to loaf and to chat,
You traded your eggs, and the grocer, you knew,
would throw liver in just for the cat (also dog
bones)
Flour was sold by the 100 pound sack,
sugar sold that way too
You could buy cornmeal for mush or cornbread
in the amount that suited you.
In season a bunch of bananas hung
in the window of the store
The grocer would cut off just one for you
or perhaps a dozen or more.
Licorice string and peppermint sticks
you could buy for only a penny,
a plug of tobaccy you could get for a dime,
cigarettes, there weren't any.
A delivery horse was tied out front
hitched to a wagon or sled,
sometimes the order would be a full load,
sometimes just a spool of thread.
From 7 a.m. until 9 at night the
store was open for trade (until midnight two
nights a week). Nothing was packaged
and the customers watched while the
grocer counted or weighed,
A few paid cash but many said charge,
some accounts were good, some were bad,
But we made a good living, I ought to know
for the grocer was my Dad.

Mary Marmon

*(Continued on Next Page)*

## (Grocer On Main Street - Continued)

*Mary lived her entire life in the small town of Mitchellville, 15 miles east of Des Moines. She was still publishing poetry when she was over 100 years old. The poem well describes the store her father once had as well as the store owned and run by the Gerald (Red) and Esther Brunottes from 1939-1968.*

## FOOD SPECIALS FOR SPRING APPETITES

### PRICES FOR FRIDAY and SATURDAY

| | | |
|---|---|---|
| Maxwell House Coffee | lb | 43¢ |
| Burch Saltine Crackers | 2 lb box | 39¢ |
| Rock Candy Syrup | 56 oz jar | $1³⁹ |
| WHOLE PEELED SPICED PEACHES | No. 10 can | 49¢ |
| Swansdown CAKE FLOUR | | 32¢ |
| VELVEETA CHEESE | 2 lb box | 75¢ |
| Pure GROUND BEEF | lb | 29¢ |
| SLAB BACON | lb | 43¢ |
| CRISP RED RADISHES | 4 bunches | 10¢ |
| Plastic CLOTHES PINS | doz | 19¢ |

OPAL FOODS
**Farmers Exchange Store**
Quality MEATS and GROCERIES
PHONE 3691 Gerald Brunotte, prop. MITCHELLVILLE, IA.

# Brunotte's General Store
# Mitchellville, Iowa

*By: Esther Brunotte*

As to our general store, there is a vast difference between the old century stores and the supermarkets of today.

65 years ago stores sold a variety of things, from groceries to shoes, overshoes, yard goods, novelties, even kerosene, since there was no rural electricity then, and people used kerosene lamps. During the hot summer months people used kerosene stoves when it was too hot to heat up the old coal or wood range for baking and getting meals.

There were no packaged meats. Even cookies had to be weighed out. There were no cake mixes or other packaged breads etc. There were no frozen foods except ice cream, and that was sold in ice cream stores. Lunch meats had to be sliced, wieners were in a long string, all candy weighed out. Our store had no furnace nor indoor plumbing except water, only a heating stove in one end that was usually surrounded with men playing checkers or just visiting. We sold long underwear for winter wear and men's B.V.D.'s for summer. That reminds me of an old Irishman that lived here in town with his mother. Every fall he came in and wanted his long underwear, as he was going to walk the three miles to the Skunk River to take his bath (also bought a cake of soap). Then in the spring he came in for his B.V.D.'s, the long underwear having been worn all winter. He'd never taken it off. One year he came back in the spring after his trek to the river and told us to put the B.V.D.'s back on the shelf, the water was too cold to bathe in so he'd come back in a few weeks to get them when the water warmed up.

Most people charged their groceries until pay day, and some farmers paid theirs once a year when they sold crops or livestock. I remember William and Bessie Van Dyke. They were wonderful people. They lived in Mitchellville, close to our store. When my oldest son went to collect for his paper route, Bessie Van Dyke always had cookies for him. His favorite was a Spice Dutch cookie that I still make using her recipe, just like the Dutch windmills.

# Personal Thoughts From The Editor

*By: Diana Neff*

I should know about William and Bessie Van Dyke because they were my grandparents. Noone ever left their house without some of their Dutch cookies, cake or pie. Grandma and Grandpa lived in a huge house in downtown Mitchellville, where they moved after leaving the farm I grew up on. I remember a large flower garden of delphiniums out back, an even larger vegetable garden, and a gorgeous patch of Virginia bluebells that always bloomed just in time for my May Day basket. On the other side stood a mulberry tree that was always leaving its permanent stains on something. Outside the main door were the huge orange poppies that divided the Van Dykes from the Clarks. Mostly though, I remember the white circular fence surrounding the goldfish pond in the yard, and grandpa lifting me up so I could watch.

I also remember the first time grandpa took me into Red Brunotte's general store in downtown Mitchellville. I was only three years old at the time. Just as special were my Saturday mornings when grandpa came by in his green Fraser and picked me up so we could go for our ride together. Even though grandpa passed away when I was only five, I have some very fond memories from the times we shared.

# Hot Milk Sponge Cake

2 eggs
1 cup sugar
1 cup flour
1 teaspoon baking powder
½ teaspoon salt

½ cup milk (heat with 2
   tablespoons butter)
1 teaspoon flavoring (your
   choice)

Cream eggs and sugar. Combine flour, baking powder and salt in a separate bowl. Add flour mixture to creamed ingredients. Mix in milk and butter. Add flavoring. Pour into a greased and floured 8x8-inch baking dish. Bake in a 350⁰ oven for 30 minutes. Serve warm with fruit.

Teresa Behal
(Davenport, Iowa)

# Tin Wedding Cake
*(1880's)*

Rub one cup of butter and 3 cups of sugar to a cream; add one cup of milk, 4 cups of flour, 5 eggs, 1 teaspoonful of cream of tartar, ½ teaspoonful of soda, ¼ pound of citron.

Moderate oven (It doesn't give the time. I guess you just watch it rise!). Makes 2 loaves.

*In the 1880's people in the Midwest used to give a gift of tin to those celebrating their 10th wedding anniversary. Sometimes it was an ornament, little pair of shoes or boots; some sort of a trinket. As long as it was made out of tin.*

Penelope Miller
(Princeton, Iowa)

# Surprise Cake

Bake a white cake. I usually use a box mix or use your favorite white cake from scratch.

**TOP WITH THE FOLLOWING:** **PINEAPPLE SAUCE:**
1 cup pineapple, including ¼ cup sugar
   liquid (crushed pineapple) 2-3 tablespoons cornstarch

Combine all ingredients in a small saucepan. Cook on high, stirring constantly until thick. Cool. Spread on cool white cake and frost with favorite white 7-minute boiled frosting.

**NEVER FAIL FROSTING:**
1 cup white sugar ¼ teaspoon salt
½ teaspoon cream of tartar 3 tablespoons cold water
2 egg whites

Combine all frosting ingredients in the top section of double boiler. Bring water to boil in bottom section of double boiler. Place top section in water and immediately beat the ingredients with an electric beater while the ingredients begin cooking. Beat until the frosting is fluffy and holds its shape. Remove the top section from over the water. Let set to cool slightly. Add 1 teaspoon vanilla. Fold in the vanilla. Spread frosting over the cooled cake with the sauce added. Spread frosting over the cooled cake with the sauce added. Best if eaten within 4 hours as the pineapple sauce will dissolve the frosting, but, it is still good!

*This dessert is considered an alternative to the normal birthday cake for our family. Our three children have all their birthdays within a two week period, so this is the cake the last child wanted for his birthday. These recipes are from the old community cookbook of 1948 so it has been tested and tried for many years.*

*One of the most interesting stories in regards to this cake is it really looks good on someone's face as throwing a pie at someone!*

**Donna Furrow**
**(Eldridge, Iowa)**

388

# War Cake
*(Low Calorie)*

| | |
|---|---|
| 1 cup raisins | 2 cups flour |
| 2 cups water | 1½ teaspoons soda |
| 2 tablespoons shortening | 1 teaspoon cinnamon |
| 1 cup sugar | 1 teaspoon nutmeg |

Cook and simmer raisins and water until 1 cup of liquid remains. Set aside to cool. Cream shortening and sugar. Add cooled liquid and raisins. Add flour, soda and spices. Beat until well blended. Bake in 8-inch square pan at 325⁰ for 30-40 minutes. (Approximately 182 calories for a 2x2⅔-inch piece.) Drizzle powdered sugar frosting over cake while it's warm.

## Grandma's War Cake

I can smell it now. Mixed in with the aromas of baking are the memories of Grandma, Grandpa, Aunts, Uncles and Cousins. We lived in a wonderful little town in Iowa--Atlantic.

Grandfather and Dad both worked for the Rock-Island Railroad. I will never forget my father's news that our family would have to transfer to the BIG city of Des Moines. What a heart breaker for an eight year old. It's good that children are resilient.

My heart stayed in Atlantic for many years. Times were very different then. For visits back to my Grandparents my father would put me on the train, tell the Conductor to take good care of me, and I would be off!

I can remember listening to the clackety clack of the big steel wheels, watching the farm homes whiz past and humming my favorite song, Sentimental Journey. For I was going "Home."

Grandpa was at the station waiting for me and we would walk from the depot, through the town, past the movie theater and the Library and down to Cedar Street. Grandma was at the door with a smile, a kiss and a hug.

Then to the good stuff! A warm piece of Grandma's War Cake and a glass of milk. So much was rationed during World War II, but we as children never felt denied a thing!

Delores O'Donnell
(Des Moines, Iowa)

# Mrs. Hubbell's Cupcakes

*(Reprinted from "Recipes and Recollections From Terrace Hill," of which Mrs. Chris Branstad was editor-in-chief, and with permission of the Terrace Hill Society.)*

½ cup butter (not margarine)
⅔ cup sugar
1¼ cups cake flour
1½ teaspoons baking powder
1/8 teaspoon salt
½ cup skim milk

3 egg whites
⅓ cup sugar
½ teaspoon vanilla
Chocolate frosting
Chopped pecans

In a large mixing bowl, cream the butter and the ⅔ cup sugar. Sift flour, baking powder, and salt together. Add alternately with milk. In a large mixer bowl, beat egg whites with the ⅓ cup sugar and vanilla until stiff. Fold egg whites into batter. Spoon into paper-lined 1¾-inch muffin pans, filling about two-thirds full. Bake in a 350⁰ oven for 12 to 15 minutes. Cool and frost with chocolate frosting. Sprinkle pecans on top. Makes about 40 cupcakes.

*These "little cookies" were a necessity when Anna Hubbell's great-grandchildren came to visit at Terrace Hill, which originally was the Hubbell mansion.*

# Dutch Apple Pie

9-inch unbaked pastry shell
5-6 tart apples (sliced)
¾ cup sugar
1 teaspoon cinnamon

⅔ cup flour
½ cup brown sugar
⅓ cup margarine

Preheat oven to 425°F. Combine apples, sugar and cinnamon and place in pie shell. Mix flour, brown sugar and margarine until crumbly. Sprinkle over apples and bake 15 minutes. Reduce heat to 375°F and bake 35 minutes more.

**Shirely Weller**
**(Knoxville, Iowa)**

# Cheesecake Pie

CRUST: Combine ¾ cup graham cracker crumbs, ¼ cup sugar, and ¼ cup melted margarine. Press into bottom and sides of 9-inch pie pan and chill in refrigerator for one hour.

1 (8 ounce) package cream cheese
1 cup (8 ounce) cottage cheese
½ cup Sue Bee Honey
2 eggs
2 tablespoons flour

½ teaspoon salt
1 tablespoon grated lemon rind
1 tablespoon lemon juice
1 teaspoon vanilla
Dash nutmeg

Beat cottage and cream cheese until smooth. Add all other ingredients and mix well. Pour into crumb-lined pan, and bake in a 350° oven for 30-35 minutes or until silver knife inserted in center comes clean. Top with blueberry or cherry pie filling.

**Sioux Honey Association**

# French Apple Pie

**Standard pastry crust for 9-inch one-crust pie:**

| | |
|---|---|
| 1 cup flour | 2-3 tablespoons cold water |
| ½ teaspoon salt | ⅓ cup plus 1 tablespoon Crisco |

Measure flour and salt into bowl. Cut in shortening. Sprinkle in water. Gather dough into ball. Shape into flattened round on waxed paper. Cover with waxed paper and roll out. Place into pie dish and put into freezer until ready to add pie filling.

**APPLE PIE:**

| | |
|---|---|
| ¾ cup sugar | 6 cups thinly sliced tart |
| ¼ cup flour | apples (McIntosh or |
| ½ teaspoon nutmeg | Jonathan are good as |
| ½ teaspoon cinnamon | pie apples) |

Stir together sugar, flour, nutmeg, cinnamon; mix with apples. Turn into crust and cover with crumb topping.

Crumb topping for French Apple Pie: Mix 1 cup flour, ½ cup firm butter or margarine and ½ cup brown sugar (packed) until crumbly. Bake 50 minutes at 425⁰. Cover topping with aluminum foil last 10 minutes of baking so top doesn't get too brown. Serve warm.

*We live close to an apple orchard. Every fall my three girls and I would pick apples for eating and cooking. We have an antique apple peeler that they would take turns using to peel each apple. The girls are now teenagers but have fond memories of our fall apple picking trips.*

**Mary Giesler
(Urbandale, Iowa)**

392

# Chocolate Pie

⅔ cup plus ½ cup sugar
3 tablespoons cornstarch
2 tablespoons flour
Pinch of salt

3 cups milk
4 egg yolks
5 tablespoons cocoa
1 teaspoon vanilla

Mix cornstarch, sugar, flour, salt and cocoa in pan. Add 2½ cups milk and vanilla. Cook to hot on medium heat. Add yolks and ½ cup milk and bring to a boil. Pour into a prepared pie shell and chill.

*This is a recipe from a restaurant where an aunt of mine worked.*

**Susan Severs**
**(Princeton, Iowa)**


# Easy Coconut Pie
*(around 100 years old)*

1½ cups sugar
½ cup butter

Pinch of salt
3 eggs

Melt butter, add sugar and salt. Then add beaten eggs.

**ADD TO ABOVE:**
1 tablespoon vinegar
1 teaspoon vanilla

1 cup shredded coconut

Bake 1 hour at 325⁰.

**Joyce Brockhouse**
**(Princeton, Iowa)**

393

# Custard Pie
*(Ellen Steamboat Recipe)*

4 eggs (slightly beaten)  2 cups milk
½ cup plus 1 tablespoon  Flavoring
  sugar
2 tablespoons flour

Butter a 9-inch pie pan - use plenty of butter. Bake 1 hour at 300⁰. Makes its own crust. Sprinkle nutmeg on top before baking.

*Rose Peters was my grandmother and cook on the Ellen Steamboat. She used to get up at 4:00 every morning to begin baking pies for the crew.*

**Rose Peters, Cook - Ellen Steamboat**
**(Submitted by: Lois Havenhill, Princeton, Iowa)**

# Graham Pie
*(1860's recipe for graham pie)*

For a healthful pie take 2 eggs, ⅔ cup of sugar, 2 teacups full of sweet skimmed milk, a teaspoon of salt, and a pint of graham flour. Beat the ingredients together, pour in a deep dish, and bake. The flour settles to the bottom and makes a crust.

**Penelope Miller**
**(Princeton, Iowa)**

# French Silk Pie

2 packages of instant French vanilla pudding
2 packages of instant chocolate pudding
1 package of instant butter pecan pudding
5 cups of milk

5 cups of vanilla ice cream
Whipped cream
Hershey chocolate bar (shaved)
Graham cracker crust in 9x13-inch pan

Combine 1 package of vanilla pudding, 2 packages of chocolate pudding, 3 cups of ice cream and 3 cups of milk. Beat until smooth. Pour over graham cracker crust and chill until set. Combine 1 package of vanilla pudding, 1 package of butter pecan pudding, 2 cups of ice cream and 2 cups of milk. Mix and spread over first layer and chill. Once set, spread layer of whipped cream over top and then top shaved Hershey chocolate bar shavings over whipped cream.

**(US Representative Jim Nussle of Iowa)**

Dear Diana:

Thank you for writing me to request a family recipe for your 1996 Iowa Sesquicentennial: 150 years of statehood, cookbook. I was honored to receive your letter and am pleased to provide you with one of my favorite recipes. Please find it enclosed.

Diana, thank you for including me in your cookbook. I hope that you enjoy the Sesquicentennial planning.

Good luck and best wishes.

Sincerely,
Jim Nussle
Member of Congress

# Dreamy Ice Cream Pie

1 cup cornflake crumbs
2 tablespoons sugar
⅓ cup butter (melted)
1 cup milk or half and half
1½ packages of the 3¾ ounce
    package vanilla instant
    pudding mix

1 pint vanilla ice cream
    (slightly softened)
1½ cups crushed pineapple
    (drained)
½ cup pineapple juice
1 tablespoon cornstarch

Blend crumbs, sugar and butter together and press into 9-inch pie shell. Chill. Pour milk into mixing bowl. Add pudding mix and ice cream. Beat slowly until well blended (1 to 2 minutes). Pour into crust. Refrigerate while making glaze. Drain pineapple. Measure syrup. Add the syrup to cornstarch gradually. Stir to keep mixture smooth. Cook over low heat stirring constantly until thickened and clear. Add pineapple and cool. Spoon over pie and chill one hour.

**Marguerite Vens**
**(Davenport, Iowa)**

# Lemon Pie
*(Ellen Steamboat Recipe)*

1⅓ cups sugar
4 tablespoons cornstarch
½ teaspoon salt

2 cups boiling water
3 egg yolks (beaten)
Rind and juice of 1 lemon

Blend sugar, cornstarch and salt. Stir in boiling water, cook until clear. Stir in egg yolks and cook 2 minutes. Stir in lemon rind and juice. Pour mixture into baked and cooled pie shell. Frost with meringue. Bake 10 to 15 minutes at 375° until meringue is lightly brown.

**Rose Peters, Cook - Ellen Steamboat**
**(Submitted by: Lois Havenhill, Princeton, Iowa)**

# Mincemeat for Pies

*(over 100 years old)*

Boil a beef roast until done.

| | |
|---|---|
| 3 cups finely shredded beef | 1½ teaspoons salt |
| 5 cups apples (cut up) | 1½ teaspoons cinnamon |
| 2 cups raisins | 1½ teaspoons nutmeg |
| 4½ cups sugar | 1½ teaspoons allspice |
| 1½ cups cider vinegar | 1½ teaspoons cloves |
| 1 cup molasses | |

Cook 1 hour. Just before done, add ¼ cup flour, mixed with a little cold water.

*All my recipes included are around 100 years old. They are from my ancestors, the Schmalz family. Christian and Anna Schmalz homesteaded next door to Earl and me. They had 4 daughters and one son (my grandfather). One of the daughters and her husband built and ran the hotel in Princeton. Their name is on the front, above the door where the barber shop is, POPE. Another daughter was an ardent seamstress with a shop next to the McGinnis Funeral Home on Front Street in Princeton. My grandfather Andrew was instrumental in founding the Farmer's Saving Bank of which he was president as well as a successful farmer. My grandparents, Andrew and Alvena Schmalz did a lot of entertaining. Therefore, I learned at an early age the pride of serving tasty dishes with the added touch of love to each recipe.*

**Joyce Brockhouse**
**(Princeton, Iowa)**

# Green Tomato Mincemeat

| | |
|---|---|
| 1 peck green tomatoes | Juice of 2 lemons |
| 4 pounds sugar | 1 teaspoon cloves |
| 2 pounds raisins | 1 teaspoon cinnamon |
| 1 pound fat salt pork | 1 teaspoon nutmeg |
| ¾ cup vinegar | Boiling water |

Wash tomatoes. Put them through a food chopper, using the coarse knife. Pour enough boiling water over them to just come to top. Let cool. Drain. Again cover with boiling water. Let cool, and drain throughly. Chop raisins. Cut salt pork into small pieces. In large preserving kettle put tomatoes and all other ingredients. Cook slowly until well done. This will keep indefinitely. OPTION: Omit pork and dot filling with bits of butter when making a pie.

*This is from a book my mother made when she was first married (in 1906), from recipes printed in Capper's Weekly and The Des Moines Register. Green Tomato Mincemeat was usually made in late summer or early fall as the tomatoes began to diminish and frost threatened. Above quantities are for a large family and could be reduced for average use.*

**Hubert W. Wilson**

# Never Fail Meringue

Put 1 tablespoon cornstarch in just enough water to moisten. Mix and add ½ cup of boiling water. Boil until clear. Then cool. Beat 3 egg whites until stiff. Gradually add 6 tablespoons sugar and a pinch of salt. Beat in cornstarch mixture until it peaks well. Bake at 350⁰ until brown.

**Bessie Sierk**
**(Bettendorf, Iowa)**

# Party Pie
*(around 100 years old)*

**MERINGUE CRUST:**

4 egg whites
½ teaspoon cream of tartar
1/8 teaspoon salt

1 cup sugar
½ teaspoon vanilla

Beat egg whites until thick. Add the rest of ingredients. Put in well buttered pie tin. Bake 1 hour at 275⁰. Cool.

FILLING: 4 egg yolks, ½ cup sugar, pinch of salt, 2 tablespoons lemon juice, 1 grated lemon rind, ½ cup drained crushed pineapple. Cook and stir until thick. Spread on meringue crust. Top with ¾ cream (whip) and mix 2 tablespoons sugar, ½ teaspoon vanilla and some coconut. Set in refrigerator for 24 hours.

Joyce Brockhouse
(Princeton, Iowa)

# Peanut Butter Cream Pie

8 ounces cream cheese at
   room temperature
¾ cup confectioners sugar
½ cup crunchy peanut butter
2 tablespoons milk

4 cups heavy cream whipped
   until thick (divided use)
1 graham cracker crust
½ cup chocolate shavings and
   curls (or use chocolate
   chips)

Using an electric mixer, beat the cream cheese with the confectioner's sugar until creamy. Add the peanut butter and milk; beat well. Fold half the whipped cream into the peanut butter mixture and spoon into the crust, smoothing the top. Refrigerate for at least 1 hour until set. To serve, spoon some of the remaining whipped cream over each wedge of pie. Top with 1 tablespoon chocolate curls or chips. Makes 8 servings.

Glenn Maynard
(Princeton, Iowa)

399

# Peach Custard Pie
### (Ellen Steamboat Recipe)

1 unbaked 9-inch pie shell
1 cup sugar
1/8 teaspoon salt
1 tablespoon flour

⅓ cup cream
½ cup milk
3 egg yolks (slightly beaten)
4 large ripe peaches (peeled and thinly sliced)

Combine sugar, salt and flour. Beat egg yolks slightly. Add cream and milk, then stir in flour-sugar mixture, blending until smooth. Place peach slices over bottom of dough lined pan, pour custard mixture over peaches. Bake in 450⁰ oven 12-15 minutes to lightly brown the crust; reduce heat to 350⁰ and bake for 35 minutes longer. Remove pie from oven and frost with meringue; and put back in oven and brown.

**MERINGUE:**
3 egg whites
1/8 teaspoon salt

6 tablespoons sugar

Beat egg whites until frothy, add salt. Gradually add sugar. Continue beating until stiff and glossy.

**Rose Peters, grandmother of Lois Havenhill
(Submitted by: Lois Havenhill)**

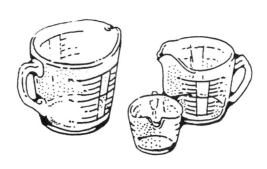

# Pilgrim Pie

2 eggs (slightly beaten)
1 (16 ounces) can of pumpkin
  or 2 cups of cooked,
  mashed pumpkin
¾ cup Sue Bee Honey
½ teaspoon salt

1 teaspoon cinnamon
½ teaspoon ginger
1/8 teaspoon cloves
1 cup evaporated milk
1 (9-inch) unbaked pastry
  shell

Prepare single pastry for 9-inch pie pan. In a bowl, beat eggs slightly, and then mix in the remaining ingredients. Pour into pastry-lined pie pan and bake at 425° for 15 minutes. Reduce oven temperature to 350° and bake 45 minutes longer or until pie is set or silver knife inserted in center comes out clean. Top with whipped cream.

**Sioux Honey Association**

# Prune Pie

Line deep pie dish with rich pastry. Cover bottom with stewed pitted prunes (cooked).

**BEAT TOGETHER:**
1 beaten egg
½ cup sugar
½ cup milk

½ cup cream
Pinch of nutmeg

Pour mixture over top of prunes. Bake without upper crust at 325°-350° (watch closely), like a custard pie. I stick a knife in the center to see if it is done.

**Regina Portz
(Princeton, Iowa)**

# Heavenly Pumpkin Pie

| | |
|---|---|
| 1 unbaked 9-inch pastry shell | ¼ cup sugar |
| 1 (8 ounce) cream cheese (softened) | 1 teaspoon cinnamon |
| ¼ cup sugar | ¼ teaspoon salt |
| ½ teaspoon vanilla | ¼ teaspoon nutmeg |
| 1 egg | ½ cup chopped pecans |
| 1½ cups pumpkin | 2 tablespoons oleo (softened) |
| 1 cup evaporated milk | 2 tablespoons flour and |
| 2 beaten eggs | brown sugar |
| ¼ cup brown sugar | |

Beat together the ¼ cup sugar, vanilla and egg until smooth. Chill for 30 minutes. Turn into prepared pie shell. Combine pumpkin, milk, the 2 eggs and ¼ cup brown and white sugars, cinnamon, salt and nutmeg. Carefully pour over cream cheese mixture. Cover edge of pie with foil. Bake in 350° oven for 25 minutes. Remove foil and bake 25 minutes more. Combine pecans, oleo, flour and 2 tablespoons brown sugar. Sprinkle over pie and bake for an additional 10-15 minutes or until knife inserted in center of pie comes out clean. Cool on wire rack.

*A prize winner in Anamosa's 1994 Pumpkinfest recipe contest.*

**Jeanne Stump**
**(Thanks also to: Sarah Schoon, Executive Director,**
**Anamosa Chamber of Commerce)**

# Rhubarb Cream Pie

One 9-inch plain pastry
3 cups fresh rhubarb
1½ cups sugar
½ teaspoon nutmeg

1 tablespoon butter
2 beaten eggs
3 tablespoons flour

Line pastry shell with rhubarb. Blend together in a bowl the sugar, flour, nutmeg, butter, and eggs. Pour over rhubarb. Top with lattice pastry if desired. Bake at 450⁰ for 10 minutes. Then reduce to 325⁰ and bake 45 to 60 minutes.

**Billie Turley**
**(Mount Pleasant, Iowa)**

# Mother's Fresh Rhubarb Pie

3 heaping cups fresh rhubarb
1½ cups sugar
1/8 teaspoon salt
2 eggs

1 tablespoon butter
Pastry for 2 crust 9-inch pie
Cinnamon (or nutmeg)

Mix the first 5 ingredients together and let stand while preparing pastry. Put rhubarb mixture in pastry shell and sprinkle with cinnamon. Cover with a lattice of pastry. Bake at 400⁰ for 1 hour. May be frozen but then increase baking time approximately 10 minutes. Makes 6 servings.

**Bea (Mrs. Neal) Smith**

403

# Rhubarb Meringue Pie
### *(Ellen Steamboat Recipe)*

| | |
|---|---|
| 2 tablespoons butter | 2 tablespooons cornstarch |
| 1½ cups sugar | Pinch of salt |
| 2 cups rhubarb (cut fine) | ¼ cup light cream |
| 2 eggs | 1 baked pie crust (8-inch) |

Melt butter in heavy pan. Add 1 cup sugar and rhubarb. Cook slowly until rhubarb is done. Set aside. Beat egg yolks, add ½ cup sugar, cornstarch, salt and light cream; mix well. Stir this mixture into cooked rhubarb and cook until thick; cool. Pour filling over baked pie shell.

To prepare meringue: Beat 2 egg whites until frothy, gradually beating in 4 tablespoons sugar, a little at a time. Continue beating until sugar is dissolved and meringue is glossy and stiff. Bake meringue until golden brown in 450⁰ oven for 5-8 minutes.

**Rose Peters, Cook - Ellen Steamboat**
**(Submitted by: Lois Havenhill, Princeton, Iowa)**

# Fresh Strawberry Pie

| | |
|---|---|
| 1 cup sugar | 1 package (3 ounces) |
| 2 tablespoons cornstarch | Strawberry Jello |
| 1¾ cups cold water | 1 teaspoon vanilla |
| ¼ teaspoon salt | 1 quart fresh strawberries |
| Few drops red food color | |

Make 1 pie shell and bake. Cook first four ingredients until thick and clear. Add food color, then dry Jello, and stir until dissolved. Add vanilla. Chill until partially set, add strawberries and let finish setting. Top with whipped topping. Garnish with whole sugar coated strawberries.

*This is a pretty pie.*

**Thelma Smith**
**(Mitchellville, Iowa)**

404

# Sweet Potato Pie

3 large baked sweet potatoes
  (about 2 cups)
¼ cup butter (melted)
¾ cup sugar
½ teaspoon salt
1 teaspoon vanilla extract

½ teaspoon lemon extract
2 eggs (separated)
1 cup half and half or
  evaporated milk
1 9-inch unbaked pie shell
  (deep dish)

Bake potatoes at 400⁰ until tender, cool; remove skins. Mash or whip potatoes in large mixing bowl. Add butter, sugar, salt and extracts. Set aside. In small bowl, beat egg yolks slightly, add to potato mixture with milk/cream. Set aside. Whip egg whites until soft peaks form. Fold gently into potato mixture. Pour into pie shell. Bake at 425⁰ for 15 minutes. Reduce temperature to 350⁰, bake 25-30 minutes more until center test is done.

**Glenn Maynard**
**(Princeton, Iowa)**

# Baily Vinegar Pie

1½ cups granulated sugar
3 tablespoons cornstarch
2 tablespoons flour
1 teaspoon cinnamon
Pinch of salt

Scant ½ cup cider vinegar
2½ cups boiling water
1 tablespoon butter
9-inch baked crust
Meringue (if desired)

Mix the dry ingredients and add the vinegar. Stir this mixture slowly into the water. Mix until thickened and stir in the butter. Cool about 10 minutes, then pour the filling into the crust. If meringue is used prepare it, spread on pie and brown in a 350⁰ oven approximately 15 minutes.

*This pie was a tradition on Thanksgiving or Christmas at my Grandma Baily's house. Don't let the name put you off. It is good-more sweet than sour and something like a lemon pie.*

**Mamye English**
**(Also thanks to: Sarah Schoon)**

# Strawberry Pie

| | |
|---|---|
| 1 baked, cooled pastry shell 9-inch | 4 tablespoons cornstarch |
| 1 quart fresh strawberries | 1 cup water |
| 1 cup sugar | 1 cup whipped cream |
| ¼ teaspoon salt | 2 tablespoons powdered sugar |

Pick out the 6 prettiest berries and save them for the top. Divide the remainder in half. Crush ½ of the berries and combine with sugar, salt, cornstarch and water. Cook over direct heat until thick and clear, stirring constantly. (A few drops of red food coloring can be added). Place the remaining berries in the baked pie shell. Pour the cooked mixture over the berries; chill. Garnish with the sweetened whipped cream and top with the six reserved berries.

*An Iowa weekend not to miss is the Strawberry Days Celebration held the second weekend in June, an event begun years ago as a show of appreciation from the chamber of commerce to the surrounding community. Little Miss Strawberry is crowned Saturday noon with a parade following. On Sunday, after a chicken barbecue, the chamber serves free strawberries and ice cream.*

**Charlotte Fliehler**
**(Secretary, Chamber of Commerce, Strawberry Point, Iowa)**

# My Grandmother's Shoofly Pie

This is a little of the background story of:

"My Grandmother's Shoofly Pie"

On September 18, 1878, Rebecca Burkhard became the bride of Jacob G. Snyder at Freeport, Illinois. A few days later they loaded their possessions into a crowded wagon and started west over the prairies, arriving at Ayr, Nebraska, a month later. This recipe was among her most treasured recipes.

While the original read something like this:
-Butter the size of a large egg
-A heaping coffee cup of flour
-A teacup of brown sugar
Work these together to make the crumbly mixture.

For the liquid part:
Mix well together - not quite a cup of molasses, a spec of salt, a pinch of nutmeg, a couple dashes of cinnamon and a hint of ginger and cloves. Now add almost a cup of boiling water. Stir.

Line pie tin with pastry made of:
Lard - the size of a couple large hen eggs
Boiling Water - not so much as the lard, quite a good pinch of salt and flour to make a soft dough.

Now layer the crumb mixture and the liquid part alternately in the un-baked pie shell. Begin and end with a crumb layer.

Bake in a hot oven a short while and let it cool down and bake a longer spell until it is all set up.

The recipe on the next page is what my mother, daughter of Jacob G. and Rebecca Burkhard Snyder, worked out in more definite measurements and had the best luck with.

*(Continued on Next Page)*

# My Grandmother's Shoofly Pie

**HOT WATER PIE CRUST:**

| | |
|---|---|
| ½ cup lard | 2 cups flour |
| ⅓ cup boiling water | ½ teaspoon salt |

Put lard and salt in bowl; add boiling water, blend with wire whip or fork until creamy. Add the 2 cups flour, mix with fork to make dough. Chill in refrigerator an hour or so for easier handling when rolling it out. Makes 2 large pie shells.

Line the pan with half of the above pastry.

**For the liquid part:**

| | |
|---|---|
| ¾ cup hot water | ¾ cup molasses |
| ¾ teaspoon baking soda | ¼ teaspoon salt |
| 1/8 teaspoon nutmeg | ¼ teaspoon cinnamon |
| 1/8 teaspoon cloves | ¼ teaspoon ginger |

Mix together well, adding the hot water last.

Into the unbaked pie shell, combine the crumbs and liquid in alternate layers, using crumbs on bottom and top. Bake 15 minutes at 450°, reduce temperature to 350° and bake 10 minutes longer. "Don't eat yourself full, there's pie back yet."

**Mrs. Melvin Dobbins
(Wilton, Iowa)**

408

# Triple Layer Party Pie

1 (4-serving) package JELL-O
Sugar Free Instant
Butterscotch Pudding Mix
1⅓ cups Carnation Nonfat
Dry Milk Powder
2½ cups water
1 (6 ounce) Keebler Chocolate
Crumb Pie Crust

1 (4-serving) package JELL-O
Sugar Free Instant
Chocolate Pudding Mix
½ cup Cool Whip Lite
2 tablespoons (½ ounce)
chopped pecans
1 tablespoon (¼ ounce) mini
chocolate chips

In medium bowl, combine dry butterscotch pudding mix, ⅔ cup dry milk powder, and 1¼ cups water. Mix well using wire whisk. Pour into pie crust. In same medium bowl, combine dry chocolate pudding mix, remaining ⅔ cup dry milk powder, and remaining 1¼ cups water. Mix well using a wire whisk. Pour chocolate mixture evenly over butterscotch layer. Refrigerate 5 minutes. Evenly spread Cool Whip Lite over chocolate layer. Sprinkle pecans and mini chocolate chips evenly over top. Refrigerate at least 1 hour. Cut into 8 servings. Each serving equals: HE: ½ bread, ½ skim milk, ¼ fat, 1 slider, 8 optional calories 215 calories, 7 grams fat, 6 grams protein, 32 milligrams carbohydrate, 487 milligrams sodium, 1 gram fiber. DIABETIC: 2 starch, 1 fat, ½ skim milk

JoAnna Lund
Editor and Publisher, Healthy Exchanges Newsletter
(DeWitt, Iowa)

# Pie Crust

2 cups flour
1 teaspoon salt

¾ cup Crisco
5 tablespoons cold water

Mix flour and salt. Cut in Crisco until fine, then add 5 tablespoons water to form ball. Put into a 9 or 10-inch pie pan.

Mrs. Rainsford A. Brown, Jr.
(Bettendorf, Iowa)

# Oil Pie Crust

1½ cups flour
1 teaspoon salt

½ cup oil
¼ cup milk

Mix flour and salt. Then add oil and milk to form ball. Roll between wax paper. Put into a 9-inch pie shell.

Mrs. Rainsford A. Brown, Jr.
(Bettendorf, Iowa)

# Press In Pie Crust

IN 9-INCH PIE PAN: Mix
1½ cups flour
1 teaspoon salt

½ cup oil
2 tablespoons milk

After mixing press on the bottom and sides.

Mrs Rainsford A. Brown, Jr.
(Bettendorf, Iowa)

# Christmas Plum Pudding

*(Reprinted with permission from "Dining With The Hoover Family: A Collection of Reminiscences and Recipes by Dale C. Mayer.)*

*This is an old English recipe from the Minthorn side of Herbert Hoover's family.*

*It is supposed to be made on Advent Sunday (4 Sundays before Christmas.) It is a terrific job to mix, so entice the whole family to help by telling each he can make a wish on the 25th stroke.*

2 ground nutmegs
½ pound chopped almonds
2 pounds raisins
2 cups milk
2 pounds currants
12 eggs
2 cups brandy
2 pounds brown sugar

4 cups flour
2 pounds suet, chopped fine
1 quart bread crumbs (about
  2 loaves)
2 pounds prunes, soaked
  and ground
2 pounds mixed candied peel

Mix all ingredients together well and let stand in a covered bowl overnight. This makes a lot of puddings so you can use them for gifts. Don't forget to put a shiny dime in each one. To cook, fill molds (or tin cans) ⅔ full and put in a large steamer on a rack. Fill with boiling water ⅔ of the way up outside of the molds, (or instead of molds put the puddings in cloth and tie four corners together. Set on a rack out of the water.) Cover pot and steam for 12 hours. Keep a kettle of boiling water at hand to replace water in steamer. The puddings I am going to save (they keep well over a year) or those I am giving for gifts, I chill in the refrigerator and then dunk, cloth and all, in hot paraffin. I tie a red bow around them. They make elegant gifts because who else wants to go to all the trouble of making steamed plum pudding? To serve, heat throughly, stick a sprig of holly on top, pour brandy over, light brandy and serve flaming. Or if you are like me and can't make the brandy flame, put the pudding on an inverted saucer in the platter and then pour alcohol on the platter (NOT on the pudding) and light it. Very effective. Serve with hard sauce.

**Mrs. Lou Henry Hoover**

411

# Once-A-Year Plum Pudding

| | |
|---|---|
| 1 cup bread crumbs | 1 teaspoon salt |
| 1 cup suet (finely chopped) | 1 teaspoon nutmeg |
| 1 cup sugar | 1 teaspoon baking powder |
| 1 cup milk | 1 teaspoon baking soda |
| 4 eggs (beaten) | 1 cup currants and 1 cup |
| 1 cup flour | raisins |

HARD SAUCE:

| | |
|---|---|
| 1 cup sugar | 2 tablespoons butter |
| ½ cup water | ¼ teaspoon nutmeg |
| 1 teaspoon flour | 1/8 cup brandy |

Mix all pudding ingredients and pour into greased two-quart mold. Cover tightly. Steam two and one-half hours. (I use a spaghetti steamer.) Prepare hard sauce by bringing hard sauce ingredients to boil. To flame pudding; warm one-half cup brandy in small saucepan over low heat. Ignite with match and pour over unmolded pudding. Cut into individual servings and serve with hard sauce.

*I let my butcher know ahead of time when I'll need the suet and he puts a fine piece aside for me. The suet's the ingredient responsible for the recipe's name. Serve it more than once a year and you might have to call 911 (very rich pudding, due to suet).*

**Kay Patrinos**
**(Milwaukee, Wisconsin, formerly Luxemburg, Iowa)**

# Chocolate Pudding

| | |
|---|---|
| 6 tablespoons flour | 1 tablespoon cocoa |
| 1 cup sugar | 1 quart milk |

Mix all ingredients and cook over medium heat until boiling. Pour into individual bowls and chill until set.

**Susan Severs**
**(Princeton, Iowa)**

# Sophia's Brazil Pudding

1 cup sugar
1 cup flour
1 teaspoon baking soda
½ teaspoon salt
1 teaspoon cinnamon

1 cup toasted bread crumbs
  very dry, rolled fine
*1 cup suet (ground very fine)
1 cup Brazil nuts rolled or
  chopped very fine

**WASH AND DRY:**
1 cup dark raisins
1 cup white raisins

1 cup sweet milk

*Obtainable at butcher counters

Combine first five dry ingredients, then stir in crumbs. Stir rest of ingredients. Mix well and steam well for two hours in large container. Serve with lemon sauce.

**LEMON SAUCE:**
**Mix Together:**
½ cup sugar
2 tablespoons flour

¼ teaspoon salt

**ADD:**
1 cup boiling water
1 teaspoon vanilla

½ of lemon (juice)
1 tablespoon butter

Cook very slowly until thick. Serve hot over pudding.

*My mother Sophia Banwell of Fort Dodge, made this pudding as a substitute for the usual plum pudding served, during the yuletide.*

**Mary Banwell Powers**
**(Omaha, Nebraska, formerly of Fort Dodge, Iowa)**

# Mom's Bread Pudding

1 cup bread cubes
2 tablespoons melted butter
1 egg (slightly beaten)
¼ teaspoon salt
¼ cup sugar

½ teaspoon vanilla
¼ teaspoon cinnamon
2 cups milk (scalded)
½ cup raisins

Combine sugar, salt, vanilla, butter, cinnamon and egg. Add milk slowly, stirring constantly. Add bread cubes and raisins. Mix thoroughly. Pour into well-buttered baking dish. Set in pan of warm water. Bake in moderate oven (350⁰) about 1 hour or until an inverted knife comes out clean. Cool. Serve with cream.

Jeanne Roths

# Hot Fudge Pudding

1 package dark chocolate cake
  mix (regular size)
1 cup brown sugar
¼ cup cocoa

1 cup chopped nuts
1¾ cups boiled water

Mix above ingredients together. Prepare cake mix as directed on package. Pour cake batter in greased 9x12-inch pan. Pour sugar, cocoa, nuts and boiling water mixture over top of cake batter. Bake in 350⁰ oven for 45 minutes. Serve with whipped topping.

*This recipe was popular in the early 1950's. I was teaching school in Fort Dodge at that time. Many of the young working women belonged to an organization called Business Girls. I got this recipe from a member of the group.*

Iva Bentzin
(Stillwater, Minnesota, formerly Klemme, Iowa)

## Rommegrot
### *(Norwegian Cream Pudding)*

*This traditional Norwegian Cream Pudding is everyone's favorite. Countless gallons are served at Vesterheim's Dayton House Cafe and at the museum's special events throughout the year.*

| | |
|---|---|
| 1 quart milk | ½ cup sugar |
| 1 cup half and half | ¼ cup margarine (melted) |
| 1 cup margarine | Sugar and cinnamon |
| ¾ cup flour | |

Heat milk and half and half (either on stovetop or in microwave). In a large heavy pan, melt margarine and add flour; cook 5 minutes, stirring constantly. Pour in milk and half and half; cook over low heat, stirring constantly until mixture bubbles and thickens (this can take up to 15 minutes). Stir in sugar. To serve, pour small amount of melted margarine on top and sprinkle with sugar and cinnamon. Yield: one-half gallon.

NOTE: This may be kept warm and served from a Crock-pot. Use low heat. Leftover pudding may be stored in the refrigerator and heated in the microwave.

**Vesterheim Norwegian-American Museum**

# Norwegian Rommegrot (Cream Pudding)

*Vesterheim Norwegian-American Museum tells the story of the Norwegian immigrant from his Old World roots to New World experiences. It's main complex, located in downtown Decorah, has fifteen historic buildings. In addition, there is a church and farmstead in the country.*

*(Continued on Next Page)*

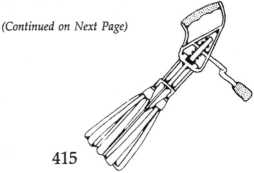

415

## (Norwegian Rommegrot (Cream Pudding)

*MAIN BUILDING: The main building of the Vesterheim complex was originally built as a luxury hotel in 1877. In 1975 it was restored to its original appearance. The building itself sets the stage for the America that the newly arrived Norwegians were to discover.*

## Ostakaka (Swedish Pudding)

1 gallon whole milk (fresh)
1 cup flour
½ cake rennet
½ cup lukewarm water
2 eggs

1¼ cups sugar
1½ cups thin cream (½ & ½)
1 tablespoon almond extract
½ teaspoon salt

Heat milk to 101° (lukewarm). Make thickening of flour with one cup of the milk. Dissolve rennet in warm water. After milk is warm, remove from stove and add thickening and rennet. Stir well. Let stand about ½ hour. During this time beat the eggs, add sugar, salt, extract and cream. Cut through the thickened milk and let stand another ½ hour. Drain off half the whey (liquid) and then add the egg mixture to the curds, which have been put into a 9x12-inch greased baking dish. Mix the egg mixture with fingers to break up the curds. Bake in 400° oven for ten minutes and then reduce to 350° for an hour or until brown on top. Serve with thickened grape juice (sweetened). It is best served warm (the pudding, that is). Serve with Spritz Cookies.

*Ostakaka is a Swedish pudding that used to be served only at Christmas time. Now there are other Swedish events celebrated in the U.S. so it is being served most any time of the year.*

Dorothy Ossian
(Stanton, Iowa)

# Rice Pudding

½ cup rice                          ½ cup water

Cook in double boiler until tender.

**ADD:**
**1 quart milk**                    **1 egg (beaten)**
**⅓ cup sugar**                     **½ cup raisins (optional)**

Mix well, chill. Serve with sugar and cinnamon.

*This dish was a favorite of my dad's. No one could make it like his mom did.*

**Susan Severs**
**(Princeton, Iowa)**

# Almond Rice Pudding

**2 cups milk**                     **¼ cup almond bits**
**¼ cup rice**                      **5 tablespoons sugar**
**1 package gelatin**               **1 teaspoon vanilla**
**1 tablespoon water**              **2 cups whipped cream**

Bring 2 cups milk to a boil in a double boiler. Add ¼ cup rice and boil until done. Add 1 package gelatin dissolved in 1 tablespoon of water, whatever it takes to soften. Add ¼ cup almond bits, 5 tablespoons sugar, and 1 teaspoon vanilla. Cool. Add 2 cups whipped cream.

*My husband is Danish. Every Christmas dinner we serve this dessert with several whole almonds dropped in it. The one or ones who find the whole almonds in their serving are not to eat them until everyone is through with dinner. You keep the whole almond in your mouth to prove that you have it. The ones who can prove they have one get a prize. One year my sister-in-law had 3 in her mouth. You try to keep visiting with the almond in your mouth. You don't want others to know you have it until the meal is finished. Drop in as many almonds as you want. I go according to how many children are present.*

**Vivian Andersen**
**(Soldier, Iowa)**

417

# Yummy Pudding

1½ cups milk
Pinch of salt
2 tablespoons butter
4 tablespoons flour

1 cup sugar
2 eggs
1 tablespoon vanilla
½ pound vanilla wafers
6 large bananas

Scald 1 cup of the milk, add salt and butter. Mix flour, sugar and the other ½ cup milk together to form a smooth batter. Add the beaten egg yolks and the scalded milk. Cook in a double boiler until thick (about 15 minutes) stirring constantly. Remove from fire, add vanilla; when cool add stiffly beaten egg whites. Cool in ice box!

(Instructions for Banana Ice Box Cake)
Have ready large dish lined with crushed vanilla wafers, then cover with a layer of bananas which have been peeled and sliced. Cover with custard. Repeat layers. Crumble some of the wafers on top. Chill 3 hours. Serve with or without whipped creme. Makes 8 large servings.

*This is a recipe my husband loved when he visited his grandparents as a boy in Sully, Iowa during the late 30's and 40's. They lived on a farm near Sully. There was no electricity, and they farmed with a team of horses.*

*I now just fix the pudding, often times doubling the recipe. My husband says "it's better than ice cream."*

*As we travel the world over, Iowa is a wonderful place in which to return. Our growing up years, education and steady place to raise our family could not be duplicated in any other state or place in this world.*

*The Indians looked across the rolling plains, and called this "Ioway", meaning this is the place. We couldn't agree more. This is the place for us too!*

**Ann Brown (Mrs. Rainsford Brown, Jr.)**
**(Bettendorf, Iowa)**

418

## Butterscotch Nut Torte

6 eggs (separated)
1½ cups sugar
1 teaspoon baking powder

2 teaspoons vanilla
2 cups graham crackers
1 cup chopped nuts

Beat egg yolks well, slowly adding sugar, the baking powder and flavoring. Mix well. Beat egg whites until they hold stiff peaks, then fold into yolk mixture. Fold in crumbs and nuts. Pour into 2 (9-inch layer pans) greased and lined with wax paper. Bake in slow oven (325⁰) 30 to 35 minutes, cool 10 minutes, then remove from pans. Frost when completely cooled.

TO FROST: Whip 2 cups heavy cream, slowly adding 3 tablespoons sugar. Spread frosting between layers and over top.

FAIR SAUCE: Add ¼ cup water to ¼ cup melted butter in saucepan. Blend in 1 cup brown sugar and 1 tablespoon flour. Add 1 egg, well beaten, ¼ cup orange juice, ½ teaspoon vanilla. Mix well, bring to boil and cool until thick. Cool thoroughly and pour over top of cake.

**Marvella Hans**
**(Ankeny, Iowa)**

## Kolacki (Polish)
*(Dessert Pastry)*

4 cups unsifted flour
½ pound butter
1 small Philadelphia Cream
   Cheese
1 teaspoon vanilla

8 heaping tablespoons sugar
½ pound Blue Bonnet
   Margarine
2 tablespoons cream

Combine flour and sugar, work in butter, margarine and cheese. Add cream and vanilla. Roll into balls. Press in the middle with palm of your hand. Fill with ½ teaspoon filling and put on ungreased cookie sheet. Preheat oven, bake at 375⁰ for 12-15 minutes. Cool and sprinkle with powdered sugar.

**Alice Totosz**

419

## Sour Cream Twists

4 cups flour
1 teaspoon salt
1 cup shortening (Crisco)
1 envelope yeast dissolved
    in ¼ cup water

1 teaspoon vanilla
2 eggs
1 cup sour cream

Sift flour and salt, cut in shortening. Soak yeast in warm water. Add vanilla. Beat 2 eggs. Mix eggs, sour cream, yeast, and vanilla, add to dry ingredients. Roll out in sugar on board (12-14 inches). Fold into thirds. Repeat 3 times adding more sugar. Cut into 1-inch strips. Sprinkle with cinnamon and sugar. Twist and put on ungreased cookie sheets. Bake at 375⁰ for 20 minutes.

*I got this recipe from a neighbor about 25 years ago. It has gone to many school events and is still one of our favorites.*

**Doris Myers**
**(Iowa City, Iowa)**

## Carrot Cake Frosting

1 small cream cheese
1 cube butter or margarine
1 box powdered sugar

1 cup nuts (optional)
1 cup coconut
1 tablespoon crushed pine-
    apple out of can for cake

If too thick use pineapple juice.

**Betty (Schneckloth) Nelson**
**(Davenport, Iowa)**

420

# Coconut Pecan Frosting

**COMBINE IN SAUCEPAN:**

| | |
|---|---|
| 1 cup evaporated milk or half and half | 3 eggs |
| | ¼ pound butter |
| 1 cup sugar | 1 teaspoon vanilla |

Cook over medium heat 12 minutes, stirring constantly until mixture thickens. Add one (3½ ounce) can flake coconut and 1 cup chopped pecans. Beat until cool and of spreading consistency. Use these quantities if two cakes are made from above recipe: 1½ cups evaporated milk or half and half, 1½ cups sugar, 5 eggs, ½ pound butter and 2 teaspoons vanilla.

Margaret Schneckloth (Raymond)

# White Frosting

| | |
|---|---|
| 2 tablespoons water | 1 egg |
| 4½ tablespoons granulated sugar | ⅔ cup vegetable shortening |
| 2⅓ cups sifted confectioners sugar | 1 teaspoon vanilla |

Boil water and granulated sugar for 1 minute and set aside to cool. Mix confectioners sugar and egg together and blend with syrup. Add remaining ingredients and beat until creamy. Will frost a 9x13-inch loaf cake.

Bea (Mrs. Neal) Smith
(Altoona, Iowa)

421

# Hot Fudge Sauce/Butterscotch Variation

1 cup sugar
⅓ cup cocoa
2 tablespoons flour
  (I use 3)

¼ teaspoon salt
1 cup boiling water
1 tablespoon butter
1 teaspoon vanilla

Blend dry ingredients. Add water and butter. Cook until thick, stirring constantly. Remove from heat and add vanilla. Serve hot or cold. Butterscotch Variation: Use brown sugar instead of white sugar. Omit cocoa.

*This is a favorite from a friend in Iowa.*

**Barbara Ann (Mrs. Charles) Grassley**

# Yellow Sauce for the Christmas Pudding
*(Once-a-Year Indulgence)*

1 cup sugar                    ½ cup butter (soft)

Cream together well in medium size bowl.

4 egg yolks                    Pinch of salt

Add to above and cream well. Heat 1 cup of cream to simmer and gradually add to above mixture. Pour all into heavy bottom pan or double boiler and cook carefully, stirring until thickened, 7-12 minutes. NEVER let it boil. Then remove from heat and add 1 teaspoon vanilla. When completely cooled, immediately store in refrigerator up to 2 or 3 days and reheat only amount needed.

*I can only recall two times that I have not had this sauce at Christmas since I was 4 years old in the early 20's. It was always made by one of 3 great, great aunts, 2 grandmothers, my mother, my daughter, my son or myself.*

**Mary Fischbeck**
**(Mason City, Iowa)**

# Chocolate Dip

1 cup sugar
2 tablespoons cocoa
½ cup cream

¼ cup Karo
¼ cup butter

Combine above ingredients. Boil slowly and eat on favorite ice cream.

**Bessie Sierk**
**(Bettendorf, Iowa)**


# Extra Special Chocolate Sauce

½ cup oleo
½ cup cocoa
½ teaspoon salt
¼ cup light corn syrup

3 cups sugar
1 can evaporated milk
1 teaspoon vanilla
½ teaspoon burnt sugar
    flavoring

Mix first 4 ingredients and heat over low, slowly adding 3 cups of sugar. Add 1 can evaporated milk, 1 teaspoon vanilla and ½ teaspoon burnt sugar flavoring. Heat until sugar dissolves and mixture is smooth and creamy. Chill to store.

*My mom made this sauce. It was our version of a hot fudge sundae.*

**Susan Severs**
**(Princeton, Iowa)**

423

# Apple Crisp

Slice enough apples to fill a deep pie pan. Mix in ½ cup sugar and 1 teaspoon cinnamon. Top with:

**1 cup brown sugar**　　　　　½ **cup oleo**
**1 cup flour**

Mix this into a crumbly mass and sprinkle over the top. Bake at 350° 30-45 minutes or until apples are tender (fork tender). Place cookie sheet under pan to catch any spills.

**Susan Severs**
**(Princeton, Iowa)**

# Caramel Dumplings

*(Ellen Steamboat Recipe)*

**MELT TOGETHER IN SKILLET:**
½ **cup brown sugar**　　　　**1 tablespoon butter**

**ADD:**
**1 cup sugar**　　　　　**1 teaspoon vanilla**
**2 cups boiling water**

Boil gently for 20 minutes.

DUMPLINGS:
MIX:
1 tablespoon butter　　　　2 teaspoons baking powder
½ cup sugar　　　　　2 cups flour
1 cup milk　　　　　1 teaspoon vanilla

Mix first 3 ingredients. Sift together baking powder and flour. Mix batter well and add vanilla. Drop by teaspoon in hot syrup. Bake in moderate oven at 350° for 20 minutes. Serve with cream or extra syrup.

**Rose Peters, Cook - Ellen Steamboat**
**(Submitted by: Lois Havenhill, Princeton, Iowa)**

# Blueberry Cobbler

¼ cup sugar
1 tablespoon cornstarch
¾ cup liquid (water and blueberry juice)*
½ cup Sue Bee Honey
1 tablespoon lemon juice
1 (15 ounce) can (or 2 cups frozen)* blueberries (drained)

1 cup flour
1 tablespoon Sue Bee Honey
1½ teaspoons baking powder
½ teaspoon salt
3 tablespoons shortening
½ cup milk

Mix sugar and cornstarch in a saucepan. Stir in liquid (water and blueberry juice), ½ cup Sue Bee Honey and lemon juice. Bring to a boil, stirring constantly until mixture thickens. Add fruit. Pour into 1½ quart baking dish. Make biscuit topping by combining flour, 1 tablespoon Sue Bee Honey, baking powder, and salt in a bowl. Cut in shortening and add milk. Mix until dough forms a ball. Drop by spoonfuls over fruit mixture. Bake 25-30 minutes at 400°. Serve warm with whipped cream. Makes 6-8 servings. *(If you use fresh or frozen, rather than canned blueberries, use ¾ cup water, and increase honey by ¼ cup).

**Sioux Honey Association**

# Fruit Soup-Danish

Soak 1 package of pearl (large) tapioca in 2 quarts of water overnight. In the morning add 1½ quarts water, 1 cup prunes, 1 cup raisins, (or any dried fruit), and a cinnamon stick. Boil until clear. Take off heat and add 1 can grape juice concentrate and 1½ cups sugar. Cool and serve. Adjust to your own taste.

**Vivian Andersen**
**(Soldier, Iowa)**

# 4 Layer Cherry Dessert

**FIRST LAYER:**

3 cups graham cracker crumbs

¼ cup sugar

¾ cup melted margarine

¼ cup Sue Bee Honey

Mix and pat in 9x13-inch baking dish and bake 10 minutes at 375°. Cool.

**SECOND LAYER:**

16 ounce cream cheese (2-8 ounce packages)

¾ cup powdered sugar

¼ cup Sue Bee Honey

Mix and spread on crust.

**THIRD LAYER:**

2 cans cherry pie filling

Spread over second layer.

**FOURTH LAYER:**

2 packages Dream Whip

Make Dream Whip according to directions on the package and spread over cherries.

**Sioux Honey Association**
**(Sioux City, Iowa)**

426

# Chocolate Roll

| | |
|---|---|
| 4 egg whites | ⅓ cup flour |
| 4 egg yolks | ¼ cup cocoa |
| ¾ cup sugar | ½ teaspoon baking powder |
| 1 teaspoon vanilla | ¼ teaspoon salt |

Beat egg whites until very stiff. Beat yolks and add to egg whites. Gradually add the sugar. Add vanilla. Combine the flour, cocoa, salt and baking powder and beat into the egg mixture until just blended. Pour in a 9x12-inch pan that has been lined with greased wax paper. Bake in a 350⁰ oven for 12 to 15 minutes. Remove from pan onto a towel that has been sprinkled with powdered sugar. Roll up into roll and let cool. Then unroll and spread with whipped cream, sweetened with ½ cup sugar and vanilla extract. Roll up and chill. This will keep for 2 or 3 days if necessary, but is best if served the first day. It should be frosted with a powdered sugar, cocoa frosting. Slice and serve on individual plates.

*This is a favorite recipe of my family, and the grandchildren always look for this to be served when they come to visit. I am sorry this is not a very low calorie dessert, but calories can be cut some place else.*

**Dorothy Ossian
(Stanton, Iowa)**

# Death By Chocolate

1 recipe of chocolate
  brownies (9x13-inch pan)
  (baked)
¼ cup Kahlua (optional)

2 packages chocolate mousse
  (prepared)
1 large container Cool Whip
8 Heath/Skor bars (crushed)
1 cup pecans (chopped)

Prepare brownies. Cool and poke holes. (Pour Kahlua over brownies) Crumble and place ½ in large, pretty, glass bowl or compote. Prepare chocolate mousse according to directions and divide into two portions. Spread ½ of the mousse over the crumbled brownies. Spread ½ of the package of Cool Whip over mousse. Crush candy bars and nuts and sprinkle ½ over Cool Whip. Repeat all steps. Refrigerate and allow to set for several hours, or overnight for flavors to mingle. Serves 12 to 15.

Suzy VenHorst
(Bettendorf, Iowa)

# Norwegian Sweet Soup

½ cup tapioca
2½ cups water
½ teaspoon salt
1 tablespoon vinegar
1 cup sugar

1 cup dry apricots (cut up)
1 cup seedless raisins
1 cup stoned prunes
1 cup chopped apples
2 cups grape juice

Add tapioca to boiling water, stirring frequently, add rest of ingredients, except grape juice. Boil until fruit is tender, then add grape juice. May be served cold as a dessert with whipped cream.

Dorothy Carlson
(Ankeny, Iowa)

# Ingalls Family
# Burr Oak, Iowa

*(With special thanks to Mrs. Ferneva Brimacomb and the Laura Ingalls Wilder Park and Museum Inc.)*

The Charles Ingalls family lived in Burr Oak, Iowa in 1876-1877. They moved to Burr Oak from Walnut Grove, Minnesota when the grasshopper plague destroyed their crops and they lost their farm. Family friends, the Steadmans, had purchased the hotel in Burr Oak and asked Pa to manage it. Ma was to do the cooking for the hotel guests and the townspeople who chose to eat at the hotel.

Ma Ingalls took special pride in her churned butter. In "Little House In The Big Woods" Laura remembers Thursday of every week was set aside as Churning Day. "In winter the cream was not yellow as it was in summer, and butter churned from it was white and not so pretty. Ma liked everything on her table to be pretty, so in the wintertime she colored the butter. After she had put the cream in the tall crockery churn and set it near the stove to warm, she washed and scraped a long orange-colored carrot. Then she grated it on the bottom of the old, leaky tin pan that Pa had punched full of nail-holes for her.

Ma rubbed the carrot across the roughness until she had rubbed it all through the holes, and when she lifted up the pan, there was a soft, juicy mound of grated carrot.

She put this in a little pan of milk on the stove and when the milk was hot she poured milk and carrot into a cloth bag. Then she squeezed the bright yellow milk into the churn, where it colored all the cream. Now the butter would be yellow." (Taken from Chapter 2, of "Little House In The Big Woods.")

*(Continued on Next Page)*

## (Ingalls Family - Continued)

In addition to recipes for feeding her family, Ma Ingalls would have had a recipe for making her own soap. Perhaps it would have been much like the following recipe taken from "Woman's Exchange Cook Book" dated 1894.

### LYE SOFT SOAP

"Ashes should be made from good wood, or the lye will be weak. Keep the ashes dry until a week before using; see that they are well packed down in the leach, which can be made out of a barrel. Then pour on water until the lye begins to drip slightly; leave it to soak out the strength of the ashes for a week. Then pour on water and begin to run off lye. The proper strength can be told by its floating of a fresh egg. If it is not strong, boil it or turn it back through the ashes again. Then add clear grease or "soap grease" in the proportion of 1 pound to a gallon of lye, boil until it is dissolved, then dip in a feather and if, on taking it out, the plume part can be stripped off with the fingers, it requires more grease, which should be added until it will take no more. If a white scum rises, skim off (it is grease), or add a little more lye. Boil until it looks soapy. If the lye remains weak, on account of poor ashes, add potash until it is of sufficient strength." Taken from Woman's Exchange Cookbook.

Similar recipes, many of them recorded only in the minds of the pioneer women, are what made our early pioneer families self-sufficient and able to "live off the land." It is this pioneer spirit we pay tribute to, as we commemorate 150 years of statehood for Iowa.

Just one more recipe for you to enjoy from the Laura Ingalls Wilder recipe collection - her favorite Gingerbread which is a special favorite of all the schoolchildren who visit us each year. We always finish the schoolchildren's tour with a fresh sample of Gingerbread.

**Laura Ingalls Wilder Museum, Burr Oak, Iowa**

*(Continued on Next Page)*

# Laura Ingalls Wilder's Gingerbread

1 cup brown sugar blended with ½ cup shortening.
½ cup molasses mixed well with this.
2 teaspoons baking soda in 1 cup full of boiling water. (Be sure cup is full of water after foam runs off into cake batter.) Mix all well. To 3 cups of flour add: 1 teaspoon each of the following spices: ginger, cinnamon, allspice, nutmeg, cloves, and ½ teaspoon salt. Sift all into the mixture and mix well. Add lastly two well beaten eggs. The mixture should be quite thin. Bake in moderate oven for thirty minutes. Raisins or candied fruit may be added and a chocolate frosting adds to the goodness.

HAPPY PIONEERING!

**Kitchen area in Masters' Hotel**     **Crown Organ**
**at Laura Ingalls Wilder Museum**
**in Burr Oak, Iowa**

# Gingerbread

*Muster Day or Training Day Gingerbread is named for a New England tradition. Before the Civil War (and stemming from the time of the American Revolution) the first Tuesday of every June was set aside as Training Day for all men from the ages of eighteen to forty-five. This military training began at nine o'clock in the morning and the men were usually accompanied by the whole family and friends. It became, of course, an occasion for festivity, and this Gingerbread was one of the indispensable ingredients of the day.*

| | |
|---|---|
| ⅔ cup brown sugar (firmly packed) | ½ teaspoon cloves |
| ⅔ cup molasses | ¾ tablespoon baking soda |
| 1 teaspoon ginger | ⅔ cup butter |
| 1 teaspoon cinnamon | 1 egg (slightly beaten) |
| | 5 cups all-purpose flour |

Heat brown sugar, molasses, ginger, cinnamon, and cloves to the boiling point. Remove from heat, and add baking soda, and pour over butter in a mixing bowl. Stir until butter has melted. Then stir in the egg and flour thoroughly. Knead for a few minutes then gather dough into a ball. Refrigerate dough until firm enough to roll easily, then roll on a lightly floured board and cut with fancy cookie cutters. Place on greased cookie sheet and bake in a preheated 325⁰ oven for 8 to 10 minutes.

*I am a fifth generation Iowan whose great grandfather from Iowa fought in the Civil War.*
*My background is a combination of Scotch, Irish, English and Dutch. In fact I am a direct descendant of Henry Hudson, the famous explorer.*

**Nancy Bettis**

# Grandmother's Gingerbread

1 cup molasses
½ cup sugar
½ cup lard (melted)
1 teaspoon each--ginger,
  allspice, cinnamon

Yolks of 2 eggs
3 cups flour
1 cup boiling water with
  1 teaspoon soda added
Raisins (if desired)

Combine all ingredients except for last 3. Add flour and raisins. Last add the soda in boiling water. Bake at 350°. Use the toothpick test to check when it is done.

*A cook needs to know something about food preparation when using such recipes. Reading old cookbooks is always interesting.*

**Theo Ahrendsen**
**(Oxford Junction, Iowa)**

# Graham Cracker Dessert

14 graham crackers (crushed)
1 teaspoon baking powder
¼ teaspoon salt
3 egg whites (beaten stiff)

1 cup sugar
½ cup chopped dates
½ cup chopped nuts
1 teaspoon vanilla

Combine cracker crumbs, baking powder, and salt. Fold sugar into egg whites and beat smooth. Fold cracker crumbs into egg whites. Add dates, nuts, and vanilla. Turn into greased glass pie plate and bake in moderate oven (325°) for 25 to 30 minutes, or until delicately browned. Cool. Swirl the top with Cool Whip or it may be served topped with ice cream.

**Mrs. Eugene (Elda) Way**
**(Kalona, Iowa)**

# Hefenklosse mit Zimmetsoske

*(Yeast dumplings with cinnamon sauce from Amana)*

**DUMPLINGS:**

| | |
|---|---|
| 1 cup milk | 2 eggs (beaten) |
| ½ cup lard | ½ cake compressed yeast |
| 1 tablespoon sugar | ¼ cup warm water |
| 1 teaspoon salt | 4 cups sifted flour |

**PLACE IN SKILLET:**

| | |
|---|---|
| 1 tablespoon lard | 1 teaspoon salt |
| ¾ cup boiling water | |

**ADD:**

| | |
|---|---|
| 2 tablespoons bread crumbs | 2 tablespoons butter |

**CINNAMON SAUCE:**

| | |
|---|---|
| ¼ cup sugar | ½ cup cold milk |
| 4 tablespoons flour | 3½ cups scalded milk |
| 1 tablespoon cinnamon | |

DUMPLINGS: Heat milk, add lard, sugar, salt and beaten eggs. When cooled to lukewarm, add yeast dissolved in warm water. Add flour. Let rise overnight in a warm place. Form dough into dumplings about two inches across and let rise again on cloth covered board until double in bulk. Into heavy skillet with tight-fitting cover, put lard, boiling water and salt. Place dumplings in skillet, side by side, cover, and simmer 15 minutes without removing lid. Place in serving dish and top with bread crumbs which have been browned in butter. Serve with Cinnamon Sauce: Mix sugar, flour, and cinnamon. Moisten with cold milk, add to scalded milk, and cook in top of double boiler for 20 minutes. Serve hot with yeast dumplings. Warning! Serves 10-12 people.

*P.S.- My father's family came from Amana and they are great cooks! Choosing a favorite was difficult.*

**Marsha Hollingsworth**
**(Davenport, Iowa)**

# The Eskimo Pie
## Onawa, Iowa
*(With special thanks to the Onawa Chamber of Commerce)*

Eskimo Pies are the oldest of the ice cream novelties. Their beginning: 1920, 76 years ago, in the Missouri River town of Onawa, Iowa. Christian K. Nelson is the person given credit for their creation. Ice cream fanatics of the world can thank Mr. Nelson for his delicious contribution.

# Banana Ice Cream

**Peeled frozen bananas**
**Frozen berries can also be**
**added**

**Walnuts or other nuts**

Put bananas through a champion juicer. Use homogenizer blade. Comes out like soft serve ice cream. Grind walnuts and sprinkle on top.

*A great dessert, especially for those who can't eat sugar.*

Mary Swander

# Old Fashioned Ice Cream

**6 eggs**
**4 cups sugar**
**3 tablespoons vanilla**

**1 quart heavy cream**
**Whole milk**

Beat eggs, adding one at a time, until light. Gradually add sugar, beating constantly. Add cream and vanilla, blending well. Pour into one and one half gallon ice cream freezer container and fill with whole milk until 2 to 3 inches from top of container. If desire a less rich ice cream, use Half and Half instead of heavy cream. CAUTION: Eggs must be fresh and free from cracks. Follow manufacturer's directions for freezing. Makes 16 to 24 servings.

**Neal Smith**
**(Former US Representative from Iowa)**

# Marvelous Maple-Nut Ice Cream

| | |
|---|---|
| 3 cups light cream | 1 tablespoon vanilla |
| 1½ cups sugar | 3 cups whipping cream |
| 2 tablespoons maple flavoring | ¾ cup chopped black walnuts |

In the freezer can of a 4 to 5 quart ice cream freezer, combine light cream, sugar, maple flavoring and vanilla. Stir in the mixture until the sugar is dissolved. Stir in whipping cream and black walnuts. Freeze the mixture according to manufacturer's directions. When ready, ripen the ice cream by covering the ice and salt packed freezer with heavy cloth or layers of newspaper to keep the contents cold. Drain off water and add extra salt and ice as necessary. (As it ripens, the ice cream hardens slightly and becomes smoother.) Makes 2 quarts. NOTE: For a 2 quart ice cream freezer, use ⅔ of the recipe above and freeze according to manufacturer's directions.

**Marville Hawn**

*Jack Hawn and his wife Marville live on a farm near Perry, Iowa in a scenic setting along Iowa's Raccoon River. Jack's favorite pastime gathering black walnuts; Marville's favorite pastime: using them for her two favorite recipes: "Marvelous Maple-Nut Ice Cream" and "Chocolate-on-Chocolate Walnut Cookies." A few years ago Jack picked an unbelievable 100 quarts of walnuts. Walnuts are great to freeze. According to the Hawns who have become experts on the subject, walnuts will keep 3 or 4 years in the refrigerator or freezer.*

*Finding the best trees is easy for the Hawns who grew up in the area. Jack washes the nuts in an old electric Maytag washer using the formula: 5 gallons of nuts and 5 gallons of water for an 8-10 minute cycle. He dries them in a 10-inch deep, squirrel-proof screen box he built from an old door screen. Since black walnuts crack much better after soaking, Jack invented a chicken-wire soaker that looks like a large French-fry basket.*

*The Hawns love what they do. Although their hobbies are quite time consuming, Jack and Marville both have their arts down to a science. Look in the "Cookies and Bars" section for the "Chocolate-on-Chocolate Walnut Cookies" recipe. THEY MUST ACCOMPANY THE ICE CREAM!*

# Oreo Dessert

1 large bag of Oreo cookies
1 stick margarine
1 package (8 ounces) cream
   cheese
1 cup powdered sugar

1 carton (12 ounces) Cool
   Whip
2 packages (4-service size)
   French vanilla instant
   pudding
4 cups milk

Crush the cookies. Take ⅔ of the crumbs and line the bottom of a buttered 9x13-inch pan: Cream margarine, cream cheese, powdered sugar and Cool Whip together; then add pudding and milk. Pour over crumb layer and sprinkle with remaining crumbs. Refrigerate. Serves 15 to 20.

Kay Youngers
(Princeton, Iowa)

# Peppermint Dessert

1 large package Oreos
   (crushed)

1 stick butter (melted)
Peppermint ice cream

Mix Oreos and butter and put into a 9x13-inch pan, save back ½ cup. Spread peppermint ice cream over crust and freeze.

**TOPPING:**
1 small package chocolate
   chips
1 teaspoon vanilla

2 cups powdered sugar
1 large can evaporated milk
1 stick butter

Mix and boil 8 minutes. Let cool. Spread over ice cream. Sprinkle with remaining crumbs. Let freeze.

**Linda (Schneckloth) Grimm**

438

# Pineapple Delight

Heat 1 cup milk to boiling point. Add 1 pound marshmallows, 1/8 cup butter (melt in milk), stir with fork until marshmallows are dissolved. Set aside to cool. When cool, add small can or 1 cup crushed pineapple and 1 cup cream whipped. Stir together. Crush 24 graham crackers. Put half in bottom of pan. Put in pineapple mixture and place rest of crackers over the top. Set in (ice box) 24 hours. Serves 12.

*Mom used to put this in two of the metal ice cube trays. Served for Ladies Aid at church.*

**Pat Walker**
**(Princeton, Iowa)**

# Rhubarb Crunch

| | |
|---|---|
| **5 cups diced rhubarb (fresh** | **1 cup brown sugar** |
| **or frozen)** | **1 cup oatmeal** |
| **3 tablespoons flour** | **½ cup butter** |
| **1 cup sugar** | **½ cup shortening** |
| **1½ cups flour** | |

Mix first 3 ingredients and place in greased 9x13-inch pan. Mix other ingredients and sprinkle over fruit mixture. Bake at 375⁰ for 35 minutes or until golden brown. Serves 12.

**Carolyn Manning**
**Thanks also to: Story County Extension Service**
**(Ames, Iowa)**

# Raspberry Dessert

**CRUST:**

½ cup plus 1 tablespoon oleo (melt)

1 cup flour plus 1 tablespoon sugar

Mix flour and sugar into melted oleo. Pat into a 9x13-inch pan. Bake 300° for 20 minutes. Cool.

**FILLING:**

2 (8 ounce) cream cheese (not light)

2 cups powdered sugar

½ teaspoon salt

2 teaspoons vanilla

1 (8 ounce) Cool Whip (not light)

Mix altogether. Pour over crust and chill.

**TOPPING:**

1 (6 ounce) package raspberry Jello or 2 (3 ounce)

2½ cups boiling water

½ cup sugar

2 (10 ounce) frozen raspberries

Mix and cool slightly. Pour over cream cheese layer. Then chill until set.

**Mary Craig**
**(Mitchellville, Iowa)**

440

# Rhubarb Delight

2 cups (very full) cut up
   rhubarb
1¼ cups sugar
¼ cup butter (melted)
2 cups graham cracker
   crumbs

1 (3 ounce) package raspberry
   Jello
1 tablespoon lemon juice
1 (12 ounce) can evaporated
   milk (Pet)

Melt the ¼ cup butter. Mix with graham cracker crumbs. Press ⅔ of mixture in bottom of 9x13-inch pan. Reserve remaining crumbs to sprinkle over top of filling. Combine the 2 very full cups of cut up rhubarb and the 1¼ cups of sugar. Bring to a boil, over low heat, stirring constantly to avoid scorching. DO NOT ADD WATER! Cook a few minutes and while still hot add the 3 ounce package of raspberry Jello. Stir until dissolved. Chill until syrupy. Pour the 12 or 13 ounce can of Pet milk in large mixer bowl. Add the lemon juice. Place in the freezing compartment of refrigerator; chill until it begins to freeze. This should be done at the very beginning of preparation. Whip evaporated milk until peaks form when beaters are lifted out. Fold in the thickened gelatin mixture, blend in well. Pour over graham cracker crumbs in the 9x13-inch pan. Sprinkle reserved ⅓ of crumbs over top. Chill until firm or overnight. Cut and serve. ENJOY! This makes enough to fill 2 purchased graham cracker pie shells, if preferred.

**Ethel M. Dobbins**
**(Wilton, Iowa)**

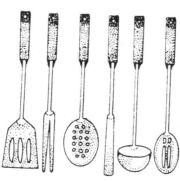

# Strawberry Mousse

½ cup canned evaporated
   skim milk
1 pint strawberries
1 envelope unflavored
   gelatin
2 tablespoons sugar

1 egg white
Dash of salt
½ cup water
2 teaspoons lemon juice
¼ teaspoon vanilla

About 4 hours before serving, put the milk in a medium bowl and put in freezer until ice crystals form throughout, about 1 hour, stirring occasionally. Meanwhile reserve 1 strawberry for garnish later. In covered blender container at high speed, puree' strawberries. Pour into medium bowl. In small saucepan, combine gelatin, sugar and salt, stirring constantly, until gelatin is completely dissolved, about 1 minute. Into pureed strawberries, stir lemon juice, vanilla and gelatin mixture. Refrigerate until mixture mounds drop from spoon, about 25 minutes. In small bowl, with mixer at high speed, beat egg white until white stands stiff, glossy peaks. In chilled bowl with mixer at high speed, beat ice milk until stiff and color turns white. Fold beaten egg white and whipped milk into strawberry mixture. Spoon into quart bowl. Refrigerate until set, about 2 hours. Cut reserved strawberry into thin slices. Garnish mousse with slices. Makes 4 servings.

**Catherine Freund**

# Yogurt Delight
### *(Lowfat)*

1 (6 ounce) package sugar-free gelatin (any flavor)
2 cups hot water
1 cup cold water

1 (8 ounce) carton lowfat yogurt (same flavor as gelatin)
1 angel food cake, homemade or purchased

Boil water. Add gelatin and dissolve. Add cold water. Chill until consistency of egg whites. Beat until frothy (10-15 minutes). Fold in yogurt. Cube cake, fold into mixture. Pour into 8x13-inch pan. Refrigerate. Cut and serve with a dollop of low calorie whipped topping. Raspberry or strawberry are great flavors. Yield - 15 servings. Nutritive value per serving: Calories 125; Fat 2 percent; Protein 10 percent; Sodium 71 milligrams; Carbohydrates 85 percent

**Carol Schneider**
**(Le Mars, Iowa)**

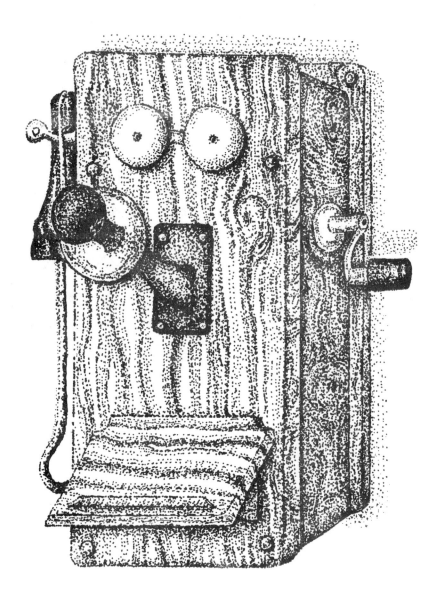

# Cookies & Bars

Illustration by Gary Nauman

446

# Dutch Symbolism

This illustration reminds us all of the Netherlands, the western European country from which many of our ancestors, (including mine), came bringing with them traditions, stories, and, of course, their recipes. In 1847 Dominie (Rev.) Hendrik P. Scholte founded Pella, Iowa, a move which began a wave of Dutch immigration to the United States. In 1870 Holland, Iowa, (later, Orange City), was founded by Henry Hospers organizing a committee to colonize northwest Iowa; an area where land was more available and less expensive.

A number of wonderful Dutch recipes included, in this book are mostly from Pella and Orange City.

Windmills have played a very important part in Dutch history. Wooden shoes, or klompen, started as inexpensive and practical footwear for farmers and fishermen. They were carved by those who wore them. Today there is still a wooden shoe factory in Orange City, Iowa. The shoes are worn during the May tulip festivals in Pella and Orange City, and by dancers dressed in costume. In the Sunken Gardens Park in Pella, the pond in between the windmill and beautiful array of tulips, is in the shape of a wooden shoe.

Tulips are a famous Dutch symbol that beautify many an American spring garden. More than 2,000 varieties have been developed in the Netherlands. The cleanliness, friendliness, and simplistic beauty of our Iowa Dutch communities are indeed impressive to the tourist, and all he or she needs is something from one of the bakeries like a Dutch Letter to keep coming back for more.

447

# COOKIES AND BARS

## COOKIES

Aggression Cookies . . . . . 449
Anise Drops . . . . . . . . . . . 449
Applesauce Cookies . . . . . 450
Butter Pecan Cookies . . . . 450
Banana Split
    Sundae Cookies . . . . . . 451
Biscotti Di Greve (Orange
    Almond Biscotti) . . . . . 452
Cherry Cookies . . . . . . . . . 453
Basic Cookie Recipe . . . . . 453
Chocolate-On-Chocolate
    Walnut Cookies . . . . . . 454
Chocolate Cream-Cheese
    Frosting for Walnut
    Cookies . . . . . . . . . . . . . 454
Crescent Cookies . . . . . . . 455
Dutch Lace Cookies . . . . . 455
Holland Lace Cookies . . . 456
Gingersnaps . . . . . . . . . . . 457
Golden Cooky . . . . . . . . . . 457
Goose Grease Cookies . . . 458
Krumkake (Norwegian) . 458
Ice Box Cookies . . . . . . . 459
Kringla . . . . . . . . . . . . . . . 459
Norwegian Kringle . . . . . . 460
Macaroons . . . . . . . . . . . . 461
Lebkuchen . . . . . . . . . . . . 461
Nurnberger Lebkuchen . . 462
Molasses Cookies . . . . . . . 463
Peanut Butter Cookies . . . 464
Pecan Cookies . . . . . . . . . 464
Oatmeal
    Chocolate Chips . . . . . 465
Oatmeal Jim Jams . . . . . . 466
Peanut Cookies . . . . . . . . 466
Olympic Cookies . . . . . . . 467
Peanut Butter 'N Chocolate
    Chip Cookies . . . . . . . . 467
Pfeffernusse . . . . . . . . . . . 468

Pride of Iowa Cookies . . . 469
Ranger Cookies . . . . . . . . 469
Rosettes . . . . . . . . . . . . . . 470
Sandbakkelse . . . . . . . . . . 471
Snowball Cookies . . . . . . 471
St. Nickolas Koekjes . . . . . 472
Van Dyke
    Christmas Cookies . . . . 472
Santa Claus
    Cookies . . . . . . . . . 473,474
Danish Sugar Cookies . . . 474
Spice Drop Cookies . . 475,476
Soft Tollhouse Cookies . . 477
Nano's Sugar Cookies . . . 477
Toll House Cookies . . . . . 478
Vanilla Crescents
    (Vanilla Kipfert) . . . . . . 479

## BARS

Brownies . . . . . . . . . . . . . . 481
Beef Brownies . . . . . . . . . . 482
Thick Chewy Brownies . . 482
Twice Baked Brownies . . 483
Championship Chocolate
    Chip Bars . . . . . . . . . . . 483
Frosted Cream Bars . . . . . 484
Mom's Date Bars . . . . . . . 485
Gram's Peanut
    Butter Bars . . . . . . . . . . 485
Frosted Creams/Cream
    Chocolate Frosting . . . . 486
Peanut Butter Fingers . . . 487
Prune Bars . . . . . . . . . . . . 487
Pecan Pie Squares . . . . . . 488
Scotcheroos . . . . . . . . . . . 488
Pumpkin Bars . . . . . . . 489,490
Sour Cream Raisin Bars . 489
Pumpkin Pie Squares . . . 490
Raisin-Spice Squares . . . . 491
Berry Berry
    Streusel Bars . . . . . . . . 492

# Aggression Cookies

3 cups oatmeal
1½ cups brown sugar
1½ cups flour

1½ cups margarine
1½ teaspoons baking powder

Mix together with hands. Mash! Pound! Squeeze! Roll into balls. Bake at 350⁰ for 10-12 minutes.

Dan Gable (Submitted by Kathy Gable)
Wrestling Coach, University of Iowa

# Anise Drops

1 cup plus 2 tablespoons
  sugar
4 small eggs

2½ cups flour (measure
  before sifting)
1 teaspoon anise seeds

Beat eggs and sugar 1 hour by hand, or 45 minutes at low speed in the electric mixer, finish by beating 10 minutes by hand. Sift and add flour and anise a little at a time. Drop by teaspoonful on greased and floured cookie sheet. Let stand in warm room for at least four hours or overnight. A dry crust will form on top. Bake at 325⁰ F for 10 to 15 minutes.

Margaret Schneckloth (Raymond)

449

# Applesauce Cookies
### *(Ellen Steamboat Recipe)*

1 cup unsweetened
    applesauce
1 cup white sugar
½ cup shortening
1 cup raisins
2¼ cups flour
1 teaspoon baking powder

1 scant teaspoon cinnamon
½ teaspoon salt
1 egg
1 cup chopped nuts
1 teaspoon soda
½ teaspoon cloves

Mix sugar and shortening. Add egg and applesauce, salt, raisins and nuts. Sift dry ingredients and add all at once. Drop by spoonfuls on greased cookie sheet. Bake at 350⁰ for 10 to 12 minutes.

Rose Peters, Cook - Ellen Steamboat
**(Submitted by: Lois Havenhill, Princeton, Iowa)**

# Butter Pecan Cookies

1 cup butter
1 teaspoon vanilla
2 teaspoons water
5 heaping tablespoons
    powdered sugar

1½ cups flour
Pinch of salt
1 cup chopped pecans (fine)

Mix in given order, bake on ungreased sheet at 350⁰ for 6 minutes. Let cool a bit. Cookie is very tender and rich. Yield: approximately 55.

*This is a very old recipe from old PTA days at Polk School, a former Davenport School.*

**Anna Schmidt**
**(Princeton, Iowa)**

# Banana Split Sundae Cookies

1 cup (2 sticks) margarine or butter (softened)
1 cup firmly packed brown sugar
1½ cups mashed ripe banana (about 4 medium)
2 eggs
2 teaspoons vanilla
2½ cups Quaker Oats (quick or old fashioned, uncooked)

2 cups all-purpose flour
1 teaspoon baking soda
¼ teaspoon salt (optional)
1 cup (6 ounce) semisweet chocolate pieces
Ice cream or frozen yogurt
Ice cream topping, any flavor

Heat oven to 350⁰F. Beat together margarine and sugar until creamy. Add banana, eggs and vanilla; beat well. Add combined oats, flour, baking soda and salt; mix well. Stir in chocolate pieces; mix well. Drop by ¼ cupfuls onto ungreased cookie sheet about 3 inches apart. Spread dough to measure 3½-inch diameter. Bake 14 to 16 minutes or until edges are light golden brown. Cool 1 minute on cookie sheet; remove to wire rack. Cool completely. To serve: Top each cookie with a scoop of ice cream and ice cream topping. About 2 dozen. Nutrition Information (1 cookie without ice cream or topping): Calories 225, Fat 11 gram, Sodium 130 milligrams, Dietary Fiber 1 gram

**Quaker Oats Company
(Cedar Rapids, Iowa)**

THYME       PARSLEY       BASIL

451

# Biscotti Di Greve
## (Orange Almond Biscotti)

2 cups unbleached all-purpose flour
1 cup sugar
½ teaspoon baking soda
1 teaspoon baking powder
¼ teaspoon salt
2 large whole eggs
1 large egg yolk
1 teaspoon vanilla
1 tablespoon orange zest (freshly grated)
1½ cups natural whole almonds (toasted lightly and coarsely chopped)

In the bowl of an electric mixer fitted with the paddle attachment, blend the flour, sugar, baking soda, baking powder and salt until the mixture is combined well. In a small bowl, whisk together the whole eggs, the yolk, vanilla and zest; add the mixture to the flour mixture, beating until dough is formed, and stir in the almonds. Turn the dough out onto a lightly floured surface, knead it several times and halve it. Working on a large buttered and floured baking sheet, with floured hands, form each piece of dough into a flattish log 12 inches long and 2 inches wide. Arrange the logs at least 3 inches apart on the sheet, and brush them with the egg wash (see note below). Bake the logs in the middle of a preheated 300⁰ oven for 50 minutes and let them cool on the baking sheet on a rack for 10 minutes. On a cutting board, cut the logs crosswise on the diagonal into ½-inch thick slices. Arrange the biscotti, cut sides down, on the baking sheet and bake them in the 300⁰ oven for 15 minutes on each side. Transfer the biscotti to racks to cool and store them in airtight containers. Makes about 48 biscotti. NOTE: An egg wash is made by beating together 1 large egg and 1 teaspoon water. Toast almonds in a 325⁰ oven for 10 to 15minutes - watch carefully. Then remove from pan to prevent further browning. (Did Columbus and his crews sail to the new world eating these traditional Ligurian biscotti? It's entirely possible, although theirs would have been cooked much longer to drive off all the moisture, allowing them to keep for an entire ocean crossing. Though these biscotti are made with enriched bread dough instead of the traditional cookie dough and have a somewhat softer texture, they keep well when stored in an airtight container.)

**Sunday Antrim**
**(Master Gardener, Johnson County)**

# Cherry Cookies

1 cup brown sugar
1 cup white sugar
1 cup butter (softened)
1 teaspoon vanilla
2 eggs (beaten)
2½ cups flour

1 teaspoon salt
1 teaspoon soda
1 cup chopped maraschino
  cherries
1 cup chopped walnuts

Cream butter, sugar, brown sugar, and vanilla until light and fluffy. Add eggs; beat well. Combine flour, baking soda and salt; gradually beat into creamed mixture. Stir in cherries and nuts. Drop by teaspoonfuls onto ungreased cookie sheet. Bake at 350⁰ for 15-18 minutes. Makes 4-6 dozen cookies.

Mollie Dudley
(Le Claire, Iowa)

# Basic Cookie Recipe

1 cup shortening
¾ cup white sugar
¾ cup brown sugar
2 eggs
1½ cups flour
2 cups (quick cooking)
  oatmeal

1 teaspoon soda in 1
  tablespoon hot water
1 teaspoon salt
1 cup nutmeats
1 package chocolate chips*
1 teaspoon vanilla

Preheat oven to 375⁰. *May use coconut instead of chocolate chips. Drop by spoonful on lightly greased cookie sheet. Bake 10 to 12 minutes until golden brown.

*A favorite for a large family, my friend and I have used this recipe for 40 years. We each had six children, and these cookies are still their favorite when they visit.*

Rose Eisele
(Cedar Rapids, Iowa)

# Chocolate-on-Chocolate Walnut Cookies

2¾ cups all-purpose flour
½ teaspoon baking soda
½ teaspoon baking powder
¼ teaspoon salt
1½ cups sugar
½ cup butter or margarine
2 eggs

1 teaspoon vanilla
2 squares chocolate
  (2 ounces) unsweetened
  (melted and cooled)
1 cup dairy sour cream
1 cup coarsely chopped black
  walnuts
Chocolate Cream-Cheese
  frosting (optional)

In a bowl, combine flour, baking soda, baking powder and salt; set aside. In a large mixer bowl, cream sugar and butter or margarine on low speed on electric mixer. Add eggs and vanilla; beat on medium speed until fluffy. Beat in cooled, melted chocolate and sour cream. Add flour mixture; beat on low speed until well-mixed. With a spoon, stir in black walnuts. Cover; chill for 1 hour. From a teaspoon, drop dough 2-inches apart onto a greased cookie sheet. Bake in a 375⁰ oven for 8 to 10 minutes. Remove cookies to a wire rack; cool. Frost with Chocolate Cream-Cheese Frosting, if desired. Store frosted cookies in your refrigerator. Makes about 60.

**Marville Hawn**

# Chocolate Cream-Cheese
# Frosting for Walnut Cookies

In a mixer bowl, beat together until light and fluffy one (3 ounce) package cream cheese, softened; 2 tablespoons butter or margarine, softened; 1½ squares (1½ ounces) unsweetened chocolate, melted and cooled; 2 tablespoons milk or light cream; and ½ teaspoon vanilla. Gradually add 2 cups sifted powdered sugar, beating until smooth. Add a little more milk or powdered sugar, if necessary for spreading consistency.

**Marville Hawn**

## Crescent Cookies

½ pound butter (room
  temperature)
3 tablespoons powdered
  sugar (sift)

2 cups regular flour (sift in)
1 teaspoon vanilla
1 package nuts (chopped)

Put all ingredients in bowl and mix. Dough looks gummy, but that's the way it should be, when mixed. Roll into crescent shape and put on ungreased cookie sheet. Bake at 350° for 20 minutes. Roll in powdered sugar, while still warm, not hot.

Alice A. Totosz

## Dutch Lace Cookies

1 cup butter
2 cups brown sugar
2 beaten eggs

1 cup flour
1 teaspoon soda
1 teaspoon cream of tartar

Melt 1 cup butter and 2 cups brown sugar together in microwave. Add 2 beaten eggs, 1 cup flour, 1 teaspoon soda and 1 teaspoon cream of tartar. Mix well. Heavily grease and flour cookie sheet each time you put batter on it. Drop by teaspoon 6-8 per sheet. I bake them on the top rack at 350° about 6 minutes. Watch carefully just after bubbles stop. If not baked long enough, they will be chewy; too long; they burn. Take out and let stand about 2 minutes. Carefully remove with spatula while still warm and place on flat surface. Cookies are very fragile, but good. Makes around 75.

*I once made 300 to serve with our Dutch meal during Orange City's annual tulip festival.*

Mrs. LaDonna Huisman
(Hospers, Iowa)

# Holland Lace Cookies

| | |
|---|---|
| 1 pound brown sugar | 1 cup flour |
| ½ cup butter or 1 stick oleo | ½ cup water |
| ½ teaspoon cinnamon | ½ cup almonds, shredded |
| ½ teaspoon nutmeg | (or slivered almonds broken up) |

Mix ingredients all together in order given. Place a sheet of foil to cover cookie sheet and grease foil. Drop cookie mixture using a scant ½ teaspoon size. As cookies bake they tend to spread out. By using small spoonfuls, cookie will be a nicer serving size. Bake at 375⁰ for about 5-6 minutes until they are a light golden brown. They will be bubbly and not look baked, but as they cool, they will become more firm. When slightly cool remove from foil-lined pan. The firmer they become the harder they are to remove so you must work quickly. By using foil you can manipulate removing the cookies better. Discard foil and use new for each batch of cookies, oiling or greasing each time.

*These cookies were a recipe I received from my mother-in-law. She called them "Aunt Rena's Cookies" because only Aunt Rena could make them so well. This was within the first year of our marriage. I made them to show her that I would have no trouble making them. Well, they were a disaster because I couldn't get them off the cookie sheet. They all broke into pieces. However, I tried again and decided to use foil over the pans so I could work around the cookie a little easier. The foil gave a little whereas the cookie sheet was too stiff. It worked much better although some were still broken. That's where the smaller they are, the easier it becomes to handle them. Also there is a certain point at which they are much easier to remove. Letting them cool too long lets them become hardened and too difficult to remove without breaking. These are definitely for an experienced cook and then some! Although persistence is a great help. They are very good; delicious and spicy, light and airy, so they are a good holiday cookie. Men especially like the flavor.*

**Idelle Vogel**
**(Orange City, Iowa)**

456

# Gingersnaps

2 cups white sugar
1½ cups shortening
4 cups flour
2 teaspoons soda
½ teaspoon salt

½ cup molasses
1 teaspoon ginger
1 teaspoon cloves
2 eggs

Combine ingredients. Form into balls and roll in sugar. They will flatten out while baking. Bake in 400⁰ oven 7 to 8 minutes.

**Marguerite Vens
(Davenport, Iowa)**

# Golden Cooky

1 cup shortening (half
   margarine, half butter)
1½ cups sugar
3 egg yolks

2½ cups all-purpose flour
1 teaspoon cream of tartar
1 teaspoon baking soda
1 teaspoon ground cardamom

Soften shortening and add sugar. Cream together. Add egg yolks and mix well. Sift flour, cream of tartar, soda and cardamom together. Add dry ingredients to creamed mixture. Mix very well. Roll in small balls. Bake in a slow oven (325⁰) for about 15 minutes. Makes about 70 cookies. Store in a tight container.

*This cooky recipe came from Germany over 125 years ago. It has been handed down to us through our Grandmother and an aunt.*
*It is always a favorite, but is a tradition in our family at Christmas.*

**Helen and Margaret Storch
(Davenport, Iowa)**

457

## Goose Grease Cookies

1 cup goose grease
1½ cups sugar
3 egg yolks
2¼ cups flour
1 teaspoon baking soda
    dissolved in 1 tablespoon
    hot water

½ teaspoon salt
1 teaspoon cream of tartar
1 teaspoon ground cardamom

Mix first 3 items together. First add water, (soda mixture), then flour etc. Roll dough into small ball and place on ungreased sheet. Press down very lightly. Cookies will have cracked top. Bake at 400° for 7 minutes, (do not over bake, will burn easily). Let set a short time before removing. Very tender. Store in covered container. Makes about 75 cookies. To render fresh fat from goose, use a heavy pan. Add small amount at a time. Pour grease off as it melts and strain as you go along. Cool. Will look like milk when cool.

*This recipe is an old one from my mother-in-law, Mrs. Henry Beuse, (deceased) of Germany.*

Anna Schmidt
(Princeton, Iowa)

## Krumkake (Norwegian)

1 cup sugar
½ cup butter
1 cup milk

2 egg yolks
1 teaspoon vanilla
1½ cups flour

Cream butter and sugar. Add milk, egg yolks, 1 teaspoon vanilla, and 1½ cups flour. Drop tablespoon of batter on krumkake iron. Bake until lightly brown and roll up while warm.

Vivian Andersen
(Soldier, Iowa)

458

# Ice Box Cookies
### (Christmas Cookie)

1 cup white sugar
1 cup brown sugar
1½ cups lard and butter
   (half of each)
3 eggs well beaten
5 cups flour

1 cup walnuts
1 cup chopped dates
1 teaspoon soda with a little
   cold water
1 teaspoon salt
1 teaspoon vanilla

Cream butter, lard, and sugar well, add eggs and other ingredients. Set in refrigerator overnight. Then roll out, but not too thin. Cut with knife into squares and bake at 375° for 10 to 12 minutes, or until brown. Roll out and cut into 1 or 1½-inch squares.

This recipe was my mother's.

Regina Portz
(Princeton, Iowa)

# Kringla

3½ cups sifted flour
1 cup sugar
½ cup buttermilk
½ cup butter (melt)
1 cup sour cream

1 medium egg (beaten)
2 teaspoons baking powder
½ teaspoon soda
1 teaspoon vanilla
½ teaspoon ground cardamon

Have buttermilk and sour cream at room temperature. Add melted butter and sugar. Mix well and add egg. Stir in flour and other dry ingredients including cardamom. Add vanilla. Cool overnight or several hours. Using a rounded tablespoon of dough, roll a strip 8-inches long and form into a pretzel shaped cooky. Bake 8-10 minutes 375°. Use (serve) with butter and coffee. Must be stored in tightly covered container or plastic bag. Makes 36. Also, flour must be used to roll these out.

*These cookies are a favorite of most midwest Norwegians and especially my family. We served them at two family weddings.*

Marilyn Ullestad
(Des Moines, Iowa)

# Norwegian Kringla

1¼ cups sugar
½ cup Crisco
2 egg yolks
1 cup buttermilk
1 teaspoon soda

3 cups flour
1 teaspoon baking powder
½ teaspoon vanilla
½ teaspoon anise
Pinch of salt

Mix flour, baking powder and salt and set aside. Cream Crisco, sugar, vanilla and anise. Add egg yolks. Add soda to buttermilk and add to creamed mixture before foaming stops. Add dry ingredients. Chill at least 3 hours. Flour a flat surface well. Drop a rounded teaspoon of dough onto floured surface. Roll into a 6-inch long rope 3/8-inch in diameter. Place on cookie sheet, making figure 8's or in a knot. Bake at 375⁰ for 8 to 10 minutes. The bottoms should be a light brown. Serve with butter on top!

*My husband is a Lutheran clergyman, and over the years we have had many groups in our home, especially during the holidays. I serve these at our open houses.*

**Dorothy Carlson**
**(Ankeny, Iowa)**

A similar recipe was submitted by Lola Tjelmeland Anderson from Nevada, Iowa.

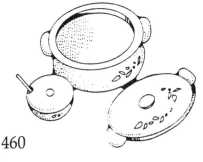

# Macaroons
### *(Non Cholesterol)*

1 cube margarine
1 egg or (¼ cup egg beaters)
1 cup sugar
1 teaspoon plus 2 drops
    coconut flavoring

1½ cups non cholesterol
    Bisquick
1½ cups Betty Crocker potato
    buds

Mix ingredients and refrigerate. Then drop by teaspoon and bake at 350⁰ for 10 to 15 minutes.

Clarice Sarchet
(Urbandale, Iowa)

# Lebkuchen

1 pint honey
1 cup sugar
2 eggs
5¼ cups flour

1 tablespoon soda, dissolved
    in 3 tablespoons whiskey
Nuts (if desired)

In a large bowl, combine sugar, honey, eggs, and baking soda. Beat until foamy. Then add flour. Mix well until a soft dough is formed. Set in a cool place overnight, safe from dough-snatchers! The next morning place part of the dough on a floured board, and roll into 1-inch thick ropes. Cut ropes into 2-inch long pieces and place pieces on greased cookie sheets. Bake at 350⁰ for about 10 minutes. Ice with vanilla, powdered sugar glaze, if desired.

Lina Unglenk
(Amana, Iowa)

# Nurnberger Lebkuchen

*(Christmas Spice Cookies)*

2 eggs
1 cup sugar
1 cup sifted flour
¼ teaspoon cinnamon
1/8 teaspoon ground cloves
1/8 teaspoon powdered
   cardamom

¾ cup blanched almonds
   (chopped fine in blender)
¼ cup candied lemon peel
½ teaspoon grated lemon
   peel

Beat eggs, gradually add sugar. Beat until thickened. Blend in flour, spices, almonds and lemon peels. Drop by teaspoonful on well greased cookie sheets or spread in a well-greased 8-inch square baking pan. Bake in a slow oven (325°) 15 to 20 minutes or until edges are beginning to brown for drop cookies; 20-25 minutes or until edges begin to pull away from sides of pan for bar cookies. If using cookie sheets, remove and cool on rack. If using pan, cut into bars about 3x1-inches (make 3 cuts in one direction, 8 in the other). Cool on rack. Store cookies or bars in cookie jar to mellow for a few days. Cookies may be sprinkled with powdered sugar or iced with a chocolate glaze. Makes 2 dozen 2-inch cookies.

**Wilma Howard**
**(Denton, Texas, formerly Cedar Falls, Iowa)**

# Molasses Cookies

2 cups molasses
1 cup (scant) lard (I use oleo)
2 beaten eggs
2 tablespoons soda
3 tablespoons boiling water
  (combine soda and water
  and mix well)

2 teaspoons ginger
2 teaspoons cinnamon
½ teaspoon salt
1 teaspoon vanilla
½ teaspoon cloves
4-4½ cups flour

Mix as any other recipe; let cool for several hours or overnight. Roll and bake for 8 to 10 minutes at 375⁰.

**FROSTING:**
1 cup sugar
1 egg white

3½ tablespoons water
6 marshmallows (cut up)

Cook in double boiler. Beat as it cooks until it stands in peaks. Take from stove. Add 1 teaspoon vanilla. Put on cookies while still hot.

*This recipe was given to me many years ago by a friend. It was from her mother-in-law's mother, who was Old Order Amish.*

**Norma Fry**
**(Kalona, Iowa)**

463

# Peanut Butter Cookies

1 cup brown sugar
1 cup white sugar
1 cup shortening
2 eggs (well beaten)
1½ teaspoons vanilla

1 cup peanut butter
½ teaspoon soda in 2½ cups
   flour
½ teaspoon salt

Mix in order given. Roll into a ball the size of a walnut. Press flat with a fork in both directions. Bake at 375⁰ for 10 minutes.

*Blue ribbon winner at early 1960's Hamilton County Fair.*

**Cheryll Entriken**
**(Thank you also to: Bertha Shaw**
**Hamilton County Extension Service, Webster City, Iowa)**


# Pecan Cookies

Whole graham crackers
1 cup chopped pecans

1 cup brown sugar
1 cup butter

Boil together 1 cup brown sugar and 1 cup butter for 2 minutes on stove top. Fold in 1 cup chopped pecans. In an ungreased 9x13-inch pan line bottom with whole graham crackers and pour mixture over graham crackers. Bake for 12 minutes in a 350⁰ oven. Cool slightly and cut into squares.

*Whenever my children came home from school and smelled these baking, they always said, "What party are you going to?" These were the special cookies that they only got the scraps from. Even though it is the simplest recipe I have, they knew they were for special occasions.*

**Mrs. Robbie (Marvin) Winick**
**(Des Moines, Iowa)**

464

# Oatmeal Chocolate Chips

| | |
|---|---|
| 2 cups white sugar | 3½ cups flour |
| 2 cups brown sugar | 4 cups oatmeal |
| 2 cups butter | 1½ cups chocolate chips |
| 2 teaspoons soda | 1 cup cut up nutmeats |
| 2 teaspoons baking powder | 4 eggs |
| 1 teaspoon salt | 2 teaspoons vanilla |

I blend the sugars and butter in the mixer until creamy. I next add 4 eggs and vanilla, then salt, soda, baking powder, and flour. These should be sifted together. I then change the mixer to dough hooks and add oatmeal, chocolate chips, and nuts. Shape into walnut sized balls and flatten until about ½ the height. Use an ungreased cookie sheet. Bake 12 to 15 minutes in 350⁰ oven.

*My brother, sister, and I own the original farm or site on which the red delicious apple tree was discovered by Mr. Hiatt. The road which goes by there now is called Hiatt Apple Road.*

*We used to use our mom's sugar cookie recipe for cookies to keep on hand, but after we got to using this Oatmeal Chocolate Chip Recipe, we use it even more.*

**Elma Tracy
(Madison County)**

# Oatmeal Jim Jams

1 cup shortening
1 cup brown sugar
2 cups flour
½ teaspoon salt

1 teaspoon soda
½ cup sour milk
2 cups ground oatmeal

FILLING: COOK UNTIL THICK
¾ cup dates (cut fine)
¾ cup sugar

½ cup water

Mix cookie ingredients in order given. Dough should be stiff. Roll on floured pastry cloth quite thin. Cut in 2-2½ -inch circles. Bake 10 minutes in 350⁰ oven. When cool put 2 circles together with date filling between.

*This recipe is an old family favorite and usually made at Christmas time.*

Mrs. Franklin (Lois) Vogel
(Orange City, Iowa)

# Peanut Cookies

1 cup white sugar
1 cup brown sugar
1 cup shortening (I use oleo)
2 eggs (beaten)
1 cup cornflakes (crushed)

1 cup oatmeal
1 cup salted peanuts
1 teaspoon baking powder
1 teaspoon soda
2 cups flour

Cream sugars and shortening. Add eggs, beat well. Add rest of ingredients and drop by teaspoon on greased cookie sheet. Bake at 350⁰ until done. Do not overbake.

Dorla Schroder
(Princeton, Iowa)

# Olympic Cookies

*(From Olympic Training Center, Colorado Springs, Colorado)*

1 cup butter or margarine
1½ cups packed light brown
  sugar
1 egg
1¼ teaspoons vanilla
2½ cups quick oats
  (uncooked)

1 cup flour
1 teaspoon baking soda
½ teaspoon salt
1 cup M&M candies
½ cup raisins
¾ cup chopped nuts
¼ cup coconut

Beat together butter and sugar until light and fluffy; blend in egg
and vanilla. Add combined oats, flour, soda, and salt; mix well. Stir
in remaining ingredients. Drop dough by rounded teaspoonfuls onto
ungreased cookie sheet about 3-inches apart. Press 2 to 3 additional
candies into each cookie. Bake at 350° for 8-10 minutes. Makes 4
dozen 2½-inch cookies. Calories 97 per cookie.

**Dan Gable (Submitted by Kathy Gable)**
**(Wrestling Coach, University of Iowa)**

# Peanut Butter 'N Chocolate Chip Cookies

¾ cup (1½ sticks) butter
  or oleo
1 cup granulated sugar
1 cup firmly packed brown
  sugar
½ cup peanut butter
2 eggs

2 teaspoons vanilla
2½ cups flour
1 teaspoon baking soda
½ teaspoon salt
1 package (11.5 ounces) milk
  chocolate chips

Heat oven to 350°. Beat butter (or oleo), sugars and peanut butter in
large bowl with mixer on medium speed until light and fluffy. Blend
in eggs and vanilla. Mix in flour, baking soda, and salt. Stir in chips.
Drop by rounded tablespoonfuls onto ungreased cookie sheets. Bake
10 to 12 minutes or until lightly browned. Cool 2 minutes; remove
from cookie sheets onto wire racks. Makes about 4 dozen.

**Mary Ahlgren**
**(Le Claire, Iowa)**

# Pfeffernusse

½ cup butter
½ cup sugar
1 egg
4 cups flour
½ teaspoon cardamom

1½ teaspoons baking soda
½ teaspoon ground cloves
1 cup molasses
Whole blanched almonds
  for top

Cream butter and sugar. Add egg and mix well. Sift together dry ingredients and add alternately with molasses. Makes a stiff dough. Put in zipper bag or tight fitting container and keep in the refrigerator for several weeks so the flavors "marry." When ready to bake, roll into little balls - roll in sugar - press whole almond in center and bake 10 minutes at 350⁰ on greased cookie sheet. When cool, pack into a container and let sit for a week or more again. These are very hard and best "dunked".

*My aunt tells me they used to sit around the breakfast table and drop a few of the cookies into their coffee and then dip them out with a spoon.*

**Doris Haesemeyer**
**(Elmhurst, Illinois, formerly Stanwood, Iowa)**

# Pfeffernusse

1 cup butter
2 cups sugar
2 cups flour
2 eggs

½ cup sour cream (dissolve
  1 teaspoon soda in cream)
5 teaspoons cinnamon
Add a little ginger and
  nutmeg

Mix above ingredients. Add about 4 cups more of flour or enough to make a stiff dough. Roll out in finger-size widths. Chill. Cut in ½ -inch pieces and bake at 375⁰ for 10 minutes on ungreased cookie sheets.

**Lorraine Habben**
**(Thank you also to: Bertha Shaw)**

## Pride of Iowa Cookies

| | |
|---|---|
| 1 cup margarine | 1 teaspoon baking soda |
| 1 cup sugar | ½ teaspoon salt |
| 1 cup brown sugar | 2 teaspoons vanilla |
| 2 eggs | 3 cups oatmeal |
| 2 cups flour | 1 cup butterscotch chips |
| 1 teaspoon baking powder | |

Cream margarine and sugars. Stir in eggs. Sift together flour, baking powder, baking soda, and salt. Add to first mixture. Blend in vanilla, oatmeal and chips. Drop by teaspoon on greased cookie sheet. Bake at 350⁰ until light brown.

*This has been a favorite cookie recipe from when I was growing up. I entered these cookies at the Jones County Fair and nearly 25 years later my daughter used the same recipe and received a Gold ribbon at the Polk County 4-H Fair.*

Carol Wenndt
(Ankeny, Iowa)

## Ranger Cookies

| | |
|---|---|
| 1 cup shortening | ½ teaspoon salt |
| 1 cup white sugar | 1 teaspoon vanilla |
| 1 cup brown sugar | 2 cups oatmeal |
| 2 eggs | 1 cup coconut |
| 2 cups flour | 2 cups Wheaties or Rice |
| 1 teaspoon baking soda | Krispies |
| ½ teaspoon baking powder | 1 cup chopped nuts |

Cream shortening and sugars. Add unbeaten eggs and vanilla. Mix well. Sift together flour, baking powder, soda, and salt. Blend into creamed mixture. Add all remaining ingredients. Dough will be stiff. Drop cookies on cookie sheet. Bake at 350⁰ for 10 to 12 minutes. Makes about 7 dozen.

Ida Weibel
(Long Grove, Iowa)

# Rosettes

### *(Scandinavian Christmas Treats)*

| | |
|---|---|
| 2 eggs | 1 cup milk |
| 1 tablespoon sugar | 1 teaspoon vanilla |
| ¼ teaspoon salt | Fat for frying |
| 1 cup all-purpose flour | Powdered sugar |

In a mixing bowl combine the eggs, granulated sugar, and salt; beat well. Add flour, milk, and vanilla, and beat until smooth. Heat a rosette iron in deep hot fat (375⁰). Dip the hot rosette iron into the batter being careful batter only comes ¾ of the way up the side of the iron. Fry rosette in the hot fat until golden, about ½ minute. Lift iron out and tip slightly to drain off any excess fat with fork, carefully pushing rosette off iron onto paper towels placed on rack. Reheat iron; make the next rosette. Sift powdered sugar over the cooled rosettes. Makes 3½ dozen.

Susan Senn
(Davenport, Iowa)

# Rosettes

Similar to recipe above.

*If rosette falls off iron in hot fat, there is not enough flour in the batter. If rosette is thick, there is too much flour and you need to thin a bit with milk.*

*Rosettes may be dusted with powdered sugar or granulated sugar before serving. In Norway they are sometimes stacked three high with whipped cream between them and topped with fruit.*

Rosalie Dunnegan
(DeWitt, Iowa)

# Sandbakkelse

1 cup butter
1 cup sugar
2¾ cups flour

2 eggs
1 teaspoon almond extract

Cream the butter, gradually add sugar. Add eggs and almond extract, beat well, and add flour. Press small pieces of dough into individual sandbakkelse tins, beginning at the bottom and working upward to the top edge of the tin, using enough dough to form a thin hollow shell. Place tins on a cookie sheet and bake in 350⁰ oven for 15 minutes, or until golden brown. When done, remove tins and place upside down on cookie rack until they drop out. Makes 4 dozen.

*These are two recipes that my mother made every Christmas. When I was old enough, she taught me how to make these Norwegian cookies. Now I am passing this tradition onto my children.*

**Rosalie Dunnegan**
**(DeWitt, Iowa)**

# Snowball Cookies

1½ cups butter
3¼ cups powdered sugar
1 teaspoon vanilla
⅔ cup coconut

2½ cups dry oatmeal
1½ cups mini chocolate chips
or part mini M&M's

Mix butter, vanilla and powdered sugar. Add oatmeal and coconut. Stir in chocolate chips and M&M's. Mix well. Shape into walnut sized balls. Roll in powdered sugar and refrigerate. Ready to eat!

**Donna Millhollin**

# St. Nickolas Koekjes
*(Dutch Santa Claus Cookies)*

| | |
|---|---|
| 2 cups brown sugar | ½ teaspoon cloves |
| 1½ cups butter | 1 teaspoon baking powder |
| 3½ cups flour | 1 egg (beaten) |
| 1 teaspoon cinnamon | 1 scant teaspoon salt |
| ½ teaspoon nutmeg | |

Cream butter and sugar and add remaining ingredients. This makes a very stiff dough. Mold cookies on a Santa Claus Cookie board or form into a roll as for refrigerator cookies and slice when thoroughly chilled. Bake 10-12 minutes at 350⁰.

**Mrs. H.P. Scholte**
**Mrs. Lenore Hettinga**

*Mrs. H.P. Scholte was the daughter-in-law of Dominie H.P. Scholte, who founded Pella in 1847. Mrs. Lenore Hettinga was his great-granddaughter.*

*We grew up enjoying these special Dutch cookies and still enjoy them at ages 88 and 90.*

**Mrs. Francis Huyser**
**(Pella, Iowa)**

Similar recipes for Santa Claus cookies were submitted by Laurie Van Dyke, Mequon, Wisconsin, and Grace Soeth, Spirit Lake, Iowa.

*Laurie Van Dyke's recipe may have originated from the same Pella source as the recipe above. Grace explains how she got hers:*

*These cookies were very popular at our dorm at Drake University when Laurie Van Dyke would bring them after a weekend at home, about 1947-'48. I got the recipe and have made them almost every Christmas since. I have named them the "Van Dyke Christmas Cookies".*

# Santa Claus Cookies

*Santa Claus cookies were a regular Christmas treat when I was grow-ing up. I don't know where the recipe originated and, of course, I didn't think about that when I helped my mother make the cookies, using special cookie cutters to make decorative shapes.*

*My father, William Van Dyke, came to this country from the Netherlands in 1913, but I don't think he brought any recipes with him. My grandmother, Johanna Vandehaar -- my mother's mother -- came from the Netherlands in the middle of the 19th Century, as a small child in a family of 10. Her family settled in the Pella area.*

*The Santa Claus cookie recipe probably came from her family and the Pella connection.*

*There was very little Christmas activity at our Mitchellville farm home. I remember being very pleased at those times when we actually had a Christmas tree.*

*We usually got together with my two uncles and their families Christ-mas Day. My father, would crank up the '27 green Chevy and it often was a cold, snowy drive those 20 miles to Prairie City or Colo.*

*Presents of any kind were scarce in our house in those depression years. But there was always plenty to eat. As I recall, my mother, Bessie Van Dyke, made the Santa Claus cookies. My sister and I sometimes helped as we got older. My aunt who lived with us, Gesiena Van Pilsum, often made what she called coffee cake. It actually has coffee in it and has little resemblance to what we call coffee cake today.*

*When I was in grade school the cooking and baking were still being done on an iron range, the kind with a water reservoir on the side. After we got an electric stove in the kitchen, the old range was moved to the basement and my mother and aunt often cooked there, maybe to save elec-tricity, or maybe just because they felt comfortable with the old stove.*

*Anyone who ever used one of those wood stoves knows it wasn't easy to keep an even fire, but I don't remember that the cookies ever burned.*

*As my mother and aunt grew older, the traditional cookies and coffee cake often didn't get made. Years later, I found the recipes and sometimes made them at Christmas, for friends and my sister's family. At least two of my friends got the cookie recipe and still make Santa Claus cookies every year.*

*(Continued on Next Page)*

473

## (Van Dyke - Continued)

*After a lapse of a few years, I made the cookies and the coffee cake again this past Christmas. I had a newly remodeled kitchen and wanted to prove to skeptical friends that I could still bake.*

*I used my fancy new touch button oven and timer. Some of the cookies got a little crisp. I was almost finished when a "fault" signal flashed in the window and an insistent buzzing began. I managed to finish before I pulled the breaker to shut off the power to the oven. If I hadn't the cookies might have burned. It might have been nice to have an old wood range in the basement.*

Laurie Van Dyke
(Mequon, Wisconsin)

# Danish Sugar Cookies

2 cups sifted flour
¾ teaspoon soda
1 teaspoon cream of tartar
¼ teaspoon salt
1 cup powdered sugar

½ cup firm butter
½ cup vegetable shortening
1 egg (beaten)
1 teaspoon vanilla
Granulated sugar for rolling

Sift dry ingredients into bowl; cut in butter and shortening with pastry blender until mixture resembles coarse crumbs; stir in egg and vanilla. Dough is fairly soft. Shape in 1-inch balls. Roll in granulated sugar and place 2-inches apart on greased cookie sheets. Flatten to ½-inch thickness with bottom of glass dipped in granulated sugar. Bake at 350⁰ about 12 minutes or until delicately browned. Makes about 6½ dozen cookies.

Glenda Underwood Mariani
(Formerly Princeton, Iowa, now living in New Jersey)

# Spice Drop Cookies

| | |
|---|---|
| 1 cup sugar | 1 teaspoon baking powder |
| 1 egg | 1 teaspoon baking soda |
| ¼ cup lard or Crisco | 1 teaspoon cinnamon |
| ½ cup sorghum | 1 teaspoon cloves |
| ½ cup hot water | 1 teaspoon nutmeg |
| 2½ cups flour | |

Cream shortening and mix with sugar. Mix dry ingredients separately. Add baking soda to hot water and mix all ingredients. Drop size of cookie you desire on a greased pan. Bake 10 minutes at 400° F. If dough flattens out like a ginger snap add more flour. If you like black walnuts or raisins, add them. If you have to ask how many you don't like them.

*Boys Cooking Class at Mitchellville High School, 1941. A short lived experiment by Mary Lee Piper, Home Ec. Teacher. She left the next year and married E. Adlebert Crosby Jr. and moved to a farm in Nebraska where they raised a nice family of girls.*

*Our first cooking project was of our own choice. I used my mother's Spice Drop Cookie Recipe. It was a success. Then we got down to technical things such as leveling off a teaspoon of baking powder with a knife and not patting the flour down in the cup after sieving it, etc. By about the 4th class session we boys wanted to make a cherry pie, so we did. I don't recall if the crusts were flaky or the fillings too thick or runny but I do recall that we had no more classes. I think possibly Miss Piper discussed the merits of the class with the Superintendent.*

*Today they might call our delving into the culinary arts as "creative cookery"—but I doubt it. Really though, our school was ahead of its time in a number of ways. We had a class called "Consumer Science" with a text book of the same name by Hausrath & Harms, hot off the press with a publishing date of 1940. Field trips were the highlights of this course. We would go to Des Moines and tour a packing plant or the Jacobsen Candy Company where we got free samples of those candies that looked like they had been formed with an ice cream scoop and had cherry cream centers*

*(Continued on Next Page)*

475

## (Spice Drop Cookies - Continued)

*with lots of crushed peanuts and chocolate on the outside. One time we toured the Meadow Gold Ice Cream plant and learned that the different qualities of ice cream were determined by how much air they pumped into it. We also got free samples there. The Superintendent taught this class.*

*Another class we tried was "auto mechanics". I can't remember that we had a teacher but it might have been one of those "other duties as assigned" that they gave to the coach to legitimize the class. We bought an old Model T Ford that didn't run for $15.00 and towed it around back of the schoolhouse. We boys proceeded to take it apart and then put it back together (mostly during study or assembly hours) but it still didn't run so we sold it for $10.00 to the Olson boys who towed it down to their dad's garage. I don't know if he got it running or not. That ended our mechanics class.*

*The most important time I spent in high school was the two years in typing class. I am convinced this skill helped me more than anything else in conning my way through college. Of course, I had to steer away from classes with too much scientific or mathematical content. The bane of college freshmen is English. I avoided it by taking "Semantics" courses and when I discovered the instructor liked true war stories, I had it made. My faithful old "Underwood" of college days went off to Goodwill Industries just this year.*

**George Wilkinson
(Lakewood, Colorado, formerly Mitchellville, Iowa)**

SAGE

## Soft Tollhouse Cookies

1 cup shortening
¼ cup white sugar
¼ cup brown sugar
2 eggs
1 teaspoon vanilla

1 teaspoon soda
1 package instant vanilla
  pudding
2 cups quick oatmeal
1½ cups flour
2 cups chocolate chips

Cream together the first 6 ingredients. Add to the creamed ingredients the next 3 ingredients. Add the chocolate chips last. Drop by teaspoonful on ungreased cookie sheet. Bake 8 to 10 minutes at 350°. Do not over-bake, but remove from oven when brown around the edges and small spots of brown are on cookies.

**Marilou Gay**
**(Master Gardener '82, Johnson County)**

## Nano's Sugar Cookies

1 cup butter
1 cup sour cream
2 cups sugar
4 egg yolks
2 teaspoons vanilla extract

1 teaspoon lemon extract
1 teaspoon salt
1 teaspoon baking soda
5 cups flour

Mix all ingredients well. Chill. Form in small balls. Pat out on cookie sheets (Grandmother Vincent used to use her hands). Sprinkle cookies with sugar. Bake at 350° until lightly brown on an ungreased cookie sheet.

**Jamia Thompson Dailey**

*This is the recipe of Jamia Thompson Dailey. Her grandfather, William Vincent, was a dairy herdsman for the Iowa Men's Reformatory—a landmark in Anamosa, often called the White Palace of the west because of the white stone used to construct it.*

**(Thanks to: Sarah Schoon**
**Executive Director, Anamosa Chamber of Commerce)**

477

# Toll House Cookies

| | |
|---|---|
| 1 cup plus 2 tablespoons unsifted flour | 8 tablespoons sugar |
| ½ teaspoon baking soda | ½ teaspoon vanilla |
| ½ teaspoon salt | 1 cup chocolate morsels |
| ½ cup butter or margarine (softened) | 8 tablespoons brown sugar |
| | 1 egg |
| | ½ cup chopped nuts |

Combine flour, soda and salt. Set aside. Combine butter, sugar, brown sugar and vanilla. Beat until creamy. Beat in egg, and add flour mixture. Mix well. Stir in chocolate and nuts, drop by rounded teaspoon on ungreased cookie sheet. Bake at 375⁰ for 10 minutes.

*We got this cookie recipe from a next door neighbor when we lived in Jefferson, Iowa some 40 years ago. I baked some again this past Christmas. Our oldest grandson and his wife brought their 2 year old daughter, our first and only great-grandchild, out to visit us last week. They brought some cookies out for us, this same recipe, and they live in Wisconsin. So it really gets around.*

Ralph W. Held
(Sun City, Arizona, formerly Jefferson, Iowa)

# Vanilla Crescents (Vanilla Kipfert)

1 cup (2 sticks) sweet butter
⅓ cup sugar
1 teaspoon vanilla
2 cups finely chopped pecans
1½ teaspoons instant coffee
   (dry)

¼ teaspoon salt
Confectioner's sugar and
   granulated sugar
2 cups all-purpose flour

Cream butter, gradually add sugar. Beat until light and fluffy. Stir in vanilla. Combine flour, nuts, instant coffee and salt. Gradually stir into creamed mixture. Press dough into a ball, cover and refrigerate at least 1 hour for ease in handling. Preheat oven to 325⁰ F. Shape rounded teaspoonful of dough into crescents. Place one inch apart on ungreased cookie sheets. Bake until set but not brown, about 15 to 20 minutes. While still warm, roll crescents first in confectioner's sugar, then in granulated sugar, and finally in confectioner's sugar. Cool completely and store in tightly covered containers.

*I always bake these Vanilla Crescents around Christmas. it reminds me of my childhood in Vienna, Austria.*

**Wilma Howard
(Denton, Texas, formerly Cedar Falls, Iowa)**

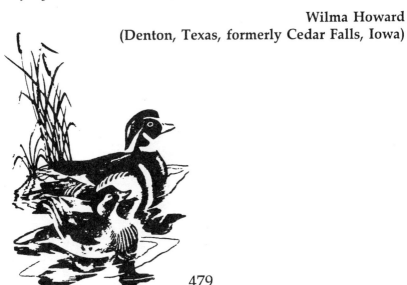

479

# A Granddaughter's Recollections

Holidays or special occasions were spent at my Grandmother's house in a little Eastern Iowa farming community. We had a wonderful dinner with the rest of the family (8 children and their families). The dining room table was extended and set for as many as possible and all the men sat down to eat first. When they finished the table was cleared, dishes all washed (by hand) (water heated in the tea kettle); then the table was reset, the food warmed up and the second sitting of women and children began. This procedure was repeated with the cooks being the last to eat. No one thought about "equal rights" - the most fun was in the kitchen anyway, where the women shared the latest gossip and jokes and just enjoyed the warmth of being together.

**Anonymous**

480

# Brownies

| | |
|---|---|
| 1 cup sugar | ½ cup butter or margarine |
| 2 eggs | ½ cup flour |
| 2 squares unsweetened chocolate | 1 teaspoon vanilla |
| | ½ cup chopped walnuts |

**FROSTING:**

| | |
|---|---|
| 1 cup sugar | 2 tablespoons butter or |
| 1 egg (beaten) | margarine |
| 2 tablespoons light cream | 1 teaspoon vanilla |
| 2 squares unsweetened chocolate | |

Add sugar to eggs; beat. Melt chocolate and butter, add to egg mixture. Blend in flour, add vanilla and nuts. Spread in greased 8x8x2-inch pan. Bake at 350⁰ for 25 to 35 minutes. Cool. Combine frosting ingredients. Bring to boil, stirring constantly. Remove from heat, stir until of spreading consistency. Spread over cooled brownies. Cut in 2-inch squares. Makes 16.

*These bars travel well. They are wonderful for school treats, potluck dinners, bake sales, and buffet dinners.*

**Beth Louise Wilimek Leutenegger**
**(Mequon, Wisconsin, formerly Newton, Iowa)**

481

# Beef Brownies

| | |
|---|---|
| ½ cup cooked ground beef (drain well) | 1 teaspoon vanilla |
| | 2 squares unsweetened |
| 3 eggs | chocolate |
| 1 cup sugar | ¾ cup flour |
| ½ teaspoon salt | 1 teaspoon baking powder |
| ½ cup butter | ½ cup nuts |

Beat eggs, sugar, salt, and vanilla until fluffy. Melt butter and chocolate. Cool. Add to egg mixture. Add nuts, flour, and baking powder. Mix well. Stir in browned beef. Bake in 8x8-inch greased pan at 350° for 35 minutes.

Emily Leonard
(Thanks also to: Bret Warnke)

# Thick Chewy Brownies

| | |
|---|---|
| 1 cup margarine | 2½ cups flour |
| 2 cups brown sugar | 1 teaspoon salt |
| 2 eggs | 1 teaspoon soda |
| 2 teaspoons vanilla | 3 cups oatmeal |

Cream margarine and sugar. Mix rest of ingredients. Put ⅔ of this in jelly roll pan and spread this mixture on top.

| | |
|---|---|
| 1 can Eagle brand milk | 2 teaspoons vanilla |
| 2 tablespoons margarine | 1 (12 ounce) package of |
| ½ teaspoon salt | chocolate chips |

Heat and melt chocolate chips, add rest of ingredients and spoon over mixture in pan. Then dot the top with remaining ⅓ of batter. Bake in 15x10-inch pan, in 350° oven for 30 to 35 minutes.

Rosemary A. Fuller
(Muscatine, Iowa)

# Twice Baked Brownies

| | |
|---|---|
| 1 German chocolate cake mix | 14 ounces light caramel |
| ⅓ cup evaporated milk | candies |
| ¾ cup melted margarine | ⅓ cup evaporated milk |
| 1 cup chopped nuts (optional) | 1 cup chocolate chips |

Mix cake mix, milk and margarine; add nuts. Press half of mixture into a greased 9x13-inch pan. Bake for 8 to 10 minutes at 350°. Melt caramels and milk together in a double boiler. Spread over baked crust. Sprinkle chocolate chips over caramel layer. Top with remaining cake batter. Spoon on and bake for another 15 to 20 minutes at 350. Cool slightly. Refrigerate for 30 minutes to set. Serves 24 to 30. First place ribbon Iowa State Fair Open Class Food Division in 1970's.

Bertha Shaw
(Hamilton County Extension Service, Webster City, Iowa)

# Championship Chocolate Chip Bars

| | |
|---|---|
| 1½ cups unsifted flour | 1 (14 ounce) can sweetened |
| ½ cup firmly packed brown | condensed milk (not |
| sugar | evaporated) |
| ½ cup cold margarine or | 1 egg |
| butter | 1 teaspoon vanilla |
| 1 (12 ounce) package | 1 cup chopped nuts |
| chocolate chips | |

Heat oven to 350°. Combine flour and sugar. Cut in margarine until crumbly. Stir in ½ cup chips; press firmly on bottom of 13x9-inch baking pan. Bake 15 minutes. Meanwhile, in same bowl, combine condensed milk, egg, and vanilla; stir in remaining 1½ cups chips and nuts. Spread evenly over prepared crust. Bake 20 to 25 minutes or until light brown. Cool completely. Store covered at room temperature. Makes 24 to 36 bars. *

Dan Gable (Submitted by Kathy Gable)
(Wrestling Coach, University of Iowa)
483

# Frosted Cream Bars

| | |
|---|---|
| 1 cup water | ½ teaspoon cinnamon |
| ¾ cup raisins | ½ teaspoon nutmeg |
| ¾ cup sugar | 1½ cups flour |
| ½ cup shortening | ¾ teaspoon soda |
| 1 egg | ½ cup nuts |
| ½ teaspoon salt | |

Pour water over the raisins and cook for 15 minutes. Reserve ½ cup liquid from raisins and set aside. Cream sugar and shortening. Add egg and beat. Dissolve soda in liquid reserved from raisins. Mix and sift flour, salt, cinnamon, nutmeg; then add to sugar mixture alternately with soda and liquid. Drain rest of liquid off and add raisins and nuts to the cookie mixture. Bake at 350° for 20 minutes on a greased cookie sheet. Frost while warm, cut into squares.

*The Frosted Cream Bars recipe is from Mother's recipe file. My mother was born in Center Point, Iowa (Linn Co.) in 1889. Her mother was named Iowa Anna Rogers as she was the first child in her family to be born in Iowa in Keokuk in 1851. We all loved the smell of these Frosted Creams when we came home from school, especially from college.*

**Jean Oxley**
**(Marion, Iowa)**

## Mom's Date Bars

¾ cup flour
1 teaspoon baking powder
¼ teaspoon salt
1 cup sugar
1 cup dates

1 cup walnuts
½ cup coconut
2 beaten eggs
1 teaspoon vanilla

Put dates, nuts, and coconut through food chopper. Add eggs and vanilla to dry ingredients. Add chopped dates, nuts, and coconut. Press into a 8-inch square pan. Bake at 350° for 15 to 20 minutes. Cut in squares and roll in powdered sugar while still warm.

*This recipe is in memory of my Mom, Caroline Neff, and one I so fondly remember her baking each Christmas.*

Carol Wenndt
(Ankeny, Iowa)

## Gram's Peanut Butter Bars

1 cup brown sugar
1 egg
½ cup peanut butter
½ cup butter
1 teaspoon soda

1½ cups flour
1 teaspoon vanilla
½ teaspoon salt
¼ cup quick oatmeal

Mix together and put into a 10x16x1-inch pan. Bake 15 minutes at 375°. Remove and frost with 1½ cups powdered sugar, 2 tablespoons butter, 2 tablespoons peanut butter, 1 teaspoon vanilla and 3 tablespoons milk.

*When my grandmother was in her 80's she still tried new recipes. I received it from her. Now my grandchildren request them. I asked an 11-year old what he wanted for Christmas this year. He said, peanut butter bars, and he got them.*

Mrs. LaDonna Huisman
(Hospers, Iowa)

# Frosted Creams/Cream Chocolate Frosting

1½ cups sugar
1 cup shortening
2 eggs
1 teaspoon cinnamon
1¼ teaspoons baking soda
1 cup liquid from cooked
  raisins

1½ cups raisins
3 cups flour
1 teaspoon salt
1 teaspoon vanilla
1 cup nuts

Cook raisins in water and keep 1 cup liquid; cool. Cream shortening, add sugar and eggs; beat until smooth. Sift together dry ingredients and add alternately with liquid and raisins, vanilla, and nuts. Spread ½-inch thick on large cookie sheet. (I use a jelly roll pan). Sprinkle chocolate chips over the top before baking. Bake at 350° until done or about 40 minutes. Frost with creamy chocolate frosting.

## CREAM CHOCOLATE FROSTING:

3 squares unsweetened
  chocolate
2 tablespoons butter
3 cups sifted confectioners
  sugar

7 tablespoons milk
1 teaspoon vanilla

Melt chocolate and butter. Add to confectioners sugar and milk mixture; beat until smooth and add vanilla. Cut in squares.

Marvella Brus
(Blue Grass, Iowa)

486

# Peanut Butter Fingers

½ cup butter
½ cup sugar
½ cup firmly packed brown
  sugar
1 unbeaten egg
⅓ cup peanut butter (either
  chunky or smooth)

½ teaspoon soda
¼ teaspoon salt
½ teaspoon vanilla
1 cup flour
1 cup quick oats
1 cup semi-sweet chocolate
  chips

Cream sugars and butter. Blend with egg, peanut butter and vanilla. Combine flour, soda and salt in sifter. Add to first mixture stirring well. Add rolled oats. Mix well. Spread in greased 9x13-inch pan. Bake at 350⁰ for 20 to 25 minutes. When done remove from oven and sprinkle with the 1 cup of chocolate chips - immediately. Let stand for 5 minutes until melted. Then spread. Cool and cut into bars. Makes approximately 4 dozen.

Ann Marie Underwood
(Formerly Princeton, Iowa)

# Prune Bars

**CRUST:**
1 cup sugar
¾ cup margarine
½ teaspoon soda
1 teaspoon salt

2 cups flour
½ cup coconut
½ cup coarse chopped nuts

Mix this all to crumbs. Pour 3 cups in a 9x13-inch pan. Press in and bake 10 minutes at 400⁰. Meanwhile, have 2½ or 3 cups prunes cooked; add to them ¾ cup sugar. Thicken with cornstarch. Spread this on the baked crumb mixture. Sprinkle rest of crumbs on top and bake 25-30 minutes at 375⁰ until some brownness appears on top. Very good!

Marguerite Vens
(Davenport, Iowa)

# Pecan Pie Squares

3 cups flour
¼ cup plus 2 tablespoons
sugar

¾ cup margarine
¾ teaspoon salt

Heat oven to 350°. Grease a (15½ x10¼ x1-inch) jelly roll pan. Beat flour, sugar, margarine and salt in large bowl on medium speed until crumbly (mixture will be dry). Press firmly in pan. Bake until light golden brown, about 25 minutes. Prepare filling. Pour over baked layer: spread evenly. Bake until filling is set, about 25 minutes, cool, cut into 1½ -inch squares. It usually needs to bake longer until center is set.

**FILLING:**
4 eggs (beaten)
1½ cups sugar
1½ cups Karo syrup

3 tablespoons margarine
1½ teaspoons vanilla
2½ cups chopped pecans

Mix all ingredients except pecans until well blended. Stir in pecans. I use brown sugar and white syrup.

**Rosemary A. Fuller**
**(Muscatine, Iowa)**

# Scotcheroos

1 cup sugar
1 cup light corn syrup
1 cup chocolate chips

1 cup peanut butter
1 cup butterscotch chips
6 cups Rice Krispies

Combine sugar and syrup in a 3 quart sauce pan. Cook over moderate heat, stirring frequently until mixture boils. Stir in peanut butter. Add Rice Krispies, stir until blended. Press into a buttered 9x13-inch pan. Melt chips in the microwave or in a sauce pan on low; heat, and pour over Rice Krispies mixture.

**Joni Lange**
**(Davenport, Iowa)**

# Pumpkin Bars

**MIX:**

4 eggs
1 cup oil

2 cups sugar
1 (15 ounce) canned pumpkin

**SIFT:**

2 cups of flour
2 teaspoons cinnamon
2 teaspoons baking powder
1 teaspoon soda

½ teaspoon salt
½ teaspoon nutmeg
¼ teaspoon ginger
½ teaspoon cloves

Mix together the above ingredients. Pour into greased pan (12x18x1-inch). Bake at 350° for 25 to 30 minutes. Serves 32.

**FROSTING:**

1 (8 ounce) cream cheese
   (softened)
¾ stick butter

1 tablespoon milk
1 teaspoon vanilla
4 cups powdered sugar

Julie Ward
(Le Claire, Iowa)

# Sour Cream Raisin Bars

1¾ cups oatmeal
1¾ cups flour
1 cup brown sugar
1 teaspoon baking soda
1 cup melted oleo

6 egg yolks
2¼ cups sugar
4½ tablespoons cornstarch
3 cups sour cream
   (commercial)
3 cups raisins

Combine oatmeal, flour, brown sugar, and soda. Blend well. Add butter (oleo) and mix well. Pat ⅔ of mixture into a 9x13-inch pan. Bake at 350° for 15 minutes. Combine remaining ingredients in pan. Cook until thickened, stirring to avoid scorching. Pour over crumb layer and cover with remaining crumbs. Bake 20 minutes at 350°.

Norma Skinner
(Mitchellville, Iowa)

# Pumpkin Bars

2 cups sugar
4 eggs
1 cup oil
2 cups flour

2 cups pumpkin
2 teaspoons baking powder
½ teaspoon salt
1 teaspoon soda
4 tablespoons cinnamon

Mix together and pour onto cookie jelly pan. Bake at 350° for 25 minutes.

FROSTING:
3 ounce package cream cheese
¾ stick oleo
1 tablespoon cream (milk)

1 teaspoon almond flavoring
1¾ cups powdered sugar

Combine all ingredients and frost when cool. They freeze well.

**Sandy Ridout
(Anchorage, Alaska, formerly Massena, Iowa)**

# Pumpkin Pie Squares

1 cup flour
½ cup brown sugar
½ cup quick rolled oats
½ cup margarine
1 (16 ounce) can pumpkin
1 (13½ ounce) evaporated
   milk
¾ cup sugar

2 eggs
½ teaspoon salt
1 teaspoon cinnamon
½ teaspoon ginger
¼ teaspoon cloves
½ cup pecans
½ cup brown sugar
2 tablespoons margarine

Combine flour, oats, brown sugar and margarine in mixing bowl. Mix until crumbly. Press into ungreased 9x13-inch pan. Bake at 350° for 15 minutes. Combine pumpkin, milk, eggs, sugar and spices in bowl. Beat well. Pour onto crust. Bake at 350° for 20 minutes. Combine pecans, brown sugar and margarine. Sprinkle over pumpkin mixture. Bake 15 to 20 minutes or until filling is set. Cool and cut into squares.

**Jeri O'Conner
(New Hampton, Iowa)**

# Raisin-Spice Squares

| | |
|---|---|
| 1 cup raisins | 2 cups water |
| ½ cup shortening | ½ teaspoon baking powder |
| ¼ teaspoon salt | 1 cup sugar |
| 1 egg | 1 teaspoon soda |
| ½ cup chopped nuts | 1 teaspoon cinnamon |
| (optional) | 1 teaspoon nutmeg |
| 1¾ cups flour | 1 teaspoon allspice |

Boil together raisins and water. Save ½ cup of the liquid. Melt shortening in raisin liquid. Mix together drained raisins, shortening and rest of ingredients. Bake in 9x13-inch pan at 325⁰ for 30-35 minutes.

*This is a family recipe from Nona Noll Fair, my grandfather's sister. Nona loved the Cubs baseball team. She and my father would argue over the Cubs or Cardinals being better! Nona and her husband lived in Laurens, Iowa and operated the movie theater.*

**Catherine Noll Litwinow**
**(Davenport, Iowa)**

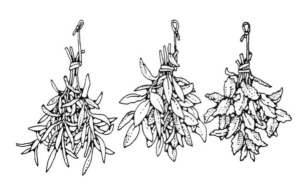

TARRAGON      SAGE      MINT

# Berry Berry Streusel Bars

1½ cups Quaker Oats (quick or old fashioned, uncooked)
1¼ cups all-purpose flour
½ cup firmly packed brown sugar
¾ cup (1½ sticks) margarine or butter (melted)

1 cup fresh or frozen blueberries
⅓ cup raspberry or strawberry preserves
1 teaspoon all-purpose flour
½ teaspoon grated lemon peel (optional)

Heat oven to 350⁰ F. Combine oats, 1¼ cups flour, brown sugar and margarine; mix until crumbly. Reserve 1 cup for topping; set aside. Press remaining oat mixture evenly onto bottom of ungreased 8 or 9-inch square baking pan. Bake 13 to 15 minutes or until light golden brown. Cool slightly. In medium bowl, combine remaining ingredients; mix gently. Spread over crust. Sprinkle with reserved oat mixture, patting gently. Bake 20 to 22 minutes or until light golden brown. Cool completely; cut into bars. Store tightly covered. Makes 16 bars. Nutrition Information (1 bar): Calories 190, Fat 9 grams, Sodium 110 milligrams, Dietary Fiber 1 gram

**Quaker Oats Company**
**(Cedar Rapids, Iowa)**

492

# Candy

# Mamie Doud Eisenhower Birthplace
## Boone, Iowa

*Restoration Drawing by*
*William J. Wagner, Dallas Center, Iowa*
*Courtesy of Mamie Doud Eisenhower*
*Birthplace Foundation, Inc.*

# Iowa's First Lady
*(Born in Boone)*

The birth of Mamie Doud Eisenhower took place on November 14, 1896. Her birthplace is one of only 2 First Lady homes in the country to be restored.

Ike and Mamie were married on July 1, 1916. They lived in 28 homes in 35 years. Wherever possible, they had a vegetable garden, and several rows of corn when there was room.

By the time Ike and Mamie moved into The White House Ike had already become quite handy in the kitchen. His culinary skills were very impressive. Although Mamie's cooking was not quite up to her husband's, her abilities to organize and be in command were. Being married to a military man had made her very strong-willed. Two weeks after taking residence in The White House she made it very clear who was wearing the 5 stars when it came to managing her home. She was to be in charge of the White House kitchen and dining room. White House menus were to be approved by Mamie and only Mamie.

# CANDY

## CANDY

Mamie's Million
 Dollar Fudge . . . . . . . . . 498
Pumpkin Chiffon Pie from
 Mamie's White House
 Recipe Files . . . . . . . . . . 498
Almond Bark
 Drop Candy . . . . . . . . . . 499
Almond Butter Crunch . . 499
Caramels . . . . . . . . . . . . . . 500
No Bake Crisp
 Caramel Clusters . . . . . 500
Caramel Pecan Turtles . . 501
Cereal Candy . . . . . . . . . . 501
Chocolate
 Covered Cherries . . . . . 502

Cherry Mash . . . . . . . . . . 502
Martha Washington
 Chocolates . . . . . . . . . . 503
Date Loaf Candy . . . . . . 503
Divinity . . . . . . . . . . . . . . 504
Peanut Butter Balls . . . . . 504
Amy Wilson's Peanut
 Butter Candy . . . . . . . . 505

Peanut Brittle . . . . . . . . . 507
Pioneer Candy . . . . . . . . . 507
Creamy Praline Patties . . 508
Salted Nut Roll . . . . . . . . 508
Pulled Taffee . . . . . . . . . . 509
Salt Water Taffy . . . . . . . . 509
Sugarless Sweets . . . . . . . 510

# Mamie Doud Eisenhower
## Early Kitchen and Recipes

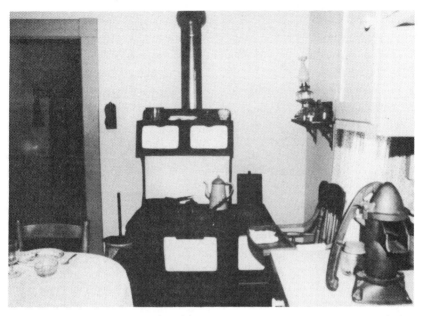

*(Used with permission of Mamie Doud Eisenhower Birthplace Foundation, Inc.)*

While visiting the kitchen you'll find an oak ice box, a wall telephone, table with cane chairs, high chair, hand pump, and wood burning cook stove. The pantry provides storage space for canning jars, crocks, utensils and food necessities. Behind the Birthplace is the summer kitchen used for cooking, preserving food, and doing laundry. Here you'll find a copper clad boiler, a gas stove, laundry tubs, washboards, and wire carpet beaters.

# Mamie's Million Dollar Fudge

4½ cups sugar
2 tablespoons butter
Pinch of salt
1 tall can evaporated milk
12 ounces semi-sweet
  chocolate bits

12 ounces German sweet
  chocolate
1 pint marshmallow cream
2 cups of nutmeats

Boil the sugar, salt, butter and evaporated milk together for 6 minutes. Put chocolate bits, German chocolate, marshmallow cream and nutmeats in a bowl. Pour the boiling syrup over the ingredients. Beat until chocolate is all melted, then pour in a pan. Let stand for a few hours before cutting. Remember it is better the second day. Store in a tin box.

*Even though fudge was Mamie's main culinary claim to fame, she did keep a recipe file of 12 or so Eisenhower family specialties. She was happy to share these with anyone who asked.*

# Pumpkin Chiffon Pie from Mamie's White House Recipe Files

3 egg yolks (beaten)
¾ cup brown sugar
1½ cups cooked pumpkin
½ cup milk
½ teaspoon salt
1 teaspoon cinnamon

½ teaspoon nutmeg
1 envelope of plain gelatin
¼ cup cold water
3 egg whites (stiffly beaten)
¼ cup granulated sugar

Combine egg yolks, brown sugar, pumpkin, milk, salt and spices. Cook in a double boiler until thick, stirring constantly. Soak gelatin in cold water, stir into hot mixture. Chill until partly set. Beat egg whites, add granulated sugar and beat until stiff. Fold into gelatin mixture. Pour into baked pie shell and chill until set. Garnish with whipped cream. Makes one big pie.

**Recipes from "Ike The Cook," Edward and Candace Rossoli**

## Almond Bark Drop Candy

1 pound almond bark (vanilla
   or chocolate)
½ cup peanut butter

1½ cups Rice Krispies
1 cup mini marshmallows
1 cup dry roasted peanuts

Melt almond bark and peanut butter in double boiler. When melted, mix together with the other ingredients, and drop on wax paper. Let cool.

Margaret Eckel
(Huxley, Iowa)

## Almond Butter Crunch

1 cup butter (only)
1⅓ cups sugar
1 tablespoon light corn syrup
3 tablespoons water
1 cup coarsely chopped,
   blanched almonds (toasted)

4 (4½ ounce) bars milk
   chocolate (melted)
1 cup finely chopped,
   blanched almonds (toasted)

Melt butter in large saucepan. Add sugar, corn syrup and water. Cook, stirring occasionally, to hard-crack stage (300°). Quickly stir in coarsely chopped nuts; spread in ungreased 13x9½ x2-inch pan. Cool thoroughly. Turn out on waxed paper; spread top with half the chocolate; sprinkle with half of finely chopped nuts. Cover with waxed paper; invert and spread again with chocolate. Sprinkle top with remaining nuts. If necessary, chill to firm chocolate. Break in pieces.

*I make this one at Christmas. It is a very good one.*

Velma E. Skola
(Kalona, Iowa)

# Caramels

2 cups sugar
½ pound butter
1½ cups dark corn syrup

1 pint cream (divided)
1 teaspoon vanilla
Nuts (optional)

Combine sugar, butter, syrup, vanilla and ½ of cream; bring to a boil. Add other ½ of cream drop by drop while mixture boils. Reduce heat, boil slowly until hard ball stage. Pour into shallow buttered pan, cool. Cut into 1-inch squares, wrap in wax paper. For Fudge Caramels; add 3 squares of bitter chocolate after removing from stove.

Susan Severs
(Princeton, Iowa)

## No Bake Crisp Caramel Clusters

½ cup butter
1 (14 ounce) package caramels
   (unwrapped)
¼ cup milk

6 cups Cornflakes (6 ounces)
   (slightly crushed)
⅔ cup chopped pecans
1 cup flaked coconut

Line several sheets with wax paper. In large saucepan, combine butter, caramels, milk. Stir over low heat until caramels are melted and mixture is smooth. Remove from heat and add remaining ingredients. Mix well. Drop by rounded tablespoonful onto lined sheets. Mixture will be hot so work where you can rinse hands often. Cool until set (about 1 hour). Store in airtight container separating with wax paper between layers. Store in refrigerator or cool room.

Anna Schmidt
(Princeton, Iowa)

## Caramel Pecan Turtles

1 pound caramels
2 tablespoons water

¾ pound pecan halves
1 cup chocolate chips

Melt caramels with water in double boiler. Arrange 36 groups of nuts (3-4 nuts per group) on greased cookie sheet. Drop caramel by teaspoon onto nuts. Cool 15 minutes. Melt chocolate chips over hot water, spoon over top of caramels, cool until set, store in air-tight container. Can be frozen.

*These have become a "must" for me to make every year at Christmastime for our family gathering.*

**Susan Severs
(Princeton, Iowa)**

## Cereal Candy

2 cups Rice Krispies
2 cups Cheerios
2 cups Total
2 cups marshmallows

2 cups dry roasted nuts
1 package almond bark
(white)
1 cup peanut butter (creamy)

Melt almond bark in large pan in oven at 200°. Takes about ½ hour. Stir in peanut butter. In large bowl put cereal, marshmallows, and nuts. Mix well. Stir into almond mix. Drop by teaspoon onto wax paper and cool.

*This is great for a Christmas present. I give it to many of my friends.*

**Lois J. Reed
(Davenport, Iowa)**

# Chocolate Covered Cherries

2 pounds powdered sugar
1 stick softened butter
1 can Eagle Brand milk
1 tablespoon almond extract

3 (12 ounce) jars maraschino
cherries
16 ounces chocolate chips
½ bar paraffin

Mix butter, milk, and extract in bowl, add sugar and put in freezer. Drain cherries on paper towels and freeze. After frozen wrap powdered sugar dough around cherries and freeze again (buttered hands help). Melt chocolate chips and paraffin. Dip frozen cherries in chocolate and set on wax paper.

Dorothy Willet
(Davenport, Iowa)

# Cherry Mash

2 cups sugar
16 marshmallows (large)
Small can evaporated milk
12 ounce package cherry
chips

12 ounce package chocolate
chips
¾ cup peanut butter
16 ounce Spanish salted
peanuts

Melt marshmallows. Boil the marshmallows, sugar and evaporated milk for 5 minutes (use heavy saucepan). Add 12 ounce package cherry chips, and pour in greased 9x12-inch pan. Melt 12 ounce package chocolate chips and ¾ cup peanut butter in double boiler. Grind your Spanish peanuts and add to the melted chips. Spread over the cherry mixture. Cool and cut in squares.

*This is very good candy.*

Margaret Eckel
(Huxley, Iowa)

# Martha Washington Chocolates

2 (1 pound) boxes powdered
  sugar
1 stick butter or oleo
1 can Eagle Brand milk
3 (6 ounce) packages of
  chocolate chips

¾ cake of paraffin
1 can coconut flakes
1 teaspoon vanilla
2½ cups nuts (crushed
  or chopped fine)

Mix all ingredients very thoroughly. Roll into small balls and chill in refrigerator. Melt the chocolate chips in double boiler with the paraffin. Dip the chilled balls using a fork, and place on waxed paper. Trim as desired before chocolate has set.

*This was my Mother's recipe (Oma Weatherholt). She made these chocolates at Christmas and decorated them with nuts or non-pareil sprinkles.*

**Willis Ann Wolff**
**(Kimberling City, Missouri, formerly Des Moines, Iowa)**

# Date Loaf Candy

1 cup milk
2 cups sugar
¼ cup butter

1 cup shredded coconut
1 cup dates
1 cup chopped nuts

Cook milk, sugar and butter over fire until it forms a soft ball when tried in cold water. Then add dates that have been stoned and cut in small pieces. Stir and cook until mixture leaves side of pan. Remove from fire and add coconut and nuts. Continue beating until quite firm. Pour on wet cloth and roll in a long roll. When cold, cut in slices.

*My Grandma used to make this candy when I was a little girl at Christmas time. We always liked receiving her box of goodies.*

**Norma Fry**
**(Kalona, Iowa)**

# Divinity

4 cups sugar
1 cup light corn syrup

¾ cup water
3 egg whites (stiffly beaten)

Place sugar, syrup, and water in a saucepan over low heat. Stir until sugar is dissolved. Then cook without stirring to 255°. Remove from heat and pour constantly in a fine stream into the three stiffly beaten egg whites. Continue beating until mixture holds its shape and loses its gloss. Add one teaspoon vanilla or cherry flavoring. Spread in a 11x7-inch pan. Cut into small squares.

Beverly Schocker
(Davenport, Iowa)

# Peanut Butter Balls

1 stick oleo
1 (18 ounce) jar of crunchy
   peanut butter
3 cups Rice Krispies
   (crushed)

1 pound powdered sugar
½ bar paraffin
1 (12 ounce) package
   chocolate chips

Melt together oleo and peanut butter. Then add Rice Krispies and powdered sugar. Roll into balls about the size of a walnut. Let stand about an hour. Then dip with ½ bar of paraffin and 12 ounce package of chocolate chips. Melt together in double boiler, melting chips on low. Dip balls in chocolate and set on wax paper.

Margaret Eckel
(Huxley, Iowa)

# Amy Wilson's Peanut Butter Candy

2 cups sugar
⅔ cup evaporated milk
¼ cup butter

1 cup peanut butter
1 teaspoon vanilla

Combine sugar, evaporated milk and butter in 3 quart casserole dish. Cook on full power in microwave for 10-12 minutes or until soft-ball stage is reached. (Stir mixture 3 times during cooking time.) Beat in peanut butter and vanilla until mixture is smooth and creamy. Pour into greased 8x8-inch dish. Let cool. Yield: 25 pieces of titillating sweet peanut butter candy!

*This is a fun recipe for peanut butter candy my grandma Amy Wilson devised from her concoctions of "throwing things together" and making wondrous sweet morsels she always had on hand for her grandchildren.*

*I used to watch her make candy, and she never once used a written recipe for it. She knew it from heart. The amazing thing about it was she never made a bad batch of the candy. It always came out perfect. I finally watched and wrote the recipe down as she made it one time when she was in her early eighties because I wanted to have it to share with my children. My wife has learned to make this candy and it is terrific!*

*My grandma Amy was raised near Moravia, Iowa born in 1898. She was a country girl who married at sixteen and lived a full and glorious life, here, in southern Iowa that took her from pioneer days of no electricity, no running water, etc. to the modern conveniences of the early 1980's. Along with our other family members, my grandmother understood the deep love and heritage of living in Iowa that was passed on to coming generations. She, along with all ancestors, is what helps make this country great and this state a blessing to live in.*

*It is a heritage my children are being taught about as well.*

Ric Wilson
(Centerville, Iowa)

# Morning, Iowa Born

The melodic song of the Cardinal
sweetens the morning air,
its pastoral-like overture a free gift
of nature's calling to a new day,
                        Iowa born.

Screen doors squeak open
then slam shut.
Pickup trucks start roughly
then move slowly on graveled roads
well marked by tractor tires.
Coffee is brewing at the local cafe.

Neighbored next to fields
of beans and corn,
cattle graze on pasture grass.
WHO radio's morning reporter
says no rain again today.

The wind stirs from the south
as yellow school busses,
stopping and starting,
dot the countryside.

        Ric Wilson
        (Centerville, Iowa)

506

# Peanut Brittle

1 cup white sugar
½ cup white Karo syrup
½ cup water

1 tablespoon butter
1 heaping teaspoon soda
1½ cups raw peanuts

Mix all but soda and cook to 234⁰. Use a 3 quart heavy saucepan. Add 1½ cups raw peanuts. Cook to 290⁰ or 310⁰. Remove from heat, add soda. Pour immediately on greased cookie sheet. Spread and cool. Break into small pieces.

Beverly Schocker
(Davenport, Iowa)

# Pioneer Candy

A good digestive candy for children and dyspeptics. It is made from the roots of the sweet-flag by washing and slicing them fine, then placing them in a pan with enough cold water to cover them, and slowly heating it over a stove or fire until the water boils. If the candy is to be used rather as a sweet meat than as a medicine, the roots should be treated 4 or 5 times in this way, each time pouring off the water. To each 2 cupfuls of the boiled roots, add a cupful and a half of white sugar. Then water sufficient to cover them, and allow the whole to simmer slowly on the stove until the water has quite boiled away. The candy is then to be emptied out on buttered plates and stirred frequently until dry.

Penelope Miller
(Princeton, Iowa)

507

# Creamy Praline Patties

| | |
|---|---|
| 2 cups sugar | 1½ tablespoons butter |
| ¾ teaspoon soda | (measure exactly) |
| 1 cup light cream | 2 cups pecan halves |

In deep 3 quart saucepan, combine sugar and soda. Mix well with wooden spoon. Stir in cream carefully. Bring to boil over medium heat; stir occasionally. Reduce heat; cook and stir to soft ball stage (234°). Double check for soft ball stage. Use both a candy thermometer and the cold water test. Remove from heat. Add butter immediately and pecans. Beat mixture until thick, 2 to 3 minutes. Drop from metal spoon on waxed paper. (If necessary, add a little hot water). Makes 24 to 30 1½-inch patties.

Terry Swails
(KWQC-TV - Channel 6, Davenport, Iowa)

# Salted Nut Roll

| | |
|---|---|
| 2½ tablespoons oleo | 2 cups miniature |
| 1 (12 ounce) package peanut | marshmallows |
| butter chips | 1 (12 ounce) jar of roasted |
| 1 can Eagle Brand condensed | nuts |
| milk | |

Melt oleo and peanut butter chips. Remove from heat, add condensed milk and stir well, add marshmallows and nuts. Put in a 9x13-inch buttered pan. Set in refrigerator until cool. Enjoy.

Mary Craig
(Mitchellville, Iowa)

508

# Pulled Taffee

2 cups sugar
¾ cup white Karo syrup
1 tablespoon butter

1 teaspoon vinegar
½ teaspoon vanilla

Boil first 4 ingredients together until a few drops of it in cold water will form a hard ball. Add vanilla, pour into buttered pie tins and cool until the mixture can be handled. Butter hands and pull, pull, pull! When candy holds shape and is creamy in color, twist to about the size of one's little finger; then cut with scissors into bite size portions and drop onto wax paper.

**Neal Smith**
**(Altoona, Iowa)**

# Salt Water Taffy

2 cups sugar
1 cup light corn syrup
1½ teaspoons salt

2 tablespoons butter
¼ teaspoon oil of peppermint
7 drops green food coloring

Combine sugar, syrup, salt and 1 cup water in pan. Cook slowly, stir until sugar dissolves, then cook to hard ball stage. Remove from heat, stir in remaining ingredients, pour into buttered 10x15-inch pan, cool until able to handle. Butter hands, gather candy and pull. When it gets light in color and is hard to pull, cut in 4ths, pull each into long strand ½-inch thick. With buttered scissors, snip into bite size pieces, wrap each in wax paper.

*This recipe goes back to my great grandmother's time of cooking.*

**Susan Severs**
**(Princeton, Iowa)**

# Sugarless Sweets
*(Great For Children)*

1 cup chopped dates        1 cup seedless raisins
1 cup chopped nuts         1/8 teaspoon salt

Combine ingredients. Form balls. Dip in chocolate, or roll in coconut
or powdered sugar.

**Lavaughn Stolba**
**(Cedar Rapids, Iowa)**

# Miscellaneous

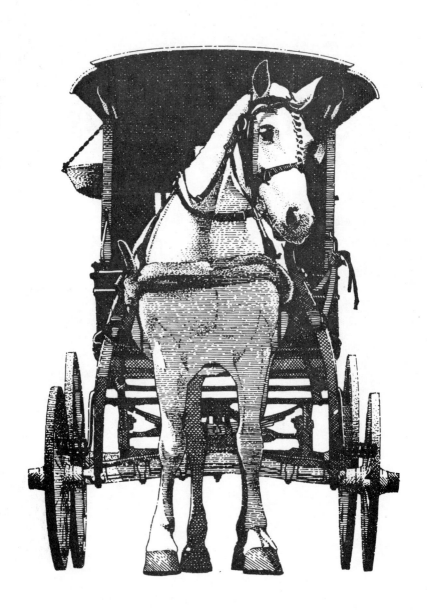

# Kalona, Iowa
## "The Quilt Capital of Iowa"

When John Gregg Myers came to the Kalona area in 1851, from Des Moines, he most likely was interested only in gaining about 700 good acres to establish a prominent farm and make a home for his wife. He was a Washington County pioneer, and a successful raiser of hogs and thorough-bred cattle. Myers was the father of 12 and was described as honest and a man of a social and courteous disposition.

In 1879 when part of the B.C.R. & N. railroad extended across the southern line of his farm, he succeeded in getting the Kalona station on his farm. He suggested Kalona for the name of the station site and it was approved. Kalona was actually the name of the registered sire of his famous herd. The first station agent for the B.C.R. & N. railroad was John Ryan. The town of Kalona, Iowa was platted in the middle of a field on August 6, 1879, on the land of John G. Myers.

The Amish and Mennonites of the area have contributed a great deal to Kalona's progress in business and community affairs. Kalona is the largest Amish-Mennonite settlement west of the Mississippi River. Over the years more and more retiring couples have chosen this location.

Today Kalona is the second largest town in Washington County, both in population and prosperity. History is a visible, living thing here. It is a place where, according to British Novelist Angus Wilson, "You can meet the 19th century coming over the hill in a horse and buggy."

## MISCELLANEOUS

Recipe for the
Language of Flowers . . 515
Canned Peaches
In Oven . . . . . . . . . . . . 516
Lydia's Dried Corn . . . . . 516
Mrs. Rowe's Kraut . . . . . . 517
Whole Tomatoes
in Oven . . . . . . . . . . . . 517
Corncob Jelly . . . . . . . . . . 518
Rhubarb Jam . . . . . . . . . . 518
Plum Jelly . . . . . . . . . . . . 519
Strawberry Jam . . . . . . . . 519
Rhubarb Conserve . . . . . 520
Pickles . . . . . . . . . . . . . . . 520
Violet Jelly . . . . . . . . . . . . 521
Pepper Relish . . . . . . . . . 521
Mother's Piccalili . . . . . . 522
Chili Sauce . . . . . . . . . . . . 522
Glazed Crystal Pickles . . 523
Cucumber Catsup . . . . . . 523
16 Day Pickles . . . . . . . . . 524
Cranberry Ice . . . . . . . . . . 525
Country Style Hot
Dog Relish . . . . . . . . . . 525

Cream Chipped Beef . . . . 526
Easy Hollandaise Sauce . 526
Fried Pumpkin
Blossoms . . . . . . . . . . . . 527
Grape Catsup . . . . . . . . . . 528
Garbage Can Dinner . . . . 528
Country Butter . . . . . . . . . 529
Cupcake Filling . . . . . . . . 530
Golden Fry Batter . . . . . . 530
Mayonnaise . . . . . . . . . . . 530
Sweetened
Condensed Milk . . . . . . 531
Cereal Pudding . . . . . . . . 531
Cottage Pudding . . . . . . . 532
Bay Leaf Swag . . . . . . . . 532
The Housekeeper's
Alphabet . . . . . . . . . . . . 533
Oddments . . . . . . . . . . 534-535
Recipes For
The Sick . . . . . . . . . . 536,537
Christmas Potpourri . . . . 538
Lye Soap . . . . . . . . . . . . . . 539
Hulda's
Homemade Soap . . . . . 540

# Recipe for the Language of Flowers

Amaryllis - Splendid beauty
Alyssum - Worth beyond beauty
Balloon Flower - Return of a friend is desired
Lemon Balm - Sharpens wit and understanding
Basil - Best wishes, hatred
Carnation - Admiration, (pink-maternal love; white-living love; striped-refusal)
Chrysanthemum - Cheerfulness, (red - I love you; white-truth)
Daisy - Innocence
Daylily - Flirt
Forsythia - Good natured
Geranium - Comfort; you are childish
Goldenrod - Encouragement
Grass - Submission; the fleeting quality
Hollyhock - Fruitfulness
Ivy - Wedded love, fidelity
Lily of the Valley - Return of happiness
Lily - Purity
Nasturtium - Patriotism
Orchid - Luxury, refinement
Pansy - Thought of love
Sweet Pea - Departure, Adieu! meet me!
Phlox - Our souls are united
Queen Anne's Lace - I'll return!
Rose - Love, beauty
Snapdragon - No! You're dazzling, but dangerous
Thyme - Activity, bravery, courage
Tulip - Fame, charity, perfect lover
Violet - Modesty
Zinnia - Thought of absent friends

Combine appropriate flowers or serve singly to express your feelings.

**Lisa MacNaughton**
**(Master Gardener '91, Johnson County)**

# Canned Peaches In Oven

Pour syrup over peaches before you put them in oven and seal. Put in oven on tray and start oven at 250º for 1 hour and 15 minutes. Turn off oven and leave until completely cold. Leave about 1-inch at top of jar if you use Kerr lids.

**Marguerite Vens**
**(Davenport, Iowa)**

# Lydia's Dried Corn

8 pints cut off sweet corn
½ cup whipping cream
1 cup whole milk

½ cup white sugar
¼ cup canning salt or just
2 tablespoons

Combine cream, milk and sugar. Heat to boiling, stir until sugar dissolves. Add cut off corn and salt, (I prefer lesser amount). Cook over low heat 20 minutes. Stir constantly to avoid scorching. Spread in jelly roll pans. Bake in oven with very low heat setting until VERY DRY (several hours). Stir often. Store in tightly covered container. To use, put desired amount in saucepan. Cover with water, simmer until tender. Very good old-time recipe from 30's or 40's. NOTE: I have used all half & half in place of milk and whipping cream. Original recipe suggested spreading corn on clean, white cloth and drying in the sun, put cloth on pans. Shake and stir often. It may take a couple days or so.

*An Old Time recipe.*

**Ethel Dobbins**
**(Wilton, Iowa)**

516

# Mrs. Rowe's Kraut

**Shred garden fresh cabbage**          **1 rounded teaspoon sugar**
**1 level teaspoon canning salt**     **¾ cup warm water**

To process, fill one quart glass canning jar with shredded cabbage, tamp lightly, DO NOT PACK. With a table knife, make a hole to the bottom of the jar. Add the salt and sugar. Pour in the very warm (not boiling) water. Seal jars with zinc lids and rubber jar rings. Turn lid back one quarter of a turn. Set outside in shady place. Cure for 3 weeks. Very Good!

**Ethel Dobbins**
**(Wilton, Iowa)**

# Whole Tomatoes In Oven

1 teaspoon of salt in bottom of quart jar. Fill with blanched tomatoes. Push tomatoes down in jar until juice appears. Don't have jar too full. Leave about an inch from top of jar. Seal before putting in oven. Put in oven on a tray and start oven at 225⁰. Leave in oven 1½ hours, then turn off. Don't take out until cold.

**Marguerite Vens**
**(Davenport, Iowa)**

517

# Corncob Jelly

12 bright red cobs
3 pints water
1 (1¾ ounces) package
   Sure-Jell

3 cups sugar
6 red hots

Boil broken cobs in water for 30 minutes. Remove from heat and strain liquid. If liquid doesn't measure 3 cups, add enough water to make 3 cups. Add Sure-Jell and bring to a rolling boil. Add sugar and boil for 2 or 3 minutes or until jelly consistency. (Put the red hots in with the liquid.) Pour into 8 small baby food jars that have been sterilized. Seal with paraffin.

*To make corncob jelly, you must use field corn not sweet corn. Field corn has red cobs and is grown to feed cattle and pigs.*

*Early pioneers could make jelly from corncobs when fruit was not available. I am sure they didn't have Sure-Jell, but knew of other ways to make their jelly set. I only make it for our own use. It is my grand-children's favorite jelly.*

**Gretchen Brittain**
**(Earlham, Iowa)**

# Rhubarb Jam

1½ pounds (2 plus cups)
   rhubarb
1 medium banana (mashed)
5½ cups sugar

½ cup water
Juice of 1 lemon
½ bottle liquid fruit pectin

Combine rhubarb and water, cover and boil about one minute or until tender. Measure 2½ cups. Add mashed banana (total 3 cups) in large saucepan; add sugar and juice of lemon, mix well. Bring to a full rolling boil over high heat; boil hard for one minute, stirring constantly. Remove from heat. Stir in pectin immediately. Skim off foam. Ladle into hot sterilized glasses or jars. Seal. A bit different, but oh so good!

**Ethel M. Dobbins**
**(Wilton, Iowa)**

# Plum Jelly
*(Pioneer Recipe)*

Put on the plums enough water to cover them; let come to boil, pour off the water, fill up this time with hot water. Boil hard until plums are perfectly soft. Then squeeze through a jelly bag. Now to every pint of juice add a pint of sugar and return to fire. Or for easier measure 1 tumbler of sugar to 1 of juice. Have your jelly bag thoroughly cleansed. After jelly comes to a boil strain once more, just to insure its being beautifully clear. Return to the fire and boil hard for 1 hour. Take a little in a spoon and when cool see if it has congealed. Be careful not to let stay a moment too long, or your jelly will be too stiff.

*(Found pasted in an old Water-Cure Advocate Book 1840's.)*

**Penelope Miller**
**(Princeton, Iowa)**

# Strawberry Jam

1 quart strawberries (washed and hulled)

2 tablespoons lemon juice or vinegar
4 cups sugar

Add lemon juice to berries and bring to a boil slowly. Add 4 cups sugar. Boil 6 minutes. Take from fire. Pour in glass bowl or crock and let stand 24 hours. Stir occasionally to "plump' berries. Put in jars. Keep in refrigerator. If more then one quart of berries is used, make only one quart at a time for best results.

*To celebrate the town's unusual name the citizens have mounted a symbolic strawberry, billed as the world's largest, at the site of the city hall.*

**Charlotte Fliehler**
**(Secretary, Chamber of Commerce, Strawberry Point, Iowa)**

519

# Rhubarb Conserve

| | |
|---|---|
| 4 cups (very full) rhubarb (cut up) | 4 cups sugar |
| 2 unpeeled, seedless oranges (quartered and sliced very thin) | 1 cup seeded (Muscat) raisins<br>1 cup walnuts (coarsely broken) |

Combine cut up rhubarb and sugar in large saucepan. Stir; let set 15-20 minutes, stirring now and then to start the sugar to dissolve and a syrup begins to flow. Add sliced oranges. Slowly bring to a boil over low heat, stirring all the while. Simmer until it reaches desired consistency, quite thick. Add raisins and nutmeats. Simmer another 5-10 minutes, continuing to stir constantly to avoid scorching. Seal in sterilized jars. Makes 3-4 pints. I DO NOT substitute seedless raisins for the Muscats. "Wunnerful good" a delightful compliment to ham, roast duck or goose. The history of this recipe is not definite, but is one of the many shared recipes among the kinfolks. The Pennyslvania Dutch are noted for their assorted sweets and sours served with their very festive meals. Amusing incident; A couple years ago I gave a jar of it to one of my in-laws. She made it into pie and was very disappointed-it was far too sweet.

**Ethel Dobbins**
**(Wilton, Iowa)**

# Pickles

| | |
|---|---|
| 7 cups thinly sliced cucumbers | 1 cup thinly sliced onions<br>2 tablespoons salt |

Soak 3 ingredients 1 hour. Stir, then drain. Add 2 cups sugar, 1 cup vinegar, 1 teaspoon mustard seed, and 1 teaspoon celery seed. Let stand 1 hour. Can and refrigerate.

**Bessie Sierk**
**(Bettendorf, Iowa)**

# Violet Jelly
*(Unusual)*

2 cups violets
Juice of 1 lemon
4 cups sugar

2-3 cups boiling water
1 package powdered pectin

Gather 2 cups of violets, remove the stems. Rinse in a bowl of cold water. Put blossoms in a quart jar and pour boiling water over them. Cover jar and let stand for 24 hours. Strain out 2 cups of liquid and add lemon juice (this will change liquid back to a violet color) and pectin. Bring to a boil. Add 4 cups of sugar and bring to a boil again for 1 minute. Pour into jars and seal. (Violets are such a herald of Spring! They are a symbol of faithfulness. Violets make a sweet jelly, with a beautiful pastel color. It is a delightful May Day item.)

Lisa MacNaughton
(Master Gardener '91, Johnson County)

# Pepper Relish

24 green tomatoes
6 green peppers
3 red peppers

6 onions
1 bunch celery

Grind all and add.

**3 tablespoons salt and 1 quart water**

Cook 30 minutes and drain in colander. Add 3 cups sugar and 3 cups vinegar. Cook 20 minutes and seal in hot jars.

*This is one of the recipes I remember eating at my grandparents home, Earl and Gertrude May.*

Betty Jane Shaw
(President and Owner of Earl May Seed and Nursery and granddaughter of Earl May, Shenandoah, Iowa)

521

# Mother's Piccalili

3 large green peppers
3 large sweet red peppers
3 large onions (size of a teacup)
1½ gallons green tomatoes
1 small head of cabbage
5 tablespoons canning salt
1 quart boiling water

½ cup cider vinegar
4 cups cider vinegar
4 cups sugar
1 tablespoon celery seed
1 tablespoon mustard seed
1 teaspoon whole cloves
½ teaspoon whole allspice

Grind the vegetables; put into earthenware crock. Add salt; mix well; let set overnight. Next morning drain well in colander for an hour or two. Return drained vegetables to crock. Add the boiling water and ½ cup cider vinegar. Let set 24 hours. Drain well once more. In the meantime, combine the 4 cups sugar and the 4 cups cider vinegar in a large kettle. Tie spices in a cheesecloth bag; add to vinegar and sugar mixture. Bring to a rolling boil. Add the well drained vegetables and again, bring to a boil. Simmer until vegetables are tender, stirring often to avoid scorching. Remove the bag of spices. Ladle into hot sterilized jars. Makes 4 or 5 pints.

*"The Pennsylvania Dutch", the people of my heritage, are noted for their many sweets and sours served with their meals. "Seven Sweets and Seven Sours" made the meal, complete. This is my favorite! A real Oldie.*

**Ethel Dobbins**
**(Wilton, Iowa)**

# Chili Sauce

12 tomatoes
12 onions
12 apples
2 green peppers
1 tablespoon salt

5 cups sugar
1 pint vinegar
1 teaspoon cloves
1 teaspoon celery seed
1 teaspoon mustard seed

Grind apples, onions, and peppers. Peel and chop tomatoes. Add rest of ingredients and cook slowly 1½ hours until done.

**Bessie Sierk**
**(Bettendorf, Iowa)**

# Glazed Crystal Pickles

| | |
|---|---|
| **Several dozen small** | **Alum** |
| **cucumbers (3-inches long)** | **Sugar** |
| **Salt** | **Pickling spices** |
| **Vinegar** | |

Make a salt brine strong enough to float an egg (1 pound salt to 9 pints of water). Soak whole cucumbers in this brine for 3 days. A 5 gallon crock works well for this, and a plate may be placed on top of the cucumbers to keep them all immersed in the brine. After 3 days, drain off brine and soak in clear fresh water for 3 days, changing the water each day. Drain. Make a solution of 1 cup vinegar and 1 scant teaspoon alum to 4 cups water. Make enough to cover pickles. Soak for 3 days in this solution. Drain well and then cube the cucumbers. Make a syrup of 2 cups of sugar, 2 cups vinegar, and 1 tablespoon pickling spices. Boil the syrup and pour hot over cucumber chunks. Let set. Each day for the succeeding 2 days pour off syrup, add 2 cups more sugar, bring to a boil, and pour over pickles. (Adding all the sugar at one time would shrink the pickles.) On the third day pack pickles in clean, hot sterilized jars and seal.

**Mrs. Judy Denniston**

# Cucumber Catsup
*(1800's Recipe)*

One dozen cucumbers, three onions, three green peppers, white and black mustard seed, white pepper whole, and vinegar enough for liquor.

**Verlena Pelo**
**(Le Claire, Iowa)**

CHIVES

523

# 16 Day Pickles

2 gallons medium cucumbers (whole)
1 pint pickling salt
7 cups vinegar (cider)
13 cups sugar
3 tablespoons alum
1 teaspoon celery seed
¼ teaspoon oil of cloves
¼ teaspoon oil of cinnamon
1 tablespoon pickling spice

In large crock or plastic bucket cover cucumbers with cold water, pour salt over top. Stir every day for seven days. Eighth day drain, rinse, and cover with boiling water, 9th day drain and cover with boiling water, add 3 tablespoons alum to water, 10th day drain and cover with boiling water, 11th day slice or chunk, make syrup: 7 cups vinegar and 8 cups sugar, 1 teaspoon celery seed, ¼ teaspoon oil of cloves, ¼ teaspoon oil of cinnamon, 1 tablespoon pickling spice (tied in a bag). Bring syrup to boil, pour over cucumbers. Each morning drain off syrup and add 1 cup sugar. Bring to boil, and pour over cucumbers for 4 mornings. 5th morning drain syrup and add 1 cup sugar. Bring to boil. Pack pickles in jars, and pour boiling syrup over pickles, and adjust lids. Hot pack 20 minutes. Makes 6-7 quarts. You can add green food color if you like greener pickles. If you don't have oil of cloves or oil of cinnamon you can use 1 teaspoon cinnamon and 1 teaspoon cloves in a bag. I prefer the oils. These take a lot of time but well worth the effort. Your house will smell really good for over a week while they are curing. Years ago my neighbor gave me this recipe. She is now gone, but every time I make these or open them up they remind me of her.

Martha McCaughey
(McCausland, Iowa)

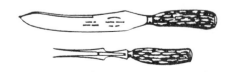

524

# Cranberry Ice

**BOIL UNTIL SOFT:**
**1 quart cranberries**         **1¾ cups water**

Strain off juice and put berries through a sieve. Add the following to the pulp and juice and boil for 5 minutes.

**1¾ cup sugar**              **¾ cup water**

Set aside to cool. Add ¾ cup ginger ale. Freeze in a 9x12-inch pan overnight. Cut in small squares to serve.

*I wanted to send you an heirloom recipe for your book. This recipe was my grandmother's. She was a great cook, but never shared recipes with anyone in the family. This is the only one my mother was ever able to get from her. It's wonderfully refreshing and different from any cranberry relish I've ever seen.*

**Ann Hutchinson**
**(Mayor, Bettendorf, Iowa)**

# Country Style Hot Dog Relish
*(Makes 9 pints)*

**4 cups chopped onions**      **12 green peppers**
**4 cups chopped cabbage**     **½ cup salt**
**10 green tomatoes**          **2 tablespoons mustard seed**

Grind first four ingredients together using coarse blade of food grinder. Drain. Sprinkle with ½ cup of salt. Let stand overnight. Rinse and drain. Combine remaining ingredients. Pour over vegetable mixture. Heat to a full boil of 5 to 10 minutes. Place in clean hot sterilized jars and seal.

**Lila Maynard**
**(Princeton, Iowa)**

# Cream Chipped Beef

1 small package Armour
　dried beef
⅓ cup oil
3 tablespoons flour

1½ cups milk
1 cup (4 ounces) American
　cheese

In saucepan bring water to a full boil. While waiting for water, in another saucepan combine oil and flour, stir together over medium heat. When hot, add milk, stir until smooth, then add cheese. Tear dried beef into bite size pieces and drop into boiling waer, remove from heat immediately and drain. Add meat pieces to sauce. Serve over toasted English muffins or regular toast. Recipe can be doubled.

Susan Severs
(Princeton, Iowa)

# Easy Hollandaise Sauce
*(Excellent)*

½ cup butter
2 egg yolks
1 tablespoon lemon juice
　or vinegar

¼ teaspoon salt
¼ teaspoon paprika
Few grains cayenne pepper

Melt butter over hot water. Beat egg yolks and lemon juice or vinegar until very light. Add melted butter a few drops at a time, beating vigorously with rotary beater, after each addition. Last, add the salt, cayenne pepper, and paprika. Serve over green vegetables-asparagus, broccoli, spinach, etc.

Ethel Dobbins
(Wilton, Iowa)

# Fried Pumpkin Blossoms

16 pumpkin or squash
  blossoms
About 4 ounces mozzarella
  cheese
1 extra large egg
1 tablespoon olive oil

1 tablespoon water
About ½ cup unbleached
  flour
Few pinches of salt
Vegetable oil for frying
Lemon wedge for garnish

Do NOT use pumpkin or squash blossoms, that have been sprayed.
Gently wash the pumpkin blossoms; remove stamens or pistils and
pat dry. Cut cheese into 16 pieces about 1½ -inches long by ½ -inch
square and place a stick in each blossom. Beat egg lightly with a
fork in a shallow bowl. Add water, olive oil and blend well. Add
flour and salt and combine well to make a smooth batter. Pour oil
in skillet so it is about ¾ -inch deep and place it over moderate heat
until a faint haze forms on oil. Holding the flower by the open end,
dip into the batter and carefully lower it into the hot oil. Repeat with
a few more flowers. Turn gently, so they turn golden brown all over.
Remove them with a slotted spoon and put them on paper towels
while frying the rest. Serve hot with lemon wedges. Makes 16
blossoms; serves 4.

**Judy Terry**
**(Master Gardener '94, Johnson County)**

# Grape Catsup
*(1800's Recipe)*

Five pounds grapes boiled and strained through a colander, two and one-half pounds sugar, one pint vinegar, one tablespoon each of cinnamon, cloves, allspice and pepper and one-half spoon salt. Boil until thick.

Verlena Pelo
(Le Claire, Iowa)

# Garbage Can Dinner

3 dozen ears of corn
30 to 40 potatoes
5 to 6 pounds carrots
4 heads cabbage (quartered)
1 dozen onions
12 to 15 Polish sausage or
    fresh pork (cubed)

A new 20 gallon metal
    garbage can (solder to
    hold water)
3 bricks
2 cement blocks
2 wire mesh screens
Foil
20 pound charcoal

Solder bottom and sides of garbage can to hold water. It must be leakproof. Place 3 bricks in bottom on edge. Cover with wire mesh and fill with water to cover bricks. Cut ends off of corn, but leave silk and husks. Stand them vertically on wire mesh. Add cleaned potatoes, carrots, cabbage and onions. Cover with another wire mesh screen. Add meat and cover with foil. Place lid on garbage can. Place bag of charcoal between 2 cement blocks. Split bag and light. Set garbage can on top. Do not remove lid while cooking. Cook 4 hours; carefully remove contents into containers to hold each item. Remove husk from corn. Serves 30 people plus.

Suzy Ven Horst
(Bettendorf, Iowa)

# Country Butter

Fifty years ago many people who lived on farms had no electricity or modern conveniences. We raised or grew our food. We had a cow, chickens, pigs, rabbits, and horses.

We milked the cow every morning and evening. The milk was poured through a clean white cloth to filter out anything that might have dropped in the bucket. Then we poured the milk into a clean pail with a tight lid and lowered it into the well by a long rope. The well was cold and acted as a refrigerator. When a fresh supply was lowered down the unused milk was given to the cats or pigs. Sometimes clabbored (soured) milk was given to the chickens.

Every morning's breakfast consisted of home cured bacon, fried potatoes, gravy and of course homemade biscuits.

While mom peeled and sliced the potatoes and made the biscuits, we had to make the butter for the day.

Mom spooned the thick cream, into a fruit jar, from the top of the milk that had been in the well overnight. We had to shake the jar until the cream formed into little balls the size of peas. All the contents of the jar were then poured through a strainer that was set over a bowl.

The buttermilk was poured into a jar and the lid was tightened. This jar was put into a pail in the well and left a while if we wanted to drink the buttermilk cold. Some was used for baking and cooking.

The lumps of butter were placed in a bowl and a butter paddle was used to press the lumps together and press out the remaining buttermilk. When all the lumps were pressed together into a ball, a small amount of salt was added. Now we had butter for our homemade bread and for mom to bake cookies. Later we had enough money to buy a cream separator, a more modern butter churn and an ice box. We still did not have electricity. Also I became old enough to milk the cow both morning and night.

**Marilyn Mason Schmitt**
**(Mitchellville, Iowa)**

# Cupcake Filling

½ cup sugar
⅔ cup Crisco
⅓ cup milk

¼ teaspoon salt
1 teaspoon vanilla

Mix ingredients and beat for 10 minutes. Add 1 tablespoon water and ¼ cup powdered sugar. Mix well. Put inside of cupcakes using decorator's tube.

**Susan Severs**
**(Princeton, Iowa)**

# Golden Fry Batter

½ cup Mazola Corn Oil
1 cup sifted flour

1½ cups milk
1 egg

Blend oil and flour. Add milk and egg. Fry in Mazola (375°) 3 to 4-inches deep until golden brown. Use chickens 2½ pounds. Fry until tender.

*This batter is also good for onions and other deep fat fry foods.*

**Lila Maynard**
**(Princeton, Iowa)**

# Mayonnaise

2 eggs (or 4-6 yolks)
1 cup sugar
1 cup vinegar
1 cup water

2 tablespoons flour
1 teaspoon salt
1 teaspoon mustard

Mix all ingredients well and store in refrigerator.

**Susan Severs**
**(Princeton, Iowa)**

# Sweetened Condensed Milk

½ cup hot water  
¾ cup sugar

1 cup plus 2 tablespoons
dry milk powder

Mix water and sugar until dissolved, add milk powder and mix well. Use right away or can be stored in refrigerator.

**Susan Severs**
**(Princeton, Iowa)**

# Cereal Pudding

½ cup Farina  
⅓ cup sugar

½ teaspoon salt

Bring to boil 3 cups milk, turn heat on low and add above ingredients, cook and stir 3 minutes.

**ADD:**
1 tablespoon butter  
3 eggs (beaten well)

1½ teaspoons vanilla

Put in small dishes and serve warm. May add fruit on top.

*I found this recipe in the 70's. It is supposed to provide an excellent breakfast for busy kids.*

**Doris Myers**
**(Iowa City, Iowa)**

531

# Cottage Pudding
*(My mother's recipe-Mary Wolfe Matlock)*

**PUT IN SMALL SAUCE PAN:**

¾ cup to 1 cup sugar          3 tablespoons (heaping) flour

Pour in boiling water and cook until thick. Add dash of nutmeg. Add about 2 teaspoons vinegar.

*Mom used this to pour over anything dry, or a cake that wasn't eaten to prevent throwing anything out.*
*It's a World War II Recipe.*

Pat Walker
**(Princeton, Iowa)**

# Bay Leaf Swag
*(Reprinted From Madison County Cookbook)*

**½ POUND OF ANY OF THE FOLLOWING:**

Whole bay leaves                Cinnamon sticks
Dried apple slices or dried     Fresh cranberries
  orange slices                 Strawflowers
Orange peels and lemon          Baby's breath
  peel

String your choice of these or other items on heavy gauge florist wire, cut to the length you need and decorate ends with ribbons.

**Teresa Hoffelmeyer**
**(Winterset, Iowa)**

# The Housekeeper's Alphabet
*(From a 1900 cookbook)*

APPLES: Keep in a dry place, as cool as possible without freezing.

BROOMS: Hang in the cellar way to keep soft and pliant.

CRANBERRIES: Keep under water in cellar; change water monthly.

DISH of hot water set in oven prevents cakes, etc., from scorching.

ECONOMIZE time, health and means and you will never beg.

FLOUR: Keep cool, dry and securely covered.

GLASS: Clean with a quart of water mixed with a tablespoon of ammonia.

HERBS: Gather when beginning to blossom, and keep in paper sacks.

INK STAINS: Wet with spirits of turpentine; after three hours rub well.

JARS: To prevent, get husband to subscribe for the home paper.

KEEP an account of all supplies, with cost and date purchased.

LOVE lightens labor.

MONEY: Count carefully when you receive change.

NUTMEG: Prick with a pin, and if good, oil will run out.

ORANGE AND LEMON PEEL: Dry, pound and keep in bottles.

PARSNIPS: Keep in the ground until spring.

QUICKSILVER and the white of an egg destroy bedbugs.

RICE: Select large, with fresh, clear look; old rice may have insects.

SUGAR: For general use, granulated is the best.

TEA: Equal parts of Japan and green are as good as English breakfast.

USE a cement of ashes, salt and water for cracks in stoves.

VARIETY is the culinary spice.

WATCH your back yard; keep it clear from dirt and bones.

XANTIPPE was a scold. Don't imitate her.

ZINC lined sinks are better than wooden ones.

**Verlena Pelo**
**(Le Claire, Iowa)**

# Oddments

*(From a 1900 cookbook)*

### CLOTTED OR DEVONSHIRE CREAM

Fresh milk, let stand for cream to rise twenty-four hours. Set the crock or pan with milk and cream over a pot of hot water, let it heat until a ring forms on the cream, set away until thoroughly cold, then skim.

### LEMON EXTRACT

Cut the yellow rind from several lemons, put in a bottle, cover with alcohol, let stand ten days, drain and cook for use.

### QUINCE HONEY

Three pounds sugar, one pint water and two grated quinces. Boil seven minutes.

### RASPBERRY VINEGAR

Take two quarts of berries, pour over them a scant quart of cider vinegar and let stand twenty-four hours. Strain and to every pint of juice add one pound of sugar; boil ten minutes or until a rather thin syrup is formed. When cold, bottle for use. Three or four tablespoons added to a glass of cold water makes a very pleasant drink. If possible use half red berries; they give a rich flavor and the black ones the color.

### WINE JELLY

One pint cold water, juice of three lemons, two tablespoons lemon essence, half pound crushed sugar, one pint good white wine (if used by a sick person, sherry is preferable), three pints boiling water and one box Cox's gelatin; strain and pour into molds to cool.

*(Continued on Next Page)*

## (Oddments-Continued)

### A Good Hair Tonic

One ounce alcohol and five grains quinine. Rub in good over the scalp at the roots of the hair at night.

### Almond Paste

Beat four ounces bitter almonds. Add to them three ounces lemon juice, three ounces almond oil and enough of weak spirits of wine and ether to make a paste. Apply to hands when retiring.

### A Perfume For Clothes

To be used in packing away clothes. Druggists say it will keep away moths. Pound to a powder one ounce each of cloves, caraway seed, nutmeg, mace, cinnamon and tonquin beans and six ounces orris root. Fill little bags of muslin with this mixture and place among the garments.

# Recipes For The Sick
*(From a 1900 cookbook)*

### Albumen Water

Gently stir the whites of two eggs into one-half pint cold water and sweeten with a little sugar of milk. This is the most simple food it is possible to obtain and may be resorted to when all others fail.

### Barley Water

Take one cup pearl barley and soak one-half hour in a little luke warm water, previously salted. Drain, put barley into a pint boiling water and let simmer one-half hour; when done strain into a pitcher.

### Beef Tea

One pound fresh meat, cut fine and soak in one-third quart of cold water over night. In the morning remove the meat and save the water in which it has been soaked. Put meat in two-thirds quart of water and let simmer for two hours, keeping the water up to the original level by replacing what is lost by evaporation. Now pour the beef broth into the cold liquor in which the meat was soaked, squeezing the meat as dry as possible. The meat should then be spread on a tin and dried in the oven. When perfectly dry it can easily be reduced to powder in a mortar. Mix this meat powder in the liquor. Salt to taste and add twenty drops muriatic acid and three grains pepsin. This is the only preparation of beef tea that contains all the elements of the meat.

### Egg Nog

One egg, one glass of milk, one dessert spoon brandy, one dessert spoon sugar. Carefully scald the milk and let cool. Beat sugar and egg to a froth, put into a glass, add the brandy and fill up with milk. If wanted in a hurry use milk without scalding.

*(Continued on Next Page)*

## (Recipes For The Sick-Continued)

### Gum Arabic Wafer

Dissolve gum arabic in water, one part to ten by bulk. For very young babies, use it in the proportion above given, for older children, barley water if bowels are loose, oatmeal water if there be constipation. A little gelatin added to the mixture of milk and water, may be substituted for any of the above.

### Mutton Broth

Take one pound fresh mutton free from fat; cut into thin slices with a sharp knife; put into a suitable dish; salt, pour over it one quart cold water and let simmer over the fire for an hour—then let boil for an hour longer. Strain off the broth, refusing the meat fiber. Season with salt.

### Oat-Meal Water

Soak one cup oat-meal in one pint water, with a little salt added, over night. Strain thoroughly through a napkin the next morning.

### Wine Whey

Bring to a boil one pint fresh milk; add slowly a wine glass of sherry wine and let simmer until a curd forms. Strain the whey through a cloth and sweeten. Nourishing and stimulating.

**Verlena Pelo**
**(Le Claire, Iowa)**

# Christmas Potpourri
*(Reprinted From Madison County Cookbook)*

**1½ QUARTS BLENDED:**

Bayberry leaves
Spruce needles
Holly leaves
Dried verbena

1 ounce orris root
5 drops pine oil or cinnamon
oil

**½ QUART BLENDED:**

Dried orange peel
Dried lemon peel
Whole allspice
Bay or juniper berries

Cloves
Cinnamon sticks
Holly

Gently combine and mix with hands in a ceramic bowl. Place in tightly covered glass jar and store in dry, dark location for about 5 weeks. Shake jar occasionally. Place in decorative containers when ready to use.

Teresa Hoffelmeyer
(Winterset, Iowa)

# Lye Soap

5 cups water (cold)
2 tablespoons Borax
  (20 Mule Team)

1 can lye
9 cups animal fat (prefer
  pork fat or lard)

NOTE: You must use enamel containers or glass and wooden spoons with long handles. Melt fat and strain, (pure lard is a lot easier). Dissolve Borax in cold water, then slowly add lye and dissolve (liquid will become extremely hot). VERY IMPORTANT TO DO IN THIS ORDER. Slowly add 9 cups of grease always stirring in the same direction. After all grease has been stirred in, stir in same direction for an additional 15-20 minutes. Then pour into a glass or enamel pan or a box lined with cloth, 9x13-inch. Let set up. Cut into bars and take from container. Air dry completely. Store 6 months before using or grating. (3 pound coffee can ¾ full of clean grease is 9 cups of grease).

*Our son and daughter grew up with a strong 4-H background. Both raised livestock and had many other 4-H interests. We had the food stands save the fat drippings from ground beef and pork during fair week.*

*After the 4-H animals were sold and all their other projects returned home the afternoon was set aside to make soap outside. With pails turned upside down for seats and long handled wooden spoons used for stirring, the soap making was in progress.*

*This was an excellent time for them to reminisce about fair week, while it was fresh in their minds; relive the successes, the disappointments, and the funny things that happened along with setting some goals for the following year.*

*Sometimes the soap would be excellent and sometimes it was stirred way beyond the amount of time the recipe required. We were still able to use almost all the flops.*

*The soap is used in bars for washing your hands and grated into fine pieces for the washing machine. It does not take stains out of clothes, but does an excellent job of washing clothes. The jeans and bath towels are much softer after being hung on the clothesline than with the detergents you buy from the store.*

**Norene Johnson**

# Hulda's Homemade Soap
### *(Recipe that Reflects the Past)*

4½ pounds grease or
   cracklings
1 can lye

7 quarts water
2 tablespoons Borax
½ cup ammonia

Put first three ingredients in an iron vessel and let stand for 3 days, stirring occasionally. Then bring to a boiling point and add last two ingredients. Pour into containers. Next day when it has hardened, cut into bars.

*I can remember the hot steamy liquid that Mother would pour into a dishpan. When she would remove it from the pan, the pan was clean and bright again. She used the soap for all her laundry by grating it. Of course, these were the days with the wringer washing machine with clothes hanging on the lines outside in the summer and all over the house in the winter. Mother only washed once a week, so we were taught to change clothes only when absolutely necessary.*

**Elaine Rosene Oles**
**(Bettendorf, Iowa)**

# —JUST FOR NOTES—

542

# Danish Windmill
## VELKOMMEN
*(With special thanks to Peggy Hansen)*

The Danish Windmill is one of Iowa's official welcome centers, as well as one of the state's top tourist attractions. Visitors can climb to the top of the Windmill, see the grinding stones, and on a windy day, see the wings go around. Elk Horn and twin village Kimballton only two miles away, in western Iowa, share this strong Danish background. In fact there is a greater concentration of people of Danish ancestry here than anywhere else in the U.S.

The 60 foot windmill, built in Norre Snede, Denmark in 1848, was dismantled, shipped to Elk Horn, Iowa, and rebuilt in 1976. The mill has four 30-foot wings, each having 80 shutters, 7 feet across. The shutters catch the wind, turning the gears and grinding grain that has been locally grown.

Since the windmill's arrival 20 years ago, over one million tourists have visited Elk Horn to view the attraction. The mill has the largest collection of Danish imports anywhere in the U.S.

The famous yearly Danish celebration is the TIVOLI FEST, held May 25th and 26th this year.

# SPECIAL IOWA FEATURES

Largest Coffee Pot In The World, Stanton, Iowa ...................3
The Amana Colonies .........................................17
The Bily Clock Museum/Dvorak Exhibit, Spillville, Iowa .........47
Macksburg, Home of the National Skillet Throwing Championship .53
Midwest Old Threshers ......................................75
The Czech Village, Cedar Rapids, Iowa.......................92
Shenandoah's Famous Field Family .......................105-107
Sidney, Iowa Championship Rodeo ...........................125
Wilton Candy Kitchen .......................................146
An En-Deere-ing Act of Kindness - Rudy Eckel ...............147
Princeton, Iowa, On The River...............................151
Will What We Eat Today Make Our Ancestors Proud?
    Mary Hopson.............................................165
Iowa Celebrates Its 150th Birthday in 1996
    Mina Baker Roelofs, Pella ...........................171-172
Growing Up In Iowa - Herb Plambeck ........................184
Iowa Fields - Pat Underwood ...............................187
The Little Brown Church in The Vale, Nashua, Iowa ...........193
Buffalo Bill Cody, Le Claire, Iowa ..........................227
Music: A Great Scout Named Buffalo Bill - Cecil Fletcher...227A-227B
The Famous Green Tree, Le Claire, Iowa .....................228
Home of Albert The Bull, Audubon, Iowa .....................239
The Old Dinner Bell, Dorothy Birdwell.......................255
Earl May Seed & Nursery, Shenandoah, Iowa .................269
Time for Thanks - Betsy Logan ..............................292
State Fair Champion - Vincent Pemble, Indianola, Iowa .........304
Willson Family Recipes .................................344-348
Discoverer and Discovery of the Delicious Apple .........353-355
Ah! Sweet Perfume - Lucille Morgan Wilson, Iowa .............368
Boyhood in Wall Lake - Andy Williams .......................381
"Grocer On Main Street" - Mary Marmon .....................383
Vesterheim Norwegian - American Museum, Decorah, Iowa ...415-416
Ingalls Family, Burr Oak, Iowa .........................429-431
Morning, Iowa Born - Ric Wilson ............................506
Kalona, Iowa - The Quilt Capital of Iowa.....................513
Danish Windmill ...........................................543